MYSTERY AND SACRAMENT OF LOVE

Mystery and Sacrament of Love

A Theology of Marriage and the Family
for the New Evangelization

Marc Cardinal Ouellet

Translated by Michelle K. Borras and Adrian J. Walker

HUMANUM
PONTIFICAL JOHN PAUL II
INSTITUTE SERIES

WILLIAM B. EERDMANS PUBLISHING COMPANY
GRAND RAPIDS, MICHIGAN / CAMBRIDGE, U.K.

Previously published in Italian as *Mistero e sacramento dell'amore: Teologia del matrimonio e della famiglia per la uova evangelizzazione* (Cantagalli, 2007) and in French as *Mystère et sacrament de l'amour* (Paris: Éditions du Cerf, 2014)

This translation published 2015 by
Wm. B. Eerdmans Publishing Co.
2140 Oak Industrial Drive N.E., Grand Rapids, Michigan 49505 /
P.O. Box 163, Cambridge CB3 9PU U.K.
www.eerdmans.com

Printed in the United States of America

21 20 19 18 17 16 15   7 6 5 4 3 2 1

Library of Congress Cataloging-in-Publication Data

Ouellet, Marc, 1944-
    [Mistero e sacramento dell'amore. English]
    Mystery and sacrament of love: a theology of marriage and the family for the
    new evangelization / Marc Cardinal Ouellet; translated by Michelle K. Borras
    and Adrian J. Walker.
        pages   cm
    Includes bibliographical references.
    ISBN 978-0-8028-7334-7 (pbk.: alk. paper)
    1. Marriage — Religious aspects — Catholic Church.
    2. Families — Religious aspects — Catholic Church.
    3. Catholic Church — Doctrines.   I. Title.

BX2250.O9313   2015
234'.165 — dc23

2015014155

Humanum is an imprint of the John Paul II Institute for Studies on Marriage and Family at the Catholic University of America in Washington, D.C.

Contents

Contents

Contents

viii

Contents

Preface

Marriage and the family are at the forefront of the burning questions being debated by civil society and the Church today. Vatican Council II, in its Pastoral Constitution on the Church in the Modern World, *Gaudium et Spes,* already identified these themes as priorities; but they have grown increasingly relevant under the influence of the sexual revolution, feminism, and most recently, attempts to redefine the institution of marriage.

Alongside this evolution, which has all the characteristics of a profound anthropological crisis, the religious convictions of citizens of secularized societies have been progressively relegated to the private, purely individual sphere. The result has been to thwart the transmission of spiritual values, which no longer find any support within the dominant sociological and cultural framework. This leads to certain consequences within the family sphere: a fear of commitment; the fragility of marriages, whether sacramental or otherwise; the instability of families; difficulties in education; and disaffection with regard to sacramental practice in the Church.

Aware of these serious challenges, Pope Francis has launched a two-year synodal path devoted to all the questions connected with them. He has proposed a "pastoral conversion" to the whole Church (*Evangelii Gaudium* 25). This conversion will bear fruit for the mission of the family to the extent that it develops "on the ground" the theological intuitions of the Second Vatican Council and the remarkable contribution of Saint John Paul II, the pope of the family. The goal of this book is to offer a theology of marriage and the family that has ripened through long contact with these sources and that is articulated according to a comprehensive vision of sacramental theology inspired by the innovative thought of Hans Urs von Balthasar.

This book will attempt to indicate a path for a "pastoral conversion" that is rooted in a "theological conversion" where the Word of God is received in faith and interpreted in an anthropologically meaningful way. Bringing together trinitarian anthropology and an ecclesial sacramental theology, our study will lay the foundations for a renewed understanding of the sacraments and a transformation of sacramental practice, which is now seriously compromised, into a resource of the first importance for the new evangelization.

The work is divided into three parts. Part One takes up the essential theological data regarding the sacrament of marriage. John Paul II called marriage the "primordial sacrament" because it belongs to the order of creation from the beginning, while simultaneously possessing a specific ecclesial meaning rooted in the New Covenant with Jesus Christ. A central insight here is that human love, as mystery and sacrament, is a real participation in the love of Christ and the Church, which is in turn the supreme manifestation of the source of all love, the Holy Trinity.

Part Two focuses on the relationship between the Church's sacraments, or more precisely, sacramental marriage, and the Church-as-Sacrament. One of the new developments of Vatican II was to highlight the sacramental dimension of ecclesiology. Despite this affirmation of the analogical character of the notion of sacrament, however, the Council did not clearly articulate the relationship between the Sacrament of the Church and the seven sacraments in the narrower sense. We will address this lacuna by adopting the nuptial paradigm of sacramental theology proposed by Saint John Paul II. This paradigm allows for a deeper understanding of the New Testament specificity of the sacramental order, especially its fundamental link with the Eucharist, the sacrament par excellence of the New Covenant.

Part Three develops more systematically the link between the mystery of the Trinity and nuptial symbolism, always from the starting point of the *mysterium fidei* of the New Covenant. The Christian family is revealed to itself by participating in the trinitarian mystery, the transcendent foundation of the *communio personarum,* and it is strengthened by the intrinsic link between the two sacraments of nuptial love, marriage and the Eucharist. In this way, the Christian family acquires a radiantly attractive sacramental beauty; and the *ecclesia domestica,* or "domestic church," becomes a mighty force to illumine and guide the pastoral and missionary conversion of the whole Church.

The following pages, which have already been published in French and Italian, offer the English-speaking public the fruit of courses that I developed some years ago at the John Paul II Institute for Studies on Marriage and the Family in Rome. The 2014 and 2015 synods on the family, together with the search for new pastoral solutions, are an opportunity for a broader theological and pastoral dialogue based both on the heritage of Scripture and Tradition and on a contemporary development of doctrine. The present book is meant as a modest contribution to such dialogue.

I hope that these pages will help the reader to enter with enthusiasm into the new missionary dynamism demanded by the present time, to which Pope Francis gives so strong a witness through his example and writings:

> If the whole Church takes up this missionary impulse, she has to go forth to everyone without exception. But to whom should she go first? . . . Today and always, "the poor are the privileged recipients of the Gospel," and the fact that it is freely preached to them is a sign of the kingdom that Jesus came to establish. (*Evangelii Gaudium* 48)

Sacramental Theology in Transition

The Preliminary Pastoral Question

The problems we encounter in the theology of the Eucharist have their source in the profound transformation of contemporary culture, which in turn has repercussions on our understanding and practice of the sacraments. We can formulate one of these problems, which is pastoral in nature, by reflecting on Jesus' dialogue with the Samaritan woman at Jacob's well. The woman asks Jesus whether one ought "to adore God on this mountain" (Mount Gerizim, the center of Samaritan worship) or in Jerusalem (the center of Jewish worship). Jesus answers, "Woman, believe me . . . the hour is coming, and now is, when the true worshipers will worship the Father in spirit and truth" (John 4:21-23). According to the vocabulary and theology of John's Gospel, to adore "in spirit and in truth" does not mean to pray in a completely interior or purely mental way, but rather to adore according to the Holy Spirit that Jesus will give after his resurrection. In any case, Jesus does not pronounce on the question of place, but speaks instead of the spirit of true adoration of the Father.

Louis-Marie Chauvet comments:

How, then, can we avoid asking why we need all these rites, with their more or less obligatory rhythm, gestures and rules that we take for granted, their pre-programmed formulae, their material elements imposed in the name of "tradition," not to mention the pomp that the Church deploys in them with such solemnity — all to adore the Father? Isn't all this, if not clearly contradictory to the spirit Jesus mentions, at least an obstacle to it? And so we find ourselves dreaming of a "truer" and thus necessarily more sober religion: a religion in which direct contact with the pure Word of God would at last be possible.[1]

The pastoral problem of the sacraments is none other than the contemporary abandonment of sacramental practice. This now universally recognized state of affairs demands a new, general and coherent reflection.[2] The pastoral problem leads us to the theological problem of the sacraments. Our question is no longer that of an earlier age, that is, how to explain the way in which rites and words communicate God's grace to us. In the Middle Ages, sacramental realities were a part of the unquestioned heritage of Christian tradition. People debated which sacraments should be included in the list of the seven, but they did not question the very idea of sacrament. The sacraments were simply received as a foundational datum of the Church. Modernity severed the link between soul and body, the intellect and the senses, faith and the sacraments. The need for a reality such as the sacraments lost its obviousness once modern Enlightenment philosophy limited religious progress to "an ever greater spiritualization of religion, which has to be purified of every relation to the senses and to matter."[3] Liberal theology limits itself to this vision and demands a "moral" justification for the entirety of Christian reality, to the detriment of the sacramental dimension of Christianity.

In a postmodern context, we have to justify the "why" of the sacraments; it is not enough to explain their "how" within a universe of meaning that no longer exists. This is why Chauvet presents his book as an effort to "reconcile with the liturgical rites," highlighting the fact that the faith, "even at its most spiritual, can be lived only within the mediation of the body."[4] Chauvet attempts this "reconciliation" through a theology of symbol that gives a profound and intrinsic account of Christian identity. We will study the merits of his proposal later on. In the meantime, we will identify the cultural matrix of the contemporary transformation of sacramental theology, as well as the

1. L.-M. Chauvet, *I sacramenti. Aspetti teologici e pastorali* (Milan: Ancora, 1997), 7.

2. G. Colombo, "Dove va la teologia sacramentaria?" (1974), in *Teologia sacramentaria* (Milan: Glossa, 1997), 3-61; H. Denis, "Les sacrements dans la vie de l'Église," *La Maison Dieu* 93 (1968): 39-59; W. Kasper, *Glaube und Geschichte* (Mainz, 1970), 287-90.

3. J. Ratzinger, Preface to the Italian edition of H. Luthe, ed., *Incontrare Cristo nei sacramenti. Sussidio teologico per una pastorale sacramentaria* (Cinisello Balsamo: Paoline, 1988), 6.

4. Chauvet, *I sacramenti*, 9: "At stake, then, in this (fundamental) theology of sacramentality is nothing less than a Christian reconciliation with the body (or better, as we will clarify, with corporeity). Aren't the sacraments the chief expression of a faith that exists only insofar as it is exposed to the risk of the body?"

theological issue underlying the pastoral problem of the devaluation of the sacraments.

The Cultural Matrix for the Renewal of Sacramental Theology

Ernesto Ruffini summarizes the cultural event represented by the rediscovery of the anthropological meaning of symbols and the symbolic dimension of human existence: "The renewal of sacramental theology has been significantly influenced by a cultural matrix that favors a recovery of symbolism as a historical and anthropological value. Moreover, we have moved from symbolism as a study of praxis to symbolism as a hermeneutical criterion."[5]

The value of the symbol and of symbolism is no longer limited to the merely instrumental function of a conceptual sign, as is sometimes the case in Scholastic metaphysics in the Western tradition. With the rediscovery of its historical and anthropological value, symbolism has become a hermeneutical key for understanding the profound meaning of human existence in general and of religious existence in particular.

This restoration of symbolism is the fruit of a combination of rejections and positive choices. The most important of these rejections bears on a Cartesian heritage understood exclusively as a method of "clear and distinct ideas." Such a method exalts logical and rational analysis but neglects the original relationship of human freedom with the real. The Freudian system has also been rejected insofar as it "reduces the 'imaginal' to the 'imaginary' (fictitious), as if the imaginal and the symbolic were nothing more than the sublimation of animal instinct."[6] Symbolic hermeneutics refuses to reduce the symbol to the pathological; it highlights the extent to which human symbolic activity is a sovereignly free act that is neither mechanical nor naturalistic. Finally, there has been a rejection of historical evolutionism, which claimed to explain history on the basis of a materialistic scientific evolutionism. Contemporary hermeneutics considers historical evolutionism to be one of the most dangerous positivist myths, which must be unmasked if we are to save the human person's capacity for creative and free choice and his ability to dominate history.

5. E. Ruffini, "Orientamenti e contenuti della teologia sacramentaria nella riflessione teologica contemporanea," in E. Ruffini and E. Lodi, *"Mysterion" e "sacramentum." La sacramentalità negli scritti dei Padri e nei testi liturgici primitivi* (Bologna: EDB, 1987), 15-56, here 28.
6. Ruffini, "Orientamenti e contenuti," 35.

Introduction

In order to understand more deeply the reason for this threefold rejection, we must mention other, positive choices. By opting for the anthropological function of the symbol, hermeneutics intends to highlight the richness of the symbol, which exceeds the merely informative or descriptive. Ruffini writes, "The symbol is a reality that the human person needs in order to live out his existence, to construct his history, and above all, to construct it in a human sense. Where the symbolic dimension is repressed, the 'sense' or 'meaning' of history is lost; in some way, it becomes dehumanized."[7]

Against this dehumanization, hermeneutics opts for the historical and cultural function and dimension of the symbol. History is not the simple realization of premises already known on the basis of the programmed, objectivistic progress of the natural sciences. Hermeneutics opposes this fatalism and affirms the human person's capacity to give meaning to the ensemble of factors that shape his destiny: "The function of art and of all its symbolic expression is to offer an 'anti-destiny.' And the function of symbolic-ritual celebration is to offer an 'anti-history,' a counter-narrative to evolutionism."[8]

We can thus count a renewed attention to the symbol among the encouraging signs of our times. Inherent in the experience of the confluence (in Greek, *symballein* means "putting together") of temporal and super-temporal, of space and the non-spatial, of the profane and the sacred, the symbol has deep roots in man's original being.[9] Hermeneutics is rediscovering the extent to which man, as a *microcosm,* a synthesis of all of creation, is himself a powerful symbol. It is precisely because man is a symbol that he naturally develops a manifold symbolic activity: language, the word, art, technical work and religious activity are its chief forms. Christian theology thus finds itself in a favorable moment, where urgent pastoral need meets a cultural openness to a fundamental renewal of sacramental theology. Even if the latter has not yet yielded satisfying results, we must take note of its discoveries and unresolved problems.

7. Ruffini, "Orientamenti e contenuti," 37. See E. Cassirer, *Filosofia delle forme simboliche,* 2 vols. (Florence: La Nuova Italia, 1961-1964); G. Durand, *L'imagination symbolique* (Paris: Quadrige, PUF, 1964).

8. E. Ruffini, "Orientamenti e contenuti," 38. See P. Ricoeur, *Finitude et culpabilité* (Paris: Aubier, 1960); Ruffini, *La sfida semiologica* (Rome: Armando, 1974).

9. See L. Scheffczyk, "Gesù Cristo, Sacramento originario della redenzione," in Luthe, ed., *Incontrare Cristo nei sacramenti,* 13-21.

4

The Basic Problematic of Sacramental Theology

The renewal of sacramental theology has its origins in the liturgical movement, which in its early stages engaged with the "theology of the mysteries" promoted by Odo Casel in the first half of the twentieth century. At the core of his reflection, the German Benedictine presented God's entire salvific work, and especially the life of Christian worship, under the rubric of "mystery." The ensuing controversy revealed the necessity of clarifying the Christian notion of mystery vis-à-vis the use of this category in the history of religions. The search for clarification led to a rethinking of the notion of revelation. As a result, the abstract perspective of "mystery-truth" was overcome in favor of the more dynamic and concrete perspective of "mystery-event." Far from a transmission of abstract truths, the liturgy is the celebration of Christ as "represented mystery," that is to say, the "present event" of salvation. Vatican II's Constitution *Dei Verbum* confirms the rightness of this new direction with a historical or dramatic interpretation of the concept of revelation. To affirm that Christ is the "mediator and the fullness of all revelation" (*DV* 2) is to see history not as a merely exterior context, but as the very content of the event of revelation. Sacramental theology respects this "historical" dimension of revelation by expanding the "analogical" concept of sacrament to Christ and the Church.

This expansion, the work of Vatican Council II, allowed for a development of ecclesiology in light of the concept of sacrament (cf. *Lumen Gentium* 1). Nevertheless, the Council Fathers introduced the concept of "Church-Sacrament" without specifying its implications or clarifying the relationship between the Church-Sacrament and the seven sacraments. The evolution of the post-conciliar doctrine of the sacraments reveals the difficulty in interpreting this concept. In 1974, Giuseppe Colombo published a critical analysis of the situation, asking with concern, "Where is sacramental theology headed?" The post-conciliar evolution of sacramental theology seemed threatened by the expansion of the category of sacrament; the term risked being emptied of content, thereby aggravating the theological and pastoral crisis. At the philosophical and theological roots of this expansion, we find the ecclesiology of Otto Semmelroth and above all the symbolic ontology of Karl Rahner.[10] The latter situates the reflection on sacrament not so much on the level of

---

10. See K. Rahner, "Zur Theologie des Symbols," in *Cor Jesu*, vol. 1 (Rome, 1959), 463-505; Rahner, *The Church and the Sacraments*, trans. W. J. O'Hara (Herder, 1963). The first thesis Rahner proposes as the fundamental principle of an ontology of the symbol is this: "A being is of itself necessarily symbolical, because it necessarily 'expresses' itself in order to find its proper essence" (467-78).

sacramental theology as on that of fundamental theology. This leads to a very broad extension of the notion of sacrament in an obviously analogical sense, as well as to a new vision of the institution of the sacraments. The relationship between the Church and the sacraments, however, is inadequately explained. Colombo comments, "In Rahner's structure, which goes from Christ to the Church [*Ursakrament*] and from the Church to the sacraments (as acts of the Church) in a way determined by his theology of symbol, the relationship or possible relationship between Christ and the sacraments remains unexplored because it is irremediably compromised."[11]

Because it is in fact fundamental theology, Colombo concludes, this ontological approach did not lead to substantial progress in the area of properly sacramental theology. And, in fact, many followers of Rahner have limited themselves to developing a theology of the symbol and of the sign.[12]

The Multiplicity of Sacramental Theologies

We thus find ourselves in a moment of transition: the Scholastic model of the sacraments has been called into question by the adoption of a symbolic ontology, but the latter has not adequately responded to the need for renewal in the area of sacramental theology. Hence the uncertain and fluid state of research, which is reflected in the multiplicity of sacramental theologies.[13]

11. Colombo, "Dove va la teologia sacramentaria?" 20: "Rahner's discussion, though concerned with recovering many aspects of the theological tradition of the sacraments, in fact ignores an aspect unequivocally held by the theological tradition and clearly expressed in the thesis: Jesus Christ is the principal minister of every sacrament."

12. Colombo confirms this judgment in his article "Teologia sacramentaria e teologia fondamentale," in *Teologia sacramentaria*, 63-86: "The 'fundamental' importance of Rahner's research in this matter *(real symbol)* is universally recognized. Historiography seems to view him less as an indispensable reference point than as an absolute starting point for contemporary sacramental theology" (70). A. Schilson, Th. Schneider, and H. Vorgrimler adopt Rahner's approach in the German-speaking world. The legitimacy of approaching the sacraments beginning from the Church remains an open question. By contrast, H. de Lubac, following the Fathers of the Church, reflects on the Church beginning with the sacraments. This latter perspective has the advantage of better expressing the fact that the Church receives everything from Christ, who acts in the sacraments.

13. L.-M. Chauvet distinguishes four perspectives in the panorama of sacramental theology: (1) the *objectivist* approach, which highlights the causality/efficacy of the sacraments, (2) the *subjectivist* approach, which so emphasizes the aspect of the subject that it nearly makes the sacrament itself superfluous, (3) the approach of *Vatican II*, which attempts a synthesis between cause and sacramental sign, and (4) the *linguistic/symbolical* approach, which Chauvet

The classical Scholastic doctrine of the sacraments was developed during the Middle Ages and received official recognition under the influence of St. Thomas Aquinas. In this logical and metaphysical perspective, the sacraments are considered "separate" instruments that prolong the "conjoined instrument" *(instrumentum coniunctum)* of Christ's humanity in order to communicate grace to believers. The sacraments are signs "containing" grace, which apply the effects of Christ's salvific work to individuals. This model emphasizes God, who sanctifies and saves human beings through the sacraments. However, it does not adequately express the response of man, who offers himself as a "spiritual offering" for the glory of God. The distancing of contemporary thought from metaphysics (cf. Heidegger, Cassirer, Ricoeur) has made this model more difficult to employ in our time.

It thus became a matter of urgency to privilege the human aspects of the question and to recover the personal dimension of the sacraments. We highlight here the anthropological school of thought represented by Louis Bouyer and Edward Schillebeeckx.[14] This approach did not receive the welcome that Rahner's did, but it could have borne more fruit in the hoped-for renewal. From within a properly anthropological dimension, these authors sought to highlight the symbolical structures that offer a universal and objective basis for understanding the religious dimension of existence. The application of symbolical categories to the sacramental sphere allows for a harmonization of meanings that still remains underexplored in theology. This approach includes the historical-salvific line of thought developed by Schillebeeckx and Jean Daniélou, who together with Henri de Lubac renewed the spiritual and symbolical exegesis of the Fathers. It will doubtless lead to new developments in the future.[15]

The radically "subjectivist" version of this perspective tends to assimilate orthodoxy to orthopraxis (correct behavior), subjecting objective truth to the criterion of subjective sincerity, and submitting the quality of faith to the criterion of generosity. This anti-institutional tendency can easily fall into elitism and neo-Pelagianism.[16] Elsewhere, in Protestant theology, the accent falls on

---

himself proposes; see Chauvet, *I sacramenti*, 11-26. We find an exhaustive study of the various approaches in A. Bozzolo, *La teologia sacramentaria dopo Rahner* (Rome: LAS, 1999).

14. L. Bouyer, *Rite and Man: Natural Sacredness and Christian Liturgy,* trans. M. Joseph Costelloe (South Bend, IN: University of Notre Dame Press, 1963); E. Schillebeeckx, *Christ, the Sacrament of the Encounter with God,* trans. Paul Barrett and N. D. Smith (London, New York: Sheed and Ward, 1965); Schillebeeckx, *I sacramenti, punti d'incontro con Dio* (Brescia: Queriniana, 1983).

15. See for example C. Rochetta, M. Semeraro, and V. Croce.

16. Chauvet, *I sacramenti*, 16-20. Chauvet points to Karl Barth as among the authors

the subject who acknowledges what God has done for him; the sacrament reveals salvation but does not effect it.

The results of this renewal are far from uncontroversial and linear: it seems to have led above all to a vague consensus surrounding a few convictions that have forged the patrimony of contemporary sacramental theology. A. Bozzolo writes:

> There has been indisputable progress in moving beyond an individualist conception of the sacrament as a "means of grace" and rediscovering its ecclesial finality and the "mystery" contained in its celebration. Similarly, the introduction of the "practice" of the sacrament as the starting-point for theological reflection has found general approval; hence the attention paid to the rite as an intrinsic component of the truth of the sacrament, the passage from the realm of the "sign" to that of "symbol" as the determining element in the new sacramental theology, and the passage from a "regional" notion of sacramentality to a sacramental re-reading of all of Christian existence, perhaps even of all of reality.[17]

We will not enter here into a consideration of the still fragmentary merits of these contributions. However, we agree with Ruffini when he highlights the need for these new approaches to be rooted in the biblical and patristic notion of *mysterion*, which lies at the basis of the sacraments. The monographs on this subject allow us to glimpse foundational elements that have not yet been fully integrated into systematic sacramental theology.[18] We still need a holistic, trinitarian presentation that can gather together the contribution of the anthropological and symbolical approaches in a satisfying manner, so as to express the objective efficacy of the sacraments while including the active and subjective aspect of faith in the sacramental event.

Finally, the results will not be convincing so long as the presentation

---

most representative of this line of thought: "Whereas the 'objectivistic' model understands the sacrament as an instrument of the *production* of grace, here it is understood as an instrument of the *translation* of the grace that God has already given in everyday existence" (19).

17. Bozzolo, *La teologia sacramentaria dopo Rahner*, 11.

18. We highlight the contribution of E. Ruffini on this question: "Sacramentalità ed economia sacramentale negli scritti dei Padri della Chiesa," in Ruffini and Lodi, *"Mysterion" e "sacramentum*," 57-212, with a bibliography; C. Rochetta, *Sacramentaria fondamentale. Dal "Mysterion" al "Sacramentum"* (Bologna: EDB, 1989). See also L. Bouyer, *The Christian Mystery: From Pagan Myth to Christian Mysticism*, trans. Illtyd Trethowan (Edinburgh: T&T Clark, 1989).

of sacramental theology is not based on revelation itself and on revelation's internal logic, which is essentially dramatic. The dramatic nature of revelation means that God communicates himself to man implicating man in God's own gift. There is no revelation without faith, just as there is no sacrament without faith. Faith is co-constitutive of the sacrament. In other words, we must high-light the nuptial structure of revelation, the faith, and the sacraments. This is how the theology of symbol, for example, will be able to receive enrichment from new contributions in ontology, anthropology, linguistics, or semiotics. Nevertheless, it will not advance decisively until it integrates all these contributions "from below" into a theological vision "from above." As Colombo insists:

> At bottom, without Jesus Christ, the notion of sign is empty of content from a rigorously theological point of view. Jesus Christ alone gives meaning to the notion of sign. The inverse is not true: the notion of sign cannot express the meaning of Jesus Christ. It seems more intelligible to begin from Jesus Christ to understand the notion of sacrament than from the notion of sacrament to understand Jesus Christ.[19]

In other words:

> Perhaps the moment has come to reverse the tendency to understand the sacrament in terms of the vague notion of symbol, and to begin at last to seek in sacramental practice the ultimate principle capable of illuminating the many forms of human symbolic experience.[20]

In distancing himself from the anthropological perspective of Karl Rahner, Hans Urs von Balthasar stressed very early the need to safeguard the priority of Christ's work and salvific gift. By itself, the anthropological is incapable of explaining the sacramental; the human situation as such cannot determine the sacrament. Already in his essay *A Theology of History* (1950) Balthasar affirms that grace defines man and not vice versa. Christ is the historical figure of the grace that defines man. In taking up our history and tradition, the life of Christ becomes an active and creative principle that fashions history. In this approach, the distinction among the various sacraments comes not so much from the typical situations of human existence as from the plenitude of the life of the risen Christ, who, in the Holy Spirit, communicates

---

19. Colombo, "Dove va la teologia sacramentaria?" 51.
20. Bozzolo, *La teologia sacramentaria dopo Rahner*, 226.

his "form" to believers through the Church's sacraments.[21] Following in the footsteps of Balthasar, Giorgio Mazzanti offers one of the most promising essays in sacramental theology, basing his presentation on the theology of the "real symbol," Christ and the Church, and on a careful analysis of the anthropological and cultural structure of the symbol.[22] We will have occasion to return to Mazzanti's symbolical sacramental theology, which privileges the nuptial symbol.

The Transformation of Sacramental Theology in a Eucharistic Perspective

In the light of the above, it is not surprising that the theology of the Eucharist has been affected both by the culture of the symbol and by attempts to reconfigure sacramental theology in general on the basis of new perspectives in ontology, anthropology, ecclesiology, and linguistics. Many such attempts at reconfiguration run the risk of applying new categories (semiotics, sociology, linguistics) to the mystery of the Eucharist in a way that imposes their logic on the content of this mystery. In order to evaluate these new perspectives, we have the criterion of fidelity to certain incontrovertible principles that the Tradition has confirmed in order to safeguard the eucharistic mystery: "The Tridentine dogma — real presence, transubstantiation, and the sacrifice of the Mass — drew out a certain number of definitive teachings that remain 'points of no return' in our understanding of the mystery."[23] The Magisterium recalls these touchstones each time they risk being forgotten or misunderstood.

That said, in presenting these "points of no return," we are not obliged to follow the order of manualist theology, which was led by the pressure of apologetic necessity to separate these elements into various chapters. The real presence, transubstantiation, and the sacrifice of the Mass do not refer to different subjects, but tend necessarily to substantial unification. This is because the Eucharist is the sacrifice of Christ, or, more precisely, the real presence of Christ's sacrifice. Colombo affirms that in clarifying the proper character of the real presence in its singularity and sacramental specificity, we must say that

---

21. H. U. von Balthasar, *The Theology of History* (San Francisco: Ignatius-Communio Books, 1994); *A Theological Anthropology* [*Das Ganze im Fragment*] (Eugene, OR: Wipf and Stock, 2010).

22. G. Mazzanti, *I sacramenti, simbolo e teologia*, vol. 1: *Introduzione generale* (Bologna: EDB, 1997).

23. Colombo, "Dove va la teologia sacramentaria?" 329.

"the Eucharist is the sacrament of Christ's sacrifice."[24] This new integration, which is now being consolidated, allows us to focus our attention on the final *"res"* of the Eucharist: the Church as mystery of communion.

Rahner's fundamental shift implied a kind of reversal in the relation between the Eucharist and the Church. Attention was focused on the "sacraments of the Church," and the Church's action moved to the foreground, in a certain sense obscuring the foundational role of Christ, and thus of the Eucharist, with respect to the Church herself. The thesis that the Church proceeds from the Eucharist, which Henri de Lubac, following the Fathers of the Church, had the merit of recovering, no longer appeared in all its clarity. The formula, "The Church makes the Eucharist and the Eucharist makes the Church," which has become a kind of slogan, is not always correctly interpreted:

> In fact, the reciprocity between the two actions is not real, but rather absolutely unequal. In the language of Scholastic philosophy, when the Eucharist "makes," this making must ultimately be understood in the order of formal causality; whereas when the Church "makes," this latter making must be understood in the order of ministerial, and thus of instrumental, causality.[25]

If the Church is essentially constituted by the Eucharist in the perspective of formal causality, we cannot then speak of the Church "before" or "without" the Eucharist.

Colombo expresses his desire for a Magisterial teaching anchored more deeply in the Eucharist-Church relationship, so that the ecclesiology of Vatican Council II can achieve the right balance between the "mystery of the Church" and the "people of God." For it is precisely the Eucharist that is the keystone of this equilibrium. We agree with Colombo that the link between the Trinity and the Eucharist offers a path toward a more profound understanding of this issue:

> Precisely because the Church is "mystery," she does not exhibit herself but is the image/symbol of the Trinity. She came from the Trinity, not simply as a postulate but according to the laws of the economic Trinity. She comes, then, from the Father, but only through the Son and the Spirit; and she is necessarily marked by the Spirit as well as by the Son, not only

24. Colombo, "Dove va la teologia sacramentaria?" 330.
25. Colombo, "Dove va la teologia sacramentaria?" 332.

by the Father. In other words, the Spirit who "makes" the Church is the Spirit of the Son. The Spirit thus leads to the Eucharist, since the Eucharist is not a marginal event in the historical adventure of the incarnate Son, that is to say, of Jesus of Nazareth; it is, rather, the concluding moment, the supreme gesture of his self-gift.[26]

The task of eucharistic theology today is to highlight the foundation of ecclesial communion in eucharistic communion, which introduces the former concretely into the communion of the Trinity. This insertion is obviously mediated by the sacrament and thus by the celebration of Christ's sacrifice, which, in the power of the Holy Spirit, prolongs the gift of Christ crucified, dead, and risen. Christ's Presence in the species of bread and wine is not a static fact: it contains in itself, albeit in the modality of the memorial of the Lord's "death," an offer of communion in the eternal life of the risen Son, who has returned to the Father. The Presence of the sacramental sacrifice thus has as its finality the gift of trinitarian communion, which passes through the kenosis of the eucharistic Christ. It would be helpful further to develop this theme, which focuses our reflection on the Eucharist, the center of gravity of the nuptial encounter between the Trinity and the Church. Moreover, it allows us the better to glimpse the ultimate, doxological meaning of human life, thanks to the decisive light that radiates from Christ's eucharistic gift to the Church, his Body and Bride. Finally, such a trinitarian and spousal approach sheds light on the eucharistic meaning of trinitarian anthropology — an eschatological and missionary meaning that emerges from the encounter of the economic Trinity and the people of God around the eucharistic table.

This dramatic, communion-centered perspective requires a theological methodology that is no longer focused merely on the (of course indisputable) aspects pertaining to the Lord's Presence (bread and wine transubstantiated into the body and blood of Christ), but now broadens to include the liturgical celebration as a whole. By centering our methodology on the metaphysical "how" of the real presence, we lost sight of the event of the celebration as God's historical-salvific encounter with his people. In recovering now the historicity of revelation, we must, following Casel, stress the "mystery-character" of the eucharistic celebration. The concrete rite contains the sacrificial gift of the incarnate Son, who died and was raised. In the humility of the rite, God comes to encounter his people in a sacramental way, which is thus historical and eschatological as well. The joint action of Christ and the Holy Spirit, with

26. Colombo, "Dove va la teologia sacramentaria?" 336.

the mediation of the ordained ministers and of the faith of Mary-Church, accomplishes in the sacramental sphere an "exchange of gifts" between the divine Persons; this exchange involves the Church, the Bride of Christ, in the mystery of the trinitarian communion. As event, the eucharistic liturgy, rooted in the intra-trinitarian drama, requires methodologically that we pay attention to the dynamic of the celebration and not only to the elements that result from it on the level of Presence *(res et sacramentum)* or of personal sanctification (grace). In short, we must restore liturgical praxis to its place as the privileged source of trinitarian and ecclesiological doctrine. *Lex orandi, lex credendi, lex theologandi.*

Our Proposal in the Wake of the Apostolic Letter
Novo Millennio Ineunte

Elaborated in response to contemporary debates in sacramental theology, the following proposal must be situated within the framework in which it arose: academic research and teaching at the John Paul II Institute for Studies on Marriage and Family, as well as in the context of the Great Jubilee of the year 2000 that celebrated the eucharistic and nuptial gift of Jesus Christ, who calls all people to holiness, committing them to the glorification of the Trinity.

By adopting the global perspective of Hans Urs von Balthasar, we have sought to follow the trinitarian logic that governs the kenotic and eucharistic gift of Christ.[27] The mystery of communion that forms the *"res"* of ecclesial unity has its roots in Christ's eucharistic kenosis. From the gift of the bodily and spiritual substance of the New Adam springs the gift of the Holy Spirit and the Church-Bride, represented at the foot of the cross by Mary Immaculate. At the end of our study, on the basis of a discussion of Christology, the Trinity,

---

27. See C. Rochetta, *I sacramenti della fede,* vol. 1: *Sacramentaria biblica fondamentale,* 7th ed. (Bologna: EDB, 1998), 43-50, "I sacramenti 'frammento' dell'estetica ecclesiale," in which the author cites at length Balthasar's theological aesthetics in order to highlight the "impoverishment of the Christian mystery when we have 'the expulsion of contemplation from the act of faith, the exclusion of "seeing" from "hearing," the removal of the *inchoatio visionis* from the *fides'* "; he cites H. U. von Balthasar, *The Glory of the Lord,* vol. 1: *Seeing the Form,* trans. Erasmo Leiva-Merikakis (New York: Crossroad; San Francisco: Ignatius, 1982), 70. While we acknowledge the importance of the aesthetic dimension (the contemplation of the *mirabilia Dei*), we believe that Balthasar's theo-dramatics (implication in God's engagement for the world) offers the most apt framework for further developing sacramental theology in a eucharistic and nuptial key. See N. Reali, *La ragione e la forma. Il Sacramento nella Teologia di H. U. von Balthasar* (Rome: PUL-Mursia, 1999).

and the unsurpassable value of the nuptial symbol, we will propose a eucharistic and nuptial trinitarian anthropology, which leads not only to an external glorification of the Trinity, but to a participation in the mutual glorification of the Father and the Son in the Spirit of Love.

PART ONE

The Mystery-Sacrament of Marriage

The Sacrament of Marriage Today

Authentic married love is caught up into divine love and is governed and enriched by Christ's redeeming power and the saving activity of the Church, so that this love may lead the spouses to God with powerful effect and may aid and strengthen them in sublime office of being a father or a mother. For this reason Christian spouses have a special sacrament by which they are fortified and receive a kind of consecration in the duties and dignity of their state.

GAUDIUM ET SPES 48 §2

The Second Vatican Council, often called the "Council of the Holy Spirit,"[1] discussed the Church's *aggiornamento* and her mission in an innovative and daring way. The Council marked a turning point in the Church's relation with the modern world. After centuries of conflictual relations, the Church, moved by the Spirit, undertook a rapprochement, a path of dialogue, with the modern world. This change was made possible by a renewed Christocentrism that permeated the reflection of the Council Fathers and reawakened in them a new missionary consciousness. The philosopher Jean Guitton called the Council the "event of the century" because of this attitude of dialogue on the part of the Church, which is rooted in Christ, the "Light of Nations" [*Lumen Gentium*].[2]

---

1. H. U. von Balthasar, "The Council of the Holy Spirit," *Communio: International Catholic Review* 17, no. 4 (Winter 1990): 595-611.

2. The Dogmatic Constitution on the Church is entitled *Lumen Gentium*, designating Christ as the "Light of Nations": *"Lumen Gentium cum sit Christus"* (LG 1).

We must keep this Christocentrism in mind if we wish to understand later developments of the Church's Magisterium, particularly under John Paul II. All the Church's teaching on the dignity of the human person and respect for life has its source in the light of Christ, who "fully reveals man to man himself and makes his supreme calling clear" (*GS* 22).

Among the "problems of special urgency" discussed by the Council, Christian marriage had pride of place. We find evidence of this in the first chapter of the second part of the Pastoral Constitution *Gaudium et Spes*, which is dedicated to "fostering the nobility of marriage and the family." After highlighting the dignity of the human person in the first part of the Constitution, the Council turned to the situation of marriage and the family, "presenting certain key points of Church doctrine in a clearer light" in order to strengthen Christians and other persons who seek "to foster the natural dignity of the married state and its superlative value" (*GS* 47). Fifty years later, the problems affecting marriage and the family mentioned in this paragraph of *Gaudium et Spes* have become real pastoral and cultural challenges, threatening the future of evangelization and of civilization itself. We must be aware of this drama as we begin our investigation of the sacrament of marriage. Our reflection will thus start with the Church's diagnosis of the current situation of marriage and the family. In the footsteps of John Paul II, we will then seek to situate our approach within the context of the renewal of sacramental theology after Vatican Council II. Our introductory chapter is divided into three parts: (1) pastoral and cultural challenges at the dawn of the third millennium; (2) John Paul II's engagement on behalf of marriage and the family; and (3) new developments in sacramental theology.

Pastoral and Cultural Challenges at the Dawn of the Third Millennium

To give a sense of the Church's diagnosis of the situation of marriage and the family today, we begin with a brief text from the Council:

> [T]he excellence of this institution is not everywhere reflected with equal brilliance, since polygamy, the plague of divorce, so-called free love and other disfigurements have an obscuring effect. In addition, married love is too often profaned by excessive self-love, the worship of pleasure and illicit practices against human generation. Moreover, serious disturbances are caused in families by modern economic conditions, by influences at once social and psychological, and by the demands of civil society. Finally,

in certain parts of the world problems resulting from population growth are generating concern. (*GS* 47)

This description, although already troubling enough, offers only a glimpse of the dramatic evolution that would lead contemporary society to a radical questioning of marriage and the family.[3] Though the Council Fathers were aware of the rapid and profound changes marking contemporary history, they do not seem to have foreseen the epochal transformation we are experiencing in the institution of the family at the dawn of the third millennium.[4]

The apostolic exhortation *Familiaris Consortio* (no. 6) further develops the Council's analysis, evaluating the situation sixteen years after its conclusion. The document mentions "bright spots and shadows." Positively, we note "a more lively awareness of personal freedom and greater attention to the quality of interpersonal relationships in marriage, to promoting the dignity of women, to responsible procreation, to the education of children." Negatively, we are overwhelmed by signs of a troubling degradation of certain fundamental values:

a mistaken theoretical and practical concept of the independence of the spouses in relation to each other; serious misconceptions regarding the relationship of authority between parents and children; the concrete difficulties that the family itself experiences in the transmission of values; the growing number of divorces; the scourge of abortion; the ever more frequent recourse to sterilization; the appearance of a truly contraceptive mentality.

Moreover, families in the "Third World"

often lack both the means necessary for survival, such as food, work, housing and medicine, and the most elementary freedoms. In the richer

---

3. See P. Morandé Court, "L'actualité de *Gaudium et Spes* et la mission de l'Église, à l'heure de changements qui font époque et de nouveaux défis," in *Gaudium et Spes, Bilan de trente années,* Lorette 95, Pontifical Council for the Laity, Revue 39 (Vatican City, 1996), 56-70; in the same issue, T. and R. Padilha, "Mariage et famille dans le Magistère pontifical après Vatican II," 113-22; H. Wattiaux, "La famille a-t-elle encore un avenir?" *Esprit et Vie* 40 (October 1992): 265-69 and 529-44.

4. I am thinking of the sociological, psychological, and juridical dimensions of marriage, all of which have been affected in specific ways. See R. Béraudy, *Sacrement de mariage et culture contemporaine. Questions et perspectives* (Paris: Desclée, 1985); H. Denis, *Le Mariage, un sacrement pour les croyants?* (Paris: Éd. du Cerf, 1990), ch. 1, 13-59.

countries, on the contrary, excessive prosperity and the consumer mentality, paradoxically joined to a certain anguish and uncertainty about the future, deprive married couples of the generosity and courage needed for raising up new human life.

The apostolic exhortation mentions the influence of this cultural situation on the conscience of the faithful. Under the pressure above all of the mass media, fundamental values have been overshadowed, giving way to the defense of divorce, the acceptance of merely civil marriage, the celebration of the marriage sacrament for reasons other than living faith, a rejection of moral norms in the area of sexuality, etc. These pressures have grown considerably in the course of the last few years, leading the Church to take a public position against population policies imposed on developing countries:

> *Demographic tendencies* certainly vary from one country to another. Every day, migration poses new challenges. The process of the reduction and stabilization of population growth, which experts call "demographic transition," can be observed in many regions. Nevertheless, in many countries a neo-Malthusian ideology, based on a false interpretation of demographic data, inspires politics of population control via contraceptives, forced sterilization, and ultimately, abortion. Sustained by wealthy nations, the agents of this false and destructive ideology are transformed into powerful international institutions, involved in what John Paul II denounced as a "conspiracy against life." (*Evangelium Vitae* 17)[5]

Despite the Church's efforts to awaken consciences, there has been no reversal of this tendency in contemporary culture at the dawn of the new millennium. To the contrary, individualistic, hedonistic and consumerist tendencies have grown stronger; homosexual unions have multiplied and have been claimed — in many places with success — as a right; the mass media exalt free sex and violence to the point of transforming them into social norms; abortion and euthanasia have become legal means for the solution of demographic problems.[6]

---

5. *Familia et Vita* 1, no. 2 (1996): 73.
6. See T. and R. Padilha, "Mariage et famille," 120-21; M. Berger, "La famille aujourd'hui. État des lieux," *La Pensée Catholique* 275 (January-February 1995): 9-27. The World Meeting of Families in Rio de Janeiro served as a platform to denounce anew the conspiracy of international organizations against the family. See also R. Cascioli, *Il complotto demografico. Il nuovo colonialismo delle grandi potenze economiche e delle organizzazioni umanitarie per sottomettere i poveri del mondo* (Casale Monferrato: Piemme, 1996).

In short, we observe more or less everywhere an aggravation of the already-mentioned problems regarding marriage and the family.

In the face of these cultural and pastoral challenges, the Church, guided by the Pope, has reaffirmed a series of important principles: the innate dignity and value of each human person, created in the image and likeness of God and thus capable of loving and being loved; the family founded on marriage, which is the union between a man and a woman, open to the transmission of life; the obligation incumbent upon the law to protect the indissolubility of marriage between a man and a woman for the good of society; and the right to life of every human being, from his or her conception to natural death.[7] In the encyclical *Evangelium Vitae,* John Paul II forcefully recalls that:

> Before the moral norm which prohibits the direct taking of the life of an innocent human being "there are no privileges or exceptions for anyone. It makes no difference whether one is the master of the world or the 'poorest of the poor' on the face of the earth. Before the demands of morality we are all absolutely equal." (*Evangelium Vitae* 57)

Today, these principles of the Church are attacked with new weapons in the name of an alarmist ideology that pursues a very definite agenda, which consists in using every possible means to limit the population of the Third World because it threatens to disturb the privileges of the rich. Some of the most powerful participants in the United Nation's notorious 1994 Cairo Conference on population, which set in motion a new global program of family planning, had sought to include abortion among the ordinary means of birth control. John Paul II, with the support of Muslim countries, succeeded in partially blocking these efforts, which were backed by the United States along with various international organizations. Unfortunately, however, the Church's influence has been too limited to prevent such birth control programs from going into effect. Between 2000 and 2015, it is predicted that 20 billion dollars a year will have been invested in limiting the growth of Third World populations. The United States and the World Bank grant foreign aid to poor nations only on the condition that the latter accept these imperialist demographic goals.

In terms of numbers and real influence, the Church does not weigh much in the power games played by the great ones of this world,

---

7. See *Familia et Vita,* 75.

and yet history has always shown that a small group of people who live freely and refuse to accept the Universal Law is enough to throw a wrench into the machine of totalitarianism. It is likely that the hardest battle will be fought on this front in the next twenty years.[8]

The Church is resolved to do everything necessary to safeguard the family. With serene strength, she affirms the truth about marriage and the family, that is, God's plan for the most basic cell of society. Christ assures us that the truth makes us free. The Church gives families a confirmation that the true freedom of loving can be found in their own midst. But we can go further. The Church now proposes to the world the gospel of the family as a way of salvation. The path of the new evangelization of cultures passes through the family and requires the missionary engagement of all, including the family itself, as it becomes more aware of its own value for the future of civilization.

The challenge posed by secularized cultures demands of both pastors and faithful a new attentiveness to the complexity of the current situation, along with a decisive commitment to responding with ardor, creativity, and urgency by means of a new evangelization. The teaching of the Church that we find both in the apostolic exhortation *Familiaris Consortio* and in later documents provides a holistic vision capable not only of renewing the family, but of recovering the family as the basis for a renewal of the Church herself. The vision of the family as "domestic church" lays the foundation for rethinking the communion and global mission of the Church today from what is, after all, her primary and most fundamental cell. Faithful to the teaching of the Council, John Paul II stressed with conviction that "the power and strength of the institution of marriage and family can also be seen in the fact that time and again, despite the difficulties produced, the profound changes in modern society reveal the true character of this institution in one way or another" (*GS* 47). In God's plan, the true nature of this institution is "ecclesial," that is, sacramental. It must, then, participate today more than ever in the universal mission of the Church, the "Sacrament of salvation" (*LG* 1). Such is the core message of John Paul II's pontificate.

John Paul II's Engagement on Behalf of Marriage and Family

John Paul II issued an urgent appeal in the encyclical *Evangelium Vitae:* "What is urgently called for is a general mobilization of consciences and a united

8. *Familia et Vita*, 198.

ethical effort to activate a great campaign in support of life. All together, we must build a new culture of life" (*EV* 95).

This is not an isolated appeal; it is the culmination of a continuous crescendo in John Paul II's commitment to the promotion of marriage and the family. The contribution of his pontificate has even been summarized in the title "the pope of the family."[9] This title reflects both his teaching and his strategy for a new evangelization, which gave priority to questions of marriage and the family.

With regard to doctrine, John Paul II took up Paul VI's argument in the encyclical *Humanae Vitae* and deepened it anthropologically and ethically. In developing his own reflections, first expressed in *Love and Responsibility*, John Paul II confirmed the orientation of Paul VI's encyclical in a personalistic and Christological key.[10] The Church's commitment to the defense of human life from conception to natural death is a consequence of faith in Christ, the Redeemer of man, John Paul II argues. The work of the redemption consecrates the dignity of the human person and the unity of love and of life. The central message of the encyclical *Humanae Vitae* — the inseparable unity of the two meanings of marriage, the unitive and the procreative — is thus reaffirmed in the face of their dissociation in the dominant culture. The apostolic exhortation *Familiaris Consortio* and the encyclical *Evangelium Vitae* represent a substantial contribution to the doctrinal development of the Church's Magisterium on questions of love and of life.

On a pastoral level, John Paul II multiplied initiatives designed to translate these convictions of the Church into practice. The creation of the John Paul II Institute for Studies on Marriage and the Family in 1981 was followed by the transformation of the Committee for the Family, founded in 1972, into the Pontifical Council for the Family in 1984. These organs of the Holy See carry forward on a doctrinal and pastoral level the vigorous impulse given by the pope in these crucial questions. We should also keep in mind the complementary reflections that we find in documents such as the apostolic letter *Mulieris Dignitatem,* the *Letter to Women,* and the *Letter to Families.* These texts exemplify John Paul II's dialogue with contemporary culture and his concern to proclaim the Gospel in the face of the cultural challenges that threaten and obscure the mission of the family in the Church and the world.

We can conclude by saying that John Paul II was profoundly interested in adopting and developing the main lines of Vatican II's teaching on marriage

9. T. and R. Padilha, "Mariage et famille," 116.

10. K. Wojtyła, *Love and Responsibility,* trans. Grzegorz Ignatik (Boston: Pauline Books and Media, 2013).

and the family. In the doctrinal content of his interventions as well as in his family-centered pastoral strategy for a new evangelization, he demonstrated how crucial this issue — already considered particularly urgent at the Council — had become in our time. We could say more. This pontificate was a constant, profoundly intelligent stimulus that raised the Church's proposal regarding marriage and the family to a new level: that of a prophetic message for the salvation of the confused and nihilistic cultures of our time. We can only hope that contemporary theology and the pastoral activity of the local churches will organically adopt the Christological re-centering of marriage and the family that John Paul II accomplished in the wake of the Council. This could result in a qualitative advance in our awareness of the dignity of the family as domestic church and, consequently, in a significant revival of the Church's mission in the world beginning with its most fundamental cell.

New Developments in Sacramental Theology

We said above that the event of the Council renewed the Church's Christo-logical consciousness, that is, her awareness of being the Church "of Christ": "*Lumen gentium cum sit Christus*" (*LG* 1). The light of nations is Christ and not the Church, but this light shines on the Church's countenance. This Christological consciousness is expressed in the first paragraph of the Dogmatic Constitution on the Church, when it uses the term "*sacramentum*" to express the relationship between the visible reality of the Church and the invisible mystery — "*mysterion*" — of God in Christ: "the Church is in Christ like a sacrament or as a sign and instrument both of a very closely knit union with God and of the unity of the whole human race" (*LG* 1). The Church is the universal sacrament of Christ: this theological claim reflects the path opened by Henri de Lubac in the 1930s.[11]

The Council's use of the term "sacrament" to describe the mystery of the Church confirmed theology's orientation toward a new approach to the sacraments:

> Drawing on already existing advances, post-conciliar sacramental theol-
> ogy seems to be well on the way to overcoming a certain received account

---

11. H. de Lubac, *Catholicism: Christ and the Common Destiny of Man*, trans. Lancelot C. Sheppard and Elizabeth Englund (San Francisco: Ignatius, 1988), 76: "If Christ is the sacrament of God, the Church is for us the sacrament of Christ."

of the sacramental event. Mainly juridical in cast, this reading was characterized by an excessive preoccupation with the "matter" and "form" of the sacraments and the "minimum" criteria of their liceity and validity.[12]

Without denying the value of such considerations for canonical purposes, post-conciliar research has turned its attention above all to the Christological and ecclesiological dimension of the sacraments. It has sought to highlight the personalist dimension of the sacraments, focusing on the celebration in its entirety, the anthropological value of symbols in their global context, and their organic relationship to the paschal mystery. Sacramental theology has learned to speak in new categories such as "encounter," "interpersonal event," "communication," "dialogue," and "relation." As Rochetta writes, "The sacraments are not 'things' but acts of the glorified Lord in the Church, and thus events in which an interpersonal encounter with God takes place, a living communication in Christ and in the gift of his Spirit."[13]

The new approach of post-conciliar sacramental theology consists precisely in grounding the ecclesial dimension of the sacraments in Christ, the "original sacrament":[14]

Faith, whose gaze has been refined over the course of salvation history, discovers in the human figure of Christ the incarnation of the mystery of God, the epiphany of the divine life, him in whom the *mysterion* of salvation has become so transparent that the fourth evangelist can place this affirmation on Jesus' lips: "Whoever sees me, [also] sees the Father" (John 14:9). Thus illuminated, faith conceives of Christ as the "original sacrament." This very recent theological expression means that all the Church's sacraments are recapitulated and concentrated in Christ in a preeminent way, before they are explicated in the liturgy as holy signs that communicate grace.[15]

---

12. C. Rochetta, *Sacramentaria fondamentale. Dal "Mysterion" al "Sacramentum"* (Bologna: EDB, 1989), 379-80. Various studies exist on this subject; see especially J.-M. Tillard, "Le nuove prospettive della teologia sacramentaria," in *Sacra Doctrina* (Bologna: ESD, 1967), 37-58, especially 45; P. Adnès, "La function sotériologique des sacrements," *Studia missionaria* 30 (1981): 89-111.

13. Rochetta, *Sacramentaria fondamentale,* 380.

14. See L. Scheffczyk, "Gesù Cristo Sacramento originario della redenzione," in *Incontrare Cristo nei sacramenti. Sussidio teologico per una pastorale sacramentaria,* ed. H. Luthe (Cinisello Balsamo: Paoline, 1988), 13-27.

15. Scheffczyk, "Gesù Cristo Sacramento originario della redenzione," 30-31.

By applying the expression "original sacrament" to Christ, we understand better how the individual sacraments are derived from him, without
needing an explicit pronouncement in Scripture to demonstrate their Christological provenance. Rather, the derivation is deduced organically from Christ's
being and action as the God-man. Thomas Aquinas already spoke of Jesus'
humanity as the *"instrumentum coniunctum"* of his divinity. The idea of the
"original sacrament" leads to the same conclusion by highlighting the revelatory and communicative instrumentality of divine grace, which characterizes
the man Jesus. This of course does not mean that we are reducing the mystery
of the God-man to a sign like that of the sacraments in liturgical action. Christ
is much more than "a" sacrament. On the other hand, the expression "sacrament" is not applied to Christ in a purely figurative or metaphorical sense. As
Scheffczyk affirms, "Christ is truly sacrament and original sacrament in a true
and preeminent sense, but he also represents a singular form of the realization
of the sacramental mystery. This form cannot subsist in the same way as the
individual sacraments."[16]

The Church's participation in the sacramental mystery of Christ is rooted
in the event of the Incarnation: "Behold, I am the handmaid of the Lord; let
it be done to me according to your word" (Luke 1:38). From the beginning,
Mary's consent contributed to the formation of the Body of Christ in her
womb. Moreover, from his birth to the Cross, she participated in the gift that
he made of himself to the world. St. Paul and the Church Fathers understood
the unity of Christ and the Church, accomplished through the work of the
Holy Spirit, as the unity of the head with the members of the body (1 Cor. 12:12-
27). This strict and organic unity remains nonetheless "nuptial," maintaining
the distinction between Christ and the Church. The Letter to the Ephesians
stresses precisely these two aspects of Christ's unity with the Church in the
famous passage addressed to Christian spouses:

> As Christ loved the church and gave himself up for her . . . husbands
> should love their wives as their own bodies. He who loves his wife loves
> himself. For no man ever hates his own flesh, but nourishes and cherishes

---

16. Scheffczyk, "Gesù Cristo Sacramento originario della redenzione," 32. P. Kuhn, "I
sacramenti della Chiesa. Un settenario," in Luthe, ed., *Incontrare Cristo nei sacramenti*, 88-89:
"Only faith is capable of recognizing in the earthly figure of the Lord the *sign* of his eternal
divinity, and of experiencing it as the *means* through which he accomplishes the redemption.
Christ is, consequently, *the* mystery of faith . . . the Sacrament that comes before the sacraments and founds them by communicating to them his own sacramental nature: Christ is the
original sacrament."

it, as Christ does the church, because we are members of his body. (Eph. 5:25, 28-30)

Hans Urs von Balthasar summarizes the patristic teaching on the unity of Christ and the Church in a single body: "The Church, in this perspective, is the broadest 'incarnation' [of the Logos] . . . since she has as her goal leading all of humanity to God."[17] In the economy of the "mystery," the Church thus appears *"in Christo"* as sacrament, that is, as "sign and instrument . . . of the unity of the whole human race" (*LG* 1). Her participation in Christ's sacramentality is simultaneously physical, spousal, and universal. Through her, Christ the "original sacrament" extends his fruitfulness through time and all human cultures.

The particular sacramentality of the seven sacraments flows from Christ's original sacramentality; they participate in the latter within the universal sacramentality of the Church. St. Augustine writes, "Christ dies so that the Church can be born. . . . After his death, his side is pierced by a lance so that from it can flow the sacraments that build up the Church." Vis-à-vis the Scholastic tradition, contemporary theology understands the institution of the sacraments from a new angle. Christ is the author of the sacraments, but not because he specified in detail the matter and form of each sacrament. The institution of the particular sacraments appears today, rather, as fundamentally present in the birth of the Church from Christ's paschal mystery.[18] Moreover, the rediscovery of the Holy Spirit in Western theology opens new perspectives for sacramental theology in general and the theology of marriage in particular.[19] The concern to establish the divine institution of the sacraments in the explicit, historical will of Christ in fact reveals a forgetfulness of the Spirit that has impoverished the theology of the sacraments in the West. The Holy Spirit's role is precisely that of confirming and universalizing the whole truth of Christ. This mission of the Spirit consists in causing the Church, Christ's Body and Bride, to exist as his "helpmate" in giving life to the world. It is, then, the Spirit's role to confirm the institution of the sacraments in the Church, in fidelity to the word of Christ, and to guide their development in the ecclesial tradition.

This new approach of sacramental theology thus overcomes an overly

17. H. U. von Balthasar, *Parole et mystère chez Origène* (Paris: Cerf, 1957), 51.
18. See K. Rahner, *The Church and the Sacraments,* trans. W. J. O'Hara (Herder, 1963), 41-74; E. Schillebeeckx, *Christ the Sacrament of the Encounter with God* (New York: Sheed and Ward), 112-32.
19. See M. Martinéz Peque, *Lo Spirito Santo e il matrimonio* (Rome: EDR, 1993), 211-18.

narrow, juridical, and essentialist view centered on a defense of the seven sacraments. It grasps more profoundly the symbolical dimension of human existence and tends toward a more trinitarian, personalist, and spousal approach. This perspective allows us to speak of the efficacy of the sacraments in terms of fruitfulness, which more accurately conveys the personal character of grace. The particular fruitfulness of the sacraments flows from the trinitarian fruitfulness of Christ as the eschatological Bridegroom of humanity. This fruitfulness consists above all in the gift of the Holy Spirit that is poured out after Easter. Mary-Church shares in this spiritual fruitfulness through the mystery of the covenant in the Spirit; this covenant involves her eucharistically in Christ's paschal and sacramental gift to all humanity. Our reflection on the sacrament of marriage will unfold within this spousal and pneumatological framework. Since this sacrament "is a great mystery . . . in reference to Christ and the Church" (Eph. 5:32), it seems obviously important to begin from the "mystery" of Christ the Bridegroom and the Church his Bride in order to understand more deeply the sacramentality specific to Christian marriage.

The text of the Council with which we began our reflection, *Gaudium et Spes* 48 §2 unveils the elements essential to presenting the sacrament of marriage — except for a reference to the Holy Spirit, which can be found immediately afterward in the same text. We are essentially interested in authentic human love as this is taken up into the divine-human love of Christ for the Church. We will therefore seek the foundations of the sacramentality of conjugal love in revelation and in the Church's tradition. This will involve exploration of the theological, ecclesiological and anthropological aspects of the question in order to understand and explain more fully the Church's prophetic response to the contemporary crisis of marriage and the family.

CHAPTER 1

The Revelation of the Marriage Sacrament

God is love and in himself he lives a mystery of personal loving
communion. Creating the human race in his own image and continually keeping it in being, God inscribed in the humanity of man
and woman the vocation, and thus the capacity and responsibility,
of love and communion.

JOHN PAUL II, *FAMILIARIS CONSORTIO* 11

In order to shed full light on the spouses' vocation to love, we must first of all
turn to the Bible, which contains God's revelation regarding marriage and the
family. We must be careful to note at the beginning that the Scriptures, from
Genesis (1–3) to the book of Revelation (21–22), contain abundant references
to the institution of marriage, from the nuptials of Adam and Eve to the wedding feast of the Lamb. Marriage occupies an important place in the Bible.
The ideal of the couple that we discover there, though conditioned by Israel's
culture and socio-political situation, differs from the mythical conceptions of
neighboring religions.[1] Moreover, this ideal of unity, fidelity, and fruitfulness
appears to be confirmed by the key role of the category of "covenant" in the
general interpretation of Scripture. It is true that this category had a primarily
legal signification, but it is also true that along the course of salvation history
the nuptial symbol gradually became the privileged expression of the "pact"
that God established with his people. This is why we begin our reflection by

---

1. See P. Grelot, *Le Couple humain dans l'Écriture* (Paris: Éd. du Cerf, 1962); A. Tosato,
"L'istituto familiare dell'antico Israele e della Chiesa primitiva," *Anthropotes* 13, no. 1 (1997):
109-74.

recalling the meaning of covenant in biblical hermeneutics, before analyzing the texts that speak more explicitly about God's design for the sacrament of marriage.

The Covenant in Biblical Hermeneutics

"The fundamental idea of the whole Bible is that God wishes to establish a covenant with men."[2] This affirmation of the biblical scholar Ignace de la Potterie provides us with a hermeneutical starting point. Without entering into the details of the relationship between theology and exegesis, we recall the necessity of rediscovering a fundamental principle governing the interpretation of Scripture: the unity of the Bible. The Scriptures are more than a collection of texts assembled more or less artificially by a tradition of scribes subject to all the influences of the culture of the time. They are the fruit of God's intimate dialogue with his people within the framework of a covenant (Hebrew *berit*: disposition) marked by the seal of the Spirit in the Ten Commandments. This first dispensation, which is the foundation of a history of love and infidelity, was called from the beginning to find its fulfillment in the New Dispensation *(berit)* sealed in the blood of Christ. The unity of the Bible is in fact rooted in the New Covenant, which, as just noted, is sealed in Christ's blood for the salvation of all. If, from a human perspective, the Bible seems to be a library of many different books, from the perspective of the divine Author, all of Scripture is "as if *one* book."[3]

The unity of the Bible is the incontrovertible presupposition of all Christian exegesis. This unity is founded on faith in Christ, the Word of God made flesh, who brings the promises of the Old Covenant to their fulfillment. This conviction shared by the Fathers and medieval doctors alike was abandoned by modern scientific exegesis, with its overly narrow focus on a historical-

---

2. I. de la Potterie, *Marie dans le mystère de l'Alliance* (Paris: Desclée de Brouwer, 1985), 20.

3. J. Ratzinger, "L'exégèse biblique en conflit," in *L'Exégèse chrétienne aujourd'hui* (Paris: Fayard, 2000). This book contains several contributions by I. de la Potterie and one by G. Colombo regarding Scriptural exegesis and the present task of reconstituting a theological, spiritual, and fully ecclesial exegesis. See also H. de Lubac, *L'Écriture dans la tradition* (Paris: Aubier-Montaigne, 1966) [*Scripture in the Tradition* (New York: Crossroad, 2001)]; R. Voderholzer, *Die Einheit der Schrift und ihr geistiger Sinn. Der Beitrag Henri de Lubac zur Erforschung von Geschichte und Systematik christlicher Bibelhermeneutik* (Einsiedeln: Johannes Verlag, 1998).

critical analysis of the texts.[4] The interpretation of Scripture must not limit itself to situating the texts in their immediate literary context or to tracing the historical genesis of events and words. The understanding of the texts requires something more of exegesis: reception of the "whole of Scripture, which is centered on Christ."[5] This means that biblical hermeneutics always unfolds within the framework of the Church's faith. If it wishes to be "scientific," it must understand itself as a "science of the faith," whose foundational principle is the Christ to whom the Church bears witness as the fulfillment of all the Scriptures. Now, if Christ is the sole reality of which Scripture speaks and thus the key to its interpretation, this reality is itself nothing other than the mystery *(mysterion)* of the covenant. As Carlo Rochetta writes:

> Within the Bible as a whole, the category of "covenant" expresses the central content of the *mysterion* in history: the gratuitous communion of love and life that God wishes to establish with humanity. This communion is manifested historically and eschatologically in Christ and is communicated in the Spirit through the Church, the community of the ultimate and definitive covenant. As such, the category of "covenant" is particularly apt for representing both God's coming among us and the unique bond that he establishes with mankind. This content is given to us through the progressive unfolding of the economy of the *mysterion*. At each stage, the God of revelation is the God of the covenant, a covenant that is first promised and prefigured, and then accomplished and established in the only-begotten Son made man, who died and rose from the dead. The Church and the sacraments — marriage among them — belong to this historical-salvific dynamism and actively make it present to human existence in its particularly crucial moments.[6]

From the earliest prophets to the book of Revelation, the image of marriage is employed to describe the covenant. As the union of man and woman,

---

4. I. de la Potterie, "L'exégèse biblique, science de la foi," in *L'Exégèse chrétienne aujourd'hui*, 138. With the example of Mary, "Daughter Zion," the author shows how, within the context of Scripture as a whole, a "symbolical" exegesis "represents a great step forward in terms of hermeneutics" (139).

5. De la Potterie, "L'exégèse biblique, science de la foi," 138.

6. C. Rochetta, *Il sacramento della coppia* (Bologna: EDB, 1996), 164. Regarding the notion of *mysterion* and marriage, see ch. 6, 135-62; see also G. Bornkamm, *"Mysterion,"* in *Theologisches Wörterbuch zum Neuen Testament* (Stuttgart, 1942), vol. 4, 823-26; R. Penna, *Il 'mysterion' paolino. Traiettoria e costituzione* (Brescia: Paideia, 1978).

marriage is the fundamental symbol of the covenant: God is the Bridegroom and Israel is the (often unfaithful) bride. According to the classical formula of the covenant, God says to Israel, "I will be your God and you shall be my people" (cf. Exod. 6:7; Jer. 7:23). This formula expresses the mutual belonging of the people to God and of God to his people. This mutual belonging explains the recurrent theme of God's jealousy in the Old Covenant. Yahweh does not want his bride to commit infidelity by seeking out other gods. The reality that the Old Testament presents in the context of the relationship between Yahweh and Israel reappears in the messianic age in the relationship between Christ and the Church. Pauline theology sets forth their nuptial relationship as the "great mystery" hidden in God in order to be revealed in the fullness of time. The theology of marriage thus finds its privileged locus in the Letter to the Ephesians, which contains the most significant scriptural data regarding the sacrament of marriage as well as for the hermeneutics of Scripture as a whole. As we will see further on, Pope John Paul II structured his catecheses on marriage around the relationship between the sacrament of creation (Gen. 1–3) and the sacrament of the redemption, which Paul places at the center of his great meditation on the mystery of man's election in Christ (Ephesians 1 and 5).

The Primordial Sacrament in the Old Covenant

The first three chapters of Genesis are a kind of Magna Charta of God's original plan for marriage. John Paul II paid particular attention to these texts, in which he saw a sketch of God's original plan for marriage as a "primordial sacrament": "Thus, in this dimension, a primordial *sacrament* is constituted, understood as a *sign that* efficaciously *transmits in the visible world the invisible mystery hidden in God from eternity.*"[7] Before presenting his complex vision of the term "primordial sacrament," we will pause for a moment to consider the

---

7. John Paul II, *Man and Woman He Created Them: A Theology of the Body,* trans. Michael Waldstein (Boston: Pauline Books and Media, 2006) [= *TOB*], 203. See especially Part I, chapter 1: "Christ Appeals to the 'Beginning'" (with an introduction by Angelo Scola in the Italian edition, "Primo ciclo. Il Principio," in *Uomo e donna lo creò. Catechesi sull'amore umano,* 4th ed. [Rome: Città Nuova–Libreria Editrice Vaticana, 1995]); and Part I, chapter 2, "Christ Appeals to the Human Heart" (with an introduction by Carlo Caffarra in the Italian edition, "Secondo ciclo. La redenzione del cuore"); and Part II, chapters 1-2, "The Dimension of Covenant and of Grace" and "The Dimension of Sign" (with an introduction by Inos Biffi in the Italian edition, "Quinto ciclo. Il matrimonio cristiano"). On the specific theme of the primordial sacrament, see catecheses no. 87, 93, and 96-98.

text of Genesis itself. The book's first two chapters offer two distinct accounts of creation: the "priestly" (Gen. 1:1–2:4a, fifth century B.C.) and the Yahwist (2:4b-25, tenth century B.C.).

The first factor common to both accounts is the unity of the couple, man and woman, which is expressed in a complementary way by the two narratives.

1. The second, Yahwist account dramatizes the theme (Gen. 2:21-24). It describes the formation of woman, who is drawn from the man's flesh by the work of the Creator: "So the Lord God caused a deep sleep to fall upon the man, and while he slept took one of his ribs and closed up its place with flesh" (Gen. 2:21; 2 Sam. 5:1). In woman, the man sees a creature who is like himself, who enables him to leave his solitude and to actualize his deepest nature. At the end of the account, Adam's exclamation leads us back to the theme of spousal union: "Therefore a man leaves his father and his mother and cleaves to his wife, and they become one flesh" (Gen. 2:24).

2. In the first, very dense creation account, the union between the spouses is expressed in a play of grammatical forms, which pass from the singular to the plural in the text. When God decides to create man, the text uses the singular: "God created *man* in his own image, in the image of God he created him"; we thus think of a single being. But when God's creative plan is realized, the text shifts to the plural: "male and female he created *them*" (Gen. 1:27). Angelo Tosato has studied these expressions and their importance in Judaism, in the Gospels, and in Saint Paul.[8] The human creature is thought and willed by God in a twofold variation, masculine and feminine, possessing an identical dignity within a specific diversity and complementarity. "Man and woman together constitute the divine image."[9]

The second fundamental datum is God's *blessing* on the two first spouses: "God blessed them, and God said to them, 'be fruitful and multiply, and fill the earth" (Gen. 1:28). Such a blessing is not a simple well-wishing; it expresses the

8. A. Tosato, *Il matrimonio nel Giudaismo Antico e nel Nuovo Testamento* (Rome: Città Nuova, 1976), 49-65.

9. C. Rochetta, "Il sacramento del matrimonio," in *Incontrare Cristo nei sacramenti. Sussidio teologico per una pastorale sacramentaria*, ed. H. Luthe (Cinisello Balsamo: Paoline, 1988), 373. See also John Paul II, Apostolic Letter *Mulieris Dignitatem* [On the Dignity and Vocation of Women], 7: "The fact that man 'created as man and woman' is the image of God means not only that each of them individually is like God, as a rational and free being. It also means that man and woman, created as a 'unity of the two' in their common humanity, are called to live in a communion of love, and in this way to mirror in the world the communion of love that is in God, through which the Three Persons love each other in the intimate mystery of the one divine life."

presence of God, it is a word which effects a reality. Marriage thus appears as an encounter between man and woman that is willed, "instituted," and sanctified by God himself. The very gift of life flowing from the conjugal encounter of the two spouses will be seen as a gift proper to God (cf. Gen. 4:1).

A third element of the Genesis text shows that the conjugal union enters into a history of trial, temptation, and sin that alters the human condition. Contrary to certain explanations of the text, the object of this temptation and sin cannot be reduced to sex, since, as Ligier notes, "the expression 'to know good and evil' has nothing to do with the union of the sexes."[10] According to Genesis 3, temptation and sin nonetheless have consequences for man and woman as well as for their reciprocal position within marriage: the woman will be dominated by her husband and will give birth in pain.[11] The husband, once the happy guardian of the garden, will have to work in the sweat of his brow (Gen. 3:19). Both of them will die and return to dust. But all of this happens without prejudice to the future: the woman receives a promise of victory over the seducer (Gen. 3:14-15). And the following chapter, which features the first human birth, begins with the woman's cry of faith: "I have gotten a man with the help of the Lord" (Gen. 4:1).

As a consequence of sin, the sacred institution of marriage was not always respected in the history of the Old Testament. From the time of the patriarchs and the spread of polygamy, Scripture records innumerable transgressions against the holiness of marriage (Gen. 16:1-4; 1 Sam. 1:6; Deut. 21:15-17). King David, though highly praised in the Bible, had his harem (2 Sam. 16:20-22), as did Solomon (1 Kings 11:1-13). In order both to stimulate the demographic growth of the people of God during the exile and to protect them from the dangers posed by their pagan surroundings, laws were established to promote the purity and sanctity of the sexual encounter. We see an example of this in all its prohibitions of Leviticus 18, for example, the prohibition of incest: "You shall not uncover the nakedness of your father . . . your mother . . . your sister" (Lev. 18:7-16). Despite the people's transgressions, the ideal of the

10. L. Ligier, *Il matrimonio. Questioni teologiche e pastorali* (Rome: Città Nuova, 1988), 16. On this theme, see Grelot, *Le Couple humain dans l'Écriture*, 41: "The sin of the first human beings was essentially an act of the 'heart' (in the biblical sense); the sacred author does not seem to consider its complete translation into some magically produced usurpation of sexuality." For an opposing view, see J. Coppens, *La Connaissance du bien et du mal et le péché du Paradis* (Louvain, Bruges, Paris: Desclée de Brouwer, 1948).

11. John Paul II, *Mulieris Dignitatem*, 10: "*The woman cannot become the 'object' of 'domination' and male 'possession.'* But the words of the biblical text directly concern original sin and its lasting consequences in man and woman."

faithful and fruitful couple is renewed in the post-exilic period, prompting a theological reflection on the drama of the original couple (Genesis 3).

The oracles of the prophets represent a significant moment in preparation for the sacramentality of marriage in the Old Testament. As we noted above, the prophets use the language of marriage to express God's covenant with his people: God is the Bridegroom, Israel and Jerusalem the bride, while their inhabitants are God's children. Israel forgets and forsakes her Bridegroom; God abandons his faithless betrothed in the desert, yet returns to her in the end (Hos. 2:4-17; 6:1-6; 11:1-9; Jer. 2:1-37; Ezekiel 16 and 20). The entire Song of Songs reprises this motif in a poetic form. It is well known that Jewish exegesis sees in this love poem a hymn to God's nuptial union with his people Israel. Since the time of the prophets, then, marriage belongs to the promise of the New Covenant, that is, the promise of the restoration of the relationship between God and humanity. Looking forward to a New Covenant symbolized by nuptials, the last prophets impart an understanding of marriage more in accord with the creation account. Malachi 2:14-16 develops a teaching on the unity of the couple that is worthy of Genesis 1:26: The two separated spouses return to their primitive unity, and so it is illicit to abandon the wife one first loved.[12]

By way of transition to the New Testament texts concerning marriage, we end this section with a passage from John Paul II's catecheses, in which he explains the meaning of the term "primordial sacrament" by referring to the origins of Genesis' teaching on marriage:

> The institution of marriage, according to the words of Genesis 2:24, expresses not only the beginning of the fundamental human community, which by the "procreative" power proper to it ("be fruitful and multiply," Gen. 1:28) serves to continue the work of creation, but at the same time it expresses the Creator's salvific initiative, which corresponds to man's eternal election spoken about in Ephesians. This salvific initiative comes forth from God, the Creator, and its supernatural efficaciousness is identical with the very act of the creation of man in the state of original innocence. In this state, already beginning with the act of the creation of man, his eternal election in Christ has borne fruit. In this way, one must recognize that the original sacrament of creation draws its efficaciousness from the "beloved Son" (see Eph. 1:6, where the author speaks about "his grace, which he has given to us in his beloved Son"). As for marriage, one can deduce that — instituted in the context of the sacrament of creation in its totality, or in the

---

12. Tosato, *Il matrimonio nel Giudaismo antico e nel Nuovo Testamento*, 32, 64.

state of original innocence — it was to serve not only to extend the work of creation, or procreation, but also to spread the same sacrament of creation to further generations of human beings, that is, to spread the supernatural fruits of man's eternal election by the Father in the eternal Son, the fruits man was endowed with by God in the very act of creation.[13]

The concept of "primordial sacrament" finds its theological justification in the Creator's institution of the man-woman relationship with a view to the covenant in the beloved Son and in his blessing it — from the beginning — with a natural and supernatural fruitfulness that flows from the grace of the Redeemer. We turn now to a more precise account of John Paul II's understanding of the sacramentality of marriage as grounded in a Christocentric view of creation inspired by Saint Paul.

The Revelation of the "Mystery of Marriage" in the New Covenant

The communion between God and his people finds its definitive fulfillment in Jesus Christ, the Bridegroom who loves and gives himself as the Savior of humanity, uniting it to himself as his body. He reveals the original truth of marriage, the truth of the "beginning," and, freeing man from his hardness of heart, he makes man capable of realizing this truth in its entirety. (*Familiaris Consortio* 13)

The revelation of the sacramentality of marriage is linked to the "mystery" of the new and eternal Covenant, which God the Father decided before all ages in his beloved Son. This mystery was accomplished in the life, death, and resurrection of Jesus Christ. The nuptial symbolism of the Old Covenant was already available to receive the meaning and breadth of this salvific event. Jesus' sacrifice, which must be understood in the light of the eucharistic mystery, is the accomplishment of the New Covenant in his blood. The paschal mystery is thus the ultimate foundation of the sacramentality of marriage. St. Paul reflected theologically on this theme in the Letter to the Ephesians, while the Synoptic authors recorded the gestures and words of Jesus that prepared the doctrinal

13. John Paul II, *TOB*, 506. As a footnote in the Italian version explains, "'Primordial' sacrament does not mean 'natural' sacrament, because the order chosen by God is in fact an order in Jesus Christ, and thus concretely supernatural. 'Primordial' means that it is already in act in the 'economic' moment of creation as a sign of the 'mystery' that is manifested in creation" (376).

development effected by the Apostle of the Gentiles. We will thus distinguish two steps in the New Testament revelation of the sacramentality of marriage.

The Gospels

The first fundamental datum of the Gospels is Jesus' awareness of being the one sent by God into the midst of his people in order to accomplish the divine Bridegroom's encounter with his bride. Three elements that are important in this context:

a. When the Pharisees accuse Jesus' disciples of not fasting, Jesus defends them, saying, "Can the wedding guests mourn while the bridegroom is with them? The days will come, when the bridegroom is taken away from them, and then they will fast" (Matt. 9:15; Mark 2:19-20; Luke 5:34-35).

b. When his disciples ask him whether he is the Christ, John the Baptist testifies: "I am not the Christ, but I have been sent before him. He who has the bride is the bridegroom; the friend of the bridegroom, who stands and hears him, rejoices greatly at the bridegroom's voice" (John 3:28-29). Of course, the bridegroom is not clearly identified in this Johannine passage, but it is legitimate to link it with the Old Testament motif of Israel as the bride of Yahweh.

c. Jesus integrates the parable of the ten virgins into his discourse about the Kingdom (Matt. 25:1-13): the attention and loving vigilance he demands are signs of his awareness of being the Bridegroom, who desires to be welcomed as such.

The second fundamental element in the Gospels is Jesus' presence at the wedding at Cana, along with the significance that the evangelist accords to this "beginning" of Jesus' signs. This episode has a symbolic meaning that also points ahead to the hour of the Cross. The evangelist thus highlights the value and importance of marriage as a symbol pregnant with mystery: "The gospel narrative of John 2:1-12 is not the description of a marriage at Cana but rather the account of the 'mystery' of this wedding feast."[14] This

---

14. De la Potterie, *Marie dans le mystère de l'Alliance*, 230. For an interpretation of the Cana episode, see E. Przywara, *Christentum gemäss Johannes* (Nuremberg: Glock & Lutz, 1954); J. P. Charlier, *Le Signe de Cana. Essai de théologie johannique* (Brussels, Paris: La pensée catholique/Office Général du Livre, 1959).

mystery is precisely the appearing of the true Bridegroom, who intervenes at the request of the "woman" to reveal, through a first sign, the imminent event of the eschatological wedding feast. The Johannine passage describing the blood and water flowing from Christ's pierced side (John 19:34) presents the final revelation of the sacramental meaning of the signs in the fourth Gospel. In John's Gospel, nuptial symbolism thus appears as central to understanding the paschal mystery, the presence of woman in the economy of the covenant, and the relationship between earthly marriage and its eschatological fulfillment.

We turn to a final fundamental element in the Gospels: Jesus' discussion with the Pharisees regarding the act of repudiation. Louis Ligier observes:

> [Jesus'] main intention is not only to abolish the Mosaic permission of divorce but to reestablish this sacred and inviolable principle: "What God has joined, let no man put asunder" (Matt. 19:6). The sanctity and inviolability of marriage have their source in *God's intervention.* Indissolubility is in fact affirmed, but the transcendent aspect of the marriage union is brought into relief at the same time.[15]

As Ligier shows, the context of this famous Matthean pericope sheds light on Jesus' profound intention to set marriage within his final teaching about the "kingdom of heaven."[16] Jesus is about to go up to Jerusalem to accomplish the paschal mystery; the declaration about marriage is immediately followed by the teaching on virginity for the kingdom (Matt. 19:10-12), voluntary poverty (Matt. 19:16-23), and aspiring to perfection (Matt. 19:21). What is involved, then, is not merely the restoration of an ancient principle. The grace needed to understand the new gift of virginity for the kingdom of heaven also sheds light on the need for grace to live the marriage established in "the beginning" according to the new order created by Jesus. "Not all can receive this precept, but only those to whom it is given" (Matt. 19:11).

The Teaching of St. Paul

Paul's teaching appears in two main passages, on which theologians have focused their attention through the centuries: the first verses of chapter 7 of the

---

15. Ligier, *Il matrimonio,* 23.
16. Ligier, *Il matrimonio,* 23.

First Letter to the Corinthians (7:1-9), which consider marriage above all as a "remedy for concupiscence," and the even more important passage from Ephesians 5 (5:21-33), which presents the "mystery" of marriage in its relationship to Christ and the Church.

First Corinthians 7:1-9: In this passage, Paul is responding to the particular questions posed by the Christians of Corinth. He does not claim to offer them a full treatment of marriage and virginity, but only to give advice on these subjects. We must keep in mind the apocalyptic anxiety that we glimpse behind the urgent questions of Paul's interlocutors.[17] He begins thus: "It is well for a man not to touch a woman. But because of the temptation to immorality, each man should have his own wife and each woman her own husband" (vv. 1-2). In fact, Paul would prefer that all be like himself, that is, celibate; but, aware of human weakness, he gives them the realistic advice that it is better to marry than to burn (v. 9). At first glance, this passage seems to offer a less than positive view of marriage, and traditionally it was used to justify a certain devaluation of matrimony. Such an interpretation, however, does not respect the Pauline text. Paul does not claim here to be giving a teaching on marriage in general, but limits himself to answering questions that seem to call into question precisely the value of sexual activity. Chapter 6 ends in an exhortation to chastity because we are temples of the Spirit and members of the body of Christ. In this light, it is evident that Paul's approach does not depend on Hellenistic prejudices against the flesh. His responses appear as a defense of sexual activity, but in the context of the early Christian expectation of the imminent inbreaking of the kingdom.

We must note, moreover, that the apostle does not oppose marriage and virginity when he says in verse 7: "Each has his own special gift from God, one of one kind and one of another." Paul's talk of charisms here applies not only to virginity, but also to marriage. We must not exaggerate the beginning of the chapter, which stresses the danger of incontinence and appears to see marriage as a simple concession, a "remedy for concupiscence." In reality, the chapter, when read in its entirety, offers a positive evaluation of marriage, for example: "If you marry, you do not sin" (v. 28), and "he who marries his betrothed does well" (v. 38). In verse 14, referring to mixed marriages, Paul affirms: "the unbelieving husband is consecrated through his wife, and the unbelieving wife is consecrated through her husband." Marriage is thus not only something good and fitting, but also a means of sanctification. Of course the positive grace of marriage appears above all in the passage addressed to

17. Tosato, "L'istituto familiare dell'antico Israele," 144-54.

the Ephesians, but we must affirm, contrary to Ligier's opinion,[18] that 1 Corinthians 7 does not limit itself to presenting marriage in a negative light, or merely as a remedy for concupiscence.

Ephesians 5:21-33: As this passage contains the fullest account of the foundation of the sacramentality of marriage in the Bible, it deserves our detailed study.

The structure of the text involves a general principle expressed in verse 21: "Be subject to one another out of reverence for Christ." The central section is then divided into two parts: an exhortation to the spouses accompanied by the reasons justifying it (vv. 22-24); an exhortation to husbands together with the reasons justifying it (v. 25ff.); and, finally, a conclusion (v. 33) that recalls the obligation of love and respect on the part of husbands and wives.

The structure of the text affords us a clear view of the analogy between the wife, who is to be subject to her husband as to the Lord (v. 22), and the Church, who is to be subject to Christ, her head (vv. 23-24). The other analogy concerns husbands, who are to love their wives "as Christ loved the Church" (v. 25), with a love that cherishes their wives as their own bodies, which is what "Christ does [for] the Church" (v. 29).

In a study of the New Testament sources for the sacramentality of marriage, Attilio Carpin observes:

> Paul thus understands human marriage in light of the spousal love between Christ and the Church, which is the model of the conjugal union between husband and wife. The union of love between Christ and the Church is reflected in the conjugal union between husband and wife, just as this conjugal union must image the union between Christ and his Church, with all the characteristics of this love, whose substance is gift to the point of self-sacrifice. A problem arises, however, above all in v. 32: *"Sacramentum hoc magnum est, ego autem dico in Christo et in Ecclesia"* ["This is a great mystery, and I mean in reference to Christ and the Church"].[19]

18. See Tosato, "L'istituto familiare dell'antico Israele," 154: "No hostile prejudice against sexuality, as if it were an *intrinsece malum*. No predilection for, or idealization of, virginity (celibacy), as if it represented in itself a state of higher perfection. No denigration of marriage, as if, by institution or by nature, it were a refuge for the incontinent. No 'aspersions' on the family, as if the network of familial relationships (conjugal, parental, filial) were in themselves an obstacle to entering the kingdom of God. Just entirely reasonable emergency arrangements tailored to the extraordinary peril of the moment."

19. A. Carpin, "Sacramentalità del matrimonio. Riferimenti scritturistici e patristici," *Sacra Doctrina* 2 (1997): 119-43, at 125.

To what does this *"sacramentum magnum,"* the "great mystery," refer? To Christian marriage? To the Christ-Church relation? Or to the text of Genesis 2:24 that Paul cites here, which speaks of the "one flesh"? It is difficult to make out a precise answer. In the history of the interpretation of this passage, the opinions of exegetes can more or less be divided among three positions.

Carpin continues:

> The first, classical interpretation, which applies the term "great sacrament" to Christian marriage (cf. St. Thomas Aquinas, *Summa Contra Gentiles* IV, 78; *IV Sent.* d. 26, q. 2 a. 1), is no longer admitted by exegetes or theologians, who, bound to the pronouncements of the Council of Trent, limit themselves to saying that Paul's text makes reference to the sacramentality of marriage. . . . The Latin translation of the Vulgate, which differs from the original Greek, doubtless led to this interpretation.[20]

In fact, the Latin term *sacramentum* does not convey the breadth and complexity of the Greek *mysterion,* "mystery."[21]

In any event, it is clear that this passage is not the direct foundation of sacramentality. Rather, as John Paul II writes:

> If [the author of Ephesians] does not speak about [the sacrament of marriage] directly and in the strict sense — here one must agree with the rather widespread opinion of scholars and theologians — it seems nevertheless that in this biblical text he speaks about the bases of the sacramentality of the whole of Christian life and in particular about the bases of the sacramentality of marriage. In an indirect way, and yet at the same time in the most fundamental way possible, he speaks about the sacramentality of all Christian existence in the Church and especially about the sacramentality of marriage.[22]

---

20. Carpin, "Sacramentalità del matrimonio," 127.

21. For a detailed analysis of the concept *"mysterion"* in its relation with *sacramentum* and marriage, see C. Rochetta, *Sacramentaria fondamentale. Dal "Mysterion" al "Sacramentum"* (Bologna: EDB, 1989), 191ff.; C. Rochetta, *I sacramenti della fede*, vol. 1: *Sacramentaria biblica fondamentale,* 7th ed. (Bologna: EDB, 1998), 135ff.

22. John Paul II, *TOB,* 488-89. The text includes an important note on the historical evolution of the concept of sacrament. The concept comes from the Greek *mysterion,* which in Paul first designates the hidden plan of God that is now revealed; then, in later letters, it is identified with the "gospel" (see Eph. 6:19) and even with Jesus Christ (see Col. 2:2; 4:3; Eph. 3:4), "which is a turning point in the understanding of the term: 'mysterion'

The most common interpretation today is that of Schlier, Gnilka, and Cambier, who see in the "great mystery" Christ's relationship with the Church.[23] Keeping in mind the global context of the Letter to the Ephesians and the meaning of the term *mysterion* as it is used elsewhere, the "great mystery" would mean the divine plan of salvation that God conceived from all eternity and that is accomplished in Christ. But this mystery is made present in the Church; Paul's use of the term "great mystery," then, designates the nuptial relationship between Christ and the Church. Linked to this relationship, the conjugal union between husband and wife appears here as "a participation in this love and holiness. The Christ-Church relation (the great mystery) is reflected in the relationship between husband and wife (the visible sign of this mystery)."[24]

The third, ancient position has recently been revitalized by A. de Marco, who is followed here by Ligier.[25] The *sacramentum* does not refer to Christ and the Church, but rather to the preceding expression, "the two shall be one flesh." The great mystery would thus be Genesis 2:24 taken in its full meaning:

> That is, the union between Adam and Eve in Genesis 2:24 would be the prototype, the prophetic anticipation of the future covenant between Christ and the Church. Why? Not only because the first was the prototype, the archetype of the future union, but also because the first was an integral part of the economy, i.e., of the mystery hidden for all ages and now revealed.[26]

This interpretation has the advantage of translating more precisely the Greek *eis* with the accusative, meaning "in view of," "with the goal of," rather than "with reference to." This is why, Ligier concludes following di Marco, "every human family ordered to Christ" helps to generate humanity and form the body of Christ, that is, the Church.[27]

---

is no longer merely God's eternal plan, but *the realization* of this plan on earth, revealed in Jesus Christ."

23. See J. Cambier, "Le grand mystère concernant le Christ et l'Église, Ep 5, 22-23," *Biblica* 47 (1966): 43-90, 223-42; H. Schlier, *Lettera agli Efesini* (Brescia: Paideia, 1965), 425-46; J. Gnilka, *Der Epheserbrief. Auslegung* (Fribourg: Herder, 1971), 272-303; Carpin, "Sacramentalità del matrimonio."

24. Carpin, "Sacramentalità del matrimonio," 126.

25. A. di Marco, "Mysterium hoc magnum est . . . Ep 5,32," *Laurentianum* 14 (1973): 43-80; Ligier, *Il matrimonio,* 24-36.

26. Ligier, *Il matrimonio,* 29.

27. Di Marco, "Mysterium hoc magnum est . . . Ep 5,32," 67.

The last two interpretations seem to us to be exegetically well-founded. Given the ambiguity of the Pauline text, it seems legitimate to adopt both of them together, without excluding either. Regardless of difficulties in interpreting the terms that figure in the text, it is clear that its theological content justifies the interpretation of human and Christian marriage as *"sacramentum magnum,"* precisely because the conjugal union participates in the nuptial relationship between Christ and the Church. We thus conclude our exegesis of Ephesians 5:21-33 with H. Schlier:

> So what idea of marriage does the apostle reveal that he holds in this chapter? Marriage is the reproduction of the relationship between Christ and the Church. . . . As a reproduction of the heavenly marriage between Christ and the Church, marriage is raised to the sublime dignity in which it participates. We must say even more. Upon this reality, which reproduces the heavenly marriage between Christ and the Church, is conferred a dignity that will later be recognized as a sacramental character. This character, as we have said, does not come from the concept of *mysterion* in v. 32 or from the Latin word that translates it, *sacramentum,* but from the reality we mentioned, that is, from the fact that it [marriage], and it alone, is the reproduction we have described.[28]

The foundations of the sacramentality of marriage are thus firmly laid in this passage, albeit in an indirect manner. The Creator's plan for man and woman is revealed and situated within, and with a view to, the fulfillment of the nuptial covenant between Christ and the Church. In the first and the second Adam, marriage is thus a sign that makes the mystery hidden in God visible and active. In the first Adam, the future union of Christ and the Church was made visible in a prophetic form. In the second Adam, that is, in Christ and the Church, and then in Christian marriage, the redemptive love with which the Father gave his Son to redeem and sanctify humanity is made visible. In both cases, the first Adam and Christ, there is a sacramental aspect, a manifestation in signs of the mystery of the love with which God loved and saved humanity.

The coming of Jesus as the eschatological Bridegroom, his teaching about marriage in the "beginning," and his nuptial self-gift for the Church, which Paul interprets as the "great mystery," explain and justify why the Church, guided by the Spirit, has understood the "mystery of marriage" to be a true

---

28. Schlier, *Lettera agli Efesini,* 440-41.

sacrament of the New Covenant. "The human couple in the image of God,"[29] this "primordial sacrament," is thus called to reproduce the mystery of Christ's spousal love for the Church.

29. See Grelot, *Le Couple humain dans l'Écriture*, 97-103.

CHAPTER 2

The Sacramentality of Marriage in the Tradition

The affirmation of the sacramentality of marriage was the fruit of a gradual process of clarification that, after the canonical and pastoral ambiguities of the tenth and eleventh centuries, came to maturity in response to the challenges posed by the Cathar and Albigensian heresies and by the Protestant Reformation. The relevant interventions of the Magisterium span a period that began with the Councils of the eleventh and thirteenth centuries, continued with the Council of Florence (1439), and ended with the solemn teaching of the Council of Trent. This process confirmed a sacrament that was part of the Church's life from the beginning but whose sacramentality was understood and clarified only gradually on the level of dogmatic reflection. Beginning with the heritage of the Church Fathers, we will survey the major developments in this growing awareness, which has led in our own day to a new and more profound understanding of the sacramental value of marriage.[1]

The Heritage of the Fathers

In order to understand the patristic teaching on marriage, we must situate it in its historical and social context. A definition of marriage in antiquity will be helpful here:

1. We can find a general summary of this development, in broad outline, in the work of D. Tettamanzi, *La Famiglia, via della Chiesa,* 2nd ed. (Milan: Massimo, 1991), 56-61; E. Ruffini, "Il matrimonio-sacramento nella tradizione cattolica. Rilettura teologica," in *Nuova enciclopedia del matrimonio,* ed. T. Goffi (Brescia: Queriniana, 1988), 177-200; L. Ligier, *Il matrimonio. Questioni teologiche e pastorali* (Rome: Città Nuova, 1988), 37-57.

Marriage in antiquity can be defined as the association of two persons of unequal social status — the man, who chooses his bride, and the woman, whose father chooses a husband for her. This association is established with a view to the management of an inheritance and the procreation of children, who will continue the family line and populate the city.[2]

This conception of marriage, marked by the woman's inferiority before the law, had a considerable influence on the Fathers of the Church. The latter combatted the moral decadence of Late Antiquity but, conditioned by cultural prejudices and by the Christian ideal of virginity (monasticism), they were unable to develop an unambiguously positive doctrine of marriage.

At that time, the Church's most serious worry came from Greco-Roman paganism. Weddings bore a taint of scandal on account of lascivious entertainments and songs, against which bishops such as John Chrysostom lifted their voices in protest. Celebrations of this kind were in need of purification. Moreover, repudiation and divorce were common, in direct contradiction of the Gospel message. The Church thus had to defend the indissolubility of marriage and respect for life. In addition to these concerns, which had their source in the customs of pagan society, the dualistic ideologies of the times, such as Gnosticism, Marcionism, and Manichaeism, threatened the dignity and sanctity of the institution of marriage.[3] Although the Fathers' work of discernment in the face of these ideologies was generally on target, the influence of a dualistic Platonism prevented them from working out a fully balanced doctrine. Hence the tendency to undervalue marriage vis-à-vis virginity and to consider sexual activity as almost inevitably marked by sin.[4]

St. Augustine was particularly concerned to explain and defend marriage. He taught that the goodness of marriage involves three, constitutive goods: *proles, fides, sacramentum*.[5] This triad frequently appears in his works

---

2. P. Adnès, *Le Mariage* (Tournai: Desclée, 1963), 44.

3. Ligier, *Il matrimonio*, 37-42.

4. Tertullian, St. Jerome, St. Ambrose, and even St. Augustine present a rather pessimistic vision of human sexuality; the Greek Fathers did not understand the matter differently; see P. Adnès, *Le Mariage* (Tournai: Desclée, 1963), 44-59.

5. St. Augustine, *De bono coniugali* 32 (*PL* 40.394). St. Augustine presents a very developed doctrine in several works: *De continentia, De sancta virginitate, De bono viduitatis, De nuptiis et concupiscentia*; he has at times been called the doctor of Christian marriage. See P. Adnès, *Le Mariage,* 44-59; F. Gil Hellín, *Il matrimonio e la vita coniugale* (Vatican City: Libreria Editrice Vaticana, 1996), chap. 1, 15-37.

with the following meaning: *proles* designates the generation and education of children; *fides* designates the fidelity of the spouses in a chastity that excludes adultery, in a mutual love and reciprocal help that allows them to control the sexual instinct; and *sacramentum* designates the symbolic value of marriage in reference to the union between Christ and the Church — a symbolism that implies the unity and indissolubility of marriage. This triad would be maintained and developed, with a few modifications, down through the subsequent history of the tradition.

Despite the limits we have mentioned, which may be more or less pronounced depending on the author, we can summarize patristic thought on the sacramentality of marriage by referring to liturgical praxis and to the theology that underlies it. Here we cite at length A. Carpin's conclusions regarding the patristic tradition:[6]

a. Christian marriage is an ecclesial and sacred reality: it is accomplished through the Church and in the Church. In order to marry, prospective spouses must obtain the bishop's consent; marriage is celebrated in a liturgy, the precursor of the nuptial mass; and an essential element of this liturgy is the priest's blessing of the spouses, a sign of God's blessing on the first marriage. . . .[7] St. Ambrose (397) offers valuable testimony in this regard: "It is opportune that the marriage itself be sanctified through the veil placed by the priest and through his blessing."[8] The rite of priestly blessing is explicitly linked to its effect, the sanctification of the marriage, and so to a divine grace.[9]

b. Patristic theology of marriage is based on chapter 5 of the Letter to the Ephesians, especially verses 31-32. Some Fathers make the link between the "great mystery" and the conjugal union of Adam and Eve, with an eye to the union between Christ and the Church (Tertullian); others situate the "great mystery" within the Christ-Church union itself (Ambrose, Augustine). Marriage, for its part, is indirectly linked to this great mystery. The union between Christ and the Church thus has a double reference: to the original conjugal union and to marriage in general. Others (Leo the Great,

---

6. A. Carpin, "Sacramentalità del matrimonio. Riferimenti scritturistici e patristici," *Sacra Doctrina* 2 (1997): 129-43. For an in-depth study, see A. Carpin, *Il sacramento del matrimonio nella teologia medievale. Da Isidoro di Siviglia a Tommaso d'Aquino* (Bologna: ESD, 1991), 7-43.

7. Carpin, "Sacramentalità del matrimonio," 142.

8. *Epistula* 19.7 (*PL* 16.1026).

9. Carpin, "Sacramentalità del matrimonio," 132.

Isidore) do not enter into exegetical questions, preferring to highlight the relationship between conjugal union and the spousal union of Christ and the Church, while referring to the text of Genesis.

c. On the scriptural basis of the Pauline letters, Christian marriage is perceived as the symbol or image of Christ's union with the Church. Particular stress is laid on the "sacramental" dimension in the marriage of the first Adam, the prophetic prefiguration of the union between Christ and the Church. Augustine stresses the indissolubility of the conjugal bond *(sacramentum)* in Christian marriage, which symbolically reflects the indissoluble union between Christ and his Church. While following Augustine's identification of conjugal sacramentality with indissolubility, Isidore reinforces this sacramental character by relating it directly to the mystery of the Christ-Church union.

d. The infusion of divine grace — guaranteed by the priest's blessing of the spouses — is linked to the celebration of Christian marriage. This grace, or divine aid in the Christian conduct of married life, is not so much the effect of marriage as it is a requirement for living it out according to God. This grace involves the couple in the Church's struggle against sin and the "mystery of iniquity" (2 Thess. 2:7). In reality, the Fathers had not yet elaborated the concept of marriage as a sacrament in the form that the concept would take in Scholastic theology, that is, as a sign and efficient cause of grace. The Fathers' theology of marriage thus remains limited, yet it provides the foundation for future developments.[10]

The evolution in the awareness of the sacramentality of marriage took on a somewhat juridical cast under the influence of Roman law.[11] We owe the first significant Magisterial intervention on the subject to Pope Nicholas I, who in the year 866 responded to an inquiry of the Bulgarians regarding the essential form of marriage. In line with Roman law, the Pope affirmed that the essential form of marriage is the spouses' consent: "And if, by chance, this consent alone is lacking in the marriage, everything else is in vain, even if solemnized by intercourse itself, as attested to by the great Doctor John Chrysostom" (Denz 643).[12]

The "consummation" of the marriage is thus not a constitutive, co-

10. Carpin, "Sacramentalità del matrimonio," 142-43.
11. Ligier, *Il matrimonio,* 45-53.
12. See H. Denzinger, *Compendium of Creeds, Definitions, and Declarations on Matters of Faith and Morals,* 43rd ed. (San Francisco: Ignatius, 2012) [= Denz].

essential element of the sacrament. Nevertheless, the contribution of consummation to the stability and fullness of the sacrament would eventually be recognized in the twelfth and thirteenth centuries under the influence of the canonical school of Bologna.

Responding to the rise of the Cathars in France, the Second Lateran Council (the tenth ecumenical Council, convoked under Pope Alexander III) declared in April 1139 that it is heretical to condemn "legitimate marriage pacts." In 1184, the Council of Verona, held during the reign of Pope Lucius III, placed marriage among the sacraments of the Roman Church (Denz 761). Marriage is again included in the profession of faith that Pope Innocent III required of the Waldensians in 1208; against those who forbade marriage to the perfect, the Pope affirms that married persons can be saved and that it is illicit to forbid further marriages after a spouse's death (Denz 794). In 1215, the Fourth Lateran Council, which also met under Innocent III, reiterated that spouses can please God and be saved (Denz 802). Florence's Decree for the Armenians (1439) upholds the sacramentality of marriage by referring to Ephesians 5:32; it establishes spousal consent as the efficient cause of the sacrament and reaffirms Augustine's doctrine of the threefold goods of marriage: children, faith, and indissolubility (Denz 1327).

St. Thomas Aquinas

The Thomistic scholar Battista Mondin notes, "St. Thomas included a comprehensive and detailed study of marriage in the *Commentary on the Sentences* (IV, d. 26-42), which was later integrated (in a different order) into the *Supplementum* (q. 41-68). He also occasionally returns to this theme in the *Summa Contra Gentiles* (III, chap. 123-126, 137; IV, chap. 78)."[13] Aquinas's principal source is St. Augustine.[14]

According to Mondin, whose summary of Aquinas's teaching we quote at length,

> The Angelic Doctor defines marriage as the union between legitimate persons, a man and a woman, for the formation of an indissoluble, lifelong community. More briefly, *marriage is the union of man and woman*

---

13. B. Mondin, *Dizionario enciclopedico del pensiero di San Tommaso d'Aquino* (Bologna: ESD, 1991), 376-77.
14. See also Hellín, *Il matrimonio e la vita coniugale*, 37-55.

ordered to the generation and education of children.[15] St. Thomas teaches that this natural institution requires stability and indissolubility in order to achieve its ends, especially that of education. He likewise insists on the love of friendship that gives the marital relationship its distinctive quality and points out that it, too, requires stability and continuity. . . .[16]

While marriage is a natural institution, it has also become, through the will and goodness of Jesus Christ, a supernatural one as well: *a sacrament.* As a natural institution, marriage is ordered to perpetuating the human race; but, as a sacrament, it is ordered to perpetuating the Church, "which consists in the collection of the faithful."[17] [St. Thomas writes]:

> Matrimony, then, in that it consists in the union of a husband and wife purposing to generate and educate offspring for the worship of God, is a sacrament of the Church; hence, also, a certain blessing on those marrying is given by the ministers of the Church. And as in the other sacraments by the thing done outwardly a sign is made of a spiritual thing, so, too, in this sacrament by the union of husband and wife a sign of the union of Christ and the Church is made; in the Apostle's words: "This is a great sacrament, but I speak in Christ and in the church" (Eph. 5:32). And because the sacraments effect that of which they are made signs, one must believe that in this sacrament a grace is conferred on those marrying, and that by this grace they are included in the union of Christ and the Church, which is most especially necessary to them, that in this way in fleshly and earthly things they may purpose not to be disunited from Christ and the Church.[18]

To those who affirm that marriage is in no way a cause of grace but only a sign of it, St. Thomas responds, "This is untrue because then marriage would in no way differ from the sacraments of the old law and there would be no reason to count it among the sacraments of the new law."[19] St. Thomas also objects to those who limit the grace of marriage to the legitimation of an act (sexual union) that would be a sin outside of mar-

---

15. Thomas Aquinas, *Summa contra Gentiles,* IV, chap. 78.

16. Mondin, *Dizionario enciclopedico del pensiero di San Tommaso d'Aquino,* 377. See Thomas Aquinas, *Summa contra Gentiles,* III, chap. 123.

17. Thomas Aquinas, *Summa contra Gentiles,* IV, chap. 78 (trans. Charles J. O'Neil [New York: Hanover House, 1955-1957], available at http://dhspriory.org/thomas/ContraGentiles.htm).

18. Thomas Aquinas, *Summa contra Gentiles,* IV, chap. 78.

19. Thomas Aquinas, *Commentary on the Sentences,* IV, d. 26, q. 2 a. 3 (as for the two following in-text citations).

riage: "This is insufficient, because such [legitimation] was already effected in the old law." St. Thomas thus concludes that "marriage contracted in Christian faith confers the grace that aids in accomplishing the duties relevant to that state. . . ."[20]

[*Regarding the essence of marriage:*] In seeking to identify the essence of marriage in metaphysical terms, St. Thomas has no difficulty in finding the right category: we are, he says, dealing with a relation *(relatio)*. What is actuated in marriage is neither a substance nor a quantity, nor even a quality, etc., but a new relationship: a personal relationship founded on the reciprocal love of the two spouses. The juridical bond as defined by civil law is posterior and subordinate to the natural bond based on love. This is why, among the goods of marriage, the most essential is the real and effective indivisibility of the spouses:

> [S]ince from the very fact that by the marriage compact man and wife give to one another power the one over the other in perpetuity, it follows that they cannot be put asunder. Hence there is no matrimony without inseparability, whereas there is matrimony without "faith" and "offspring," because the existence of a thing does not depend on its use; and in this sense "sacrament" is more essential to matrimony than "faith" and "offspring."[21]

[*Regarding the ends of marriage:*] Since marriage is both a natural (and civil) institution and a sacrament, St. Thomas keeps all these aspects in mind while discussing the ends of marriage. But whether one considers marriage as a natural (or civil) institution or sees it as a sacrament, it follows obviously for St. Thomas that its principal end is the procreation and education of children — which confirms the texts already cited. He has no doubt that if a couple unites while excluding this finality, they sin against nature because they mortify the natural inclination that is the source of marriage. It is worth noting the vigor with which St. Thomas stresses the pedagogical finality of marriage: it is the fundamental, essential, and most important element of the *bonum prolis*. We must also note the great importance that St. Thomas attributes to the father's role in the education of children.

20. Mondin, *Dizionario enciclopedico del pensiero di San Tommaso d'Aquino,* 378-79.
21. Thomas Aquinas, *Supplementum,* q. 49 art. 3 (translation from *The Summa Theologica of Saint Thomas Aquinas,* trans. Fathers of the English Dominican Province, 2nd ed. [1920], available at: http://www.newadvent.org/summa/index.html).

Mutual help between the spouses is subordinated to this principal end: "Filiation is the most important reality in marriage; afterward comes fidelity; and finally, the sacrament."[22] However, since the ultimate foundation on which marriage rests is love, or friendship between the spouses, the conservation and growth of such friendship are doubtless ingredient in the principal ends of marriage.[23] If we look at marriage from a supernatural perspective, pride of place belongs to the sacrament. As St. Thomas argues,

> This or that may be more important to a thing in two ways, either because it is more essential or because it is more excellent. If the reason is because it is more excellent, then "sacrament" is in every way the most important of the three marriage goods, since it belongs to marriage considered as a sacrament of grace; while the other two belong to it as an office of nature; and a perfection of grace is more excellent than a perfection of nature.[24]

[*Evaluation:*] It is often said that St. Thomas has a naturalistic rather than a personalistic conception of marriage. This judgment is based on a reductive use of the term "personalism," which does not take into account the fact that filiation is a part of the personalistic horizon. We have seen that St. Thomas is greatly concerned with the education of children. Moreover, we often forget that the Angelic Doctor taught that a sterile marriage is not invalid, because it still allows the spouses to attain certain essential ends of marriage: their spiritual perfection and their participation in the spousal mystery of the Church.

St. Thomas' teaching on marriage remains valuable even if here and there we glimpse . . . an overly moralistic conception of sexuality, and the biological and physiological information available to him seems rudimentary to us today. In fact, as H. Durand observes, St. Thomas "contributed more than many others not only to define Catholic doctrine on marriage, but to explain and justify it, such that many of his arguments have become classic."[25]

---

22. Thomas Aquinas, *Commentary on the Sentences,* IV, d. 26, q. 2 a. 3.
23. Thomas Aquinas, *Summa contra Gentiles,* III, chap. 123.
24. Thomas Aquinas, *Supplementum,* q. 49 art. 3.
25. Mondin, *Dizionario enciclopedico del pensiero di San Tommaso d'Aquino,* 379-80.

From the Council of Trent to Vatican II[26]

In the sixteenth century, the Protestant Reformers taught that marriage is a purely natural institution, alleging that the Letter to the Ephesians refers not to marriage but to Christ and the Church. The Reformers admitted the legitimacy of divorce and thus of successive polygamy, pointing to Matthew 5:19 and 1 Corinthians 7:15. The twenty-fourth session of the Council of Trent (the nineteenth ecumenical Council) responded on November 11, 1563. The doctrinal part of the decree recalls the main Scriptural texts on which the indissolubility of marriage is founded: Genesis 2:23ff.; Matthew 19:5-6; Mark 10:9; Ephesians 5:31 (Denz 1797ff.).

The following paragraphs address the true and proper sacramentality of marriage and the institution of the sacrament by Christ: "Christ himself, who instituted the holy sacraments and brought them to perfection, merited for us by his Passion the grace that perfects that natural love, confirms the indissoluble union, and sanctifies the spouses" (Denz 1799).

The Council then affirmed that "matrimony in the evangelical law surpasses marital unions of the Old Law in grace" (Denz 1800). The first canon is the most important: "If anyone says that matrimony is not truly and properly one of the seven sacraments of the law of the Gospel . . . let him be anathema" (Denz 1801).

The fundamental contribution of the Council of Trent thus consists in an *affirmation of the sacramentality of a marriage between baptized persons.* But the Council also resolved the serious question of clandestine marriages, which for centuries have been celebrated in secret and without parental consent. The *"Tametsi"* decree established new legislation that, while not requiring parental consent, did require, for the validity of marriage, *a public form of celebration:*

> After these announcements have been made, and if no legitimate impediment is raised in objection, the celebration of the marriage must then take place in open church, during which the parish priest will, by questioning the man and woman, make sure of their consent and then say, "I join you together in marriage, in the name of the Father and the Son and the Holy Spirit," or use other words according to the accepted rite of each province. (Denz 1814)

26. See P. Barberi and D. Tettamanzi, eds., *Matrimonio e familigia nel magistero della Chiesa. I documenti dal concilio di Firenze a Giovanni Paolo II* (Milan: Massimo, 1986).

The encyclical *Arcanum Divinae Sapientiae* (1880) further developed this teaching, introducing the term "raised to the dignity of sacrament," which is retained in the *Code of Canon Law* of 1917 (can. 1012, §1) as well as that of 1983 (can. 1055, §1). In paragraph 9, the encyclical states:

> To the Apostles . . . are to be referred the doctrines which "our holy Fathers, the Councils, and the Tradition of the Universal Church have always taught," namely, that Christ our Lord raised marriage to the dignity of a sacrament; that to husband and wife, guarded and strengthened by the heavenly grace which his merits gained for them, he gave power to attain holiness in the married state; and that, in a wondrous way, making marriage an example of the mystical union between himself and his Church, he not only perfected that love which is according to nature, but also made the naturally indivisible union of one man with one woman far more perfect through the bond of heavenly love.[27]

The encyclical *Casti Connubii* (Pius XI, 1930) explicitly reaffirms Leo XIII's teaching. However, it goes beyond the latter's rigid and institutional view of Christian marriage, opening it to a slightly more personalist conception that paid more attention to the human, moral, and spiritual aspects of the sacrament. Pope Pius XI's teaching makes systematic use of Augustine's vision of the three goods of marriage. In order to promote the moral and spiritual growth of spouses, the Pope also valorizes the sacramentality of matrimony, while stressing its permanence as a sacrament:

> In order that they may make this firm resolution, keep it and put it into practice, an oft-repeated consideration of their state of life, and a diligent reflection on the sacrament they have received, will be of great assistance to them. Let them constantly keep in mind, that they have been sanctified and strengthened for the duties and for the dignity of their state by a special sacrament, the efficacious power of which, although it does not impress a character, is undying. To this purpose we may ponder over the words full of real comfort of holy Cardinal Robert Bellarmine, who with other well-known theologians with devout conviction thus expresses himself: "The sacrament of matrimony can be regarded in two ways: first, in the making, and then in its permanent state. For it is a sacrament like to that of the Eucharist, which not only when it is being conferred, but

27. Leo XIII, *Arcanum Divinae Sapientiae* 9; Denz 3142.

also whilst it remains, is a sacrament; for as long as the married parties are alive, so long is their union a sacrament of Christ and the Church."[28]

We come, finally, to the Second Vatican Council (1962-1965). *Lumen Gentium* 11 affirms that in the midst of the people of God, Christian spouses receive a proper gift enabling them to live their state of life in holiness and to form a "domestic church":

> Christian spouses, in virtue of the sacrament of Matrimony, whereby they signify and partake of the mystery of that unity and fruitful love which exists between Christ and his Church (cf. Eph. 5:32), help each other to attain to holiness in their married life and in the rearing and education of their children. By reason of their state and rank in life they have their own special gift among the people of God (cf. 1 Cor. 7:7). From the wedlock of Christians there comes the family, in which new citizens of human society are born, who by the grace of the Holy Spirit received in baptism are made children of God, thus perpetuating the people of God through the centuries. The family is, so to speak, the domestic church. In it parents should, by their word and example, be the first preachers of the faith to their children; they should encourage them in the vocation which is proper to each of them, fostering with special care vocation to a sacred state.

Gaudium et Spes 48 marks a turning point in the personalist approach to the presentation and development of the traditional doctrine. It surmounts the primarily juridical vision of marriage and highlights the "intimate partnership of married life and love." It reaffirms the doctrine of the ends of marriage, but without establishing a hierarchy among them; all these ends "have a very decisive bearing on the continuation of the human race, on the personal development and eternal destiny of the individual members of a family" (*GS* 48 §1). The sacramental dimension is presented in a Christocentric and ecclesial key:

> Christ the Lord abundantly blessed this many-faceted love, welling up as it does from the fountain of divine love and structured as it is on the model of his union with his Church. For as God of old made himself present to his people through a covenant of love and fidelity, so now the Savior of men and the Spouse of the Church comes into the lives of married Chris-

28. Pius XI, encyclical letter *Casti Connubii* 110, citing St. Robert Bellarmine, *De Controversiis*, vol. 3: *De Matr. Controvers.* 2, C. 6.

tians through the sacrament of matrimony. He abides with them thereafter so that just as he loved the Church and handed himself over on her behalf, the spouses may love each other with perpetual fidelity through mutual self-bestowal. (*GS* 48 §2)

Immediately afterward, the text affirms that human love participates in divine love by virtue of the sacrament, which consecrates the spouses and enables them to accomplish their mission:

Authentic married love is *caught up into divine love* and is governed and enriched by Christ's redeeming power and the saving activity of the Church, so that this love may lead the spouses to God with powerful effect and may aid and strengthen them in sublime office of being a father or a mother. For this reason Christian spouses have a special sacrament by which they are fortified and receive a kind of consecration in the duties and dignity of their state.

Finally, the text refers to the pneumatological dimension of the sacrament, that is, to the mediation of the Holy Spirit who dwells in the spouses and animates their growth and self-gift:

By virtue of this sacrament, as spouses fulfill their conjugal and family obligation, they are penetrated with the spirit of Christ, which suffuses their whole lives with faith, hope and charity. Thus they increasingly advance the perfection of their own personalities, as well as their mutual sanctification, and hence contribute jointly to the glory of God.

This doctrine will be amply developed in the apostolic exhortation *Familiaris Consortio* (no. 13), as well as in the teaching of John Paul II more generally. We will return to this theme in the more systematic part of the present work. In conclusion, we can say that Vatican II opened a path to a more profound awareness of the "mystery of marriage"; it launched a "personalistic" reflection whose many implications are beginning to be fully developed today.

Conclusion

We can summarize the development of the sacramentality of marriage in the tradition in Ligier's words:

When the sacramentality of marriage is affirmed, this refers to the *bond* between two baptized persons and, above all, to the moment in which they contract it. An institution pertaining to creation, in other words, is recapitulated by Christ and raised to the level of a sacrament, that is, a sign and instrument of grace in the economy of salvation. [The tradition] concludes that marriage is first of all something "sacred," since it was instituted by the Creator and so deserves the respect of all. Above all, however, it is something "holy" owing to its status as a sacrament. We must add that at the moment of its celebration, and even beyond, the two spouses are introduced into the work of the redemption against the power of sin and for the future of the Church. In a word, marriage is a source of grace.[29]

It seems, then, that the terms "sacrament" and "sacramentality" bear a complex content, in which we can discern three main ideas:

First, the "sacred character" of marriage in the order of creation, that is, its status as a "primordial sacrament." By the will of the Creator, the human person is established as a collaborator with God who is to master his earthly future: life appears here as a mysterious force, transmitted through procreation, in which human freedom is involved with the freedom of the Creator. This first creation already aims at the covenant in Christ.

Second, "sacramentality," understood in the *biblical and patristic sense,* according to which conjugal life participates in the mystery of the Incarnation and redemption. The Fathers of the Church understood sacramentality as a sign and reference to Christ's union with the Church, from which flows the indissolubility of marriage. With the Church, the baptized couple enters into the struggle against the "mystery of iniquity" (2 Thess. 2:7), so as to hasten the coming of the "mystery" of Christ and his Body, which is the Church.

Third and finally, the term "sacrament" understood in its *definitive meaning,* that is, as *one of the seven sacraments* (defined at the Council of Trent), indicates that marriage is a source, means, and path of grace and salvation: it gives sanctifying grace to Christian spouses, while both promising and conferring on them the help needed for their state of life. Grace does not intervene only on the day they make their marriage vows, but also afterwards, and it does not come to them from outside their condition as spouses but from within it.

29. Ligier, *Il matrimonio,* 54.

CHAPTER 3

The Theology of Sacramental Marriage

The path that we have followed thus far has allowed us to gather some of the most fundamental elements of the sacramentality of marriage. We might be a little surprised, or even disappointed, to see that the history we have traced here does not present a very clear or enthusiastic message about the sacramental value of Christian marriage. The full affirmation of the sacramentality of marriage was a long and laborious conquest that followed upon the pastoral and canonical ambiguities of the Middle Ages and the radical challenge posed by the Protestant Reformation at the dawn of modernity. The Church definitively formulated her faith in the sacrament of marriage at the Council of Trent, opposing the reductive interpretations of Scripture promoted by the Reformation. Unfortunately, the polemical atmosphere of the Reformation and Counter-Reformation was not favorable to a proper development of the theology of marriage. A prevailing juridical mentality and the dominance of hylomorphic categories proved to be an obstacle to a development of doctrine concerning sacramental marriage. Vatican II marked a Christological and personalistic turning point, which encouraged new approaches and introduced a new stage in the development of the theology of marriage.

Among the new approaches that have emerged after the Council, we find the personalist "school," which seeks to integrate the intuitions of phenomenology and philosophical personalism. We also find an anthropological tendency that envisages an integration of the *humanum*, in all its aspects (spiritual, affective, sexual, etc.), into the permanent sign of marriage. There is also work being done to repair the absence of the pneumatological and trinitarian dimension in the explanation of the grace of marriage. Finally, others have proposed a comprehensive renewal of the Augustinian doctrine of the "goods" of marriage (and of the Thomistic account of its "ends") using the philosophical and theological category of "gift."[1] This last perspective, which is inspired particularly by Pope John Paul II, opens new directions that are promising not only for reevaluating marriage but also for rethinking all of sacramental theology in the light of the marital sacrament. We will attempt to integrate the most significant of these contributions into the present theological reflection, which will focus on the three fundamental levels that constitute the sacrament of marriage: the *sacramental sign,* the *reality* that the sign signifies and produces, and the *realization* of what is signified and received in the celebration of the sacrament.

The Celebration of the Sacramental Sign of Marriage and Its Permanent Dimension

The first level of our reflection concerns the *sacramental sign.* The nature of this sign involves both a liturgical dimension occurring at a specific moment and a permanent dimension extending over a whole life. In these two dimensions, the sign is constituted by the couple who, by the "word" they exchange and their reciprocal "fidelity," commit themselves to "living" a reality of grace: "It is the interpersonal, specific relationship of these two human beings that becomes a sacrament in the strict sense of the term."[2] Schillebeeckx's affirmation is a new point of departure for the theology of Christian marriage. Instead of framing the issue in the customary way, i.e., in terms of the efficient causality of the sacrament, Schillebeeckx shifts to the perspective of the final cause by beginning with marriage as an anthropological reality constitutive both of the initial sacrament and of its permanence as a state of life. In other words:

1. For the search for a new synthesis of the "gifts" of marriage, see A. Mattheeuws, *Les "dons" du mariage. Recherche de théologie morale et sacramentelle* (Brussels: Culture et Verité, 1996). For the trinitarian and pneumatological aspect, see R. Bonetti, ed., *Il matrimonio in Cristo è matrimonio nello Spirito* (Rome: Città Nuova, 1998), especially the contribution of A. Scola, "Lo Spirito Santo rivela la verità tutta intera della famiglia cristiana"; and M. Ouellet, "The Holy Spirit: Seal of the Conjugal Covenant," reprinted as chapter 5 in M. Ouellet, *Divine Likeness: Toward a Trinitarian Anthropology of the Family* (Grand Rapids: Eerdmans, 2006). The integration of the anthropological and personalist dimension predominates in the works of C. Rochetta, especially *Il sacramento della coppia* (Bologna: EDB, 1996), whereas the pneumatological aspect is stressed in M. Martinez Peque, *Lo Spirito Santo e il matrimonio* (Rome: EDR, 1993).

2. E. Schillebeeckx, *Il matrimonio è un sacramento* (Milan: Ancora, 1963), 23-24. Rochetta has amply developed this approach in his book *Il sacramento della coppia.*

It is the specific reality of the couple formed by two baptized persons, with all the density of their being human, man and woman — their sexually differentiated corporeity, their masculinity and femininity, their love and reciprocal, total, and indissoluble dedication, their promise and reciprocal commitment — that is transformed into sacrament.[3]

The marital sacrament is not a "thing" added to the reality of the couple from the outside; rather, the couple itself is and must become the living sign of an invisible reality of grace.

The couple is transformed into a sacrament insofar as it consists of two baptized persons who marry "in the Lord." The sacramental sign of marriage is founded on baptism, which creates the radical belonging of man and woman to Christ and the Church. Only Christ can give the man and the woman to each other. He alone can create a supernatural reciprocity that makes their union signify his own union with the Church. The sacramental sign of marriage is thus effected by a "word" of Christ who, through the Holy Spirit, actualizes his covenant with the Church, first in the "verbal" consent of the celebration and then in the daily, human texture of the couple's lives. As C. Rochetta explains:

> The novelty of marriage between two baptized persons consists in the fact that this "word" acquires a new, *sacramental* signification: by virtue of their baptism, this word *of* the spouses is pronounced *in* Christ and *in* the Church, and thus becomes, in the power of the Spirit, a word *of* Christ and *of* the Church on the spouses. This word is capable of introducing them into the eschatological covenant and of making of the two persons a community of grace, a kind of "word of God" incarnate in the world: a word that says what it does and does what it says.[4]

"The specific novelty of Christian marriage corresponds to the absolute novelty brought about in the mystery of God's covenant in history";[5] the latter finds its fullness in the "wedding feast" already being celebrated between Christ and his Church. The marriage of two baptized persons is *rooted* in this mystery of the covenant, which they *express and extend* within the Body of Christ, the Church, in a manner befitting their properly spousal vocation. It is

3. C. Rochetta, "É la relazione uomo-donna che diventa sacramento. Per una sponsalità sacramentale della coppia," in *Cristo Sposo della Chiesa Sposa. Sorgente e modello della spiritualità coniugale e familiare*, ed. R. Bonetti (Rome: Città Nuova, 1997), 55-87, here 57.

4. Rochetta, "É la relazione uomo-donna che diventa sacramento," 76.

5. Rochetta, *Il sacramento della coppia*, 163ff.

from within this perspective that the Church's Magisterium defined as a *dogma of faith* at the Council of Trent that *Christian marriage is truly one of the seven sacraments of the new Law, instituted by Christ the Lord, who confers on it the grace which it signifies* (Denz 1801).

Vatican II reaffirmed this doctrine in a language redolent of the history of salvation:

> Christ the Lord abundantly blessed this many-faceted love, welling up as it does from the fountain of divine love and structured as it is on the model of his union with his Church. For as God of old made himself present to his people through a covenant of love and fidelity, so now the Savior of men and the Spouse of the Church comes into the lives of married Christians through the sacrament of matrimony. (*GS* 48)

This sacramental encounter gives divine grace to the spouses, "so that this love may lead the spouses to God with powerful effect and may aid and strengthen them in the sublime office of being a father or a mother" (*GS* 48). For this reason, the Lord Jesus "abides with them thereafter so that just as he loved the Church and handed himself over on her behalf, the spouses may love each other with perpetual fidelity through mutual self-bestowal" (*GS* 48).[6] Let us pause for a moment to consider the initial event of this "encounter" that constitutes the sacrament of marriage.

The Exchange of Consent in the Context of the Liturgy

The life-long commitment that the two spouses express and exchange is taken up into God's salvific plan and becomes a *sacramental sign* of Jesus Christ's thanksgiving for his Church. *In what exactly does this sacramental sign consist?*

Reciprocal consent: On the strictly theological level, the sacramental sign of marriage consists in the *free act of the will* whereby the spouses exchange mutual *consent,* as an irrevocable pact, reciprocally giving and receiving one another in order to establish the marriage:

> The intimate partnership of married life and love has been established by the Creator and qualified by his laws, and is rooted in the conjugal cove-

---

6. See C. Rochetta, "Il sacramento del matrimonio," in *Incontrare Christo nei sacramenti,* ed. H. Luthe (Milan: Cinisello Balsamo/Paoline, 1988), 401.

nant of irrevocable personal consent. Hence by that human act whereby spouses mutually bestow and accept each other a relationship arises which by divine will and in the eyes of society too is a lasting one. (*GS* 48)

Such consent is and must be expressed perceptibly, normally by words and gestures that demonstrate the relevant interior intention. Precisely because the sacramental sign of marriage between two baptized persons is constituted by the consent of both, the marriage pact (or contract) whereby a man and a woman establish a life-long communion/community is identical with the sacrament of marriage; and there can be no valid marriage pact between two Christian spouses that is not simultaneously a sacrament. Consequently, anything that nullifies the pact (for example, a lack of freedom on the part of one of the spouses) also nullifies the sacramental act.

Elements of the Rite

In its structure and sequence, the rite of marriage synthetically expresses the sacramental meaning of the vows exchanged by the spouses. Before the exchange of vows, the priest makes a brief introduction, reminding the spouses why they have presented themselves before Christ and the ecclesial community. This is followed by three questions concerning: (1) freedom of conscience in the spouses' mutual choice; (2) their acceptance of marriage as a path of love and reciprocal respect, which implicates them totally for the rest of their lives; and (3) their willingness to welcome the children that God will be pleased to grant them and to educate them in a Christian manner within the Church. Once these conditions have been ascertained, the ordained minister invites the fiancés to join their right hands as a sign of union and commitment, and to exchange their reciprocal consent with the formula: "I, N., take you, N., to be my wife/husband. I promise to be true to you in good times and in bad, in sickness and in health. I will love you and honor you all the days of my life."

We note that, until the recent revision of the Roman Rite of Marriage (November 28, 2004), the formula of reciprocal consent included no direct reference to God or Christ. It expressed above all the truth of human love in its act of self-giving, the promise of fidelity, and consent to the gift of the other. The "truth of love" is an integral part of the truth of the sacramental sign. The formula of the rite does not express a wish or even a hope: it is "the guarantee of a promise and obligation, which both spouses speak and by which they 'are spoken' as the reality of husband and wife — a reality established by that very word/promise."[7]

The explicit reference to Christ had always been preserved in the formula by which the presiding minister officially receives and ratifies spousal consent: "You have declared your consent before the Church. May the Lord in his goodness strengthen your consent and fill you both with his blessings. What God has joined, men must not divide."

This concluding formula situates the fiancés' human act of mutual self-gift in the theological context of trinitarian communion. It reminds all those present of the Author of their love, his blessing of, and commitment to, their union: "what God has joined." Through the act of mutual consent, the spouses in fact acquire a new participation in the communion of the Trinity. Since they have been baptized, they already participate in Christ's filiation in the Spirit; but now they participate as a couple, as the union of man and woman, in the communion of the Trinity, which is eternally one, fruitful, and indissoluble. As we will see further on, the Holy Spirit is the invisible protagonist of this participation. It is the Spirit who, as the personal love of Father and Son, transforms the spouses' human love and makes it participate in Christ's spousal love for the Church.[8]

It is certain that the marriage of baptized persons is a sacrament and confers grace: this was defined at the Council of Trent. The encyclical *Casti Connubii* and the constitution *Gaudium et Spes* (48) also affirm that marriage consecrates the spouses. We must now give a more precise answer to the following question: What is the source of the sanctifying power of marriage between the baptized? Does this power come from the sign itself, that is, from consent, which would therefore be a cause of grace? Or from conjugal love, which is the more common opinion today? According to Ligier, hylomorphic explanations are insufficient, but so is recourse to conjugal love, since the latter remains an ambiguous sign:

> If we take into account that Christ accepted the pact already in use, that is, a creaturely and sociocultural reality, and elevated it to the dignity of a sacrament, we can admit that the sanctifying power of this pact does not come from its structure but from another cause, connected with the elevation of creation to grace. *It is thus linked with baptism,* which is the root of said elevation.[9]

---

7. Rochetta, "È la relazione uomo-donna che diventa sacramento," 78.
8. See Ouellet, "The Holy Spirit: Seal of the Conjugal Covenant."
9. L. Ligier, *Il matrimonio. Questioni teologiche e pastorali* (Rome: Città Nuova, 1988), 105.

In this light, we can admit the contemporary theory once it is complemented theologically by Ligier's consideration of baptism. When we are dealing with baptized persons, their conjugal love can be a "sacramental sign" of the marriage/sacrament, because the spouses' reciprocal commitment and love are bearers of grace and consecration. Here, too, baptism gives meaning and power to the "sacramental sign." Ultimately, what is essential is the starting-point: the fact that the pact between the spouses, expressed verbally at the moment of the celebration, constitutes the sacrament. It is crucial that we are dealing with a marriage between Christians, since it is baptism that enables the conjugal pact to consecrate the persons and their state of life.

The Spouses, Ministers of the Sacrament

What we have said above explains why the spouses themselves are the human ministers (or agents of the act) through whom the sign — under the conditions established by the Church — is expressed and the sacramental event accomplished. By virtue of their baptismal character, the spouses perform a true act of ecclesial and sacramental ministeriality. If this act, with the exchange of consent that it implies, in fact constitutes the sacramental sign, the spouses are ministers of the sacrament and they are therefore part of the sacramental sign understood in its fullness. As the responsible agents of the conjugal pact, the spouses, not the priest, are the true ministers of the sacrament.

Despite the uncertainties of some ancient authors, we need to stress that the blessing of the ordained minister is not part of the sign; this is the common teaching even in the East, where this blessing is nonetheless required for the validity of the marriage. In fact, the Magisterium has not officially pronounced on the question, but a relatively clear negative position is held by the majority of theologians. It is no objection to say that the intervention of laypersons in the sacramental sphere "offends" the primacy of Christ and the Church in the economy of the sacraments. Laypeople are not strangers to the Church; by reason of their baptism, they belong to Christ and to the Church, of which they are members:

> Their spiritual priesthood is the principle of an *"ex opere operato,"* of which the spouses are the ministers. By virtue of their baptismal character, their marriage contract becomes a sacrament in a way that com-

pletely surpasses their will in virtue of the pure transcendence of Christ's action.[10]

What, then, is the role of the priest in the marriage? What is his function?

The *Tametsi* decree of the Council of Trent stipulates that the priest must say the following words over the couple: "I join you together in marriage, in the name of the Father and the Son and the Holy Spirit." Like the words of absolution, this pronouncement has all the appearances of a sacramental formula. However, while the priest is the qualified and official witness of the Church, he does not intervene as the minister of the sacrament. His role is active and substantial because he asks for and receives the consent of those contracting the marriage, but his presence adds nothing essential to the celebration of the marriage; otherwise, the Church would not be able to dispense with this requirement, as she at times does (cf. *Code of Canon Law*, can. 1116). The common tradition regarding the role of the priest is not an obstacle to a debate about "the ministeriality of marriage" (C. Rochetta) in more theological than juridical terms. D. Tettamanzi has wondered whether it is not high time to reevaluate our understanding of the ministeriality of the spouses within a more Christocentric and theological perspective. The spouses are "ministers," but they are not the only ministers. The presence of the ordained minister must not be underestimated; it manifests an aspect of the fundamental ministeriality of Christ and the Church.

> The common affirmation that speaks of the spouses as "ministers" and of the priest as a "qualified witness" seeks above all to highlight the different modes of involvement in the sacrament. Further specifying these different modes is the task incumbent on a theological reflection that is still in its infancy.[11]

Such a reflection could have a positive effect on ecumenical dialogue with the Eastern tradition, which stresses the priest's sacerdotal ministry. *The spouses do not marry; they are married by the Lord in the Church:*

> The Western tradition stresses the baptismal character of the spouses and their royal priesthood. . . . The priest, as the representative of Christ and of

---

10. G. Martelet, "Mariage, amour et sacrement," *Nouvelle Revue Théologique* 95 (1963): 584, cited in Ligier, *Il matrimonio*, 110.

11. D. Tettamanzi, *Matrimonio cristiano oggi* (Milan: Ancora, 1975), 97-100; see also Rochetta, *Il sacramento della coppia*, 213-23.

the community, publicly confirms the act of the spouses. . . . In the Eastern tradition, the accent falls, rather, on the priest's sacerdotal ministry. . . . Through the person of the celebrant, the Church enters "visibly" into the constitution of the sacramental sign.[12]

For Rochetta, the two perspectives, although different, can nonetheless be complementary and mutually enriching.

The Contribution of Consummation to the Stability and Fullness of the Sacrament

When Hugh of St. Victor made consent the constitutive act or efficient cause of the sacrament, he was followed by all the schools and, indeed, by the whole Church. The famous "theory of consummation," that is, of the sexual encounter that follows the expression of the nuptial pact (as necessary for a valid marriage), was rejected; consummation was not held to be essential to the establishment of the sacramental sign. However, this theory, based on a tradition from the patristic era, allowed for a strengthening of marriage such as to render it fully indissoluble. In fact, consummation gives the sacrament its plenitude and perfection. That is, consummation gives a fullness to the sacrament's signification with respect to Christ and the Church and, therefore, to the efficacy of grace in it.

In this debate, the role of consummation was clarified in relation to the two chief texts where Genesis 2:24 is cited in the New Testament: Matthew 19:5 (here the concern was with indissolubility) and Ephesians 5:31-32 (here the concern was with biblical and patristic symbolism). Consummation reinforces indissolubility and brings the Christian symbolism of marriage to full completion. Christ's union with his Church is not only "mystical" and thus based on charity, but also "physical": it takes into account the Incarnation, in which the Son of God assumed human nature in the womb of the Virgin Mary and united himself hypostatically to this nature. This physical reality is confirmed through the realism that exists between Christ and the Church in the administration of the sacraments.

Catholic doctrine introduced these clarifications in the course of the ca-

---

12. G. Danneels, "Les ministres du sacrement de mariage," in *Mariage et sacrement de mariage*, ed. P. de Locht (Paris: Centurion, 1970), 207, cited in Rochetta, *Il sacramento della coppia*, 222.

nonical and theological debates of the twelfth and thirteenth centuries, thanks both to the criticisms voiced by the schools of Bologna and Paris and to the moderating influence of the popes, especially Alexander III and Innocent III.[13]

A Community of Life and Love

If, in the context of the liturgy, the exchange of consent constitutes the sacramental sign of marriage, the community of life and love is its permanent expression. The sacramental sign of marriage does not disappear after the liturgical celebration, but endures in the spouses' life. While the question of marriage as a permanent sacrament is not new, it has become newly relevant in the period following the Council.[14] In moving beyond the primarily juridical vision of marriage, the Council made possible an extension of the sacrament to the whole life of the spouses. The apostolic exhortation *Familiaris Consortio* clearly confirmed this direction in theology: "The gift of Jesus Christ is not exhausted in the actual celebration of the sacrament of marriage, but rather accompanies the married couple throughout their lives" (*FC* 56).

Historical Summary

In order the better to understand the importance of this approach, we must recapitulate the terms of the question and rehearse the steps leading up to the most recent developments. Historically, the terms of the question are linked to the affirmation of the consent theory, which caused theology to lose sight of the conjugal communion of life and love. We recall that the Fathers of the Church spoke of marriage more as a state and condition of life than as a liturgical celebration of the nuptial pact. But they did not ask how the sacrament could be the cause of grace. With the development of the scholastic notion of the "sign that effects grace," a new and complex question arose: How do we identify the sign that causes matrimonial grace? Under the influence of the consent theory, the sign was restricted to the initial event of the nuptial pact.

---

13. Ligier, *Il matrimonio,* 84-97.

14. G. Baldanza, "Il matrimonio come sacramento permanente," in Aa.Vv. [various authors], *Realtà e valori del sacramento del matrimonio* (Rome: LAS, 1976), 81-102: "It will be easier to understand our proposal if we keep in mind that, according to a broad theological tradition, the sacramental sign is transitory — consisting in the contract alone — whereas the effect of the contract is permanent: the bond" (81).

The community of life and love was thus reduced to a mere consequence and effect of the sacrament; it was not regarded as constituting the sacramental sign that communicates grace as such.

The influence of Robert Bellarmine would prove decisive in overcoming this vision. Bellarmine was cited in a key passage of *Casti Connubii,* where Pope Pius XI compares the visible sacramental sign of marriage to the sacrament of the Eucharist. In the Eucharist, the real presence continues under the *sacred species* even after the celebration of Mass; similarly, the grace acquired during the wedding celebration continues under the *species* of the married life even after the celebration is over. Despite the contribution of M. Scheeben in the nineteenth century, the encyclical *Casti Connubii,* and the support of theologians such as K. Adam, H. Doms, and M. Schmaus in the last century, the majority of theologians up until Vatican II did not see the sacramentality of marriage as going beyond the nuptial pact. According to Ligier,

> The movement of lay spirituality, which arose around 1930 and then underwent renewal and development in the post–World War II years, was probably at the origin of this development of doctrine, which was also assisted by theologians and priests open to Catholic Action in the context of married life.[15]

Vatican II and the Apostolic Exhortation *Familiaris Consortio*

In this regard, the constitution *Gaudium et Spes* marked a decisive development. The document no longer limited the gift of matrimonial grace to the celebration alone, but extended it to the entire life of the spouses:

> The Savior of men and the Spouse of the Church comes into the lives of married Christians through the sacrament of matrimony. He abides with them thereafter so that just as he loved the Church and handed himself over on her behalf, the spouses may love each other with perpetual fidelity through mutual self-bestowal. . . . For this reason Christian spouses have a special sacrament by which they are fortified and receive a kind of consecration in the duties and dignity of their state. By virtue of this sacrament, as spouses fulfill their conjugal and family obligation, they are penetrated with the spirit of Christ, which suffuses their whole lives with

15. Ligier, *Il matrimonio,* 211.

faith, hope and charity. Thus they increasingly advance the perfection of their own personalities, as well as their mutual sanctification, and hence contribute jointly to the glory of God. (*GS* 48)

Taking up the text of the constitution just cited, the apostolic exhortation *Familiaris Consortio* explicitly adds that "the gift of Jesus Christ is not exhausted in the actual celebration of the sacrament of marriage," so that "just as husbands and wives receive from the sacrament the gift and responsibility of translating into daily living the sanctification bestowed on them, so the same sacrament confers on them the grace and moral obligation of transforming their whole lives into a 'spiritual sacrifice'" (*FC* 56). The permanence of the grace of the spouses' sanctification logically requires the permanence of the sign that reveals and communicates this grace. The relationship between marriage and the other sacraments would have to be developed here. We will return later to the content of this relationship, and to the conditions under which the sign formed by the couple becomes a source of grace. Our main business here is simply to highlight the change of perspective that has marked the contemporary development of doctrine concerning the sacramentality of marriage. In conclusion, this doctrine, providentially taught by Pius XI, was adopted by Vatican II in the constitution *Gaudium et Spes* and taught authoritatively by John Paul II in the apostolic exhortation *Familiaris Consortio*. It has become a part of the Church.

Essential Aspects of the Couple's Spousal and Sacramental Character

Following the apostolic exhortation *Familiaris Consortio,* we can continue reflection on the spouses' "community of life and love," basing ourselves precisely on the vocation to love, which opens the exhortation's chapter on "God's plan for marriage and the family." Received from the Creator, enriched by the Redeemer, and consecrated by the sanctifying Spirit, the vocation to love comprehends the spouses' entire existence. Their total, bodily and spiritual self-gift extends in time the "yes" of mutual love solemnly pronounced before the assembly of the faithful:

> The only "place" in which this self-giving in its whole truth is made possible is marriage, the covenant of conjugal love freely and consciously chosen, whereby man and woman accept the intimate community of life and love willed by God himself, which only in this light manifests its true meaning. (*FC* 11)

The institution of marriage, understood as a permanent state of life, is not an exterior formality added from without, but an interior requirement of the pact of conjugal love, which of itself demands indissoluble fidelity. "A person's freedom, far from being restricted by this fidelity, is secured against every form of subjectivism or relativism and is made a sharer in creative Wisdom" (*FC* 11).

The mutual "yes" expressed verbally in the liturgical celebration is then translated into the "language of the body," that is to say, not only into the conjugal encounter (consummation), but also into the spouses' shared life, daily fidelity, friendship, reciprocal forgiveness, fecundity, education, etc. The sacramental sign prolongs itself in time. The spiritual act of self-gift "in the Lord," enriched by the redemptive power of Christ and the salvific action of the Church, establishes the *couple* as a permanent sacrament and transforms its history into salvation history — in other words, into a sign that bears the gift of God to his people. We must note, however, that the sacramental signification of the couple is not automatic or independent of the moral quality of the gestures performed by both. For example, the couple's sexual relationship bears inward grace only if it is accomplished according to the Creator's will; it remains possible for Christian spouses to seek their own pleasure egotistically, and to abuse marriage, its finality, and its laws. We cannot, then, claim that the spouses are automatically instruments of grace. This fact explains why numerous theologians hesitate to acknowledge the sacramental character of human love: human love is ambiguous and wounded by sin, and the sphere of marital relationships is no exception. Needless to say, we have no intention of denying this truth. Nevertheless, we must acknowledge that when spouses are faithful to the norms and ends of marriage, their conjugal relationship is in itself an occasion and instrument of grace. Ligier stresses:

> The life of the spouses must not be reduced solely to the sexual sphere, but rather extended to the totality of their existence as persons, to the encounter of the two persons who live together with their children. In this context, shared work and conversations, culture and prayer can have an effect of grace. All the more in that the spouses and their children complement one another. In this sense, the spouses' and the family's entire life is an occasion and means of grace.[16]

C. Rochetta has taken this approach a step further by seeking to identify the essential elements of the couple's spousal and sacramental character. The

---

16. Ligier, *Il matrimonio*, 214.

five he mentions facilitate a more concrete purchase on the fundamental anthropological features of the couple's being and lived experience: masculinity and femininity, the love between man and woman, the body and its sponsality, sexuality, and the word as promise and reciprocal gift.[17] As *Familiaris Consortio* explains, "This conjugal communion sinks its roots in the natural complementarity that exists between man and woman" (*FC* 19). With this premise in mind, Rochetta proceeds to reflect on the difference between masculinity and femininity as a richness of gift and welcome:

> It is the loving reciprocity between the spouses, with the fullness of their sexually differentiated being and their transcendent vocation, that in the sacramental act of marriage begins to enter into the *historia salutis* and to participate in the *eschaton* of Easter. God's love fully respects the difference between man and woman, which he himself willed as a reflection, image, and likeness of his own mystery of trinitarian communion.[18]

The love between man and woman that is the Creator's gift does not remain external to the sacramental sign. It is assumed from within by Christ and healed, confirmed, and sanctified by the Holy Spirit, precisely in order to signify the invisible reality both of the love of the triune God and of the love between Christ and the Church: "Consequently, there is a radical continuity between the truth of conjugal love and the sacramental event." In other words, there is no dualism between the spouses' human love and the love of God given in the sacrament of marriage. Both grow together, and human love finds its sustenance within the love of God: "The more the couple grows in the truth of the reciprocal love that grounds it, the more it grows in the grace of the sacrament of marriage. The converse is also true: the more it grows in the grace of the sacrament, the more it is able to grow in mutual love."[19]

Conjugal spirituality must be based on this unity. But a reflection on love that is integrated with a theology of the nuptial body has another consequence as well: a re-evaluation of the meaning of sexuality within the sacrament of marriage. From the patristic era to the Middle Ages, the conjugal act was generally associated with at least venial sin, unless it was directly and deliberately intended

17. Rochetta, "È la relazione uomo-donna che diventa sacramento," 68ff.; Rochetta, *Il sacramento della coppia*, Part I: "Antropologia teologica della coppia," 17-131.
18. Rochetta, "È la relazione uomo-donna che diventa sacramento," 69. See also C. Giuliodori, *Intelligenza teologica del maschile e del femminile. Problemi e prospettive nella rilettura di von Balthasar e P. Evdokimov* (Rome: Città Nuova, 1991), 230-48.
19. Rochetta, "È la relazione uomo-donna che diventa sacramento," 71.

for the sake of generation and preserving reciprocal fidelity. Contemporary theology perceives the need to overcome an overly moralistic vision and to:

> reinsert matrimonial sexuality within a more positive and personalistic anthropological framework, so as to show the extent to which the human aspects of sexuality are an integral part of the sacramental dynamic of marriage and must be understood within the domain of the grace that flows from it.[20]

The grace of marriage touches precisely sexuality, healing it, freeing it — at least in principle — from the danger of dissociation from love, and making it the sign of the union of Christ and the Church. We can thus understand the idea that sacramental marriage is a *remedium concupiscentiae* in a positive sense. This means realizing that *eros* and *agape* must progressively unite in the power of purifying grace to overcome both false spiritualism and materialism:

> The *remedium* has to do with the search for a profound integration between spirituality and corporeity, tenderness and sexuality, the communion of hearts and the communion of bodies; the sacrament of marriage is the symbol of this tension, an event of healing, a promise and a guarantee.[21]

To conclude this reflection on the first level of the sacramental "sign" of marriage, we must recall our starting point: it is precisely the man-woman relationship, blessed by God, that is called to be, and to become more and more, the sacrament of trinitarian love through its sacramental participation in the love between Christ and the Church. On the level of the sign that produces grace, we have seen that the initial event, i.e., of the exchange of consent within the liturgy, is an essential element of the sacramentality of marriage. But we have also clearly seen that this foundational act, in both its anthropological and its sacramental aspect, is simply the opening of a source of grace that springs up throughout the spouses' communion of life and love. The symbolic and sacramental function of the couple thus unfolds in time and embraces all its constitutive human dimensions. Through the matrimonial state of life lived as a vocation to holiness, not only is a natural institution raised to a higher level, but (according to the explicit teaching of Vatican II) the Church herself is established in her first cell, the "domestic church."

---

20. Rochetta, "È la relazione uomo-donna che diventa sacramento," 74.
21. Rochetta, "È la relazione uomo-donna che diventa sacramento," 75.

Marriage, Virginity, and Spousal Love

Christian revelation recognizes two specific ways of realizing the vocation of the human person in its entirety, to love: marriage and virginity or celibacy. Either one is, in its own proper form, an actuation of the most profound truth of man, of his being "created in the image of God." (*FC* 11)

On the Christian path, the marriage of the baptized marks an entry into a specific state vis-à-vis the general state of the faithful: the "conjugal state" (*Code of Canon Law* [= *CCL*], can. 226, §1). The spouses' existential decision to form the marriage bond, which is permanent and exclusive in nature (*CCL*, can. 1134), corresponds to the decision of religious, who, through the profession of the evangelical counsels by means of vows or other sacred bonds, consecrate themselves in a special way to God (*CCL*, can. 207, §2). It also corresponds to the decision of candidates to the priesthood, who, by means of a written and signed declaration, consecrate themselves freely to the ecclesiastical ministry (*CCL*, can. 1036; see *Pastores Dabo Vobis* no. 70). Like the choice of the consecrated life or the priesthood, the marriage pact introduces the spouses into a new state (*CCL*, can. 1063, §2), which determines the particular way in which they should and can seek holiness, the end of all Christian life (*LG* 42): the perfection of love, that is, unreserved self-abandonment into God's hands. Balthasar describes this attitude in the following passage:

> The "yes" of the marriage vow and the "yes" of the counsels correspond to what God expects man to be in imitation of Jesus Christ, who, on the Cross, gave all he possessed, body and soul, for the Father and the world. In the state of election, the Christian gives his body and soul to God, and God dispenses the fruit of his sacrifice to his brethren, conferring on the one who has made the sacrifice a mission within the Church. In the married state, the Christian, by his sacramental "yes," gives his body and soul to his spouse — but always in God, out of belief in God, and with confidence in God's bountiful fidelity, which will not deny to this gift of self the promised physical and spiritual fruit.[22]

Following this comparison between the state of virginity and that of marriage, Balthasar proposes his theological category of the "state of life":

---

22. H. U. von Balthasar, *The Christian State of Life*, trans. Mary Frances McCarthy (San Francisco: Ignatius, 1983), 238.

Within the Church, a state of life is a definite life-form that differentiates the ordinary, generic Christian state by a bond, a *differentia specifica*, that has Christian (that is, not simply civil or professional) relevance. Such a life-form binds the Christian irrevocably *(cum immobilitate, sine facultate resiliendi)* in his inmost being. By this bond, which establishes him in a state of life, he is enabled to participate with supernatural fecundity in the mystery of "losing his soul" and thus in the mystery of the Cross and of redemption.[23]

For Balthasar, this definition applies to both states of life, virginity and marriage. Marriage is thus the state in which a man and a woman give their lives. Of course, all Christians are called to give their lives. It is clear that the general Christian state opens to a form of life constituting a radical and profound bond. Nevertheless, when we compare this general state with the two states of life, marriage and virginity, we see that it does not establish a concrete bond radically committing body and spirit to a supernatural service. In order to arrive at this "service," a personal choice of "state" is required in response to the call of Christ. The specific states of marriage and virginity are thus characterized by a bond that *confers the form of a supernatural service, since it lays claim to both body and spirit.* The perfection of love is always a gift of self to another; such a self-gift occurs in truth with a dialogical gift that only marriage and consecrated virginity make possible. He who does not give his own body and spirit remains on the near side of what Christ calls us to.

Thus, "marriage and virginity or celibacy are two ways of expressing and living the one mystery of the covenant of God with his people" (*FC* 16). *Familiaris Consortio* continues:

> In virginity or celibacy, the human being is awaiting, also in a bodily way, the eschatological marriage of Christ with the Church, giving himself or herself completely to the Church in the hope that Christ may give himself to the Church in the full truth of eternal life. The celibate person thus anticipates in his or her flesh the new world of the future resurrection. (*FC* 16)

By virtue of this witness, which actualizes the covenant eschatologically, "virginity or celibacy keeps alive in the Church a consciousness of the mystery of marriage and defends it from any reduction and impoverishment" (*FC* 16). The supernatural service of consecrated persons illumines, orients and pro-

---

23. Balthasar, *The Christian State of Life*, 238.

tects the supernatural service of the spouses, that is to say, the sacramental efficacy of their lives:

> Virginity or celibacy, by liberating the human heart in a unique way, "so as to make it burn with greater love for God and all humanity," bears witness that the Kingdom of God and his justice is that pearl of great price which is preferred to every other value no matter how great, and hence must be sought as the only definitive value. (*FC* 16)[24]

We can now understand better how the theological category of state of life, as defined above, extends the sacramentality of marriage to the spouses' whole existence. By virtue of their decision in faith to give themselves to each another "in the Lord," their whole life unfolds within a "state of matrimonial grace." The spouses' stable and irrevocable common life constitutes as such a supernatural service rooted in the fruitful grace of having been given to Christ, and in Christ, to each other. In this robust vision, the entire life of the spouses and the family appears as an occasion and means of grace:

> The husband's speech and action make Christ present to his wife; in the same way, the wife's speech and action make the action of the Church herself present to her husband. In being present to each other, they are mutual signs of Christ's presence. Like the priest before the assembly, they represent Christ and make the Church present.[25]

The Charism of Marriage and Sacramental Grace

We come to the heart of our enterprise: the exploration, affirmation, and definition of the sacramental character of marriage less as sign *(sacramentum)* than as the very reality signified *(res et sacramentum)*. This requires a deeper understanding of the charism of marriage and sacramental grace. The sacra-

---

24. *Familiaris Consortio* 16: "It is for this reason that the Church, throughout her history, has always defended the superiority of this charism to that of marriage, by reason of the wholly singular link which it has with the Kingdom of God." See also Pius XII, encyclical letter *Sacra Virginitas*. For a further study of the complementarity of the two vocations, see R. Bonetti, ed., *Virginità e matrimonio. Due parabole dell'Unico Amore, Percorsi pastorali* (Milan: Ancora, 1998).

25. Ligier, *Il matrimonio*, 215.

ment of marriage establishes a bond and communicates grace to those who receive it worthily. As we have seen, the awareness of this sacramental grace developed through a long and complex process in the Church's history. At the beginning of the twelfth century, the only grace recognized was a medicinal one, insofar as marriage was seen as a remedy for concupiscence.

The ensuing clarification made possible the identification of two dimensions of marital grace. The first, so to speak objective and institutional, dimension, which St. Thomas called the *res et sacramentum* of marriage, consists in the conjugal bond. The second, more personal and subjective dimension, which St. Thomas called the *res* of the sacrament, is the effect of sanctification resulting from the gift received in faith. Developing this perspective, certain contemporary authors speak of a "charism of consecration" and a "grace of sanctification."[26] We will take up the reflection on these two, complementary dimensions of the sacrament of marriage in what follows.

The Charism: A Bond Sealed by the Irrevocable Gift of Christ's Spirit

The starting point for understanding the gift of marriage in the two above-mentioned dimensions can be found in baptism and confirmation. Through the gift of baptism, persons are established as God's sons and daughters, because their being has been assumed "into Christ." Baptism signifies a radical belonging to Christ, which leaves an indelible mark on the person's being. This ontological bond, sealed by the Holy Spirit, is completed and perfected by confirmation, which signifies a new relation of belonging to Christ's Spirit. Baptism and confirmation are thus sacramental consecrations in the strong sense of the term. They create a new mode of being, which manifests itself in the Christian's new way of living. This mode of being and living is essentially filial and fraternal; it is modeled on Christ and animated by the Spirit as a public witness to God's Truth and Love in the Church and in the world.

The apostolic exhortation *Familiaris Consortio* authoritatively summarized the rooting of the grace of marriage in baptism:

> Indeed, by means of baptism, man and woman are definitively placed within the new and eternal covenant, in the spousal covenant of Christ with the Church. And it is because of this indestructible insertion that the

---

26. See Ligier, *Il matrimonio*, 114, which employs a distinction developed by H. Mühlen, *Una mistica persona* (Rome: Città Nuova, 1968), chapter 3 §9, pp. 352-438.

intimate community of conjugal life and love, founded by the Creator, is elevated and assumed into the spousal charity of Christ, sustained and enriched by his redeeming power. (*FC* 13)

The Objective Form of the Charism of Marriage in a Pneumatological Perspective

We have seen the extent to which the event of the marriage celebration involves the believing couple in an offering of themselves and their love to Christ, who is already objectively their Lord by reason of baptism. He receives their offering, assuming, healing, and perfecting this gift of the couple, which comes from the Father and Creator, while enriching it with the manifold treasures of his redemptive grace. From the initial act of the celebration, then, Christ commits himself, the Father and the Holy Spirit to blessing the spouses' communion of life and love. This commitment means that Christ assumes the totality of the persons, with their love and responsibility, into his own redemptive love — that is, into his prayer and sacrificial suffering. From this assumption there flows for the couple a treasury of grace, forgiveness, and renewal that is always available in faith.

Christ's redemptive involvement pleases the Father, who in turn "blesses" the couple with a specific gift of the Holy Spirit: "The Spirit which the Lord pours forth gives a new heart, and renders man and woman capable of loving one another as Christ has loved us" (*FC* 13). The Holy Spirit is not given only as a force that produces the created effects of goodness, unity, etc.; he is also given as a Person-*Communion*. He is given precisely in his personal modality, as the bond of love between Father and Son, that is, as the objective witness to the unity of love in the Trinity.[27] *Familiaris Consortio* thus affirms: "By virtue of the sacramentality of their marriage, spouses are bound to one another in the most profoundly indissoluble manner. Their belonging to each other is the real representation, by means of the sacramental sign, of the very relationship of Christ with the Church" (*FC* 13). The text continues:

the Holy Spirit who is poured out in the sacramental celebration offers Christian couples the gift of a new communion of love that is the living

27. See H. U. von Balthasar, *Theo-Logic*, vol. 3: *The Spirit of Truth*, trans. Graham Harrison (San Francisco: Ignatius, 2005), 343ff. See also M. Ouellet, "The Holy Spirit: Seal of the Conjugal Covenant."

and real image of that unique unity which makes of the Church the indivisible Mystical Body of the Lord Jesus. (*FC* 19)

The Holy Spirit, who seals the indissoluble covenant-relationship between Christ and the Church, thus also appears as the indissoluble trinitarian bond uniting the Christian couple within the sacramental mystery of the Church.

This pneumatological approach facilitates a better understanding of the charism of marriage in its objective dimension, that is, as a sacramental (institutional) bond. The Spirit-bond definitively introduces the spouses into the nuptial mystery of Christ and the Church, beyond the fluctuations of their subjectivity. The charism of marriage signifies above all the couple's insertion into the mystery of the covenant between Christ and the Church through an irreversible bond of belonging that is sealed by the Holy Spirit:

> The spouses participate in [the event of salvation] as spouses, together, as a couple, so that the first and immediate effect of marriage *(res et sacramentum)* is not supernatural grace itself, but the Christian conjugal bond, a typically Christian communion of two persons because it represents the mystery of Christ's Incarnation and the mystery of his covenant. (*FC* 13)

The sacramental dimension of this bond is rooted less in the natural complementarity of the couple than in the very Person of the Holy Spirit himself, the irrevocable gift that seals the spouses' objective belonging to the mystery of the covenant.[28] The marriage bond should be situated within this perspective, where it can be acknowledged as a true consecration, inasmuch as it establishes an indissoluble, sacramental kind of union.

The Charism of Consecration

The arguments in favor of a "charism of consecration" are founded in Scripture and supported by the patristic tradition. In the New Testament, entry into conjugal life is decided under the impulse of a "charism," which does not come from nature alone but from God himself. Here there is agreement

---

28. See H. U. von Balthasar, *Theo-Logic*, vol. 3: *The Spirit of Truth*, 344: The "subjective love [of the couple] . . . is elevated beyond itself to become an objective love of the Holy Spirit; such is the love that is realized between Christ, giving himself for his Church (Eph. 5:25), and the Bride he has purified so that she is holy and spotless (v. 27)."

between *Christ's teaching* (Matt. 19:11) and Paul's (1 Cor. 7:7). We owe the term "charism" to Paul's comparison between marriage and virginity. But the idea itself comes from Jesus, especially when we consider that the doubt to which he responds in Matthew 19:11 does not directly concern celibacy but the fittingness of taking a wife: "Not all can receive this precept, but only those to whom it is given." Paul, for his part, takes up the comparison between marriage and virginity, introducing the notion of "charism" and applying it to the two states of life. This theme, common to both Jesus and Paul, is further developed by Origen and St. Augustine, who wrote: "And, therefore, for this reason the Lord was invited and came to the wedding, that conjugal chastity might be given support and the mystery of marriages might be shown forth."[29]

In presenting the marriage bond as a charism of consecration, we can appeal to Vatican II, which itself furthered discussion of the grace of marriage along the lines indicated by Pius XI in the encyclical *Casti Connubii:* "They have been fortified, sanctified, and as if consecrated by so great a sacrament."[30] We see a first step in this development in *Lumen Gentium* 11's declaration that

> Christian spouses, in virtue of the sacrament of Matrimony, whereby they signify and partake of the mystery of that unity and fruitful love which exists between Christ and his Church (cf. Eph. 5:32), help each other to attain to holiness in their married life and in the rearing and education of their children. By reason of their state and rank in life they have their own special gift among the people of God (1 Cor. 7:7).

Incorporating this teaching, the constitution *Gaudium et Spes* retains the nuance of *Casti Connubii*'s expression "as if consecrated" (*GS* 48) and unfolds its implications: the "state of life" and the "function" of the spouses, defined concisely as their "mission." *Lumen Gentium* 11 had indicated the ecclesiological condition of the spouses, who are, so to speak, a "domestic church." The document thus acknowledges that the spouses have a "proper mission," i.e., the Church's general "mission" in the world. This mission is expressly defined in *Gaudium et Spes* 50:

29. Ligier, *Il matrimonio*, 113 n. 4: "*Et ostenderetur sacramentum nuptiarum.*" Translation from St. Augustine, *Tractates on the Gospel of John 1–10*, trans. John W. Rettig (Washington, DC: CUA Press, 1988), 195-96.

30. Pius XI, *Insegnamenti pontifici. Il matrimonio*, no. 304 (221); *Acta Apostolicae Sedis* 22 (1930): 555.

Parents should regard as their proper mission the task of transmitting human life and educating those to whom it has been transmitted. They should realize that they are thereby cooperators with the love of God the Creator, and are, so to speak, the interpreters of that love.

The language of the liturgy suggests the consecratory power of the charism of marriage in its objective or institutional dimension as a bond between the spouses that is not only personal but also ecclesial: "Father, you have made the union of man and wife so holy a mystery that it symbolizes the marriage of Christ and his Church" (Marriage Rite During Mass, Nuptial Blessing A). As the sign or symbol of the Church's sacramental economy, Christian marriage is *an efficacious act,* an act that objectively effects what it indicates and signifies. And what it indicates and signifies is *participation in the mystery of the covenant that supernaturally and indissolubly binds Christ to the Church and the Church to Christ.* Such is the profound reality of the sacrament of marriage, which gives the spouses a new mode of being in the Church, establishing them in a particular state of life within the people of God. From the moment they exchange their consent, the relation between Christ and the Church becomes the model structuring their ecclesial condition, which it does thanks to their *"own* [sacramental] *gift."* According to Ligier, this gift, understood as a charism of consecration, is "the traditional Augustinian 'marriage bond,' only now expressed in an ecclesial key."[31]

We can conclude that the sacramental character of marriage is founded on the sacramental sign that situates the spouses' mutual consent within the mystery of love between Christ and the Church. Christ receives and blesses their consent with a particular gift of the Holy Spirit; the spouses are thus assumed and consecrated into Christ's love in order to become, as a couple, an efficacious sign of Christ's gift for the Church. From the beginning of their consent (marriage *in fieri*), they receive an objective gift of the Spirit (charism), which, touching the intimacy of their conjugal love, transcends their subjectivity and commits them definitively and indissolubly to being credible witnesses of the fidelity of God, who is Love.

This is why, as a charism that consecrates the couple to Christ, the marriage bond causes them, and their conjugal love in all its dimensions, to participate in Christ's love for the Church. The sanctification of the spouses, founded on baptism and marriage, will increase to the extent that they live out the charism that has made them "one flesh," a task requiring their openness

---

31. Ligier, *Il matrimonio,* 119.

to the particular graces that heal, purify, perfect, and even divinize their love. This last dimension leads us to a deeper understanding of the theological and sacramental aspect of the grace of marriage.

Sacramental Grace: Participation in Christ's Nuptial Love for the Church

The Content of Matrimonial Grace[32]

Even if the Church had to wait until Vatican II for a clear Magisterial affirmation of the "charism" of marriage, the presence of "grace" in the sacrament was solemnly defined in the sixteenth century by the Council of Trent. The biblical foundation for this definition is, again, Ephesians 5:22-32. The Council Fathers wished to affirm three points with respect to grace: (a) the perfection of natural love; (b) the confirmation of indissolubility; and (c) the sanctification of the spouses. This teaching develops crucial insights of St. Thomas Aquinas.

It is true that St. Thomas's early teaching, set forth in his *Commentary on the Sentences* of Peter Lombard,[33] does not yet acknowledge the union between Christ and the Church as the grace "contained" in, and thus communicated by, marriage. At the beginning of his career, Aquinas saw the Christ-Church pair exclusively as a *figure* and *prophecy* of grace.[34] Nonetheless, the aforementioned position would become his teaching in the *Summa Contra Gentiles* IV, chapter 78.

Pius XI's encyclical, *Casti Connubii,* recovers the teaching of the Council of Trent in order to develop an understanding of the grace proceeding from the enduring gift of the "marriage bond." The pope adds that matrimonial grace is rooted in habitual sanctifying grace; that the spouses receive "special gifts," dispositions and seeds of grace that give them strength to perfect their natural powers; and, finally, that they are entitled to the assistance of actual grace whenever they are in need of it.

Vatican II deserves our attention here above all because of three documents: along with *Lumen Gentium* 11, *Lumen Gentium* 41 (on the holiness of

32. See G. Baldanza, "La grazia sacramentale al concilio di Trento. Contributo per uno studio storico-critico," *Ephemerides Liturgicae* 97 (1983): 83-140; A. di Marco, "Teologia della famiglia," *Rivista Biblica* 31 (1983): 189-209.

33. Thomas Aquinas, *Commentary on the Sentences,* IV, d. 26, c. 6.

34. Thomas Aquinas, *Commentary on the Sentences,* IV, d. 26, q. 2 a, ad 4m et 5m; see *Supplementum,* q. 42 a. 1, ad 3m et 5m.

the spouses), and *Sacrosanctum Concilium* 77 (which calls for a revision of the liturgy designed to highlight the gift of grace), the constitution *Gaudium et Spes* is particularly significant for our purposes. The latter text demonstrates how human love is healed, perfected, and elevated by the marital sacrament (no. 49), and states, "Authentic married love is caught up into divine love and is governed and enriched by Christ's redeeming power and the saving activity of the Church" (48). Marriage is thus a source of grace because God has instituted it with a view to human love, but also because it has been saved by the love of Christ, who sacrificed himself for his Church.

Familiaris Consortio is richer still. Number 13 of the document stresses that the principle of the sacrament is the coming of "Jesus Christ, the Bridegroom who loves and gives himself as the Savior of humanity, uniting it to himself as his body." In the same passage, we read that marriage, "like every sacrament, is a memorial, actuation and prophecy" of the event of salvation, and that as a memorial it gives the spouses grace. Further on, the document links the grace of marriage to the grace of baptism in an original way, adding that this grace of the sacrament gives rise to the "requirement of an authentic and profound conjugal and family spirituality" (*FC* 56).

This Magisterial teaching shows that the grace of marriage communicated by the sacrament has two main ends: first, that of *healing,* i.e., of repairing the consequences of sin in the individual and in society; and second and above all, that of *perfecting* persons and the conjugal institution. *Gaudium et Spes* summarizes all of this as follows: "This love God has judged worthy of special gifts, healing, perfecting and exalting gifts of grace and of charity" (*GS* 49). In *Familiaris Consortio,* John Paul II specifies the content of this grace:

> The content of participation in Christ's life is also specific: conjugal love involves a totality, in which all the elements of the person enter — appeal of the body and instinct, power of feeling and affectivity, aspiration of the spirit and of will. It aims at a deeply personal unity, the unity that, beyond union in one flesh, leads to forming one heart and soul; it demands indissolubility and faithfulness in definitive mutual giving; and it is open to fertility (cf. *Humanae vitae,* 9). In a word it is a question of the normal characteristics of all natural conjugal love, but with a new significance, which not only purifies and strengthens them, but raises them to the extent of making them the expression of specifically Christian values. (*FC* 13)

As Ligier remarks, a presentation as rich and dense as this deserves further reflection and commentary. The theme of healing, which has always been acknowledged, needs no discussion. This is not true of the second theme mentioned alongside it, i.e., that of elevation. First of all, conjugal love, and indeed marriage itself, must be elevated to the dignity of a sacrament. In themselves, they are natural realities pertaining to the order of creation, or better, socio-cultural realities. It is through Christ's institution of the sacrament that they are integrated into the structures of the Kingdom so as to become effective within the economy of salvation. The proper effect of marriage is realized when the spouses, who have received their own gift or charism (*LG* 11), receive something else as well: together with this divine call, they are given the grace proper to them, a grace that enables them to accomplish their divine vocation. The spouses "signify and partake of the mystery of that unity and fruitful love which exists between Christ and his Church" (*LG* 11). This is the *"gratia coniugalis."*[35]

A Genuine, Specific Participation in Christ's Love for the Church

Our account of the grace of marriage can appeal to three key concepts that the Council mentions in relation to Christ's spousal covenant with the Church: encounter, assumption, and participation.[36] We can understand these concepts either more anthropocentrically or more Christocentrically.

From an anthropological perspective, the encounter with Christ means that the spouses are helped, healed, and perfected in their love and in the fulfillment of their natural conjugal duties. This approach begins with nature and then seeks to determine what grace adds, or how it heals and perfects. The fact that the spouses are taken up into, and participate in, Christ's spousal love is interpreted above all by means of the model of imitation privileged in the pre-conciliar juridical and theological tradition.[37]

The Christocentric approach does not break with the tradition but marks a change in perspective, which highlights the primacy of incarnate grace, that is, the presence of Christ himself and of the Holy Spirit in the spouses' union.

---

35. Ligier, *Il matrimonio,* 124ff.

36. See G. Baldanza, *La grazia del sacramento del matrimonio. Contributo per la riflessione teologica* (Rome: CLV Liturgiche, 1993), 283ff.

37. This is the predominant approach in A. Miralles, *Il Matrimonio. Teologia e vita* (Milan-Cinisello Balsamo: San Paolo, 1996); Ligier also follows this approach, whereas Martinez Peque, Rochetta, and Mattheeuws, while remaining within the same general horizon, open new Christocentric and trinitarian perspectives under the influence of recent pneumatological developments.

In fact, Christ himself comes to encounter them, remain with them, and make them participate in the grace of his spousal love:

> We can thus affirm that Christ the Bridegroom enters into the lives of Christian spouses and assumes their love into his own spousal love for the Church. . . . Christ and the Church allow Christian spouses to participate in their mission as Bride and Bridegroom.[38]

To be sure, this perspective respects the validity of the imitation model, but it shifts the main emphasis to the model of gift. The gift of Christ himself is expressed through the reciprocal gift of the spouses in him. A proper and authentic conjugal spirituality is the normal fruit that should emerge precisely from this participation. In a beautiful speech to the Teams of Our Lady in 1982, John Paul II remarked:

> [T]he reality of Christian marriage is as if indwelt and transfigured by the New Covenant. . . . The Covenant not only inspires the life of the couple, but it is accomplished in it, in the sense that the Covenant unfolds its own energy within the life of the spouses. It "shapes" their love from within: they love one another not only *as* Christ loved, but already, mysteriously, *with* the very love of Christ, since his Spirit has been given to them.[39]

Thanks to the gift of the covenant, "the love of the spouses is interiorly transformed and supernaturally elevated, such as to be, really albeit mysteriously, a true and proper participation in the love that Christ has for the Church."[40] According to *Familiaris Consortio,*

> The Spirit which the Lord pours forth gives a new heart, and renders man and woman capable of loving one another as Christ has loved us. Conjugal love reaches that fullness to which it is interiorly ordained, conjugal charity, which is the proper and specific way in which the spouses participate in and are called to live the very charity of Christ who gave himself on the Cross. (*FC* 13)

38. Baldanza, *La grazia del sacramento del matrimonio,* 285ff.

39. John Paul II, Address to the Members of the Teams of Our Lady Movement, September 23, 1982. Translated as John Paul II, "God's Gift of Life and Love: Marriage and the Eucharist," *Communio: International Catholic Review* 41 (Summer 2014): 462-71.

40. Tettamanzi, *Matrimonio cristiano oggi,* 85.

The sacrament of marriage reaches its fullest fruitfulness when it brings spouses to this theological awareness, transforming their mutual love into charity — a charity that joins them to the triune God and calls them to live the logic of gift, welcome, and communion in the "today" of their conjugal life.

This insight invites us to draw out the subjective consequences of the spouses' assumption into Christ's love through the Holy Spirit. Among these consequences is of course a perfecting of natural marriage and of human love as realities pertaining to the order of creation but the chief consequence is the fulfillment of a mission of *service* rendered to the Love of God. This mission flows precisely from participation in trinitarian Love, which assumes, elevates, and transforms the reality of marriage in Christ. The human love of the couple and of the family in all of its modalities — spousal, paternal and maternal, filial and fraternal — is thus reinforced by the Spirit to express, in the Church and in the world, the exchange of love between the divine Persons. The specific sacramental meaning of marriage is thus to be an "ecclesial sign," that is, a "relational reality at once human and divine," in subjective harmony with the objective gift of the Holy Spirit. This sign or reality is actualized to the extent that the fruitful couple (a fruitfulness that is first spiritual, based on faith in the Holy Spirit, but also natural) lives, experiences, reveals, and shares with others the fact of having been "assumed into the relations of love between the divine Persons." We will return to this point in the following section.

The newness of sacramental marriage, when seen in a Christocentric perspective, lies in the fact that the real symbol of the marriage event is the couple itself, and thus the conjugal pact that the fiancés make with one another. It is the human and worldly reality of marriage that becomes sacrament: an event of the covenant and a sign of grace. Rochetta reminds us that no other sacrament exhibits so clearly the incarnational structure of salvation and faith. Moreover, as Balthasar notes, the *novum* of Christian marriage corresponds to "the fundamental figure of grace . . . Jesus Christ himself," to such an extent that "in matrimony . . . it is not the human event of a covenant entered into by husband and wife that specifies a grace which in itself is undifferentiated. Rather, this is effected by the nuptial relationship between Jesus Christ and the Church."[41] The newness of marriage between the baptized transcends their creaturely state, though

---

41. H. U. von Balthasar, *The Glory of the Lord*, vol. 1: *Seeing the Form*, trans. Erasmo Leiva-Merikakis (New York: Crossroad; San Francisco: Ignatius, 1982), 560.

it remains rooted in the latter, because the reality in which the spouses participate flows from the specific gift of Christ's redemption and cannot be reduced to what constitutes the couple solely as an immanent reality.[42] This newness of Christian marriage appears clearly in the dimension of the spouses' ecclesial mission.

Charism and Grace with a View to an Ecclesial Mission

Marriage is a reality of the order of creation that is taken up into the spousal mystery of Christ and the Church. This integration of course involves an elevation, and thus a promotion, of the natural reality of marriage beyond the human horizon. We see this promotion in the fact that conjugal charity perfects human love in all its dimensions. But the chief point about the promotion of marriage in Christ is that *human love is placed at the service of a greater love:* God's love for humanity in Christ. The center of gravity of conjugal love thus shifts to Christ, who becomes the ultimate Subject of the gift of the spouses. Consequently, the marriage bond (charism) and conjugal love (grace) begin to fulfill an instrumental or sacramental function vis-à-vis Christ's love for the Church. Christian marriage takes on an ecclesial and missionary dimension, which *Familiaris Consortio* expresses in the following terms:

> [T]he family has the mission to guard, reveal and communicate love, and this is a living reflection of and a real sharing in God's love for humanity and the love of Christ the Lord for the Church his bride. (*FC* 17)

This mission is above all a participation in the mission of the Holy Spirit, as mutual, intra-divine Love, who gives himself through Christ and in Christ and draws the couple into his self-gift. The Holy Spirit thus assumes the sacrament of the couple into the threefold signification that characterizes the whole sacramental order: memorial, actuation, and prophecy.

> As a memorial, the sacrament gives them the grace and duty of commemorating the great works of God and of bearing witness to them before their children. As actuation, it gives them the grace and duty of putting into practice in the present, towards each other and their children, the

---

42. See Rochetta, *Il sacramento della coppia,* 175ff.

demands of a love which forgives and redeems. As prophecy, it gives them the grace and duty of living and bearing witness to the hope of the future encounter with Christ. (*FC* 13)

To Attain the Ends of Marriage and Involve Oneself in Its Gifts

At the level of its earthly reality, marriage already has an end in the complementarity and reciprocal growth of man and woman and in the generation and education of children, in which the complementarity of the spouses is expressed and fulfilled:

> Thus a man and a woman, who by their compact of conjugal love "are no longer two, but one flesh" (Matt. 19:6), render mutual help and service to each other through an intimate union of their persons and of their actions. Through this union they experience the meaning of their oneness and attain to it with growing perfection day by day. (*GS* 48 §1)

"By their very nature, the institution of matrimony itself and conjugal love are ordained for the procreation and education of children, and find in them their ultimate crown" (*GS* 48 §1): this finality (or double, co-essential end) is assumed and transfigured, in all its plenitude, by the sacrament of marriage.

In fact, by reason of the sacrament, the couple is called to do more than grow as a dual unity in the procreation and education of new human beings. The call inscribed within the sacrament is above all a matter of acknowledging and consciously welcoming the gift of Christ and the Church. This gift requires the couple to grow together in faith, hope, and charity. Only in this sphere of theological growth can the couple give glory to God for his gifts, receiving the "most excellent" gift of children not only as a natural event but also as an incarnate sign of the gift that the Father-Creator makes to their love for the sake of Christ and the Church. Such an awareness is nourished by the couple's active and conscious participation in the Church's sacramental life. In this sense, the sacraments of reconciliation and the Eucharist play an essential role in the spouses' deeper spiritual growth: these sacraments root them in trinitarian love and guarantee their sacramental fruitfulness within the Church's mission.

Realizing the Vocation to Conjugal Holiness

In this way, "Christian spouses are fortified and receive a kind of consecration" from the grace of the sacrament of marriage:

> By virtue of this sacrament, as spouses fulfill their conjugal and family obligation, they are penetrated with the spirit of Christ. . . . Thus they increasingly advance the perfection of their own personalities, as well as their mutual sanctification, and hence contribute jointly to the glory of God. (*GS* 48 §2)

The call to holiness in conjugal life is not extrinsically added to the reality of marriage between baptized persons; to the contrary, it is *rooted* in their baptism — which is a universal call to holiness (see *Lumen Gentium* 39-42) — and *finds its specificity* in relation to the gift and condition proper to spouses in the Church.

This specificity is essentially characterized by the spouses' *communion*, since they henceforth fulfill their proper vocation not only as individual persons, but together *as a couple.* With the sacrament of marriage, the bond of love becomes a sacramental one: two lives are sacramentally united forever; two beings who love each another commit themselves to living out this new condition of grace, which God created in them and through them, and they do so by helping each other grow in faith. They do not merely support each other; they also *sanctify each other by giving themselves* to each other, indeed, precisely to the extent that they do so. Their salvation, too, is accomplished together, and each spouse is to a certain extent responsible for the other.[43]

In summary, the sacramental grace of marriage has its source in baptism, which, through the spouses' ecclesial consent, inserts their conjugal love "into Christ." This specific grace, "the grace of the conjugal union," gives them a share in the union between Christ and the Church. By the same token, it enriches their conjugal union with the spousal mode of being revealed in Christ's paschal mystery and actualized in the mystery of his Eucharist. As the fructification of the charism of marriage, the gift of sacramental grace enables the spouses to "follow Christ" in his paschal act of total self-gift, which is commemorated, actualized, and realized through the entire extent of their married life. The initial event in which they receive the conjugal charism is thus prolonged by, and bears fruit in, a permanent event: the grace of the

---

43. Rochetta, "Il sacramento del matrimonio," 406.

couple's fidelity, unity, and fecundity within their family, which becomes a "domestic church" in miniature.

The Implications of the Sacramentality of Marriage

We come in this last section to the conclusion of our reflection on the sacramentality of marriage. So far we have examined three points: the constitutive dimension of the sacramental sign (the *sacramentum,* which is at once the couple's consent at the moment of their wedding and the permanent gift of themselves); the institutional dimension of the charism (the *res et sacramentum,* or the bond of marriage); and the real content of conjugal grace (the *res,* or the participation of conjugal love in the spousal union between Christ and the Church). These three dimensions contain what is essential in the sacrament of marriage.

The foregoing reflection must nonetheless be complemented by a presentation of the fundamental attributes of marriage: unity, fecundity, and indissolubility in light of sacramental grace. Though these attributes have a foundation in the created reality of marriage, their immediate and essential source is the grace of the sacrament. Following the Christological approach adopted at the beginning, we will first explore the Christological and pneumatological foundation of these attributes, since in the divine plan the human couple, the dual unity of man and woman, was conceived in function of, and with a view to, the union of Christ and the Church. The accent of this approach falls on (uncreated) grace, in contrast to a once dominant treatment of the Church's doctrine on marriage that began with nature and, in our opinion, placed undue emphasis on the proper consistency, autonomy, and near self-sufficiency of the created order.[44] We must move beyond the extrinsicism between nature and grace, creation and redemption, that marked pre-conciliar theological

---

44. The issue underlying our presentation is the intrinsic relationship between the natural order and the order of Christ's grace. Those who seek to explain the gratuity of grace by hypothesizing a "pure nature" tend toward a maximalist account of the proper and autonomous consistency of the natural order, as if Christ were an extrinsic *superadditum* (the theory of two ends). See, for example, Miralles, *Il Matrimonio,* 172: "Creation that is not oriented toward Christ, toward the recapitulation of all things in him (cf. Eph. 1:10), proves to be a possibility not realized in fact. It is a true possibility, inasmuch as salvation in Christ is gratuitous with respect to human nature, but according to the eternal divine decree, this possibility is not real." Vatican II seems to adopt a more markedly Christocentric perspective; following Cardinal Henri de Lubac, it stresses the intrinsic bond between the order of creation and the order of grace, while maintaining the distinction between the two orders.

anthropology, an extrinsicism expressed in the theological opinion that the marriage pact can be detached from the marital sacrament.

The Christocentric approach to the doctrine of marriage highlights the priority of grace over nature, that is, the inscription of the created order within the order of Christ's grace from the "beginning" of the salvific plan. Christian marriage, in all its anthropological richness, is predestined to perform its sacramental function within the personalistic and transcendent covenant of Christ the Bridegroom, who gives himself nuptially to his Church. The couple consecrated to Christ is thus assumed through him, with him, and in him, into the sphere of the trinitarian relations. Consequently, all the gifts of nature and grace that bless the couple in the sphere of their marriage and family are predestined in Christ to be placed at the disposal of the triune God, to serve "unto the praise of his glory" (Eph. 1:1ff.).

Unity, Fecundity, and Indissolubility

The consecration of the spouses to Christ opens a source of grace that is made manifest in the unity and indissolubility of the marriage bond and in the spouses' (natural and spiritual) fecundity. These properties are the fruit above all of the Holy Spirit, who joins the spouses objectively (the bond) and subjectively (communion) in the unitive and procreative love that builds up the community of the family. The Holy Spirit thus inserts the natural and personal complementarity of this man and this woman into the divine and human spousal complementarity of Christ and the Church. This insertion and assumption demands a response from the couple, a response that, by virtue of their real participation in the mystery of the Trinity, entails the unity, fecundity, and indissolubility of their marriage pact, consummated and lived as a divine and human covenant. These attributes are thus essential implications of the sacrament of marriage. Throughout her history, the Church has constantly reaffirmed them in the face of challenges, separations, and divergent interpretations on the part of different ecclesial traditions.

The Unity of Marriage

The indivisible unity of conjugal communion is a consequence of the pact of conjugal love, by which a man and a woman "are no longer two, but one flesh" (Matt. 19:6; Gen. 2:24). This unity contains a call to grow ceaselessly in communion, "through day-to-day fidelity to their marriage promise of total mutual self-giving. This conjugal communion sinks its roots in the natural complementarity that exists between man and woman, and is nurtured through the personal willingness of the spouses to share their entire life-project, what they have and what they are" (*FC* 19). Hence, *Familiaris Consortio* continues,

> such communion is the fruit and the sign of a profoundly human need. But in the Lord Christ God takes up this human need, confirms it, purifies it and elevates it, leading it to perfection through the sacrament of matrimony: the Holy Spirit who is poured out in the sacramental celebration offers Christian couples the gift of a new communion of love that is the living and real image of that unique unity which makes of the Church the indivisible Mystical Body of the Lord Jesus. (*FC* 19)

Such communion is radically contradicted by polygamy. In fact, the latter directly negates the plan of God revealed to us from the beginning; it is contrary to the equal dignity of man and woman, who give themselves to each other in marriage with a total, and therefore unique and exclusive, love. Vatican II affirmed in the strongest terms this requirement of unity and stressed its foundation in the dignity of the persons: "Firmly established by the Lord, the unity of marriage will radiate from the equal personal dignity of wife and husband, a dignity acknowledged by mutual and total love" (*GS* 49). Amid cultures that often tend to oppress women, the Church has constantly maintained the divine institution of monogamous marriage, which Christ's redemptive love has confirmed and elevated to the dignity of a sacrament of his unique nuptial relation with the Church.[45]

The theological grounds for the unity of marriage, then, are the divine institution of monogamy, Christ's will to reform marriage, the gift of the Holy Spirit as a charism of consecration, and the dignity of conjugal love and its vocation as a sacramental symbol of the union between Christ and the Church.[46] The same reasons undergird the indissolubility of marriage as well:

> Christ renews the first plan that the Creator inscribed in the hearts of man and woman, and in the celebration of the sacrament of matrimony offers

---

45. Council of Trent, canon 2 on the sacrament of marriage: "If anyone says that it is lawful for Christians to have several wives at the same time and that this is not forbidden by any divine law [cf. Matt. 19:9], let him be anathema [cf. *1798]" (Denz 1802).
46. See C. Forconi, *Antropologia cristiana come fondamento dell'unità e dell'indissolubilità del patto matrimoniale* (Rome: PUG, 1996).

a "new heart": thus the couples are not only able to overcome "hardness of heart" (Matt. 19:8) but also and above all they are able to share the full and definitive love of Christ, the new and eternal Covenant made flesh. Just as the Lord Jesus is the "faithful witness" (Rev. 3:14), the "yes" of the promises of God (cf. 2 Cor. 1:20) and thus the supreme realization of the unconditional faithfulness with which God loves his people, so Christian couples are called to participate truly in the irrevocable indissolubility that binds Christ to the Church his bride, loved by him to the end. (*FC* 20)

Under the influence of the Christian ideal of monogamous marital unity, the legitimacy of second marriages after the death of the first spouse was contested and debated during the patristic age. Some of the greatest Fathers of the Church — Origen, Gregory Nazianzen, and Basil — condemned such second marriages in the name of the Christian ideal. Certain heretical sects, such as the Montanists and Novatianists, also denied the legitimacy of second marriages. The Church finally decided for the more lenient approach of St. Jerome and St. Augustine as the more adequate pastoral position and recognized the sacramental value of marriages following the death of one of the spouses.[47] A second marriage, it was argued, does not destroy the unity of the first sacramental union, since the "one flesh" that constituted the latter's sacramental character ceases to exist after death. To be sure, a profound, "spiritual" unity continues between those once united on earth, but this unity, which now resembles that existing among virgins, does not prevent the surviving spouse from contracting a new union in the sacramental "one flesh." The surviving spouse who decides to remarry is not "unfaithful" to the first spouse, or even to the unity of the marriage between Christ and the Church expressed by the first union. Death sunders the exclusivity of the "one flesh," but it does not break — in fact, it fulfills — the spiritual communion between those who were married. This more profound sponsality can of course justify a decision not to remarry, but it does not exclude the possibility of remarriage, inasmuch as the first "sacramental sign" has already reached its fulfillment.[48] It is important not to lose sight of the complementarity of marriage and virginity in the promotion of the Christian ideal.[49] Though brief, the foregoing sketch makes it clear that

47. For more details, see Miralles, *Il Matrimonio*, 229-41.

48. Rather than seeing death as the rupture of the conjugal bond, ought we not to speak of it as fulfilling this bond in the sphere of virginal relations?

49. See A. Sicari, *Breve catechesi sul matrimonio*, 6th ed. (Milan: Jaca Book, 1994), especially the preface by Luigi Giussani and the concluding dialogue between Sicari and Giussani, 91-109.

in the Roman Catholic Church, the power of the sacrament has safeguarded the monogamous unity of marriage throughout history, despite opposition and resistance stemming from the contrary mores of many cultures.

The Indissolubility of Marriage

Indissolubility has been by far the most hotly contested question concerning marriage from the beginning of the apostolic Church to our own day.[50] The question appears in the New Testament, while the tradition brings to light shifting positions reflected in diverse canonical and civil legislation. Though many elements of the question pertain to canon law and are more appropriately treated in that context, we must nonetheless highlight the scriptural and dogmatic bases for the indissolubility of marriage.

Five New Testament passages touch directly on indissolubility. The most ancient is 1 Corinthians 7:10-11, which was written around the year 55. In Mark and Luke, we find a single text each: Mark 10:1-12 and, in a shorter version, Luke 16:18. In Matthew, on the other hand, we find two texts: Matthew 5:32, which occurs in the Sermon on the Mount, and Matthew 19:1-9, which tackles the issue of divorce. While Paul, Mark, and Luke limit themselves to a general condemnation of divorce, which implies an exceptionless, absolute law, the two Matthean texts preserve the general law but make an important addition: "except in the case of concubinage." The problem consists in determining whether or not these words constitute a true exception.

The interpretation of this passage has important consequences in ecclesial praxis. The Orthodox Church interprets this well-known clause in Matthew as an exception that justifies divorce and permits remarriage. Protestants follow the same interpretation. The Catholic Church understands the clause, "in the case of *porneia*," as a confirmation of indissolubility, since *porneia* is understood as "concubinage" or "illegitimate union" — in which case the legitimacy of repudiation, and even the necessity of separation, is clear. Moreover, in the case of *porneia* in the sense of "adultery," the Roman Church, following the tradition of St. Augustine and St. Jerome, does not admit the possibility of remarriage but only of separation, with the ensuing obligation of continence. The various opinions of exegetes concerning the meaning and importance of the Matthean clause are summarized by Ligier, who offers a very nuanced

50. See P. Dacquino, *Storia del matrimonio cristiano alla luce della Bibbia*, vol. 2: *Inseparabilità e monogamia* (Leumann [Turin]: LDC, 1988), with an ample bibliography.

evaluation of the discussion.[51] The difficulty in determining the precise sense of the Matthean clause (Matt. 5:32; 19:9) highlights the importance and the role of the Church in the interpretation of Scripture.

The tradition of the primitive Church, founded on the teaching of Christ and the apostles, thus affirms the indissolubility of marriage even in the case of adultery. This principle appears clearly despite misguided exegesis and cases of (early Christian) indulgence towards persons in extreme situations. On the other hand, as the International Theological Commission has noted, it is not easy to ascertain the precise extent and frequency of such cases. The Council of Trent declared that the Church is not deceived when, following Christ and the Apostles, she teaches that the marriage bond cannot be broken by adultery (Denz 1807). However, Trent's anathema extends only to those who deny the Church's authority in this area: "It cannot be said, then, that the Council had the intention solemnly to define marriage's indissolubility as a truth of faith."[52]

The grounds for the indissolubility of marriage are manifold, and they derive both from the sphere of creation and from that of the sacraments, that is to say, from natural law and from divine positive law.[53] First of all, natural law reveals the qualities proper to nuptial love, which is *personal, irreplaceable, and absolute.* Moreover, the generation and education of children require the presence and stability of two parents. Finally, *history urges us* to add the example of the decadence of certain cultures, especially the Hellenistic and Roman, which was caused at least in part by their moral decline and by the rise of divorce. The positive law established by Christ demands the observance

51. Ligier, *Il matrimonio,* 165ff. For the Eastern tradition, as well as for certain Catholic authors such as A. M. Dubarle and U. Moingt, the clause supposedly reflects, on an exegetical level, "an attempted compromise between Jesus' first position (the categorical and absolute law) and the demands of certain Judeo-Christian sects, which retained the above-mentioned concept of adultery and considered it to be a kind of legal 'death' granting the right to a new marriage" (169). But this interpretation, which makes sense in the Jewish milieu, is not shared by other exegetes such as J. Dupont, who underscores how the practices of the Corinthian community (cf. 1 Corinthians 7) attest to an overcoming of this position already at the beginning of the apostolic Church. The most widely shared exegetical position today is that which translates *porneia* as "concubinage." It has been adopted by the most widely read Catholic and ecumenical editions of the Bible *(Jerusalem Bible; Traduction Œcuménique de la Bible. Édition intégrale* [Paris: Éd. du Cerf/SBF, 1977]); see *Traduction Œcuménique de la Bible. Édition intégrale,* Matthew 5:32, footnote h; see also Miralles, *Il Matrimonio,* 246-55.

52. International Theological Commission, *Propositions on the Doctrine of Christian Marriage* (1977), 4.2, which also explains that this reserve was "because of historical doubts (opinions of Ambrosiaster, Catharinus, and Cajetan) and for some more-or-less ecumenical reasons."

53. Ligier, *Il matrimonio,* 179ff.

of indissolubility in marriage, since Christ condemned and abolished Moses' permission to repudiate one's wife. The law promulgated by Jesus was received and taught by the apostles,[54] expounded and developed by the early Fathers despite human fragility, maintained by bishops despite the betrayals of human legislators (Justinian, Pepin the Younger), defended by the popes in the face of worldly power (Nicholas I against King Lothar, Innocent III against Philip II of France), and formulated by the Council of Trent in canons 5 and 7. Within the continuity of this tradition, the indissolubility of marriage remains an instance of Christianity's witness to non-Christians, a witness that the Catholic Church has consciously retained vis-à-vis the Eastern Churches and the Protestant dissent that emerged in the sixteenth century.

Though their treatment pertains chiefly to canon law, two privileges of the Church, which illustrate her limited but real powers regarding indissolubility, require mention in this context. The *Petrine privilege* allows the Sovereign Pontiff to dissolve a marriage that has been ratified but not consummated. This privilege is based on the fact that the absence of carnal copulation renders the sacramental sign incomplete and thus open to dissolution for serious reasons. The *Pauline privilege,* or *privilege of faith,* applies to pagans who marry and then enter into conflict due to the conversion of one of the spouses: "But if the unbelieving partner desires to separate, let it be so; in such a case the brother or sister is not bound" (1 Cor 7:15). If the non-baptized person refuses the faith and is unwilling to cohabit peacefully with the baptized partner, their marriage, even if consummated, can be dissolved in favor of the faith.[55]

In conclusion, we recall the idea with which we began: the indissolubility of Christian marriage flows above all from its structure as a spousal covenant "in Christ." God willed marriage in the order of creation as an indissoluble reality that man cannot put asunder (Matt. 19:6). The marriage-sacrament confirms and ratifies this indissolubility, inserting it into the mystery of Christ's covenant with the Church. Thanks to the marriage-sacrament, the bond between the spouses is completely removed from the arbitrary fluctuations of human sentiment. It is established as a sign and actualization of the nuptial bond by which Christ bound himself forever to his Church. We are dealing, then, with a bond of love realized in the spouses as a participation in the bond of love that unites the *Kyrios* to the Church, i.e., with a covenant as definitive as the one into which man and wife have been inserted (Eph. 5:21-33). They can fail to recognize this bond; they can lose the life of grace, but they will never

54. Luke 10:1-12; 16:18; 1 Corinthians 7:10-11.
55. *Code of Canon Law,* can. 1143 §1; see Miralles, *Il Matrimonio,* 243-52.

be able to revoke the event of the covenant that has been inscribed in them through the sacrament of marriage. Once it has been celebrated "in the Lord," this bond gives them a share in Christ's irrevocable consent to the Father, and so becomes an irrevocable event in its turn. The covenant into which the baptized spouses are inserted is not entrusted to them alone; it is given as an event of Christ and the Church, and it actualizes God's irrevocable commitment to them, "perfecting, confirming, and sanctifying" their love as husband and wife through a permanent pact. The spouses' "yes" is a part of Christ's "yes" to the Father for the Church.[56]

The Fecundity of Marriage

Our Christocentric and trinitarian approach could, indeed should, have given pride of place to the fruitfulness of marriage, but out of respect for the traditional manner of presenting the doctrine of marriage we began with unity and indissolubility, while reserving fecundity for the conclusion. The fruitfulness of marriage remains an underexploited topic in theology. The predominance of a juridical and naturalist perspective "from below" led to a stress on procreative and educative fecundity, while love was relegated to a quasi-extrinsic dimension of marriage. The task of theology today is to rethink the "goods" (St. Augustine) and "ends" (St. Thomas) of marriage from the Christocentric perspective of "gifts" (Mattheeuws)[57] and "fruitfulness" (Balthasar), in order to integrate all the dimensions of marriage and conjugal life within love. As we shall see, a deeper understanding of the grace of marriage in light of Pneumatology allows the integration of natural fecundity into supernatural fruitfulness, which is all too often overlooked. Hans Urs von Balthasar and Adrienne von Speyr offer the most pertinent reflections on this question and so open the path to a new and promising approach to the theology of marriage.[58]

---

56. See Rochetta, *Il sacramento della coppia,* 184ff.

57. A. Mattheeuws, *Les "dons" du mariage. Recherche de théologie morale et sacramentelle* (Brussels: Culture et Vérité, 1996). For a review of this work, see M. Ouellet, "Pour une théologie des "dons" du mariage," *Anthropotes* 13, no. 2 (1997): 495-503.

58. See Hans Urs von Balthasar, *The Christian State of Life,* trans. Mary Frances McCarthy (San Francisco: Ignatius, 1983), 224-49, especially 243-49; *Explorations in Theology,* vol. 4: *Spirit and Institution,* trans. Edward T. Oakes (San Francisco: Ignatius, 1995), part 2, "The Encounter in Marriage," 217-24; and *Epilogue,* trans. Edward T. Oakes (San Francisco: Ignatius, 2004), "Fruitfulness," 109-23. See also Adrienne von Speyr, *John: The Word Become*

The first fruitfulness of sacramental marriage belongs to the act of faith that founds it. This act establishes the couple as a sacred sanctuary and holy source of God's fruitfulness. By reason of this faith, a new gift of the Holy Spirit springs up from the fountain of baptism and draws the couple as such into the process of intra-divine fruitfulness:

> Whoever thirsts, come to me; drink, whoever believes in me! As scripture says: "Streams of living water will flow from within" (John 7:37). In fulfill-ment of these promises, we can feel the most overwhelming experience of God, an awakening to the presence of God that is much more than vision: it is a participation in the very surging life of God himself.[59]

Balthasar explains this participation, which involves not only the future life but also the present life in faith, as follows:

> By being born with the Son from the womb of the Father, we simultane-ously receive a part of the active gift of begetting or giving birth — for the Lord calls those who believe in him not only his brothers and sisters but also his "mothers" (Mark 3:35). . . . [I]t is already given to believers, even on earth, not only to possess the Holy Spirit but to "exhale" the Spirit, as was already made clear in the passages cited above of the living source springing up within them.[60]

In this light, Christian marriage can be seen as an overflowing source of trinitarian life, a specific participation in the very fruitfulness of God in Christ. From the moment of the consecration of marriage, this participation is no longer received by two individuals, but by a new *community:* by an "I-thou" that has become a "subjective and objective we." From that point on, this "we of love" rests on the foundation of faith, that is, on grace. Adrienne von Speyr explains the manner in which this occurs: "The mystery of the natural as of the supernatural fruitfulness of Christian marriage is grounded in that mutual Yes, given in God."[61] For von Speyr, the specificity of marital fruitfulness is rooted in the sanctification of conjugal love, which generates a

---

Flesh — Meditations on John 1-5, trans. Lucia Wiedenhöver and Alexander Dru (San Francisco: Ignatius, 1994), 75-93, especially 88-91; and *The Letter to the Ephesians,* trans. Adrian Walker (San Francisco: Ignatius, 1996), 224-41.

59. Balthasar, *Explorations in Theology,* vol. 4: *Spirit and Institution,* 442.
60. Balthasar, *Explorations in Theology,* vol. 4: *Spirit and Institution,* 442-43.
61. Von Speyr, *John: The Word Become Flesh,* 89.

total, unreserved openness in faith to the fruitfulness that God wishes to share with the couple: "The grace of marriage is, of course, primarily the sanctification of the life of married people, for it bestows what the one possesses on the other and makes it fruitful for him. The faith and love and sacrifice of the one sanctifies both."[62]

The sanctification that flows from the couple's initial "yes" includes their "yes" to the child, not as the chance result of their interpersonal love, but as a gift of grace, since their love was consecrated to God in faith. Love and its spiritual and/or bodily fruit are thus gifts of God which are to be received with grateful joy.

Adrienne von Speyr continues:

> The mutual love of husband and wife is on the one hand so wide that God alone can fill it, and on the other side so much the gift of grace that it bears with it the promise of fruitfulness, a promise that in fact remains entirely with God and is not in the hands of the parents.[63]

Consequently, the logic of gift demands of the couple an attitude of openness and availability that does not "calculate" a child. To calculate a child in this way, to exclude it a priori (contraception) or to claim it as a right (in vitro fertilization), is not a meaningful option for Christian spouses who live by grace: "Children are an expression of the freedom of fruitfulness and are therefore a symbol of the Holy Spirit."[64] The fulfillment of the promise of fruitfulness included in their love is thus left to God and to the freedom of his grace:

> Every Christian marriage is blessed by God and is fruitful in him, whether through the blessing of children or the blessing of sacrifice. If God chooses the second alternative, the spiritual fruitfulness of marriage is increased and widened out invisibly so that it flows into the whole community.[65]

In the latter case, the fruitfulness of the spouses approaches, through the path of sacrifice, the supernatural fruitfulness of the consecrated virgin.

The act of faith that consecrates conjugal love to Christ thus receives a

---

62. Von Speyr, *John: The Word Become Flesh*, 89.
63. Von Speyr, *John: The Word Become Flesh*, 89.
64. Von Speyr, *John: The Word Become Flesh*, 89-90.
65. Von Speyr, *John: The Word Become Flesh*, 90-91.

participation in the fruitfulness of the sacrifice of the Cross, the source and model of all fruitfulness, which directly forms the fruitfulness of virgins and indirectly shapes that of the spouses. As Balthasar writes:

> *This gift of self in life and death is not unlike the ineradicable, eternal vow that is immanent in all love;* it is an act of such finality that it resembles a true "loss of [one's] own soul" (Matt. 16:25). Only because the soul has sacrificed the right to dispose of its life as it will can the right so to dispose of the body also be sacrificed: "The wife has not authority over her body, but the husband; the husband likewise has not authority over his body, but the wife (1 Cor. 7:4).[66]

Through this greatest possible gift, the spouses become "cooperators with God for giving life to a new human person" (*FC* 14). The child is not merely the result of their "natural" love, but the fruit of their offering to God in faith, an offering that God blesses either with the gift of a child or with a gift of supernatural fruitfulness.

In this context, Balthasar criticizes the distinction between the "ends" of marriage: the end consisting in the procreation and education of children, and the end consisting in reciprocal self-gift, which are then conceived as the "goal" and the "meaning" of marriage, respectively. "*But this distinction disappears* (and with it many an embarrassment to which it leads) when marriage is regarded in its sacramental character."[67] While the distinction is justified in the perspective of a "natural" love that is then "raised" by the sacrament to the level of grace, it is overcome in the Christocentric perspective, which from the beginning integrates natural love within the act of faith. Balthasar continues:

> For now the spouses are no longer opened only to each other — and hence closed to all others; they stand primarily in openness to God and, from this stand before God, give themselves to him and, at the same time, expect to receive from him the unexpectable: the fruit of his grace.[68]

Clearly, then, the act of faith that constitutes the sacrament situates the couple's horizontal love within the vertical covenant with God. This act con-

---

66. Balthasar, *The Christian State of Life*, 245.
67. Balthasar, *The Christian State of Life*, 246.
68. Balthasar, *The Christian State of Life*, 246.

verts their love into a sacrament, that is, a "sign" and "instrument" of Christ's love for the Church. It demands of the spouses an attitude of openness, availability, and service, which eliminates for them the distinction between a primary and secondary end of their marriage, between its goal and its meaning. Since they have consecrated their love to God, they wish to receive from God only the kind and degree of fruitfulness that he chooses. Balthasar argues that this unification (and simplification) is ultimately rooted in the fact that the spouses' faith participates in the grace of the Cross, whose fruitfulness opens out onto the infinite:

> Their love — exteriorly something that is expended between the two of them — shares in a hidden manner in the unlimited love of the Lord, which is always universal and eucharistic, and whose fruitfulness surmounts every barrier and extends itself infinitely. It can do so because, in the fruitfulness of the Lord's love on the Cross, *the law of trinitarian love is itself revealed* — the love that is not exhausted between Father and Son, but has as its fruit the Third Person, the Holy Spirit, whose prerogative it is to be, in a special way, the love that exists in God himself.[69]

Lived in faith, sacramental conjugal love possesses an intrinsic opening to the divine and human "third," which undercuts any extrinsicism between the natural and personal ends. Those couples who love each other in faith, and thus in and through God, want nothing more than to correspond to Love's triune nature. This by virtue of the Christological fulfillment God planned from the beginning, which draws conjugal love within, and into the service of, the eternally open and fruitful love of the Trinity. Do we not find here a path to a new, personalistic synthesis of the traditional doctrine? The "ends" of marriage are integrated into the "gifts" of Christ and the couple, which open conjugal and family life to the ever-fruitful source of trinitarian Love.

The Mystery and Ministry of the Domestic Church

The *Catechism of the Catholic Church* tells us that "Christ chose to be born and grow up in the bosom of the holy family of Joseph and Mary. The Church is nothing other than the 'family of God'" (*CCC* 1655). Further on, the *Catechism* continues in a similar vein:

69. Balthasar, *The Christian State of Life*, 247.

The Christian home is the place where children receive the first proclamation of the faith. For this reason the family home is rightly called the
"domestic church," a community of grace and prayer, a school of human
virtues and of Christian charity. (*CCC* 1666)

Theological reflection on the sacramentality of marriage naturally leads
us to the mystery and ministry of the Christian family as "domestic church."
Rediscovered by Vatican Council II, the topos of the "domestic church" has
its roots in the New Testament and in the writings of the Fathers, especially
St. John Chrysostom.[70] After the Council, it was enthusiastically received and
developed both by theologians and by the Magisterium of Paul VI and John
Paul II. *Familiaris Consortio*'s substantial account of the ecclesial character of
the family is just one evident proof of this reception. By way of example, we cite
the following passage, which highlights the ecclesial mission of the Christian
family as one of its several tasks:

> In turn, the Christian family is grafted into the mystery of the Church to
> such a degree as to become a sharer, in its own way, in the saving mis-
> sion proper to the Church: by virtue of the sacrament, Christian married
> couples and parents "in their state and way of life have their own special
> gift among the People of God" (*LG* 11). For this reason they not only
> receive the love of Christ and become a saved community, but they are
> also called upon to communicate Christ's love to their brethren, thus
> becoming a saving community. In this way, while the Christian family
> is a fruit and sign of the supernatural fecundity of the Church, it stands
> also as a symbol, witness and participant of the Church's motherhood
> (cf. *LG* 41). (*FC* 49)

This growing awareness of the family's participation in the Church's salvific mission represents a qualitative leap not only in the development of the
theology of the family, but also in the development of ecclesiology as a whole.
In fact, reflection on the relationship between the family and the Church enables ecclesiology to recover one of the most fundamental and most neglected
aspects of the mystery of the Incarnation: the Holy Family of Nazareth.[71] It

---

70. See *Lumen Gentium* 11; and *Apostolicam Actuositatem* 11. On the theme of the domestic church, see D. Tettamanzi, *La famiglia via della Chiesa,* 2nd ed. (Milan: Massimo, 1991),
ch. 4: "Fate della vostra casa una chiesa," 70-92.

71. See John Paul II, apostolic exhortation *Redemptoris Custos* [On the Person and the

is incumbent on contemporary theology to deepen our understanding of the relationships that the Redeemer nurtured with his own family. Ecclesiology cannot abstract from the original model of human and supernatural community in which the humanity of the incarnate Word was formed. The virginal relationships between Jesus, Mary, and Joseph are a key to understanding the mystery of the Church as communion, as well as the complementarity of the states of life within the Church.

The family, then, is truly an integral part of the Church's being and acting. The Christian family is not only an "image" of the Church reflecting this or that aspect of ecclesial communion; the Christian family is an "ecclesial reality" by virtue of the sacramental reality that constitutes it. Indeed, it is a veritable "domestic church," not only metaphorically, but in the strong sense of the term. This insight represents a step forward in the thinking of Church and theology that is rich in promise for the future of mission. We cannot show all the implications of this fact here, but will limit ourselves to summarizing the various aspects of the sacramentality of the family that emerge from our theological reflection thus far.

The numerous foundations of the family's participation in the being and the mission of the Church, the community of salvation, are intimately linked. First of all, the baptism of the spouses and their children makes them members of the body of Christ, which is the Church. Confirmation then strengthens the child of God with the gift of the Holy Spirit, so that he or she can bear witness to Christ. The sacrament of marriage specifies the character of baptism and confirmation through a spousal charism, which consecrates the couple to Christ; the source of the nuptial love between Christ and the Church thus flows freely at the heart of the spouses' conjugal love. Finally, through the outpouring of the Holy Spirit, the grace of marriage — this trinitarian *"communio personarum"* — renders fruitful the familial relationships of sponsality, fatherhood and motherhood, filiation, and fraternity (*FC* 15). Of course, we must not forget the organic relation between marriage, the Eucharist, and Reconciliation, which forms an essential condition for the permanent actualization of this conjugal Pentecost (*FC* 57-58).

All of these sacramental realities place the family at the heart of the Church's mystery and ministry. Through the sacraments, the fruitful dual unity of man and woman, which is already an *image* of the Trinity on the level of creation, becomes a *likeness* of intra-trinitarian gift, because it participates in

---

Mission of Saint Joseph in the Life of Christ and of the Church]. See also J. Blanquet, *La sagrada familia, icono de la Trinidad* (Barcelona: Hijos de la Sagrada Familia, 1996).

Christ's spousal gift for his Church. The sacramental couple, together with its fruitfulness, is thus taken up into the gift of Christ the Bridegroom, symbolized at Cana and fulfilled on the Cross.[72] Thanks to this union with Christ the Bridegroom and the Church-Bride, the family is plunged into participation in the trinitarian communion, signifies it, and communicates it to others:

> The family has become an "icon" in the order of the new creation, thanks to the salvific commitment of the Father and the Son in the Spirit; it proclaims that the loving communion of two of the baptized constitutes a revelation and a living realization of the eternal communion of the Father and the Son in the Spirit.[73]

The "ministry" of the Christian family has its source in this "mystery." It is a prophetic, priestly, and kingly ministry exercised through the first proclamation of the faith to children, the search for unity in spousal charity (the form of conjugal holiness), and the worship of God in prayer. As the *Catechism* expresses this,

> It is here that the father of the family, the mother, children, and all members of the family exercise the priesthood of the baptized in a privileged way "by the reception of the sacraments, prayer and thanksgiving, the witness of a holy life, and self-denial and active charity."[74]

The Church's ministry, which is a participation in Christ's priesthood, thus finds a privileged expression in the domestic church.

This conjugal and familial ministry does not enclose the family within the circle of domestic relations. It also is not limited to the confines of the family: the family is impelled by the Holy Spirit to unite with the great family of the Church and even with all humanity. Christ's presence in the sanctuary of the family, as Head and Bridegroom of the domestic church, calls the family to go beyond the centripetal tendencies of natural love and to embrace all the dimensions of its vocation to love. Adrienne von Speyr writes:

---

72. See I. de la Potterie, "Le nozze messianiche e il matrimonio cristiano," in "Lo Sposo e la Sposa," *Parola, Spirito e vita* 13 (1986): 87-104; Tettamanzi, *La famiglia via della Chiesa*, ch. 2: "Come a Cana di Galilea: Cristo incontra gli sposi," 31-51.

73. L. Gendron, "Le foyer chrétien, une Église veritable?" *Communio: Revue catholique internationale* 11, no. 6 (1986): 77.

74. *Catechism of the Catholic Church*, 1656, quoting *Lumen Gentium* 10.

[This] closed circle . . . is broken open by the sacramental grace of marriage. The essence of this grace is that it enables one to love the child in God and God in the child; it opens out the earthly sphere of love in order to introduce God, and with God of course the Church.[75]

Familiaris Consortio offers a rich treatment of the mission of the family in all its dimensions: "the family has the mission to guard, reveal and communicate love, and this is a living reflection of and a real sharing in God's love for humanity and the love of Christ the Lord for the Church his bride" (*FC* 17). The text highlights four essential aspects of this mission of the family: "1) forming a community of persons; 2) serving life; 3) participating in the development of society; 4) sharing in the life and mission of the Church" (*FC* 17). This rich program deserves a fuller treatment than we can give it here.

By way of conclusion, we recall that the communion of persons at the heart of the domestic church not only reveals a new likeness between the "gifts" of the Trinity and those of the family. In addition, there is a mutual immanence of these two "gifts." The domestic church is an "icon of the Trinity," or *"sacramentum Trinitatis."* The communion of life and love in the Christian family, founded on the "sincere gift of self"[76] in the *sequela Christi,* goes beyond likeness to the trinitarian communion. It sacramentalizes the gift of the divine Persons to the world in Christ; it participates in, and grants access to, the exchange between the divine Persons in the Holy Spirit. Under the "species" of the spouses' fidelity, unity, and fecundity, a mystery of the covenant is accomplished: the covenant between the Trinity and the family, the domestic church. From this covenant are born sons and daughters of God, who bear witness that human love and divine love are capable not only of true reciprocity, but above all of a *shared fruitfulness* in the grace of the Holy Spirit.

75. Von Speyr, *John: The Word Become Flesh,* 88-89.
76. John Paul II, *Letter to Families* 11.

CONCLUSION

> This is a great mystery, and I mean in reference to Christ and the Church.
>
> EPH. 5:32

The greatness of sacramental marriage has its source above all in the spouses' participation in the trinitarian mystery of love between Christ the Bridegroom and the Church-Bride. Our study has enabled us to do several things. First, we identified the revealed origin and foundation of the sacramentality of marriage and traced the growing understanding of this sacramentality down through the Tradition. We then grasped something of its essence as sign, charism, and grace and distinguished its attributes. Finally, we explored the "ministerial" meaning of the spouses' love as an expression of its permanent sacramentality in the "domestic church."

This deepening of our understanding of the greatness of marriage was made possible by the encyclical *Casti Connubii,* which opened the path to the development of a specific conjugal spirituality rooted in the sacrament. There remains much to be done in this sphere, but in the wake of Vatican II and *Familiaris Consortio,* this conjugal and familial spirituality recommends itself more and more as a participation in Christ's paschal gift to the Church and thus as an authentic vocation to holiness.

In order to cultivate this spirituality, we must ceaselessly contemplate Christ the Bridegroom, who humbled himself for love in order to espouse, purify, and sanctify fallen humanity eucharistically. He leads humanity to the Father as a holy and immaculate Bride, with a view to the eschatological wedding feast in the Spirit of Love. United in faith, Christian spouses participate in this eternal event of Love made flesh; with Mary and John at the foot of the Cross, they find themselves immersed in the source that springs from the pierced heart of Christ. From this source, they receive countless graces of fidelity and fruitfulness, in order to radiate the glory of God in the Church and in the world.

Love is the first and last word of Christian marriage. The spouses' love is taken up into the love of Christ and the Church so that the God who is Love might be loved, served, and glorified, and so that the world might believe in Love.

PART TWO

The Theology of Marriage and the Sacramentality of the Church

Marriage and the Family, an Essential Dimension of the New Evangelization

There is no historical epoch whose salient characteristics cannot be discerned by looking at its view of marriage and the family. Upon close examination, marriage and the family turn out to be more than just one aspect or sector of life; they are an essential dimension without which man cannot be understood as an individual (identity) and personal being (relation).[1] The whole of anthropology, then, is at stake in the understanding and experience of marriage and the family.[2]

This objective fact appears even more clearly when we consider the radical cultural transformation that has taken place in our Western societies. Angelo Scola observes:

While the "traditional" conception of the family . . . is to a certain extent still present in the collective imagination, the couple as such finds itself in the midst of a serious crisis (common law unions, homosexual unions, etc.). This crisis is in its turn due to a weakening of freedom and is tied to the absence of paternity (maternity). These phenomena are interdependent and rest upon a widespread mentality that no longer acknowledges

---

1. See A. Milano, *Persona in teologia* (Rome: EDR, 1996).

2. See A. Scola, *The Nuptial Mystery*, trans. Michelle K. Borras (Grand Rapids, Cambridge: Eerdmans, 2005), 337-56, here 337. Our approach is based on the direction given by Cardinal Scola, former president of the John Paul II Institute for Studies on Marriage and Family, to further theological research in the area of marriage and family. The following reflections draw largely on appendix 4 of *The Nuptial Mystery*, which deals with the renewal of priestly formation in this area.

marriage as the root of the family or the family as the fundamental cell of society.[3]

John Paul II was well known for his tireless and prophetic commitment to promoting marriage and the family as an essential dimension of the new evangelization: "The family . . . is at the heart of the Church's mission and of her concern for humanity."[4] The pope translated his keen awareness of the family's centrality into a permanent call to all the faithful, including priests, to have a special concern for families. He recalled this in the apostolic exhortation *Familiaris Consortio* (no. 73) as well as in the document of the Congregation for Catholic Education, *Directives on the Formation of Seminarians Concerning Problems Related to Marriage and the Family* (March 19, 1995). The latter text vigorously states that "this aspect of the formation program must be accurately revised and, if necessary, qualitatively improved" (13). This qualitative improvement is not simply a matter of adding particular courses on marriage and the family to the seminarian's curriculum; rather, these themes must become "an internal dimension of pastoral and intellectual formation" itself (16).

The present study seeks to contribute to this renewal of philosophical and theological research on marriage and the family by adopting the man-woman polarity and its constitutive relations as the starting point for a new approach in systematic theology. Presupposing anthropological insights treated elsewhere, we will look at this fundamental relation and its sacramental value in connection both with the sacramentality of the Church in general and with the sacramentality of the seven sacraments in particular. Our reflection will center on the specific nature of Christian marriage since, according to D. Tettamanzi, "reflection is still . . . generic, timid, and uncertain" in this area.[5] As Tettamanzi explains, this specificity "is based on the fact that the sacrament of marriage is not something different from the pact, or conjugal love, but is this very pact/conjugal love 'elevated' to the level of an efficacious sign of grace."[6]

---

3. Scola, *The Nuptial Mystery*, 337. See also, by the same author, *Crisi della libertà e vita familiare* (Grosseto: Centro Studi S. Lorenzo — I Portici Editore, 1995); "Matrimonio e famiglia luoghi visibili dell'umanità redenta," *La Rivista* 29, no. 1 (1994); J. E. Dizard and H. Gadlin, *La famiglia minima. Forme della vita familiare moderna* (Milan: Angeli, 1996).

4. John Paul II, Recitation of the Holy Rosary, St. Patrick's Cathedral, New York, October 7, 1995. John Paul II repeated this central message of his pontificate during his apostolic journey to America on the occasion of the publication of the post-synodal apostolic exhortation *Ecclesia in America* in 1999.

5. D. Tettamanzi, *La famiglia via della Chiesa*, 2nd ed. (Milan: Massimo, 1991), 67.

6. Tettamanzi, *La famiglia via della Chiesa*, 67.

A deeper understanding of this nuptial sacramentality is certainly one of the most necessary and pressing tasks of contemporary theology. But scholarship in this area will not bear fruit for the new evangelization unless the man-woman relation truly becomes the starting point for a new approach in systematic theology.

In what follows, we attempt to meet this challenge in the field of dogmatic theology. Our first step will be to lay the basic groundwork for a sacramental theology in a nuptial key. We will then deploy a nuptial Christology in order to explore the foundations of the Church's sacramentality: participation in the communion of the Trinity through the covenant in the incarnate Word. Finally, we will treat the sacramentality of marriage in its twofold dimension: as primordial sacrament in the order of creation and as sacrament of the covenant between Christ and the Church in the order of redemption. While distinct, these two orders are intrinsically related, since Christ is the foundation of creation. The man-woman polarity, as both symbol and sacrament, thus reveals its intimate connection with the Eucharist, which is the key to understanding the entire sacramental order. This connection becomes clear in light both of the nuptial meaning of the body and of the sacraments and of the interaction between marriage and the other sacraments. Our approach seeks to place the domestic church at the center of ecclesial sacramentality, as a key point in the renewal of the Church's mission. *Familiaris Consortio's* presentation of the ecclesial mission of the Christian family points in the same direction: "For this reason they not only receive the love of Christ and become a saved community, but they are also called upon to communicate Christ's love to their brethren, thus becoming a saving community" (*FC* 49).

Although we cannot address all the anthropological and philosophical aspects of the question here, we hope at least to introduce nuptial sacramentality as a theological horizon in whose light we can properly value the sacrament of marriage within the mystery-sacrament of *Christ the Bridegroom and the Church-Bride.*[7]

---

7. See R. Bonetti, ed., *Cristo Sposo della Chiesa. Sorgente e modello della spiritualità coniugale e familiare* (Rome: Città Nuova, 1997); by the same editor, *Il matrimonio in Cristo è matrimonio nello Spirito* (Rome: Città Nuova, 1998). These publications, sponsored by the Italian Bishops' Conference, seek to deepen the theology and spirituality of marriage and the family, encouraging an interdisciplinary study that is linked to the lived experience of couples and families.

CHAPTER 4

Presuppositions for a Nuptial Sacramental Theology

The construction of a nuptially oriented sacramental theology rests on biblical, theological, and ontological bases that, while belonging to other disciplines, need to be mentioned at the beginning of our reflection. Angelo Scola offers a synthetic overview of these foundational elements in the appendix cited in the introduction to this section. We take inspiration from his work, to which we refer the reader for further study. Given that we are dealing with presuppositions, we cannot engage in an exhaustive study of them here. Nevertheless, a brief review of them will serve to set our reflection, as an exercise in sacramental theology, within its larger framework and horizon. We will begin with the Bible, examine its dramatic logic, and end with a reference to ontology. The latter deploys the resources of reason to undergird the conceptual elaboration of the content of revelation: the covenant reveals the *mysterion* of Being-Love, which calls the human person to freedom in a gift of himself.

Salvation History as the History of the Spousal Union between God and Man[1]

We recall a passage of Carlo Rochetta cited in an earlier chapter:

> Within the Bible as a whole, the category of "covenant" expresses the central content of the *mysterion* in history: the gratuitous communion of love

---

1. See C. Rochetta, *Sacramentaria fondamentale. Dal "mysterion" al "sacramentum"* (Bologna: EDB, 1990). The following synthesis takes its inspiration from another book by the same author: *Il sacramento della coppia* (Bologna: EDB, 1996), chap. 7.

and life that God wishes to establish with humanity. This communion is manifested historically and eschatologically in Christ and is communicated in the Spirit through the Church, the community of the ultimate and definitive covenant. As such, the category of "covenant" is particularly apt for representing both God's coming among us and the unique bond that he establishes with mankind. This content is given to us through the progressive unfolding of the economy of the *mysterion*. At each stage, the God of revelation is the God of the covenant, a covenant that is first promised and prefigured, and then accomplished and established in the only-begotten Son made man, who died and rose from the dead. The Church and the sacraments — marriage among them — belong to this historical-salvific dynamism and actively make it present to human existence in its particularly crucial moments.[2]

In the language of the ancient Near East, the biblical term *berit,* corresponding to "covenant," means an accord established between two groups or individuals and juridically ratified by a rite and clauses of engagement. Among the most ancient peoples, this rite consisted in an exchange of blood in token of communion and of the mutual bond. We read in the book of Genesis, "When the sun had gone down and it was dark, behold, a smoking fire pot and a flaming torch passed between these pieces. On this day the Lord made a covenant with Abram, saying, 'To your descendants I give this land . . .'" (Gen. 15:17-18).

The rite performed by Moses echoes a different but no less significant ritual usage. He immolates young bulls as a thanksgiving sacrifice, then collects the sacrificial blood in basins and sprinkles part of it on the altar, the symbol of God, and part of it on the people, which has just accepted the words of the Lord: "And Moses took the blood and threw it up on the people, and said, 'Behold the blood of the covenant which the Lord has made with you in accordance with all these words'" (Exod. 24:8). The covenant is God's institution of a unique bond between him and the people he has chosen: by virtue

2. Rochetta, *Il sacramento della coppia,* 164. See also L. Bouyer, *The Christian Mystery: From Pagan Myth to Christian Mysticism,* trans. Illtyd Trethowan (Edinburgh: T&T Clark, 1989), 18: "Isn't the eschatological meaning of human espousals that union of God with his people which all the Old Testament expressed by the image of Marriage? In the mystery in which the love of God is revealed, the image becomes reality because Christ, the eternal Son, espouses fallen humanity, which he raises up by the Cross to the height of his own assimilation to his creatures, and it is in this marriage of blood that his sonship becomes ours: we are all made sons with the Son, in the Son."

of this bond, God commits himself to his people, guaranteeing his protection and the fulfillment of his promises. Israel, for its part, declares itself ready to observe the code of the covenant and to remain faithful to it.

For Israel, this covenant represents a totalizing experience; it concerns the past, the present, and the future and determines the very identity of the chosen people. Its content is synthetically expressed in the formula that runs like a guiding thread through the Old Testament: "I will be your God and you will be my people" (Exod. 6:7; Jer. 31:33; Ezek. 36:28).

A recurrent and especially meaningful image is used to describe the event of the covenant: that of a wedding. The God of biblical faith offers himself to the community of Israel as a Bridegroom, a demanding Bridegroom who does not allow the love his people owes him to be given to others (Exod. 20:5; Deut. 4:24). He is a Bridegroom who loves and who wishes to be loved in return, who saves Israel and leads it to the promised land with a Bridegroom's fidelity. Israel pursues its journey entirely under the sign of this nuptial love. We find an example of this in the inclusion of the Song of Songs in the Hebrew canon of the Scriptures: while originally a poem about a wedding, it is reread as representing the loving encounter between Yahweh and his people, which includes all the stages belonging to the experience of love: origins, exile, and the rediscovery of love. The message of the prophets makes striking use of the same motif, especially in Hosea, Jeremiah, Ezekiel, and the book of Isaiah.[3]

At the time of Hosea's message, the worship of Yahweh was influenced by a strong tendency toward syncretistic fusion with the religion of Baal. Hosea uses nuptial terminology to denounce Israel's infidelity to its God and to show that fruitfulness and prosperity come only from Yahweh. The prophet's own conjugal life becomes a symbolic teaching. Hosea marries a woman who has been initiated into cultic prostitution; the names of his three children allude to acts contrary to the relationship of fidelity between Yahweh and his people (Hos. 1:6). But Yahweh does not abandon his people; he continues to seek out the heart of his bride (2:7-15), attempting a new betrothal (2:23).

The prophet Jeremiah contrasts Israel's infidelity to the time of wandering in the desert, when Israel was like a young fiancée, full of affection and love toward Yahweh, the husband who chose her (Jer. 2:2-3). Despite the alienation of the people, who are attracted by Canaanite idols, Jeremiah becomes the messenger of a new pact of intimate union between God and his people: "But this is the covenant which I will make with the house of Israel after those

3. See Rochetta, *Sacramentaria fondamentale*, 167-71.

days, says the Lord: I will put my law within them, and I will write it upon their hearts; and I will be their God, and they shall be my people" (Jer. 31:33).

Ezekiel retells the history of his people using the allegory of the unfaithful bride: on the one hand, he recounts God's good gifts, and on the other, Israel's sins (Ezekiel 16). The second part of Isaiah develops the same idea in the context of salvation history: Yahweh is the God of the new creation who makes all things new. As Israel's Bridegroom and Creator, then, he can renew the spousal union with his people. This new wedding feast is at once a continuation of the first covenantal bond and an absolutely new beginning.

John Paul II summarizes this understanding of salvation history as the story of the spousal union between God and man:

> The analogy we are discussing [i.e., the analogy of spousal love] allows us to understand to a certain degree the revealed mystery of the living God, who is Creator and Redeemer (and as such at the same time God of the covenant); it allows us to understand this mystery in the manner of spousal love, just as it allows us also to understand it (according to Isaiah) in the manner of "merciful" love, or in the manner of "fatherly" love (according to Ephesians, especially chapter 1). . . . The analogy of the love of spouses (or spousal love) seems *to emphasize* above all *the aspects of* God's *gift of himself* to man who is chosen "from ages" in Christ (literally, his gift of self to "Israel," to the "Church"); a gift that is in its essential character, or as gift, total (or rather "radical") and irrevocable.[4]

John Paul II's reflection on the spousal dimension of salvation history concludes with a reference to Christ, who is the supreme Mediator of the nuptial relationship between God and his people. We will thus reflect at some length on the event of the Incarnation as the mutual self-gift of God and man, in order to understand better the foundation of the covenant and the Church's participation in it. Angelo Scola suggests the need for such reflection in the article that gives us our basic orientation:

> The principal advances that we have mentioned must all flow together to enrich the theology of marriage: the analogy between trinitarian communion and spousal communion; the "one flesh" in analogy to the union of two natures in the single person of Jesus Christ; the relationship of Christ

4. John Paul II, *Man and Woman He Created Them: A Theology of the Body,* trans. Michael Waldstein (Boston: Pauline Books and Media, 2006) [= *TOB*], 501.

the Bridegroom to the church-bride (whose basis is Mariological) must reveal its character as the ontological symbol of the union between man and woman in the sacrament.[5]

We will see how the Church-Bride proceeds from the salvific event of Christ the Bridegroom, who died and rose from the dead: nourished and made fruitful by the sacraments, she also participates in the latter's fecundity. The Eucharist and marriage bring to light the mystery of the spousal covenant that God willed and accomplished with his people in Christ.

A Dramatic Understanding of Revelation and Anthropology

As Angelo Scola notes, Vatican II considerably enriched theology with a renewed concept of revelation that complemented Vatican I's *Dei Filius*. While Vatican I gave pride of place to the cognitive and doctrinal aspects of revelation, Vatican II highlighted its historical and existential dimension. We cite this passage of Scola at length:

> There is no antithesis between Vatican I and Vatican II on this point. Nevertheless, *Dei Verbum* effects an essential development.
> Borrowing the words of de Lubac, we can say that the Second Vatican Council replaces an "abstract idea of truth with the idea of a truth that is as concrete as can be imagined. I mean the idea of personal truth that has appeared in history, works in history and, from within the womb of history, is capable of sustaining all of history; I mean the idea of that truth in person which is Jesus Christ, the fullness of revelation."[6] This centrality of revelation as *truth in person,* however, does not lead to a concept of truth which is not addressed to man's reason. In this sense an "anti-intellectualist" position that undermines the necessity of dogmatic formulation can find no support in the conciliar texts.[7] The true renewal

5. A. Scola, *The Nuptial Mystery,* trans. Michelle K. Borras (Grand Rapids: Eerdmans, 2005), 351-52.

6. H. de Lubac, "La Révélation divine," in *Oeuvres complètes,* vol. 4 (Paris: Éd. du Cerf, 2006), 88.

7. De Lubac, "La Révélation divine," 70: "There is thus no antagonism between a revelation as knowledge and a revelation as event. The Council itself removed this danger, by following the phrase *'doctrinam et res'* with the phrase *'gesta verbaque'* in the same sentence. The intellectual sense of 'doctrine' leaves no room for doubt."

consists in the intuition of the profound unity between absoluteness and historicity, between necessity and freedom, that is implied in the notion of *truth in person*. The unity of these elements is possible because *Dei Verbum* proposes truth as an event.[8] This consideration is, upon close examination, the fruit of the Council's Christological focus. In fact, in the language of Vatican II, truth and Jesus Christ are identified: in this way "Vatican II frees the notion of truth from the ahistorical pre-comprehension that tends to reify it, thus restoring truth to its identity as a historical event. Truth is in fact inseparable from event; otherwise we drift into formalism."[9] The consideration of revelation as an "event which occurred in the past and continues to occur in faith, the event of a new relation between God and man,"[10] presupposes a renewed approach to revealed truth.[11]

We have called this renewed approach "dramatic" because from the very beginning of revelation in the Old Testament, human freedom is involved in the event of God's self-disclosure and is called in faith to take an active role in it.

The foregoing demands a complementary stress on the dramatic character of anthropology, whether philosophical or theological. As Balthasar puts it, "[I]f we want to ask about man's 'essence,' we can do so only in the midst of his dramatic performance of existence. There is no other anthropology but the dramatic."[12] Now, "dramatic anthropology" implies a dialogue, characterized by free self-opening and self-gift, between human subjects ontologically structured for communion. But it also means an opening and free response to God's gift in Christ. The dual unity of man and woman is a foundational element of dramatic anthropology. Man's reflection on himself is awakened by

8. J. Ratzinger, *Natura e compito della teologia* (Milan: Jaca Book, 1993), 119 [*The Nature and Mission of Theology*, trans. Adrian Walker (San Francisco: Ignatius, 1995); the English edition does not include the chapter from which this citation is taken].

9. G. Colombo, *La ragione teologica* (Milan: Glossa, 1995), 80.

10. J. Ratzinger, *Natura e compito della teologia*, 120.

11. Scola, *The Nuptial Mystery*, 348-49.

12. Hans Urs von Balthasar, *Theo-Drama*, vol. 2: *Dramatis Personae: Man in God*, trans. Graham Harrison (San Francisco: Ignatius, 1990), 335. Inspired by the Spanish playwright Calderón de la Barca, Balthasar uses the metaphor of the theater to describe the encounter between divine and human freedom in the "great theater of the world." After the *Prolegomena* (vol. 1 of Balthasar's *Theo-Drama*), and the presentation of the characters, *God and Man* (vol. 2) and *Persons in Christ* (Christ and Mary, vol. 3), the author presents the *Action* (soteriology, vol. 4), and concludes with *The Last Act* (eschatology, vol. 5). The idea of the "theo-drama" is meant to suggest not only God's involvement in the "human" drama, but also the participation of created freedom in uncreated freedom: "God's" drama with man.

the other, who provokes him and calls him to the unity of love — the archetype of which is spousal love.

This horizontal drama is the sign of a vertical, theological drama that takes place when man is called to an exchange of freedom with Christ on the stage of history. It is man's response to this call in faith that achieves his personhood; theologically, man becomes a "person" by involving himself in the "role" or "mission" that the Spirit entrusts to him in the Great Theater of the world. By accepting the "theo-dramatic" mission for which he is destined — and by integrating into it the constitutive polarity of masculine and feminine, along with the further polarities of body and spirit, individual and community that are implicit in the first — man attains his deepest personal identity "in Christ."[13] This brief sketch of dramatic anthropology in Balthasarian categories suggests its importance as a counterpart to the nuptial event of revelation.

Trinitarian Ontology and the Man-Woman Symbol

A theology founded on the dramatic nature of revelation cannot claim to be "scientific" unless it takes up the challenge of basic human reflection on the relationship between man and being. To that end, we need to leave behind the modern prejudice against metaphysics, which has led to relativism and nihilism, that is, to the abolition of man. It is Christianity's task to "safeguard metaphysics" as an inalienable dimension of human life and thought.[14] Without it, our understanding of revelation itself would be obscured; we would lack an anthropological foundation for dialogue with God. If we are to fulfill this philosophical task, we must deploy a new metaphysical creativity, in order to reflect more adequately on being in the light of the Christian mystery — and thus within the horizon of the Trinity.

The overcoming of modern rationalism, and of the separation it has introduced between nature and grace, faith and reason, opens space for a new, "trinitarian ontology" and for the symbolic realism it naturally engenders. Indeed, this development proves necessary for renewing the foundation both of meaningful human and ecclesial life and of sacramental theology. This ontology builds organically on the heritage of St. Thomas Aquinas, whose

13. See M. Ouellet, *L'Existence comme mission. L'anthropologie théologique de Hans Urs von Balthasar* (Rome: PUG, 1983), 60-97.

14. John Paul II, encyclical letter *Fides et Ratio* [On the Relationship Between Faith and Reason], 82-84.

conception of *esse* as *actus essendi* is open to new developments that take their starting point from the absolute a priori of all human knowledge: love. Rather than contenting ourselves with a set of instructions for the leisurely construction of some system, then, let us open ourselves to a reawakening of ontological reflection that without embarrassment or narrowness proceeds from the Christian mystery as its starting point.

Being-Gift, the Original Light for Living and Thinking

The history of Western thought has been marked by what Heidegger called a "forgetfulness of being." *Being* was replaced by the *idea,* and theology itself took the form of onto-theology, leaving love on the margins of its reflection. German Idealism provided a particularly clear illustration of this tendency in the person of Hegel and his absolute knowledge. But Heidegger's analysis, though for the most part correct, overlooks St. Thomas Aquinas, whose metaphysical thought remains anchored in the transcendence of *esse ut actus, actus essendi* — which is not an idea but a radical act that can be neither deduced from, nor reduced to, anything else. This act, which is "simple and complete but not subsistent," serves as a mediation between divine Being and created being.[15] On the one hand, it points to the fullness of transcendent Being, and on the other hand, to the contingence of created beings. For the Angelic Doctor, Love — though still underthematized in his thought — is the ultimate horizon of *esse,* because *esse* proceeds from the free, creative communication of divine Goodness.

Thomistic *"esse"* was the subject of numerous studies in the twentieth century, many of them the work of authors who have most inspired our own approach such as Étienne Gilson, Gustav Siewerth, Cornelio Fabro, Hans Urs von Balthasar, and Ferdinand Ulrich.[16] In the footsteps of these masters, a new generation of philosophers has reflected on being as "gift": Klaus Hemmerle, Claude Bruaire *(odontology),* Michel Henry, Jean-Luc Marion, etc. Without

---

15. Thomas Aquinas, *Quaestiones disputatae de potentia,* q. 1 a. 1 co.: *"Verbi gratia esse significant aliquid completum et simplex sed non subsistens."*

16. See G. Siewerth, *Das Schicksal der Metaphysik von Thomas von Aquin bis Heidegger* (Einsiedeln: Johannes Verlag, 1959); Siewerth, *Der Thomismus als Identitätssystem,* 2nd ed. (Frankfurt: Schulte-Bulmke, 1961); H. U. von Balthasar, *Theo-Logic,* vol. 1: *Truth of the World,* trans. Adrian J. Walker (San Francisco: Ignatius, 2000); F. Ulrich, *Homo Abyssus. Das Wagnis der Seinsfrage,* 2nd ed. with an introduction by Martin Bieler (Einsiedeln: Johannes Verlag, 1998).

reducing or betraying reason, they integrate the logic of love (and of faith) into the act of human thinking.[17]

This interweaving of faith and reason is the matrix of a "trinitarian and symbolical ontology" that displays being as gift, that is, the communicative act of a love that gives, calls, and welcomes. By the same token, ontology takes on the form of a "meta-anthropology." The meaning of being is unveiled phenomenologically in human love and grounded ontologically in trinitarian love. On the basis of his being-gift — a gift received and given again, a gift shared and fruitful — man discovers the source of meaning; he finds himself in a vital communion with the mystery of Being, learning to think in this light.[18] Human life then becomes a "sign-symbol" of the mystery, the icon of a Presence; human thought becomes dialogical and transcendental, that is, a function of the Love who communicates himself to man and makes him free.[19] With thought as a compass, then, man seeks his self-realization (which is also his freedom) in a love that assents to Love. In this sense, ontological and symbolical reflection represents a recovery of the transcendental orientation of human desire. It teaches man not to enclose himself within the gift of the material cosmos, but to open himself, with the help of revelation, to the love of God and the service of his Kingdom.

The Family, Epiphany and Dramatic Symbol
Par Excellence of Being

The pontificate of John Paul II developed the line of thought we have just mentioned in a specific and characteristic manner by centering it on the fun-

17. See K. Hemmerle, *Thèses pour une ontologie trinitaire. Un manifeste* (Paris: Ad Solem, 2014) [original in German in 1976]; C. Bruaire, *L'Être et l'Esprit* (Paris: PUF, 1983); J.-L. Marion, *Étant donné. Essai d'une phénoménologie de la donation,* 2nd ed. (Paris: PUF, 1997).

18. In theology, authors such as Angelo Scola, Alain Mattheeuws, Piero Coda, and Giorgio Mazzanti explicitly seek a new foundation for anthropology and sacramental theology in a trinitarian ontology.

19. See M. Ouellet, "Hans Urs von Balthasar et la métaphysique. Esquisse de sa contribution à partir d'Épilogue," *Path* 5, no. 2 (2006): 473-83. See also Scola, *The Nuptial Mystery,* 347: "Event, revelation and the act of consciousness thus appear ontologically indistinguishable. In particular, the act by which consciousness intends the real, grasping it as the sign (trace) of Being which calls on freedom to decide, belongs intrinsically to the concept of revelation. . . . The lines of this ontology, which has rightly been defined as symbolic precisely because being reveals itself in the sign, enable us better to understand, if we take the path glimpsed by Vatican II, the correct theological concept of revelation."

damental meaning of the family. One of the most representative themes of the pope's philosophical and theological anthropology was his reflection on the man-woman relationship as an expression of the ontological principle of dual unity.[20] A passage from the apostolic letter *Mulieris Dignitatem* expresses this clearly:

> [M]an cannot exist "alone" (cf. Gen. 2:18); he can exist only as a "unity of the two," and therefore *in relation to another human person.* . . . Being a person in the image and likeness of God thus also involves existing in a relationship, in relation to the other "I." (*MD* 7)

Following Angelo Scola's account of this text, we can distinguish a number of fundamental elements that allow us to ground the theology of the family in a trinitarian ontology. First, as Scola observes:

> Man exists always and only as a masculine or feminine being. There is not a single man (or woman) who can by himself alone be the whole of man. He always has before himself the other way of being human, which is to him inaccessible. In this way we discover in the relation of man and woman the contingent character of the human creature: the "I" needs the other and depends upon the other for his fulfillment. . . .[21] This contingence identifies not only man's limits, but also his capacity for self-transcendence in the discovery of the other-than-himself as positive for himself. In this sense contingence reveals that man, like every creature, is a sign.[22]

He is a sign that points to a destiny of communion (union within distinction). Balthasar argues that the reciprocity between man and woman "can stand as

---

20. On this subject, see G. Chantraine, *Uomo e donna* (Parma: CUSL, 1986); C. Giuliodori, *Intelligenza del maschile e del femminile. Problemi e prospettive nella rilettura di von Balthasar* (Roma: Città Nuova, 1991); A. Scola, "*L'imago Dei* e la sessualità umana," *Anthropotes* 1 (1992): 61-73; Scola, "La visione antropologica del rapporto uomo-donna. Il significato dell'unità dei due," in Aa.Vv., *Dignità e vocazione della donna* (Vatican City: Libreria Editrice Vaticana, 1989), 91-103.

21. John Paul II affirms: "In this way, the meaning of man's original unity through masculinity and femininity expresses itself as an overcoming of the frontier of solitude and at the same time as an affirmation — for both human beings — of everything in solitude that constitutes man" (*TOB*, 162).

22. Scola, *The Nuptial Mystery*, 7.

a paradigm of that community dimension which characterizes man's entire nature."[23]

Second, Scola affirms that "from a more theological point of view, human sexuality, and therefore the difference of the sexes, belongs to man's being as image of God."[24] This affirmation introduces us to the radical difference between human sexuality and animal sexuality, with which the former remains closely linked on the level of biological instinct. Scola continues, "The inclusion of sexual difference in the *imago Dei* allows us to speak — under precise conditions, to be sure — of a certain analogy between the relation of man and woman and the trinitarian relations.[25] *Communio* — the *communio personarum* — "as an essential dimension of man is part of his being in the image of God."[26]

Finally, Scola observes:

> What we have said thus far allows us to see in spousal love the *analogatum princeps* of every kind of love and, at the same time, to consider it a privileged metaphor for man's relation with reality. On this subject the pope [John Paul II] affirms: "The nature of one as well as the other love [virginity and marriage] is 'spousal,' that is, expressed through the complete gift of self. The one as well as the other love tends to express that spousal meaning of the body, which has been inscribed 'from the beginning' in the personal structure of man and woman."[27]

It follows that spousal love, and thus the family, appear as an epiphany of being and as the dramatic symbol par excellence of Being. Being expresses

23. Balthasar, *Theo-Drama*, vol. 2: *Dramatis Personae: Man in God*, 365.

24. Scola, *The Nuptial Mystery*, 9.

25. Hans Urs von Balthasar, *Theo-Logic*, vol. 3: *The Spirit of Truth*, trans. Graham Harrison (San Francisco: Ignatius, 2005), 160: "If, in imagination, we were to exclude from the act of love between man and woman the nine months' pregnancy, that is, the temporal dimension, the child would be immediately present in their generative-receptive embrace; this would be simultaneously the expression of their reciprocal love *and,* going beyond it, its transcendent result. . . . [I]t must be said that this form of 'excess' and 'fruit' (which can be spiritual-intellectual) belongs to every love, including the higher forms. To that extent, perfect creaturely love is a genuine *imago trinitatis.*"

26. Scola, *The Nuptial Mystery*, 9.

27. John Paul II, *TOB*, 431 [translation altered with respect to citation in *The Nuptial Mystery* so as to reflect the revised *TOB* translation]. See also B. Castilla y Cortazar, "La Trinidad como familia: Analogia humana de la processions divinas," *Annales Theologici* 10 (1996): 371-416, with an ample bibliography.

itself in them, and it communicates itself in a privileged way in the fruitfulness of conjugal, paternal, maternal, filial and fraternal relations. The value of this symbolical and real language of the body then reflects back on, and illumines, the spousal nature of consecrated virginity.[28]

The presuppositions we have briefly touched upon here far from exhaust the essential themes related to Christian teaching on marriage and the family. Nevertheless, they represent the basic elements needed to ground both a theology of marriage and a coherent reflection on the family. Without these elements, it would be impossible to give an organic, systematic, and critical account of God's plan for marriage and the family. We must keep them in mind and integrate them into our discussion over the course of the following chapters, which will explore the link between the sacrament of marriage and the sacramentality of the Church from the theological and symbolical perspective of nuptiality.

---

28. Regarding the relation between physical and spiritual fatherhood/motherhood, see John Paul II's illuminating reflection: "On the other hand, spousal love that finds its expression in continence 'for the kingdom of heaven' must lead in its normal development to 'fatherhood' or 'motherhood' in the spiritual sense (that is, precisely to that 'fruitfulness of the Holy Spirit' we have already spoken about), in a way analogous to conjugal love, which *matures in physical fatherhood and motherhood* and is confirmed in them precisely as spousal love. On its part, physical generation also fully corresponds to its meaning only if it is completed by fatherhood and motherhood *in the spirit,* whose expression and fruit is the whole educational work of the parents in regard to the children born of bodily conjugal union" (*TOB,* 432).

CHAPTER 5

Jesus Christ, the Sacrament of the Covenant and the Church-Sacrament

According to the New Testament, the history of the spousal union between God and man attains its fulfillment with the coming of God's Son into the world. With the incarnation, passion, death, and resurrection of the only-begotten Son of God (John 1:14), the new and eternal Covenant, which God had preordained for the sake of mankind, reaches the apex of its universal, eschatological fecundity. The mission of the Holy Spirit in the sacramental economy of the Church is both the fruit and the confirmation of this fulfillment. Through his nuptial gift, actualized in the sacraments, Christ continues to generate the Church as a holy and immaculate Bride (Eph. 5:25-26) who is called to share in his fruitfulness. The sacramental economy thus flows from the spousal relationship between Christ and the Church, which the Spirit keeps ever alive and fruitful. The seven sacraments concretize this relationship founded on Christ's bodily sacrifice for the benefit of each individual, the community, and all humanity.

To deepen our understanding of the link between the sacramentality of the Church and the sacrament of marriage, we must dwell for a moment on the relationship between Christ and the Church, since, according to John Paul II, this relationship contains what Paul calls the *"mysterion."*[1] Our reflection seeks to develop both John Paul II's catecheses and contemporary

---

1. See R. Penna, *Il "mysterion" paolino. Traiettoria e costituzione* (Brescia: Paideia, 1978). For the lexical history of *mysterion,* see G. Bornkamm, "Mysterion," in *Grande Lessico del Nuovo Testamento,* vol. 7 (Brescia: Paideia, 1971), col. 645-716. See especially John Paul II, *Man and Woman He Created Them: A Theology of the Body,* trans. Michael Waldstein (Boston: Pauline Books and Media, 2006) [= *TOB*], catechesis #93, "This Mystery Is Great," 487-91.

theology's reflection on Christ, the original Sacrament, and the Church, the universal sacrament of salvation.[2]

We will work out this sacramental and spousal approach following Hans Urs von Balthasar and his account of the pneumatological and Marian dimension of ecclesiology.[3] How do Christ the Bridegroom and the Church-Bride relate with respect to the sacramental economy sustained by the mission of the Holy Spirit? How do we define the relation between the spousal fruitfulness of Christ and the Church, on the one hand, and the particular efficacy of the sacraments, on the other? The Church's sacramentality/fruitfulness is based on the ontological efficacy of the sacraments *(ex opere operato)*; can we also say that the efficacy of the sacraments relies somehow on the immaculate Church's response to the gift of the divine Bridegroom *(ex opere operantis)*? The answer to these questions requires a theological and symbolical analysis that also takes account of the ontological dimension of the covenant. We will develop this analysis in three steps, beginning with Christ the Sacrament, whose spousal fecundity generates the Church. Secondly, we will explore the mediation of the Holy Spirit, who is the spousal bond between Christ and the Church. Finally, we will conclude with the Church, the sacrament of Christ the Bridegroom, while seeking to clarify the relationship between the baptismal and the ministerial priesthoods. This procedure will afford us a point of departure for understanding how the other sacraments — and in particular marriage — take their place within the shared fruitfulness of Christ and the Church.

2. See L. Scheffczyk, "Gesù Cristo Sacramento originario della redenzione," in *Incontrare Cristo nei sacramenti*, ed. H. Luthe (Milan: Cinisello Balsamo/Paoline, 1988), 41: "If 'sacrament' is synonymous with the gift of an invisible salvation in a historically tangible and outwardly perceptible form, we must say that this definition of sacrament finds its fullest realization in Christ. In him, what appears visibly is not only created grace, which we might understand as dissociable from God, but uncreated grace itself: in him, the divine being has become tangible and visible." See also, by the same author, "La Chiesa, sacramento universale di Gesù Cristo," in Luthe, ed., *Incontrare Cristo nei sacramenti*, 49-85; and E. Schillebeeckx, *Christ, the Sacrament of the Encounter with God,* trans. Paul Barrett and N. D. Smith (London-New York: Sheed and Ward, 1965).

3. Hans Urs von Balthasar, *Theo-Drama,* vol. 3: *Dramatis Personae: Persons in Christ,* trans. Graham Harrison (San Francisco: Ignatius, 1992), 428-35; Balthasar, *Epilogue,* trans. Edward T. Oakes (San Francisco: Ignatius, 2004), 89-123, especially 109-17.

The Wedding of God and Man in Jesus Christ, Crucified, Dead, and Risen

The Application of Nuptial Symbolism to Christ in the New Testament

Like the Old Testament before it, the New Testament expresses the mystery of the covenant by means of nuptial symbolism, which it refers to Christ and the Church. Christ is repeatedly described as the Bridegroom par excellence. In the Gospels, Jesus is designated as the Bridegroom by John the Baptist (John 3:29). Jesus also attributes this title to himself (Matt. 9:15) and uses it in the eschatological parables of the Kingdom (Matt. 22:1-14 and 25:1-13). The Pauline letters allude to this title (2 Cor. 11:2 and Eph. 5:23-25), and the book of Revelation mentions it twice (19:7 and 22:17-20). In the Gospel of John, Jesus' first miracle takes place during a wedding feast at Cana; it points forward to the hour of the Pasch, the fulfillment of the Son's spousal love for the world and the actualization of the wedding mentioned by the Baptist (John 2:1-11, with John 13:1 and 3:27-30).[4] As Gustave Martelet notes, "Although the title of Christ the Bridegroom is habitually neglected by Christology, we must rediscover its full meaning. . . . The Christology of marriage must begin from the title of Bridegroom and the mystery it indicates."[5] This nuptial Christology leads to a nuptial ecclesiology, to which the New Testament alludes in two decisive passages: 2 Corinthians 11:2 and Ephesians 5:25-27. We will treat these further on. For the moment, let us pause on the ontological and sacramental dimension of the covenant between finite and infinite freedom in the person of Christ.

The Hypostatic Union of Jesus Christ, the Original Archetype of the Covenant

The Unity of the Two Natures as the Unity of Two Freedoms

According to Angelo Scola:

> The event of Jesus Christ . . . in whom divine nature and human nature are hypostatically united in one person, is the point of reference for every

---

4. See C. Rochetta, *Il sacramento della coppia* (Bologna: EDB, 1996), 172.
5. G. Martelet, "Sedici tesi cristologiche sul sacramento del matrimonio," *Il Regno-Documenti* 17, no. 4 (1978): 390.

"unity of two," which always ultimately derives from him. Man, in his concrete existence as male or female, was created in the image of the Image, which is Jesus Christ.[6]

The event of Jesus Christ, which is the event of the covenant, thus expresses God's "yes" to man, but it also guarantees man's "yes" to God. This means that while the man Jesus is the Son of God, he is also a free man within the covenant. All human beings, moreover, are predestined and called to share his freedom, which is simultaneously divine and human.

Elsewhere, Scola describes the anthropological implications of this nuptial mystery under the inspiration of Balthasar's theo-dramatics:

> To say that Jesus Christ is the center of the cosmos and of history, or more properly, to speak of creation in Christ, signifies that Christ's freedom becomes the central axis for the understanding of human freedom and that the person of Christ, in his singular humanity, is the form for understanding man. This person is the exemplar and norm of freedom and the form of all those who are predestined to be sons of God in him. In Christ, by the mystery of hypostatic union, finite freedom is enveloped, *"indivise et inconfuse,"* in the infinite freedom of the Son of God. In this way, through the grace of the Incarnation, the great story of God's accompaniment of man in the bond of love with the Holy Spirit is placed before our eyes.[7]

We must bear in mind, however, that the event of the covenant in Jesus Christ takes place as an interchange between *God* and *man,* and so deploys the full range of the *analogia entis.* The distance and distinction between the created and the uncreated are not suppressed but rather reinforced in the unity of being found in the hypostatic union. Nevertheless, a real, bilateral covenant exists between the two as the fruit of God's unilateral grace. As Balthasar explains:

> When God's Word became man, the *fides Dei* was incorporated into Christ, and God's Covenant of fidelity became one with humanity. This man who is, as the expression of God's essence and deliberate love, his Son,

---

6. A. Scola, *The Nuptial Mystery,* trans. Michelle K. Borras (Grand Rapids: Eerdmans, 2005), 350.

7. A. Scola, *Hans Urs von Balthasar: A Theological Style* (Grand Rapids: Eerdmans, 1995), 96-97.

is the incarnate "faithfulness of God" . . . in whom "all of the promises of God have found their Yes" (2 Cor 1:18, 20). He is, as Dionysius says, the ecstasy of the divine eros flowing out of itself, in which God hands himself over and entrusts himself to the world. Because, and insofar as, he is this, he can answer God as perfect man with a faith that gathers and establishes the faith of all mankind in order also to be the incarnate Covenant of humanity with God. But he does not go back and forth along these two ways but rather is such simultaneously. Indeed, he is the hypostatic identity of these two ways, and thus he is the substantial Covenant, the ontic [ontological] bond between God and the world.[8]

The incarnation of the eternal Logos in a human nature thus represents the new and eternal Covenant of God with man. Rochetta comments:

A human nature has now been irrevocably assumed into the hypostatic union of the second Person of the Holy Trinity. However grave men's sins may be, they can no longer break this bond. We are dealing with a new and indestructible marriage: *new* with respect to the old economy, though rooted in the vinestock of the "faithful remnant" of Israel; *indestructible* because it is accomplished in the theandric, i.e., divine and human reality of Christ, and is thus absolutely indissoluble.[9]

In Jesus Christ, God and man have become a single reality. *This reality is the original, archetypical union:* the original covenant, the original pact. In the Incarnation, the human and the divine unite to generate the highest and most paradoxical form of nuptiality. This took place, St. Augustine says, in "the Virgin's womb, where the human creature was married to Him."[10] This is why the great Latin Doctor can also define the incarnate Word as the "sacrament of divinity and humanity, the sacrament revealed in the flesh."[11] Nevertheless, the ontological and spousal dimension of Christ, the original sacrament of

---

8. H. U. von Balthasar, *Explorations in Theology,* vol. 2: *Spouse of the Word* (San Francisco: Ignatius, 1991), 78.

9. Rochetta, *Il sacramento della coppia,* 171.

10. St. Augustine, *Confessions* 4.12.19. Translation by J. G. Pilkington (http://www.newadvent.org/fathers/110104.htm).

11. St. Augustine, *De Natura et Gratia* 2.2. Augustine influenced the clarification of the term "sacrament," stressing that the sacraments are sacred signs that resemble and also confer what they signify. He thus contributed to the development of the Scholastic definition of sacrament as *"signum efficax gratiae."*

the covenant, still calls for a complementary analysis of his obedience, which causes its saving power to unfold in history.

The Spousal Meaning of Christ's Obedience

If God made a covenant with Moses and the other prophets, it was in view of this new and definitive covenant with man in his Son Jesus Christ. But as we have already noted, the covenant willed by God is not limited to an abstract union of two natures, "without confusion or separation." The New Covenant is the dramatic event par excellence. Balthasar brings out this dramatic character in his trinitarian Christology using the twofold category of *mission and obedience*.[12] Balthasar shows that salvation takes the form of covenant precisely in Jesus' extreme obedience, which represents the last rung of the "ladder of obedience" of the Old Testament prophets.[13] God came among us by descending to the bottom of this ladder of obedience, whose gradual intensification culminates in the mutual commitment of God and man in Jesus Christ. This commitment is so total and irreversible that it takes on a spousal meaning that transcends history into the dimension of eschatology. The passion, death, and resurrection of Christ accomplish in one — real and sacramental — flesh the historical-eschatological marriage described in the book of Revelation as the "wedding feast of the Lamb." Christ's obedience to the Father in the Holy Spirit is thus the transcendent source of the *mysterion*. Balthasar insists that this archetypical obedience opens a dramatic space for a real play of freedoms between the divine Bridegroom and the created Bride. Jesus Christ's obedience and mission is thus the concrete unfolding of the hypostatic union; they are the latter's "incarnation" and "historical-salvific" manifestation.

The spousal meaning of Christ's obedience also appears in the nuptial mystery of the new Adam and the new Eve. John Paul II stresses this point in his catecheses on human love, explaining how the Church receives herself from Christ's obedience on the Cross:

> That gift of self to the Father through obedience to the point of death (see Phil 2:8) is at the same time, according to Ephesians, an act of "giving

---

12. See Balthasar, *Theo-Drama*, vol. 3: *Dramatis Personae: Persons in Christ*, 149-259.

13. See H. U. von Balthasar, *The Glory of the Lord*, vol. 6: *Theology: The Old Covenant*, trans. Brian McNeil (San Francisco: Ignatius, 1991), 215-98; see also G. Marchesi, *La Cristologia trinitaria di Hans Urs von Balthasar* (Brescia: Queriniana, 1997), 405-90, 516-46.

himself for the Church." In this expression, *redeeming love* transforms itself, I would say, into *spousal love:* by giving himself for the Church, with the same redeeming act, Christ united himself once and for all with her as the Bridegroom to the Bride, as the husband with the wife, giving himself through all that is included once and for all in his "giving himself" for the Church.[14]

The Church proceeds from the gift of the Bridegroom who, through the bath of water (baptism), makes her appear before him as a holy and immaculate Bride. The mission and obedience of the incarnate Word thus culminates in the "yes" by which the Church welcomes the fidelity and fruitfulness of the divine-human Bridegroom. From the "yes" that the new, perfectly obedient Adam utters to the Father *pro nobis* there flows the "yes" of the new Eve. She becomes Bride out of the sacrificial and nuptial gift of the Bridegroom's body. In the real sacramental order, then, this body, which is at once personal and eucharistic, contains more than just the entire fruitfulness of the divine Bridegroom; it also contains the entire fidelity of the created Bride and the principle of her fruitfulness. We will return to this point later.

In this light, the relationship between Christ and humanity can be seen as the universal extension of the Lord's nuptial mystery through the Church. This is the context in which we must situate both the mission of the Holy Spirit and the sacramentality of the Church. First, however, let us respond to the anthropological question formulated by Angelo Scola:

> What is the relationship between the freedom of Christ and the dramatic freedom of man? What is Christ's relationship to man? Putting it synthetically, we could say that Christ, through the events of his life and resurrection, in which he reveals himself to be true God and true man, resolves the enigma of man yet without settling the drama in advance.[15]

Put in terms of spousal logic: Rather than abolishing, Christ enables the nuptial "yes" of man, of every human being. In principle, his original sacramentality reaches all people, as Vatican Council II affirms:

> For, since Christ died for all men, and since the ultimate vocation of man is in fact one, and divine, we ought to believe that the Holy Spirit in a

14. John Paul II, *TOB*, 478.
15. Scola, *Hans Urs von Balthasar*, 96-97.

manner known only to God offers to every man the possibility of being associated with this paschal mystery. (*GS* 22)

The Church's mediation is not spelled out in this text, but the principle remains: we must avoid separating the Holy Spirit from the Church, the Body of Christ. There is a tendency today to distinguish the Church from the Kingdom, reducing the Church's sacramentality to a mere exterior sign of a salvation supposed to be universally available already. Consideration of the nuptial mystery of the Marian Church allows us to move beyond an overly sociological vision of the Church and to understand it as the universal sacrament of salvation in the strong sense: as a real participation in Christ's universal sacramentality.[16] Christ's spousal fruitfulness does not transcend the Church if by that we mean that its universality somehow leaves the Church out of account. To the contrary, while safeguarding the handmaid's dependence on, and total subordination to, the Lord, we must say that the "nuptial mystery" of the Cross involves both Bridegroom and Bride in the universal and sacramental gift of grace.

We conclude this section by recalling the supreme meaning of Christ's loving obedience: the nuptial encounter of the Trinity with humanity. The fact that this obedience culminates in the Resurrection confers both a trinitarian seal and an anthropological confirmation on the accomplishment of the new and eternal Covenant. A trinitarian seal, because the Resurrection means precisely the irruption of the Holy Spirit, the fruit of the reciprocal Love between the Father and the Son, in the flesh of Christ. We touch here on the deepest dimension of spousal sacramentality, namely, its rootedness in the intra-trinitarian nuptial mystery, of which the human person created in Christ is the image.[17] Angelo Scola does not hesitate to call this insight the ultimate

16. See Balthasar, *Epilogue*, 114: "[T]he Church is the originating sacrament springing up from Christ's material, physical nature. . . . She participates in Christ's universal mission of salvation and in the power he has to effect it (in this sense, the otherwise easily misunderstood maxim is true that 'outside of the Church there is no salvation'). She is, like Christ himself, a particular body with a universal mission and a universal effect for the world." On this theme, see Aa.Vv., " 'Tout récapituler dans le Christ'. Propos d'un ouvrage de J. Dupuis," *Revue Thomiste* 98, no. 4 (1998): 591-630, especially 613-18.

17. See H. U. von Balthasar, *The Glory of the Lord,* vol. 1: *Seeing the Form,* 2nd ed., trans. Erasmo Leiva-Merikakis (San Francisco: Ignatius, 2009), 577: "A fundamental bridal and covenantal relationship exists between God and the world as such (compare the covenant with Noah) which from all time has arisen from the Logos' mediation at the creation and from the Spirit's hovering over the abyss. This fundamental relationship makes man, in the reciprocity of husband and wife, an image and a likeness of God: of the God who, in his

foundation of the "nuptial mystery."[18] Christ the Bridegroom bears in himself his entire relationship to the Father in the Holy Spirit, which Scripture autho-rizes us to understand nuptially in light of the *imago Dei* (Gen. 2:24; Eph. 5:32).

Moreover, the Resurrection confirms the full, spousal assumption of man into God, for it allows the intra-trinitarian fruitfulness to flow forth from the vivifying and sacramental flesh of this man. The Risen One is the confirmed witness of trinitarian Love, fully given and received for all by the man Jesus. In this mystery, the spousal union between the triune God and humanity thus receives its irrevocable and indissoluble seal. Jesus Christ is the divine-human Bridegroom, exalted and established in the full power of his trinitarian fruitfulness through the Holy Spirit who raises him from the dead (Rom. 1:4). His original sacramentality results in the gift of the Holy Spirit to the Church, and the Spirit is the principle and foundation of the common, spousal fruitfulness of Christ and the Church for the salvation of the world.

The Gift of the Spirit, Fruitfulness of the Covenant

The Role of the Spirit in the Event of Christ

If Christ is the mediator of the new and eternal Covenant, this covenant is ac-complished and realized in the Church through *the gift of the Holy Spirit*. This gift was destined to characterize the time when the definitive covenant would be fulfilled. On the day of Pentecost, Peter proclaims that the Spirit is now at work (Acts 2:14-36) and can therefore greet the first Christians as "the sons of the prophets and of the covenant which God gave to your fathers, saying to Abraham, 'and in your posterity shall all the families of the earth be blessed'" (Acts 3:25). Carlo Rochetta claims that "reflection on the Holy Spirit's action in Christian marriage and in conjugal life is only at its beginning stages and is still in need of a comprehensive and thorough exploration."[19] It seems to us that this tardiness is due to two factors: sacramental theology's failure to develop along pneumatological lines; and on the other hand, its lack of a systematic

---

eternal trinitarian mystery, already possesses within himself a nuptial form." Balthasar often revisits this relatively early passage (1961), especially in the volumes of *Explorations in Theology* and finally in *Theo-Logic,* vol. 3: *The Spirit of Truth,* trans. Graham Harrison (San Francisco: Ignatius, 2005), 159-60.

18. Scola, *The Nuptial Mystery,* 96-104.

19. Rochetta, *Il sacramento della coppia,* 255. See also M. Martinez Peque, *Lo Spirito Santo e il matrimonio* (Rome: EDR, 1993), 251-60, with a bibliography.

nuptial approach.[20] The dominant perspective in sacramental theology has been narrowly limited to the question of causal efficiency addressed within the systematic framework of hylomorphism. We must forge new paths beginning from the Holy Spirit's work of placing the man-woman symbol within the spousal relationship between Christ and the Church.

Hans Urs von Balthasar's theological reflection on conjugal intersubjectivity offers some illuminating suggestions for this project. Aware that all analogies remain fragmentary, Balthasar nonetheless contemplates human love in the light of the intra-divine processions. He notes the surprising nature of "the economic reversal of the relation between Son and Spirit. Whereas the Spirit immanently proceeds from the Father and the Son (or through the Son), the Son becomes man through the Spirit and is led by this same Spirit in his mission."[21]

The goal of this reversal is to enable the event of the Incarnation as obedience. The Son does not take on human nature by himself; he allows himself to be incarnated by the Spirit, in obedience to the Father. Following the "kenotic" logic of the Trinity, the Son

> lets the Spirit made available by the Father (and who also proceeds from the Father) have power over him as a "rule" of the Father's will. He does this in order to permit this Spirit resting upon him in all fullness to stream out from himself at the end of his mission in death and Resurrection (and Eucharist). And the direction of this outpouring goes both to the Father ("into your hands . . .") as well as to the Church and the world ("and so he breathed on them . . .").[22]

At the end of his passive obedience, which is sealed by the shedding of his blood out of love, the "reversal" is overcome. In the Resurrection, the Holy Spirit is clearly poured out equally by the incarnate Son, as the evangelists attest.

The Holy Spirit is sent into the world at the precise moment when the Son's work is accomplished: "And this release of the Holy Spirit abolishes the kenotic 'inhibition' and lets the eternal mutuality of the breathing of the Spirit

---

20. See M. Ouellet, "The Holy Spirit, Seal of the Conjugal Covenant," chap. 5 in *Divine Likeness: Toward a Trinitarian Anthropology of the Family* (Grand Rapids: Eerdmans, 2006).

21. H. U. von Balthasar, *Explorations in Theology*, vol. 4: *Spirit and Institution*, trans. Edward T. Oakes (San Francisco: Ignatius, 1995), 231-32.

22. Balthasar, *Explorations in Theology*, vol. 4: *Spirit and Institution*, 232.

now also be actual and real in the world as well."[23] John situates the sending of the Spirit at Easter, while Luke retains another version that connects the breathing forth of the Spirit, as a trinitarian event, with the Son's return to the Father at the Ascension. According to Balthasar, these facts illumine the logic of the covenant, which culminates in the gift of the Holy Spirit. The Spirit is poured forth when the "incarnate Son who has returned to the Father . . . even in his perfected humanity . . . has become the *one* principle of breathing the Spirit (Lk 24:49; Acts 2:33)."[24]

The very event of the Incarnation thus proves to be an event of the covenant, in which the entire Trinity is involved in the fruitfulness of the incarnate Son who died and was raised. In the Holy Spirit, the Father generates his Son in the flesh in order to give him to the Church, the fruit of the Son's redemptive work. The risen Son — as head of the Church — also has power to send the Spirit, who now pours forth from "his body" as a source of living water (John 7:38; 19:34; 3:14). The elevation and exaltation of the crucified and risen Lord, confirmed by Pentecost, realizes in the economy the moment of the Spirit's procession in the immanent Trinity. The inner fruitfulness of the Trinity is now totally open to humanity, as the fruit of the covenant accomplished in Christ's broken flesh and outpoured blood. And the most excellent fruit of this covenant is the Holy Spirit. He is poured out into hearts as the Spirit of reconciliation and of divine, reciprocal Love, becoming the nuptial bond between Christ the Bridegroom and the Church-Bride as well as their intimate, shared fruitfulness. Our next task is to explore this bond so as to understand how the Church's sacramentality emerges precisely from her character as Spouse.

The Church-Bride, Sacrament of Christ the Bridegroom

The Nuptial Symbolism of the Church in the New Testament

The nuptial symbolism of the Church figures in at least two fundamental passages of the New Testament: 2 Corinthians 11:3, which describes the Christian community as a chaste virgin promised to a single Bridegroom, that is, Christ the Lord; and Ephesians 5:25-27, which describes the Church as a bride that Christ acquired for himself in the paschal mystery, "having cleansed her by the washing of water with the word, that he might present the church to himself in

---

23. Balthasar, *Explorations in Theology*, vol. 4: *Spirit and Institution*, 235.
24. Balthasar, *Explorations in Theology*, vol. 4: *Spirit and Institution*, 236.

splendor, without spot or wrinkle or any such thing, that she might be holy and without blemish." The book of Revelation, for its part, presents the Church as the heavenly Jerusalem, the Bride of Christ, who is adorned and ready for the eschatological wedding feast (Rev. 19:7-9; 21:2). In order to appreciate the full import of the symbol of the bride, we must keep in mind its connection with the symbol of the body, as does St. Paul when speaking of the "great mystery" in the Letter to the Ephesians. We will examine this connection more closely when we comment on Ephesians 5 below.

In recent years, there has been much discussion of the nuptial theme in the fourth Gospel. Nuptiality appears as the key to reading the entire Gospel of John. Ignace de la Potterie frequently stressed this point in his writings. The biblical scholar Renzo Infante has recently defended the same thesis on the basis of a very well-documented study:

> The use of spousal metaphors and symbols has a twofold goal. On the one hand, it aims to produce a deeper understanding of the relationship between Christ and the Church. On the other hand, it aims to influence ecclesial praxis by proposing modes of action meant to realize and demonstrate the newness of life with Christ.[25]

The spousal vision of John's Gospel finds its center in the account of the wedding at Cana. This is the first of Jesus' signs (2:11) not only chronologically but also in order of importance *(archē tōn sēmeiōn)*. It is the chief sign, the key to reading all the other salvific signs that Jesus will accomplish, which explains why it can found the disciples' faith. The protagonists of this account are not so much the newlyweds as Jesus (the true Bridegroom) and, conjoined with him, his Mother and the disciples (the Church-Bride). Together, they mark the beginning of the messianic wedding feast and the fulfillment of the covenant prefigured in the Old Testament by Yahweh's spousal relationship with his people. The wine of the Old Covenant has run out; Christ gives us the choice new wine and, by means of this "archetypical sign," prefigures the decisive hour of the gift of the Eucharist (see Matt. 26:28; Luke 22:44; John 19:34) and the Last Supper of the Lamb (see Rev. 19:9). The exegete Lorenzo Zani concludes his rich analysis of the symbolism of John 2 by noting that:

---

25. R. Infante, "Lo sposo e la sposa. Contributo per l'ecclesiologia del quarto Vangelo," *Rivista di Teologia* 37 (1996): 451-81, here 479. See also I. de la Potterie, "Le nozze messianiche e il matrimonio cristiano," in "Lo Sposo e la Sposa," *Parola, Spirito e Vita* 13 (1986), and *Maria nel mistero dell'Alleanza* (Paris: Desclée de Brouwer, 1985).

This [the miracle at Cana] was not only the first of Jesus' miracles; it was the archetypical sign, the prototype of the signs, the interpretive key for the various signs worked by Jesus. At Cana in Galilee, a new relationship between Jesus and the community begins: here, the marriage between Jesus and the disciples and his servants is established.[26]

The Participation of the Church-Bride in the Fruitfulness of the Covenant

In Mary, the prototype of the Church, humanity has already taken on the countenance of the bride — that bride, whom the Father prepared for himself, Christ united to himself indissolubly for eternity, and the Spirit filled with his gifts. The spousal "sketch" of Adam and Eve is filled out in Christ's union with his Church through the womb of Mary. In these nuptials between the human and the divine, the new existence of the children of God takes on flesh.[27]

The position laid out here by C. Giuliodori sees in the Church more than an instrument used by Christ to proclaim the faith and dispense the sacraments. The Church, the fruit of the redemption, is the Bride who sprang from Christ's side and who becomes fruitful through her spousal union with the eucharistic gift of the Bridegroom.[28] Balthasar stresses that "the way the Church fulfills

---

26. L. Zani, *Lo Spirito e la sposa dicono vieni!: Ap 22, 17* (Trent: Argentiarum, 1992), 40.

27. C. Giuliodori, "La sponsalità di Cristo e della Chiesa a fondamento della vita nello Spirito della coppia cristiana," in *Cristo Sposo della Chiesa Sposa,* ed. R. Bonetti (Rome: Città Nuova, 1997), 98-99.

28. It would be helpful to reread the numerous patristic texts that develop the analogy between Eve's being drawn from Adam's side and the Church's emerging from Christ's side on the Cross. Balthasar draws out this analogy against its trinitarian background: "God's command to Adam and Eve to be fruitful and multiply was not just a moral command . . . it was, at the same time, the result of the physical fecundity that God effected in Adam while he slept and that became, by the formation of Eve from the one living body of Adam, a direct physical image of the origin from the Father's substance of the eternal Son who shares his nature. . . . The removal of the rib was for Adam an infinitely ennobling grace: the grace of being allowed to participate in the mystery of the Father's self-giving to the Son, by which the Father empties himself of his own Godhead in order to bestow it on the Son who is eternally of the same nature as he is. It was a wound of love that God inflicted on Adam in order to initiate him into the mystery, the lavish self-prodigality, of divine love" (H. U. von Balthasar, *The Christian State of Life,* trans. Mary Frances McCarthy [San Francisco: Ignatius, 1983], 227-28).

her mission ('through,' 'with' and 'in Christ') must be seen in connection with the way she is constituted by him as such."[29] This way or modality is specified by the Letter to the Ephesians, which shows that she is "bride" only as "body."

Ephesians 5:21-33 places the image of Christ as head first, in order to underscore that his body, the Church, owes everything to him, since it was he who caused her to spring forth from his own fullness. The whole Church is like Eve, who was passively drawn from the side of the new Adam: the Church in her entirety flows from Christ's plenitude. It is only afterward that we can speak of the Church as Bride, insofar as she is derived from him: Head-Body, Bridegroom-Bride. The image of the bride allows us to put concrete flesh on the image of the body by highlighting its feminine identity. This is why Eve is drawn from Adam's side, just as the Church is drawn from the side of Christ. We see here that the Church is fundamentally feminine: she conceives and bears in herself what she has received from him for safekeeping, namely, Christ's fruitfulness. He gives to the Church-Bride the seed that belongs to him, not to her; and she, as woman, is charged with receiving this seed that has been transmitted to her and with carrying that seed within her. This is why, before administering the sacraments through the mediation of her ministers, the Marian Church always first receives the "Word of Life" in the womb of her faith. This receptivity constitutes the radically bridal character of the Church, which accompanies the work of her ministers and communicates to the faithful, her children, not only a generic grace of incorporation into Christ, but an authentic participation in her own sponsality.[30]

A text from Balthasar summarizes the richness contained in this spousal approach to sacramentality:

> If Christ is the originating sacrament as appearance, surrender, and ex-
> pression of God's love for the world, then by means of the eucharistic
> universalizing of this personally surrendered body, the Church receives
> a share in this original sacramentality. Moreover, the Church shares this
> reality by drawing the faithful into his "life-creating spirit [body]" (1 Cor
> 15:45; or "Mystical Body") as well as by being the "Bride" who is "one flesh"
> (Eph 5:31) with him and who comes forth from him, for she is the fruit of
> his sacrificed body. In both these aspects the Church owes her fruitfulness

29. Balthasar, *Theo-Drama*, vol. 3: *Dramatis Personae: Persons in Christ*, 426.

30. See Balthasar, *Theo-Drama*, vol. 3: *Dramatis Personae: Persons in Christ*, 430: "This means, in turn, that while the Church has authority to administer the sacraments, she herself is always a receiver, too." The priestly ministry is the sacramental organ that guarantees this receptive attitude of the Church with respect to Christ.

to the sacrifice of Christ's body; this is why she is forbidden to fall into the temptation of equating her primal sacramental character with his.[31]

Note Balthasar's stress on the difference between Christ's fruitfulness and the entirely derived fruitfulness of the Church-Bride. The latter adds nothing to Christ's fruitfulness — as if it were somehow lacking — but allows the transcendent, yet spousal gift of Christ's body to bear fruit in her.

Each Christian, whether man or woman, has his or her first and most fundamental spousal experience as a member of the Church-Bride, who daily weaves her dialogue of love with her Bridegroom, Christ. According to M. J. Scheeben, it is fundamentally important to see the incorporation of all the Church's members in Christ as a *mysterious wedding* with the God-Man:

> By the Incarnation Christ has assumed our nature in order to yoke himself with us. The Fathers view the Incarnation itself as a marriage with the human race, inasmuch as it virtually contains everything that can lead to the full union of the Son of God with men. But the relationship of unity it sets up comes to full fruition only in the Church. Man is to attach himself to his divine bridegroom by faith; and the bridegroom seals his union with man in baptism, as with a wedding ring. But both faith and baptism are mere preliminaries for the coming together of man and the God-man in one flesh by a real Communion of flesh and blood in the Eucharist, and hence for the perfect fructifying of man with the energizing grace of his head. By entering the Church every soul becomes a real bride of God's Son, so truly that the Son of God is able, in the Apostle's words, not only to compare his love and union with the Church and her members with the unity achieved in matrimony, but can even propose it as the ideal and model of the latter. Is not such unity an ineffable, stupendous mystery, which infinitely transcends all the notions of natural man? If the Church in all its members is thus the body of Christ and the bride of Christ, the power of its divine head, the Spirit of its divine bridegroom, must be gloriously operative in it.[32]

This clarification affords us a better grasp of the link between the Church's spousal identity and her sacramentality. The Church's sacramentality/fruitfulness, which manifests itself above all in baptism and in the Eucharist, in

---

31. Balthasar, *Epilogue*, 113-14.

32. M. J. Scheeben, *The Mysteries of Christianity*, trans. Cyril Vollert (St. Louis, London: B. Herder, 1946), 543-44.

fact plunges its roots deep in her feminine identity. We recall that she does not precede the gift of the Bridegroom, but is established and made sacramentally fruitful by his seed (his eucharistic body) and by the Holy Spirit. The Church, who is Bride and Mother, continually emerges from this living presence, which remains the initating source of the "nuptial mystery." Angela Scola asks, "How can this be?" and answers:

> Through the sacramental dynamism (an experience full of logos) by which the Risen Lord dwells bodily with the Trinity, and through all moments in time and space with his body, the church, which has her foundation in his mystical body (the Eucharist). In this way the dual unity of the two natures in the one person of Christ appears as the source from which springs the dual unity between Christ the Bridegroom and his bride the church.[33]

The Church-Bride is thus the sacrament of Christ the Bridegroom because he has given himself, and continues to give himself, totally to her, entrusting to her his broken body and his shed blood in order to purify and nourish her, making her holy and giving her a role in the world's redemption and sanctification *(Sacramentum mundi)*. Her spousal relationship to Christ in faith is the source of a shared fruitfulness for the sake of all of humanity.[34]

The Feminine "Common" Priesthood and the Masculine "Ministerial" Priesthood

From the beginning of Christianity until the Middle Ages, Christians understood the Church as feminine, *Mater Ecclesiae, Sponsa Verbi* (Mother Church, Spouse of the Word). While the hierarchy is made up of men, they themselves are first participants in the Church's Marian mystery. Although they have the function of representing Christ the Head, they are nonetheless ontologically enfolded within the mystery of Mary, Mother of the Church and Bride of Christ. They are representatives of Christ the Bridegroom, to be sure, but only insofar as they take their place within the encompassing femininity of the Church, that is, within the mystery of Mary, Virgin and Mother.

---

33. Scola, *The Nuptial Mystery*, 101.

34. We must not forget that the concept of sacrament is analogical and does not apply to the Church in the same way that it applies to Christ or to the seven sacraments. See John Paul II, *TOB*, 487-91.

In classical terms, this means that no one can become a ministerial priest except within the framework of a fundamental, life-long grace that constitutes the common priesthood. We must not forget that the priesthood is before all else the common priesthood, which is also that of Mary. This participated, derived priesthood — the baptismal priesthood — is accessible to all, men and women. The other, ministerial priesthood is one of representation, insofar, of course, as it participates in the unique and eternal Priest, who is Christ alone. No one, in fact, can be called *alter Christus* (another Christ) in the proper sense, because no one can be in his person what Christ is: true God and true man. Only one possibility remains for us: to be a priestly people in Mary-Church, Christ's Body and Bride. The common priesthood thus bears the mark of the Church's femininity, which is rooted in the unsurpassable privilege of Mary's divine motherhood and her spiritual motherhood at the foot of the Cross.

By the same reason, this Marian and priestly people needs to find itself face-to-face with Christ the Head and Bridegroom, whom the ministerial priesthood represents before the community of Marian priests. It is above all in Mary, then, that we find the fulfillment of the ideal relationship described in the Letter to the Ephesians, which speaks of the bride "without spot or wrinkle or any such thing that she might be holy and without blemish" (Eph. 5:27). Mary is immaculate not only with regard to her conception, but also with regard to her Assumption. We know that at the foot of the Cross, the immaculate Virgin participates in the suffering of the Lamb who was slain and that by this participation she receives her role as Bride and Mother: as the Bride of Christ and thus as the Mother of John, that is, of the chosen people.[35] She is the Mother of Jesus who becomes the Bride of Christ (see John 19:25-27) and, as the immaculate Bride, she begets children to newness of life. In the same act, she becomes the Mother of the Church, as Paul VI declared her to be.

We can summarize our reflection on Jesus Christ, the Sacrament of the Covenant, and on the Church-sacrament with a passage from C. Giuliodori:

> The synthesis is established in the personal unity of Christ, within which the duality between human and divine endures. This duality can be recognized even in the new formulation of his singular ecclesial body, from

---

35. See Scola's reflections on the category of welcome as an expression of the fruitfulness of the nuptial mystery in Mary and John, in *The Nuptial Mystery*, 106-9. See also A. von Speyr, *Handmaid of the Lord*, trans. E. A. Nelson (San Francisco: Ignatius, 1985), chap. 10, "Mary and John."

the way in which the members of the Church-Bride are joined to the head, who is Christ the Bridegroom.[36]

The interweaving of corporality, sponsality, and sacramentality in the Letter to the Ephesians thus points us to the nuptial mystery par excellence: the hypostatic union. The latter, in turn, ultimately leads us to the mystery of the Trinity:

> First of all, there is the relationship between Christ and the church that is presented, particularly in chapter 5 of Ephesians, as a relationship between a bridegroom and a bride. Then there is the existence of the two natures in the one person of Jesus Christ as the foundation that makes possible the "one flesh" of the two spouses that stems from the sacrament of marriage. Finally, there is the nuptial dimension within the Trinity, where the difference between the divine persons dwells in perfect unity as the cause and reason for the possibility of unity in difference which is proper to the man-woman relationship.[37]

We must still clarify the consequences of this opening of trinitarian nuptiality to creatures through the nuptial relationship between Christ and the Church. The relation between the hierarchical minister and the Marian priesthood has already brought to light a fundamental point regarding the sacramentality of Christ and the Church: while Christ is the first and original sacrament, the Church is the derived and universal sacrament, because she is his Body and his Bride. The participation of the Church-Bride in Christ's original sacramentality is based on the permanent actualization of his eucharistic sacrifice, which the Holy Spirit universalizes through Marian faith and the priestly ministry. It is not the Church's response *(ex opere operantis)* that gives Christ's gift its sacramental efficacy. Rather, it is always Christ's gift *(ex opere operato)* that makes the Church fruitful, to the extent that the Church allows God to act and completely trusts his Word. In receiving the Word and allowing it to bear fruit in her, the Church-Bride continually remembers *(anamnesis)* the absolute primacy of the Bridegroom's grace over each of her own contributions to the mystery.

---

36. C. Giuliodori, *Intelligenza del maschile e del femminile. Problemi e prospettive nella rilettura di von Balthasar e P. Evdokimov* (Rome: Città Nuova, 1991), 175. See also Scheffczyk, "Gesù Cristo Sacramento originario della redenzione," 30-77; C. Rochetta, *Sacramentaria fondamentale. Dal "mysterion" al "sacramentum"* (Bologna: EDB, 1990), 442-58; B. Testa, *I sacramenti della Chiesa* (Milan: Jaca Book, 1995), 45-54.

37. Scola, *The Nuptial Mystery*, 97-98.

CHAPTER 6

The Sacrament of Marriage, Paradigm of the Sacramentality of the Church

"All the sacraments of the New Covenant find their prototype in some way in marriage as the primordial sacrament."[1] Having reflected on the nuptial mystery of Christ and the Church as the foundation of the sacramental order, we will now consider how the different sacraments are connected in light of what John Paul II called the "primordial sacrament." The sacraments are "gifts" of Christ the Bridegroom, which the Church-Bride receives in faith in order to beget and nourish the lives of her children, to make them grow. What is the place and the role of the sacrament of marriage in the sacramental structure of the Church, the family of God? In what sense is marriage a "primordial" sacrament, a sacramental "prototype"? Can sacramental marriage be taken as a paradigm of the sacramental mystery of the Church? John Paul II explains the sacramentality of marriage in light of the biblical and patristic concept of "*mysterion*." He is very aware that he is using the term "sacrament" in an analogical sense — and yet also in a more original sense than the Scholastic tradition of the past few centuries.[2] His spousal approach merits reception and further development.

The first step towards this development is to consider the man-woman relation within the framework of biblical anthropology. Our guiding thread here will be the human person who, as man and woman, is "*imago Dei*"; this is the insight that must be integrated into the Christocentric and personal-

1. John Paul II, *Man and Woman He Created Them: A Theology of the Body*, trans. Michael Waldstein (Boston: Pauline Books and Media, 2006) [= *TOB*], 511.

2. See E. Ruffini, "Il matrimonio-sacramento nella tradizione cattolica. Rilettura teologica," in *Nuova encyclopedia del matrimonio*, ed. T. Goffi (Brescia: Queriniana, 1988), 180-200, which offers a historical summary of the theological development following the Fathers of the Church.

istic renewal of sacramental theology. The theology of marriage cannot progress until we clarify the meaning and sacramental import of the dual unity formed by man and woman. What is the sacramental value of the conjugal relation in the economy of signs Christ instituted to express the *"mysterion"* of the new and eternal Covenant? Is it a more or less symbolic figure? Or is it, as we argue here, a real and living reproduction of the nuptial mystery of Christ and the Church? What is the anthropological foundation on which the couple's participation in the "great mystery" of Christ and the Church rests? We can do no more than sketch a rough response to these questions, a suggestion about how to link the "mystery-sacrament of marriage" to the "great mystery" of Christ the Bridegroom and the Church-Bride. We will begin with marriage as the "primordial sacrament" of the New Covenant, in order then to clarify its function as prototype and paradigm, a task that will take us through an exploration of the mystery of the "shared fruitfulness" of the Trinity and the family.

Marriage, the Primordial Sacrament

> Man appears in the visible world as the highest expression of the divine gift, because he bears within himself the inner dimension of the gift. And with it he carries into the world his particular likeness to God. . . . A reflection of this likeness is also the primordial awareness of the spousal meaning of the body pervaded by the mystery of original innocence. Thus, in this dimension, a primordial *sacrament* is constituted, understood as a *sign that* efficaciously *transmits in the visible world the invisible mystery hidden in God from eternity*. . . . In fact, through his bodiliness, his masculinity and femininity, man becomes a visible sign of the economy of Truth which has its source in God himself.[3]

In his catecheses on human love in God's plan of salvation, John Paul II speaks of the "primordial sacrament." This expression refers to the original, "most ancient" sacrament belonging to creation itself. This sacrament also bears a fundamental anthropological significance whose investigation is incumbent on the theology of marriage. For Rochetta, "one of the most significant tasks of contemporary theology consists in . . . demonstrating how the marriage-sacrament takes up and integrates into itself the complete reality

---

3. John Paul II, *TOB*, 203.

of the couple, in each of its components or levels of realization."[4] As both a phenomenologist and a theologian, John Paul II made a crucial contribution to this task based on the identity of the couple as image of God. This insight was the source of a sacramental catechesis highlighting the specific contribution of conjugal love, the value and spousal meaning of the body, and the positive significance of sexuality. The reciprocity between man and woman is thus a fundamental and important basis for the sacrament of marriage, since "it is in this 'being a couple' that Christ's spousal covenant with the Church is incarnated."[5]

Let us pause to reflect on the anthropological bases of the sacrament of marriage. Since John Paul II developed his reflection on the sacramentality of marriage in light of biblical anthropology, we will begin by testing his approach, centered, as we have seen, on the "primordial sacrament," against the findings of contemporary exegesis regarding the *imago Dei*. Our presentation will necessarily be cursory and limited, as we must leave aside numerous issues in order to highlight the essential elements pertinent to our spousal perspective.[6]

The Couple, Image of God[7]

First of all, we note the work being done by contemporary exegesis to move beyond the classical interpretation of the *imago Dei,* which reduces it to the spiritual dimension that explains man's ability to dominate the earth. The majority of exegetes hold that Genesis 1:26-27 refers to the fact that "'*ādām* is the royal representative of God himself, embodying and exercising God's own authority in regard to the earth and all that lives on it."[8] Another group of exegetes maintains, with Claus Westermann, "the image of God is to be found

4. C. Rochetta, *Il sacramento della coppia* (Bologna: EDB, 1996), 277.

5. Rochetta, *Il sacramento della coppia,* 277.

6. See A. Scola, *The Nuptial Mystery,* trans. Michelle K. Borras (Grand Rapids: Eerdmans, 2005), 3-52; also P. Grelot, *Couple humain dans l'Écriture Sainte* (Paris: Éd. du Cerf, 1962); E. Przywara, *L'uomo. Antropologia typologica* (Milan: Fabbri, 1968), 189-203 [*Mensch. Typologische Anthropologie,* 2 vols. (Nürnberg: Glock und Lutz, 1959)]; H. U. von Balthasar, *Theo-Drama,* vol. 2: *Dramatis Personae: Man in God,* trans. Graham Harrison (San Francisco: Ignatius, 1990), 365-82.

7. The following section draws on material presented in M. Ouellet, *Divine Likeness: Toward a Trinitarian Anthropology of the Family* (Grand Rapids: Eerdmans, 2006), 27-39.

8. F. Martin, "A Summary of the Teaching of Genesis Chapter One," *Communio: International Catholic Review* 20, no. 2 (Summer 1993): 240-65, here 247.

in the divinely conferred capacity to relate to God."[9] In this perspective, the account of man's creation, understood in its context, expresses God's will to give himself a *partner* capable of dialogue with his Creator.

Still more interesting is the interpretation of the man-woman relationship as an integral part of the *imago Dei*. If, instead of separating the two creation narratives, we explain the first account (Gen. 1:26-27) using the second (Gen. 2:18-24) in tandem with Genesis 5:3, the following becomes clear. The image of God contains the reciprocity between masculine and feminine, which in turn enables the human person to represent God on earth and to imitate him by participating in his creative power. Exegetical interpretation of the priestly tradition has good grounds for concluding, "'*Ādām* images God, that is, makes his power and authority present and interacts with God, in the relating of man and woman."[10] Regine Hinschberger argues that Genesis 1:26 suggests "a relation of likeness between God, who creates, and man as male and female, who procreate with his blessing." Consequently, "the expression, 'God made them in his likeness' means that God made man to be fruitful, like himself."[11] According to Walter Brueggemann, the fact that God created *them*, man and woman, as an image and likeness in which to reflect himself, authorizes us to conclude: "Only in community of humankind is God reflected. God is, according to this bold affirmation, not mirrored as an individual but as a community."[12] Finally, we add the deliberative plural, "Let us make," which introduces the teaching on the image. All of these factors, then, enable us to conclude that this exegesis of the *imago Dei* in the priestly tradition constitutes a first, relatively well-founded step toward the development of the analogy between the fruitful couple — that is, the family — and the Trinity.

Of course, the book of Genesis does not make explicit the analogical correspondence between created persons and the Persons of the Trinity. Exegesis of the "image and likeness" simply establishes a dialogical relationship between the fruitful couple and an undetermined divine "we," who manifests his cre-

9. Martin, "A Summary of the Teaching of Genesis Chapter One," 258. See C. Westermann, *Genesis I–II: A Commentary* (Minneapolis: Augsburg, 1984), 147-61, especially 157-58.

10. Martin, "A Summary of the Teaching of Genesis Chapter One," 259.

11. L. Gendron, "La famille. Reflet de la communion trinitaire," in *La famille chrétienne dans le monde d'aujourd'hui* (Montreal: Bellarmine, 1995), 142-43. The first citation is taken from an article of R. Hinschberger, "Image et ressemblance dans la tradition sacerdotale," *Recherches de Science Religieuse* 59 (1985): 192. This article is a brief presentation of the author's thesis, *Image et ressemblance dans la tradition sacerdotale* (Strasbourg, 1983), the source of the second citation.

12. W. Brueggemann, *Genesis,* Interpretation (Atlanta: John Knox Press, 1982), 34.

ative power in the procreative union. Hinschberger writes: "In other words, our (priestly) tradition does not draw an analogy between the being of God and the being of man, but rather between the creative making, by which God makes life come into being, and man's pro-creative making, through which he multiplies on the earth."[13]

This dynamic vision of the image of God that actualizes its likeness to him through procreative union aligns very well with the idea of covenant, which forms the general context of biblical teaching on the *imago Dei*. God created man in his image for the sake of an exchange with man, and thus with a view to the covenant that finds privileged expression in the history of Israel and culminates in Christ. The book of Genesis shows that the structure of the covenant is already inscribed in the complementarity between man and woman, since the fruitful couple resembles and corresponds to the gift of the Creator. When Eve gives birth to her first child, she exclaims, "I have gotten a man with the help of the Lord!" (Gen. 4:1), highlighting God's intervention and the human couple's participation in the gift of life.

The Couple as Primordial Sacrament according to John Paul II

John Paul II substantially adopts these conclusions of biblical exegesis in the apostolic letter *Mulieris Dignitatem,* which may be the Magisterium's most daring text on the theme of the *imago Dei*. In the third part of the document, which deals with the "image" and with man and woman's likeness to God, John Paul II reaffirms the traditional doctrine of the human person's spiritual nature before going on to develop the personal and interpersonal dimension of the divine image: "*The woman is another 'I' in a common humanity.* From the very beginning they appear as a 'unity of the two,' and this signifies that the original solitude is overcome, the solitude in which man does not find 'a helper fit for him' (Gen. 2:20)" (*MD* 6). Sexual difference thus appears as part of the original character of the *imago Dei.*[14] The end of the paragraph confirms

13. R. Hinschberger, "Image et ressemblance dans la tradition sacerdotale," 192.

14. Scola, *The Nuptial Mystery,* 32-53 (chap. 3). See also H. U. von Balthasar, *The Christian State of Life,* trans. Mary Frances McCarthy (San Francisco: Ignatius, 1983), 103: "If this were not so, Christ could neither have pointed to the relationship of the sexes to describe his mysterious union with the Church, nor have given to the sacrament of marriage the power and the real possibility of symbolizing this perfect relationship in the relationship of the sexes"; and Balthasar, *Theo-Drama,* vol. 3: *Dramatis Personae: Persons in Christ,* trans. Graham Harrison (San Francisco: Ignatius, 1992), 288-89.

this when it refers to sexual difference "as an indispensable condition for the transmission of life to new generations, the transmission of life to which marriage and conjugal love are by their nature ordered" (*MD* 6).

A complete account of the couple's primordial sacramentality requires more than this presentation of the fruitful "unity of the two" that characterizes Genesis' teaching about the divine image. An explicit reference to the supernatural mystery is still lacking — that is, to the mystery of the redemption, within which man and woman are created and called to fruitfulness. A rich passage of John Paul II clearly explains how his vision is rooted in a Christocentric view of creation:

> *The institution of marriage,* according to the words of Genesis 2:24, expresses not only the beginning of the fundamental human community, which by the "procreative" power proper to it ("be fruitful and multiply," Gen 1:28) serves to continue the work of creation, but at the same time *it expresses the Creator's salvific initiative,* which corresponds to man's eternal election spoken about in Ephesians. This salvific initiative comes forth from God, the Creator, and its supernatural efficaciousness is identical with the very act of the creation of man in the state of original innocence. In this state, already beginning with the act of the creation of man, his eternal election in Christ has borne fruit. In this way, one must recognize that the original sacrament of creation *draws its efficaciousness from the "beloved Son"* (see Eph 1:6, where the author speaks about "his grace, which he has given to us in his beloved Son"). As for marriage, one can deduce that — instituted in the context of the sacrament of creation in its totality, or in the state of original innocence — it was to serve not only to extend the work of creation, or procreation, but also to spread the same sacrament of creation to further generations of human beings, that is, to spread the supernatural fruits of man's eternal election by the Father in the eternal Son, the fruits man was endowed with by God in the very act of creation.[15]

The concept of "primordial sacrament" finds its theological justification in the fact that the Creator established the relationship between man and woman with a view to the covenant in the beloved Son and that he blessed it — from the beginning — with a natural and supernatural fruitfulness flowing from the grace of the Redeemer. This Christocentric grounding of creation

15. John Paul II, *TOB,* 506.

is thus the deepest theological reason for the "primordial" sacramentality of marriage.[16] On the basis of this Christocentrism, John Paul II can contemplate Genesis 2:24 in light of Ephesians 5:32 and see the intimate link between the creation of man as male and female in the image of God, on the one hand, and the great spousal mystery of Christ and the Church in the order of the redemption, on the other. From the beginning, God willed marriage not only as a figurative sign of a future reality, but also as a mystery bearing within itself a supernatural fruitfulness. Sin made us lose this supernatural fruitfulness, but it did not destroy the prototypical sign of the fruitful couple, which was destined to be restored and elevated in the sacramental economy of the New Covenant.[17]

Marriage, the Sacrament of Christ the Bridegroom and the Church-Bride in the New Covenant

The communion between God and his people finds its definitive fulfillment in Jesus Christ, the Bridegroom who loves and gives himself as the Savior of humanity, uniting it to himself as his body. He reveals the original truth of marriage, the truth of the "beginning" (cf. Gen. 2:24; Matt. 19:5) and, freeing man from his hardness of heart, he makes man capable of realizing this truth in its entirety. (*FC* 13)

The sacramentality of marriage is linked to the "mystery" of the new and eternal Covenant, which God decreed before all ages in his beloved Son. This mystery was actualized in the life, death, and resurrection of Jesus Christ,

16. John Paul II employs the term "sacrament" in the biblical and patristic sense, which does not exactly coincide with the Scholastic concept of "signs instituted by Christ and administered by the Church, which express and confer divine grace on the person who receives the sacrament"; the pope refers to the *mysterion* hidden in God and revealed in history through the spousal relationship between Christ and the Church, which marriage sacramentalizes and makes visible in a privileged way. See *TOB*, 489-90, 513.

17. See the following footnote in the Italian edition of *TOB*, *Uomo e donna lo creò. Catechesi sull'amore umano,* 4th ed. (Rome: Città Nuova–Libreria Editrice Vaticana, 1995), 382: "The 'prototypical' character of marriage is based on the fact that . . . the sacrament of marriage 'synthetically' expresses the spousal love of Christ and the Church, to which all the sacraments are efficaciously related. On the other hand, we must acknowledge the primacy of the Eucharist in the order of the sacraments, defining it more intensively as the 'principal' sacrament, inasmuch as it 'contains' the Body given and the Blood poured out of Christ — that is, his charity for the Church in the realism of his 'absolutely unique' Presence."

which the nuptial symbolism of the Old Covenant allows us to interpret in a spousal key. Jesus' sacrifice — which we must understand as a "redemptive and spousal love" in light of the Eucharist — is the fulfillment of the New Covenant in his blood. The Resurrection itself has a nuptial meaning, since the Holy Spirit, the fruitfulness of the Trinity, irrupts in Jesus' personal and eucharistic Body, causing the Church to stand forth as his body and Bride. The paschal mystery is thus the ultimate foundation of the sacramentality of marriage. St. Paul reflected theologically on this question in the Letter to the Ephesians, just as the Synoptics recorded the gestures and words of Jesus that prepared the doctrinal development achieved by the Apostle to the Gentiles. We refer the reader to the Scriptural data laid out in the first part of this work, which remain the basis for our further reflections.

In the Gospels, Jesus appears as the Bridegroom who brings God's plan for his people to fulfillment. Through gestures and parables, Jesus reveals himself to be the Messiah and Bridegroom of humanity. He reveals God's will to become "Emmanuel," sharing all of human life, from birth to death, and its most universal symbolic moments — the home, food, the nuptial chamber, and fruitfulness — and all under the form of a virginal sponsality for the Kingdom of heaven.

The sacramental significance of the Word's Incarnation appears in the account of the wedding at Cana, which points to the "wedding feast of the Lamb" on the Cross. We find ourselves at a crossroads, at which two mysteries meet and shed light on each another. On the one hand, the mystery of the Cross is illumined and made intelligible by the symbol of the wedding feast. On the other hand, it is equally true that the symbol of marriage is illumined by its connection with the "great mystery" of the Lamb's wedding feast. The encounter of the two mysteries is further illumined and confirmed by the spousal symbol of Christian virginity. *Familiaris Consortio* strongly affirms this: "Marriage and virginity or celibacy are two ways of expressing and living the one mystery of the covenant of God with His people" (*FC* 16); "Either one is, in its own proper form, an actuation of the most profound truth of man, of his being 'created in the image of God'" (*FC* 11).

This means that the spousal language of the body — masculinity and femininity, the complementarity of the sexes, reciprocal and fruitful love — is the adequate language for expressing the "great mystery." The analogy between (i) the relationship of husband and wife and (ii) the virginal relationship of Christ and the Church — two relations intimately linked in the Letter to the Ephesians and symbolically expressed in the Gospel of John — allows us to perceive how these mysteries are intrinsically connected and reciprocally illuminating. It is no longer possible to understand the Cross without marriage, just as it is impossible to understand marriage without the Cross. John Paul II explains, "Spouses are therefore the permanent reminder to the Church of what happened on the Cross" (*FC* 13).

John Paul II's long meditation in his Wednesday catecheses on the correspondence between Genesis 1–2, Matthew 19, and Ephesians 5, leads to a presentation of marriage as the prototype of the "new" sacramental economy:

> Thus, as the primordial sacrament, marriage is assumed and inserted into the integral structure of the new sacramental economy, which has arisen from redemption *in the form, I would say, of a "prototype."* It is assumed and inserted, as it were, from its very basis. In the dialogue with the Pharisees (Mt 19:3-9), Christ himself confirms first of all its existence. If we reflect deeply on this dimension, we have to conclude that all the sacraments of the New Covenant find their prototype in some way in marriage as the primordial sacrament.[18]

The pope adds that marriage has the value not only of a "figurative" model, but also of a sign and real symbol of the economy of grace:

> However, the relation of marriage to the whole sacramental order, which has arisen from the Church's endowment with the benefits of redemption, is not limited only to the dimension of model. In his dialogue with the Pharisees (see Mt 19), Christ not only confirms the existence of marriage instituted from the "beginning" by the Creator, but he declares *also that this is an integral part of the new sacramental economy,* of the new order of salvific "signs" that draws its origin from the sacrament of redemption, just as the original economy emerged from the sacrament of creation; and in fact, Christ limits himself to the one and only sacrament, which was marriage instituted in the state of original justice and innocence of man, created as male and female "in the image and likeness of God."[19]

In this sense, the most recent exegesis and hermeneutics of Ephesians 5:21-33 confirms the pope's interpretation. In a recent comprehensive monograph on this pericope, K. H. Fleckenstein undertakes a careful study of the

18. John Paul II, *TOB,* 511.
19. John Paul II, *TOB,* 511.

most representative opinions about the passage. His conclusion is to propose a novel reading very close to the pope's: "It is no longer the Christ-Church relationship that is the model of the human plan; to the contrary, the author of the Letter begins from the human reality of marriage and then applies the schema of spousal union to the reality of Christ and the Church."[20]

This does not mean that the Christ-Church relationship ceases to be the spousal model for Christian marriage; to the contrary, it gains in exemplary value precisely because the whole point of the analogy is that the human spousal union is an apt expression of the mystery of the union between Christ and the Church. The author continues:

> We are convinced that Christian marriage is fundamentally related to the mystery of the spousal relationship between Christ and the Church. It is not merely a symbol of this mystery, but participates in its nature and supernatural character, which make marriage efficacious in itself as a holy and sanctifying bond. In this way, the human union of the spouses becomes an image of the relationship between Christ and the Church.[21]

Fleckenstein concludes, "We can call 'great' not only the mystery of Christ and the Church, but also marriage as a created reality that sheds light on this mystery."[22] There is no doubt that Trent's prudent formulation[23] caused Catholic exegetes to become more cautious in their use of Ephesians 5:21-33 to prove the sacramentality of marriage. Nevertheless, this caution did not compromise their general willingness to do so. In reality, Catholic doctrine

---

20. K. Fleckenstein, *"Questo mistero è grande": Il matrimonio in Ef 5, 21-33* (Rome: Città Nuova, 1996), 116.

21. Fleckenstein, *"Questo mistero è grande": Il matrimonio in Ef 5, 21-33*, 117.

22. Fleckenstein, *"Questo mistero è grande": Il matrimonio in Ef 5, 21-33*, 118.

23. In its twenty-fourth session, the Council of Trent solemnly defined the sacramentality of marriage against the Protestant Reformation: "Can. 1. If anyone says that matrimony is not truly and properly one of the seven sacraments of the law of the Gospel, instituted by Christ the Lord, but that it was devised in the Church by men and does not confer grace, let him be anathema" (Denz 1801). In the introduction to the canons, the Council refers to the Scriptural texts on which the Church's doctrine is based: Genesis 2:23; Matthew 19:5; Mark 10:9; Ephesians 5:31. Regarding the Letter to the Ephesians, it says, "Christ himself, who instituted the holy sacraments and brought them to perfection, merited for us by his Passion the grace that perfects that natural love, confirms the indissoluble union, and sanctifies the spouses. St. Paul suggests this when he says: 'Husbands, love your wives, as Christ loved the Church and gave himself up for her' (Eph 5:25), adding immediately: 'This is a great mystery, and I mean in reference to Christ and the Church' (Eph 5:32)" (Denz 1799).

no longer needs to appeal to the erroneous Latin translation *sacramentum,* which does not adequately capture the Greek *mysterion,* but can rely on the entire analogy employed by St. Paul. Read in light of this analogy, Paul's use of the term *mysterion* means that the Christian couple does not merely reproduce the relationship between Adam and Eve, but also images the salvific relationship between Christ and his Church.[24] Catholic exegesis therefore holds that marriage possesses a sanctity and dignity making it worthy of the term "sacrament":[25]

> The Christian who lives this sacrament, receiving the institution of the sign on the part of the Church, becomes a minister of the mystery of God. Since the mystery of the Church is hidden in God from the beginning of creation, in giving one another love — including through their bodies — the spouses give one another the love of God.[26]

Exegesis confirms John Paul II's sacramental approach, which aptly develops Vatican Council II's Christocentric focus. A few texts illustrate the bases of his reflection. *Gaudium et Spes* 48 certainly represents a shift in the way of presenting and developing the traditional doctrine. It moves beyond a predominantly juridical vision in order to highlight "the intimate partnership of married life and love." The text also reaffirms the doctrine of the ends of marriage without establishing a hierarchy among them, since "all of these have a very decisive bearing on the continuation of the human race, on the personal development and eternal destiny of the individual members of a family" (*GS* 48).

Moreover, the sacramental dimension is presented in a Christocentric and ecclesial key:

> Christ the Lord abundantly blessed this many-faceted love, welling up as it does from the fountain of divine love and structured as it is on the model of his union with his Church. For as God of old made himself present to

24. R. Penna, *Lettera agli Efesini. Introduzione, versione, commento* (Bologna: EDB, 1988), 243.

25. See R. Schnackenburg, *Der Brief an die Epheser* (Zurich: Benzinger; Neukirchen-Vluyn: Neukirchener Verlag, 1982), 262 n. 669; H. Schlier, *Lettera agli Efesini* (Brescia: Paideia, 1965); J. Gnilka, *Der Epheserbrief* (Fribourg: Herder, 1971), 272-303; A. Carpin, "Sacramentalità del matrimonio. Riferimenti scritturistici e patristici," in *Sacra Doctrina* 2 (March-April) (Bologna: ESD, 1997), 119-43.

26. Fleckenstein, *"Questo mistero è grande": Il matrimonio in Ef 5, 21-33,* 173.

his people through a covenant of love and fidelity, so now the Savior of men and the Spouse of the Church comes into the lives of married Christians through the sacrament of matrimony. He abides with them thereafter so that just as he loved the Church and handed himself over on her behalf, the spouses may love each other with perpetual fidelity through mutual self-bestowal. (*GS* 48)

The conciliar text affirms that human love participates in divine love by virtue of the sacrament, which consecrates the spouses and enables them to accomplish their mission:

Authentic married love is caught up into divine love and is governed and enriched by Christ's redeeming power and the saving activity of the Church, so that this love may lead the spouses to God with powerful effect and may aid and strengthen them in the sublime office of being a father or a mother. For this reason Christian spouses have a special sacrament by which they are fortified and receive a kind of consecration in the duties and dignity of their state. (*GS* 48)

This teaching is adopted and clarified in *Familiaris Consortio* 13, which states that, like the other sacraments, marriage is

a real symbol of the event of salvation, but in its own way. "The spouses participate in it as spouses, together, as a couple, so that the first and immediate effect of marriage *(res et sacramentum)* is not supernatural grace itself, but the Christian conjugal bond, a typically Christian communion of two persons because it represents the mystery of Christ's incarnation and the mystery of his covenant." (*FC* 13)

John Paul II unfolds the content of this grace and draws out its anthropological components:

The content of participation in Christ's life is also specific: conjugal love involves a totality, in which all the elements of the person enter — appeal of the body and instinct, power of feeling and affectivity, aspiration of the spirit and of will. It aims at a deeply personal unity, the unity that, beyond union in one flesh, leads to forming one heart and soul; it demands indissolubility and faithfulness in definitive mutual giving; and it is open to fertility (cf. *Humanae Vitae* 9). (*FC* 13)

The Fruitfulness of Marriage and Trinitarian Fruitfulness

Familiaris Consortio teaches: "the marriage of the baptized is one of the seven sacraments of the New Covenant. Indeed, by means of baptism, man and woman are definitively placed within the new and eternal covenant, in the spousal covenant of Christ with the Church" (*FC* 13). Dual unity, created in Christ from "the beginning," finds its fulfillment by participating in the fruitfulness of Christ and the Church. In the sacrament of marriage, the couple's "natural" fruitfulness is taken up into the "spiritual" fruitfulness of faith and becomes a living expression of the trinitarian mystery. The couple, the image of God, discovers its likeness to God within the fruitfulness of Christ and the Church, which transforms its *communio personarum* into a domestic church.

The Christocentric and sacramental approach that we have worked out thus far needs to be complemented by a reflection on fruitfulness. The privileged symbol that is man and woman needs this dimension if it is to be understood in all its depths as the paradigm of the sacramental order. The event of the Lord's cross-death-resurrection is an infinitely fruitful "nuptial mystery" that culminates in the gift of the Holy Spirit. All the sacraments, especially the Eucharist, come from this nuptial mystery, which marriage and virginity express analogically in an anthropological and ecclesial language. In order to grasp more deeply this interconnection between the sacraments in their spousal dimension, we must consider the grace of marriage in light of fruitfulness.

We have already noted that marital fruitfulness has been undertreated in theology on account of a hitherto predominant juridical and naturalist mentality that practically reduced love to an extrinsic addition. We limit ourselves here to recalling the contemporary Christological and pneumatological renewal and deepening along the lines indicated by Hans Urs von Balthasar and Adrienne von Speyr. The first fruitfulness of sacramental marriage is that of the act of faith that founds it. From this flows a new participation of the couple in the fruitfulness of trinitarian love — a love revealed in Christ crucified and risen, the source and model of all fruitfulness.

In the splendor of the initial and permanent act of faith, the couple becomes Church. Husband and wife are taken up into the relationship between Christ and the Church in order to be placed at the disposal of trinitarian love. The couple makes a gift of itself to Christ in the sacramental celebration and receives a corresponding gift: the Holy Spirit (1 Corinthians 7), who transforms their "community of life and love" into a temple and icon of the Trinity. The mission of the family, the domestic church, flows precisely from the gift of the ecclesial bond *(res et sacramentum)* that consecrates and transforms the personal bond of love into a source of grace. Christ abides with them, blessing their conjugal and family life with the eucharistic gift of trinitarian communion, a prelude to the supreme gift of children or to the gift of spiritual fruitfulness when the couple cannot have children:

> Every Christian marriage is blessed by God and is fruitful in him, whether through the blessing of children or the blessing of sacrifice. If God chooses the second alternative, the spiritual fruitfulness of marriage is increased and widened out invisibly so that it flows into the whole community.[27]

As we have seen, the spouses' fruitfulness in this case approaches the supernatural fruitfulness of consecrated virgins.

Beyond mutual help, the healing of wounds, and the perfecting of their love, Christ integrates the self-gift and communion of the spouses into his own spousal self-gift for the Church. This ultimate gift impels the couple and the family to live no longer for themselves but for Christ and the Church, according to the grace received and the faith kept in their vocation to holiness in marriage.

In conclusion, let us summarize the trajectory of our spousal approach to sacramentality. "The figure of the wedding feast underlies the mystery of all sacramentality": in these words, A. Mattheeuws nicely captures John Paul II's signature thesis that marriage is the paradigm of the sacramental order. To call marriage the "primordial sacrament" is to say that God has established marriage for, and presupposed it in, the fulfillment of the "nuptial mystery" of Christ the Redeemer. Marriage is the most ancient sacrament, destined to be rediscovered and elevated in Christ — in relation to virginal fruitfulness — as the real symbol, reproduction, or living incarnation of his love for the Church. Although it is one of the seven sacraments, marriage, together with the Eucharist, in some sense represents the *"telos"* of them all. All the sacraments serve the goal of building up the Church, Christ's Body and Bride. As the primordial sacrament instituted for the sake of Christ and the Church, marriage incarnates the spousal figure of Christ and the Church at the heart of the world. It translates the reality of the eucharistic mystery into the spouses' flesh.

The Eucharist and marriage illumine each other as nuptial mystery. The sacrament of marriage receives and bears the nuptial grace of the Eucharist into the heart of the family, the domestic church sent into the world. The do-

---

27. Adrienne von Speyr, *John*, vol. 1: *The Word Become Flesh: Meditations on John 1-5* (San Francisco: Ignatius, 1994), 90-91.

mestic church, in turn, sinks deep roots into the plan of God, who created man in his image and likeness. The dual unity of man and woman can be taken up into Christ in order to become the sacramental expression of trinitarian love in the language of the body — the language of masculinity and femininity, of sexual difference and fruitfulness.

The Church has needed time and effort to understand the full sacramentality of marriage and to plumb its anthropological significance. At the beginning of the third millennium, it seems that we are called to a qualitative advance in our awareness of the value of Christian marriage. May it please God that marriage, articulated according to the original, spousal sacramentality of Christ and the Church, become not only a key to understanding the entire sacramental order, but above all a source of grace for the renewal of the Church's mission in the world.

CHAPTER 7

Marriage and the Other Sacraments

The sacrament of marriage elevates the conjugal relationship of man and woman to the level of a paradigmatic sign-symbol of the sacramental order founded in Christ the Bridegroom and the Church-Bride. If we have found in marriage a hermeneutical principle that enables us to understand the sacraments in general, we must now clarify how that principle can be applied to the other sacraments: How do the sacraments fit together in the structure of the spousal relationship between Christ and the Church? How do they contribute to its fruitfulness? In what way does the specific grace of each sacrament introduce individuals into the "nuptial mystery" of Christ and the Church?

St. Thomas Aquinas explains the pattern linking the sacraments using the analogy of natural human life: the sacraments realize on a spiritual level the anthropological structures and fundamental stages of human existence.[1] While essentially important and perennially valid, this principle fails to stress the covenantal dimension of the sacraments. It gives us a way of understanding the supernatural fulfillment of the human person "from below," according to the model of natural life, but it risks overshadowing Christ's role and reducing it to a kind of extrinsic cause of grace. Giuseppe Colombo, for his part, proposes "treating marriage as a function of the Eucharist in line with the well-known thesis that all the other sacraments are relative to the Eucharist, while the Eucharist is prior to all the other sacraments. So much so that the Eucharist has the function of 'making' the Church."[2] We will adopt these

1. St. Thomas Aquinas, *Summa Theologica* IIIa, q. 65, a. 2; *Summa Contra Gentiles,* Book 4, chap. 58.
2. G. Colombo, *Teologia sacramentaria* (Milan: Glossa, 1997), 588.

two approaches and try to develop them further with the help of Balthasar, who, it seems to us, offers the most comprehensive principle of integration in this area.

Our essay will be Christocentric and trinitarian. Its "architectonic principle" is the mystery of trinitarian fruitfulness extended to mankind in the form of the covenant in Christ. Its hermeneutical principle, on the other hand, is the "dual unity" of the *imago Dei,* which allows us to explore the connection among the sacraments in a spousal perspective.[3] The Church-Sacrament emerges from the sacraments and at the same time expresses itself through them as a means of responding to Christ in faith. The Eucharist represents the source and summit of the spousal mystery of Christ and the Church, a mystery that marriage translates and describes in the "language of the body." Our discussion of the sacraments will thus unfold within the horizon of the spousal *mysterion* that we find in the Bible and the Fathers. Our intention is to show how trinitarian fruitfulness emerges from the eucharistic mystery, generates a filial and spousal identity through the sacraments of Christian initiation and holy orders, renews and makes fruitful the spousal relationship between Christ and the Church through the sacraments of penance and the anointing of the sick, and finally attains its supreme anthropological expression in the (spiritually and bodily) fruitful couple, who are the domestic church. We will thus begin with (a) baptism, confirmation, and marriage; then treat (b) the Eucharist and marriage; and conclude with (c) holy orders, marriage, and reconciliation.

Baptism, Confirmation, and Marriage

The Anthropological and Christocentric Foundation of the Sacraments

> One of the areas where the Church establishes her efficacy is in her life as it is configured by the individual sacraments radiating out from her. In the sacraments she presents in *bodily* form the decisive incorporation into Christ's and the Church's salvific efficacy for us physical beings in the most notable situations in life.[4]

3. A. Scola, *The Nuptial Mystery,* trans. Michelle K. Borras (Grand Rapids: Eerdmans, 2005), 77-81.

4. H. U. von Balthasar, *Epilogue,* trans. Edward T. Oakes (San Francisco: Ignatius, 2004), 114-15.

In this passage, Balthasar enunciates a principle that reformulates the approach of St. Thomas Aquinas: "since the spiritual remedies of salvation . . . have been given to men under sensible signs, it was suitable also to distinguish the remedies provided for the spiritual life after the likeness of bodily life."[5] Birth, growth, the need for nourishment, healing, and death, which already possess the value of a sacral rite or "natural sacrament," are assumed into Christ, who incorporates them, with their entire meaning in the order of creation, into the economy of saving signs.

In the history of Israel, this indispensable "natural" dimension is enriched by the pact between God and his people. This pact confers a distinct additional element, as we see, for example, in the bodily rite of circumcision, the prelude to baptism. Balthasar continues:

> But in the New Covenant all of this is overtaken by the underivable reality of Christ as *Verbum-Caro*. This new and utterly unexpected reality places the Eucharist in the center of sacramental reality, as the immediate incorporation into the bodily saving efficacy of Christ and the Church. From this center all the other sacramental situations are related to this Body.[6]

Balthasar highlights the centrality of the Eucharist not only because of the unsurpassable and substantial presence of Christ's body and blood effected by transubstantiation, but above all because of the spousal relationship between Christ and the Church that emerges from his absolute and irreversible sacrificial self-gift in the sacramental event.

The foregoing suggests a new way of understanding the sacraments in function of the event of the Incarnation rather than merely in function of the spiritual fulfillment of natural human life. This new perspective considers Christ's life as the "form" of man rather than as the meritorious cause of a grace that takes its pattern from human nature. Grace is above all an encounter "with," and incorporation "into," Jesus Christ, the Son of the Father, in the Holy Spirit. Balthasar explains:

5. St. Thomas Aquinas, *Summa Contra Gentiles,* Book 4, chap. 58: "Now, in bodily life we find a twofold order: for some propagate and order the bodily life in others; and some are propagated and ordered in the bodily life." To this latter order correspond birth-baptism, growth-confirmation, food–the Eucharist, healing–the anointing of the sick/penance in the bodily as in the spiritual life; to the first order correspond priesthood and marriage, as sacraments that exercise a function of propagation and education in the bodily or spiritual life. Cf. also *Summa Theologica,* III, q. 65 a. 2.

6. Balthasar, *Epilogue,* 115.

Thus what happens in the seven sacraments is this: the one who brought salvation to the world did so by living a fully human life. . . . Because he was the bearer of our salvation, his various life situations thus touch the basic situations of human existence in such a way that the latter (whose symbolic and sacral value every healthy culture recognizes through ritual) are marked and grounded in the foundational events of Jesus' life, which means all the turning points of human life in a Christian are thereby made fruitful for generating Christ's own life in the Church.[7]

It is not the situations of human life that define Christ's grace; rather, it is this grace that defines and determines from above the meaning and fulfillment of the human. In this sense, the hypostatic union, having been made Eucharist and interpreted within a nuptial horizon, becomes the *sacramentum mundi,* the "symbol of symbols," bearing the full ontological weight that Mazzanti attributes to this expression.[8]

Baptism and Marriage: The "Nuptial Continuity" of the Gift[9]

The spousal dimension of the sacraments already appears in baptism, which plunges the human being into Christ's paschal act. St. Paul evokes the nuptial meaning of baptism in the Letter to the Ephesians 5:25-27:

Husbands, love your wives, as Christ loved the church and gave himself up for her, that he might sanctify her, having cleansed her by the washing of water with the word, that he might present the church to himself in splendor, without spot or wrinkle or any such thing, that she might be holy and without blemish.

The action of the baptizing Christ is determined by the Church's need for purification in view of the nuptial encounter. The gift of baptismal purity tends toward the gift of the spousal relationship.

7. Balthasar, *Epilogue,* 116.

8. G. Mazzanti, *I sacramenti, simbolo e teologia,* vol. 1: *Introduzione generale* (Bologna: EDB, 1997), chap. 2, 99-152. In our opinion, the author's nuptial approach makes this work one of the most penetrating essays in fundamental sacramental theology. It holds great promise for the renewal of the entire discipline.

9. See A. Mattheeuws, *Les "dons" du mariage. Recherche de théologie morale et sacramentelle* (Brussels: Culture et Vérité, 1996), 432ff.

From the Church's perspective, baptism first of all signifies incorporation into Christ and thus an introduction into his spousal ethos. This incorporation excludes fornication because of the bodily realism of the Christian's relationship with Christ. St. Paul proclaims without hesitation: "Do you not know that your bodies are members of Christ? Shall I therefore take the members of Christ and make them members of a prostitute?" (1 Cor. 6:15). The apostle immediately adds: "Do you not know that your body is a temple of the Holy Spirit within you, which you have from God? You are not your own" (1 Cor. 6:19). Alain Mattheeuws comments:

> Through baptism, man and woman belong to Christ even in their body. They are no longer their own. They are Christ's. Their bodies no longer belong to them. Christ himself, then, must give the spouses to each another and must hand over the body of each to the other, just as he himself handed over his body. The work of marriage is accomplished in such a way that through baptismal grace the spouses' mutual self-gift is and becomes a gift of Christ. Through the grace of baptism, then, conjugal union can be union with the Body of Christ. The nuptial realism of baptism leads to the sacramental sign of marriage.[10]

The "nuptial continuity" of gift linking baptism and marriage is reinforced by confirmation, since this sacrament is the sign of maturity and mission. According to Balthasar,

> The distinction between the sacraments of confirmation and baptism arose for two reasons: first, because of the "natural sacrament" of human maturation, but also because of the distance between Christ's own baptism and the pouring out of the Holy Spirit during the *Triduum Paschale* (or at Pentecost). The institution of human marriage and its fruitfulness in children is expressly placed in the context of the relations of Christ and his Church (Eph 5).[11]

Confirmation adds to baptism a gift of the Holy Spirit designed to reinforce Christian maturity by giving Christ's disciple a particular charism of witness for the sake of Christian mission. Filial grace is thus confirmed by a new bond with the Person of the Holy Spirit. This bond is personal and not

10. Mattheeuws, *Les "dons" du mariage,* 433-34.
11. Balthasar, *Epilogue,* 115-16.

merely functional; it makes the man and the woman capable of committing themselves in marriage and receiving its specific nuptial charism. The seal of the Holy Spirit thus opens wide the doors to a new missionary dynamism that takes concrete shape in Christian marriage. Such dynamism is already present in the grace of baptism, but it is further reinforced and fortified by the particular charisms that the Holy Spirit freely grants to those who follow the Lord definitively, whether in the sacrament of marriage or in consecrated virginity for the Kingdom.

We can say, then, that birth and growth, two fundamental stages of human life, receive a Christological shape through baptism and confirmation for the sake of a spousal commitment within the Church's faithful response to Christ. This faith-commitment of the Christian in the Church is never an autonomous act that we perform before Christ, but rather the first and fundamental grace that we receive from him. In fact, "it is he who through the Church baptizes, teaches, rules, looses, binds, offers, sacrifices . . . and by his divine power permeates his whole Body" (Denz 3608).[12] If the Church realizes herself most fully in the sacraments of faith (K. Rahner), this self-realization means above all a radical, feminine welcome and ratification of the grace that always comes from her Head, Bridegroom, and Lord.

Nuptiality and Consecration

We can also consider the relation between baptism, confirmation, and marriage from the angle of the consecration bestowed by these sacraments. The sacramental "character" of baptism and confirmation, on the one hand, and the "nuptial bond" or conjugal consecration, on the other, are objective and irrevocable gifts that inscribe in the subjects a sign (Greek *sphragis*) of personal belonging — or of the couples' belonging — to Christ. Of course, the tradition does not attribute to marriage an indelible "character" as it does to baptism, confirmation, or holy orders, but there is nonetheless an analogy between this sacramental "character" and the conjugal bond. All of these realities are objective consecrations that produce irreversible effects. In our opinion, a deeper reflection on the theology of the sacramental "character" in light of the Holy Spirit contains the answer to certain hesitations regarding this analogy.[13]

12. Balthasar, *Epilogue*, 117.
13. See Part I of the present volume, chapter 3.

We note that the *res et sacramentum* of marriage (the conjugal bond), which presupposes these sacraments, not only produces a fundamental Christian state of life, expressed either maritally or socially, but also constitutes the family as the fundamental cell of the Church *(ecclesia domestica)*. The ecclesial character of the Christian family is rooted first of all in the objective charism (1 Cor. 7:7) that further determines the baptismal character by indissolubly binding the couple to the nuptial union between Christ and the Church. This "charism of consecration"[14] remains an inexhaustible source of supernatural grace *(res)* for the sanctification of the spouses and the mission of the Christian family. On this sacramental basis, wherein baptism, confirmation, and marriage converge, the couple itself becomes a stable source of grace (state of life), a state in which "a man and woman come together to beget offspring and to rear them in divine worship."[15]

A more complex question, at least on the pastoral level, arises when baptized persons no longer living the faith received in baptism nonetheless request the sacrament of marriage. While this is not the place to determine how the pastor should deal practically with such requests, it is opportune to recall the link between baptismal faith and marriage. In the ongoing debate about this question, we find a variety of positions. The predominantly juridical perspective, centered as it is on the marriage contract, tends to reduce to a minimum the faith required for reception of the sacrament of marriage. Since marriage is above all a natural reality, this position argues, the fiancés need only be baptized and wish to marry in the Church: "The mere intention of marrying as Christians suffices."[16] This minimalistic vision fails to encourage evangelization and contributes to perpetuating a "naturalistic" pastoral approach to the sacraments that is not entirely in harmony with the Christocentrism of Vatican Council II.

The search for a more adequate position leads us to stress the necessity

---

14. See L. Ligier, *Il matrimonio. Questioni teologiche e pastorali* (Rome: Città Nuova, 1988), 113ff., where Ligier notes that the charism of consecration "makes conjugal life a specific state, which characterizes the married life of the baptized . . . it is the bond that unites them, the inviolability of their state of life, the *res et sacramentum* of their marriage" (114). See also H. Mühlen, *Una mistica persona* (Rome: Città Nuova, 1968), 352-438.

15. St. Thomas Aquinas, *Summa Contra Gentiles*, Book 4, chap. 58.

16. A. Miralles, *Il Matrimonio. Teologia e vita* (Cinisello Balsamo: San Paolo, 1996), 155-57: "In marriage, those who marry act in their own name to accomplish the gift of self; hence the specific nature of the questions put to prospective spouses." Given this premise, the author argues that the exchange of consent between the baptized suffices to constitute the sacrament; "the fact that the questions imply a sacramental intent, which can be present without explicit awareness, flows from the very nature of the sacrament of marriage."

of objective faith as the link between the contract and the sacrament, between conjugal love and its insertion into Christ's paschal mystery. As Martelet writes, "The conjugal covenant does not become a sacrament in virtue of some juridical status that is automatically efficacious apart from any free Yes to baptism. Rather, it becomes a sacrament by virtue of the publicly Christian character belonging to the very heart of this reciprocal commitment."[17]

If the fiancés were not sustained and accompanied by the objective faith of the Church in which their marriage is celebrated, then the sacramental gesture of reciprocal self-gift, their action as "ministers" of Christ and the Church in the sacrament, would be pointless. We must thus avoid two extremes: on the one hand, the attempt to measure the fiancés' faith with an overly subjective criterion; and on the other hand, the reduction of the foundation of marital sacramentality to the fact of already having received baptism. Faith does in fact contain implicit dimensions; they are genuine and they can be presumed, on the condition that the fiancés do not openly contradict the Church's faith or the fundamental requirements of the sacrament.

In our opinion, the relation between baptism, faith, and marriage should not be defined on the basis of the minimum requirement for validity, but rather in terms of the Christian vocation to holiness in marriage.[18] It would be helpful if those preparing couples for the sacrament would directly proclaim the anthropological and sacramental meaning of marriage, calling the individuals to faith and showing them the value and implications of the sacrament. In the contemporary, secularized context, the right pastoral approach is not so much a matter of making sure couples have faith already as it is a matter of inviting them to embrace it in the first place. Those who request the sacrament should receive a positive welcome and should be confronted with the exciting and demanding mystery of Christian marriage. This would give them the chance to choose, that is, either to commit themselves or, supposing a real resistance to faith on their part, to seek an alternative. For this purpose,

---

17. G. Martelet, "Seize thèses de christologie sur le sacrement de mariage," *La Documentation catholique* 75, no. 1744 (1978): 571-75. For a discussion of this theme, see J.-B. Sequeira, *Tout mariage entre baptisés est-il nécessairement sacramentel?* (Paris: Éd. du Cerf, 1985); H. Denis, *Le Mariage, un sacrement pour les croyants?* (Paris: Éd. du Cerf, 1990).

18. See E. Ruffini, "Il matrimonio-sacramento nella tradizione cattolica. Rilettura teologica," in *Nuova enciclopedia del matrimonio,* ed. T. Goffi (Brescia: Queriniana, 1988), 204: "Just as in baptism the believer is called by God to be a grace and an offer of salvation for mankind in general, in marriage he is called to be this for a particular person.... To the extent that the spouses try to be a grace of God for one another, they mutually become the efficacious sign of God's love for both."

a pre-matrimonial catechumenate could certainly be useful, even if it is not a comprehensive or fully satisfying solution.[19]

The Eucharist and Marriage

In 1975, A. Ambrosanio wrote that "the relationship between the Eucharist and marriage has not yet been developed by theology. This is a chapter that remains to be written."[20] His observation remains valid, despite an increasing awareness of the challenge. We will touch on only a few essential points within the framework of the systematic nuptial approach pursued here.

The Mystery of the Covenant

> The Eucharist is the very source of Christian marriage. The Eucharistic Sacrifice, in fact, represents Christ's covenant of love with the Church, sealed with his blood on the Cross. In this sacrifice of the New and Eternal Covenant, Christian spouses encounter the source from which their own marriage covenant flows, is interiorly structured and continuously renewed. (*FC* 57)

The mystery of the covenant is the keystone of the relation between the Eucharist and marriage. The Eucharist is the source of marriage because it seals the nuptial bond of man with God in Christ's body and blood:

> The centrality of the Eucharist means above all that it is the seal of the definitive Word-made-flesh. If "man lives by everything that proceeds

---

19. See Colombo, *Teologia sacramentaria*, 590: "Pastors would do well to prioritize the various goals of their work: the first (logical) priority is to form 'groups of married couples' who live marriage and, in so doing, proclaim the good news of marriage and the Christian family; the second priority would be a 'catechumenate' for those who need conversion to the reality of marriage and the Christian family."

20. A. Ambrosanio, "Matrimonio ed Eucharistia," *Asprenas* 22 (1975): 203-19. See also M. Martinez Peque, *Lo Spirito Santo e il matrimonio* (Rome: EDR, 1993), 169-78; D. Tettamanzi, *La famiglia, via della Chiesa*, 2nd ed. (Milan: Massimo, 1991), 249-65; Tettamanzi, "L'Eucharistia al centro della famiglia," *La Famiglia* 97 (1983): 23-42; John Paul II, Address to the Members of the Movement "Teams of Our Lady," September 23, 1982 ["God's Gift of Life and Love: Marriage and the Eucharist," *Communio: International Catholic Review* 41 (Summer 2014): 462-71].

out of the mouth of the Lord" (Deut 8:3 = Mt 4:4; Jn 4:34), in the words of Jesus are "spirit and life" (Jn 6:63), for the Word has become flesh and is given for us as "food indeed" and "drink indeed" (Jn 6:55).[21]

Already in the Old Covenant, the pact on Sinai concluded with a final banquet. In the same way, the New Covenant is sealed in the eucharistic flesh of the Bridegroom; this is the daily nourishment offered to the Church-Bride to guarantee the permanent actualization of the nuptial mystery. It is worth looking more closely at the intimate link, at once symbolic and sacramental, between the supper and the wedding feast. We will take Balthasar as our guide in this examination.

In the New Testament, Jesus invites us to share in his intimacy, in which he is not only the host (Rev. 3:20), but also the food. Hence his promise: "The bread which I shall give for the life of the world is my flesh" (John 6:51). Moreover, Balthasar observes, Jesus offers himself as food containing the nuptial truth of the "one flesh" and the "one Spirit" when he affirms: "He who eats my flesh and drinks my blood abides in me, and I in him" (John 6:56). We can add the texts where Paul shows how the eucharistic mystery of the supper (1 Cor. 10:16; 11:23ff.) essentially entails a nuptial union: "The body is . . . for the Lord, and the Lord for the body. . . . But he who is united to the Lord becomes one spirit with him" (1 Cor. 6:13, 17).[22]

Since "the grace of marriage consists essentially in participating in Christ's bond of love with the Church,"[23] marriage receives its entire sacramental significance from this context: the representation of the paschal sacrifice that establishes the nuptial bond between Christ and the Church. In the Eucharist, then, the spouses find access to all the dimensions of the nuptial mystery. They perform not only an *anamnesis* of the history of the covenant, or even an *epiclesis* for a nuptial Pentecost; they also accomplish a real *methexis*, a participation in the "nuptial mystery" that they are called to translate into their conjugal life.[24] This is why the Church traditionally celebrates weddings within the eucharistic liturgy.

21. Balthasar, *Epilogue*, 117.

22. See H. U. von Balthasar, *Theo-Drama*, vol. 5: *The Last Act*, trans. Graham Harrison (San Francisco: Ignatius, 1998), 470-87 ("Meal and Marriage"); also G. Mazzanti, *I sacramenti*, vol. 1: *Introduzione generale*, 95-97.

23. G. Baldanza, *La grazia del sacramento del matrimonio. Contributo per la riflessione teologica* (Rome: CLV Liturgiche, 1993), 285.

24. A. M. Triacca, "'Celebrare' il matrimonio cristiano. Suo significato teologico-liturgico (*Anamnesis-Méthexis-Epiclesis*)," *Ephemerides liturgicae* 93 (1979): 407-56.

Encounter, Assumption, Participation

Vatican II's decisive breakthrough in this area can be expressed in three key concepts that refer marriage to Christ. According to G. Baldanza, "the guiding thread [consists in] three concepts: encounter, assumption, and participation in Christ's spousal covenant with the Church. . . . Christ the Bridegroom and the Church-Bride take up the generative power of marriage in order to actualize their fruitfulness as bridegroom and bride."[25] Now, the Eucharist is the source and summit of this encounter, assumption, and participation, because it gives the spouses access to the sacramental heart of their identity: the gift of Christ for the Church his Bride. The love that the spouses are called to incarnate and attest is Christ's spousal love for the Church transmitted through the Eucharist. The spousal Spirit that they receive in their exchange of consent "makes them capable of participating in the Eucharist as the supreme expression of the self-gift contained in the paschal mystery."[26]

The conjugal encounter sealed by the Eucharist thus manifests the Church's very nature as a covenantal mystery. The Church loves Christ the Bridegroom, is faithful to him and belongs to him forever; fully and indissolubly united to him, she is the fruitful bride. Nourished at the source of redemptive spousal love, the spouses learn to love not only "as" Christ loved, but with his very divine and human love itself, which is poured into their hearts by the Holy Spirit.[27] The real gift of the Bridegroom in the Eucharist, to which virgins also bear witness in a different but complementary way,[28] makes possible the love of the spouses unto the cross. This participated love does not diverge from its archetype: it is faithful and indissoluble; it is an agapic love, into which conjugal *eros* is assumed, healed and perfected, becoming an actualization of the exchange between Christ the Bridegroom and the Church-Bride in the history of the couple and of the family.

The relationship between marriage and the Eucharist in this spousal approach can also be illustrated on each of the three levels of sacramentality: *sacramentum, res et sacramentum,* and *res.* First of all, the sign of the eucharistic celebration corresponds to the sign of the exchange between bridegroom

---

25. Baldanza, *La grazia del sacramento del matrimonio,* 285.

26. Martinez Peque, *Lo Spirito Santo e il matrimonio,* 174.

27. See John Paul II, Address to Members of the Movement "Teams of Our Lady," September 23, 1982.

28. See Balthasar, *Theo-Drama,* vol. 5: *The Last Act,* 476: "In the Christian dispensation, the connection between bodily (corporal) self-surrender, sacrifice and fruitfulness is revealed in the renunciation of marriage 'for the sake of the kingdom.'"

and bride. Moreover, just as the Presence effected by transubstantiation binds Christ's body to the eucharistic species to the point of substantial identity, the conjugal bond binds the spouses indissolubly in "one flesh." Finally, the grace of unity, looked at as communion in the body and blood of Christ, penetrates the spouses, healing, elevating, and perfecting their conjugal *communio personarum* after the model of Christ the Bridegroom and the Church-Bride. In these two intimately linked sacraments, the visibility of the sign is accompanied by the objectivity of the gift that founds, nourishes, and constantly renews the spouses' sanctity, lived as a grace of conjugal and familial communion.

The Eucharist and Marriage, the Intimately Linked Sources of Spousal and Missionary Charity

> As a representation of Christ's sacrifice of love for the Church, the Eucharist is a fountain of charity. In the eucharistic gift of charity the Christian family finds the foundation and soul of its "communion" and its "mission": by partaking in the eucharistic bread, the different members of the Christian family become one body, which reveals and shares in the wider unity of the Church. Their sharing in the Body of Christ that is "given up" and in his Blood that is "shed" becomes a never-ending source of missionary and apostolic dynamism for the Christian family. (*FC* 57)

The apostolic exhortation *Familiaris Consortio* rightly highlights the missionary dimension inhering in the bond between the Eucharist and marriage. By virtue of its participation in Christ's love for the Church, this bond exceeds its function of "healing, elevating, and perfecting" conjugal love. The grace flowing from the Eucharist intrinsically bears a missionary and eschatological dynamism that involves the couple in the Church's mission. The second paragraph of Vatican II's constitution on the sacred liturgy, *Sacrosanctum Concilium,* affirms that the liturgy supremely contributes to believers' ability to express in their life and manifest to others the mystery of Christ and the genuine nature of the true Church. This attribute of the liturgy, centered on the divine Sacrifice, is entrusted to the family. Baldanza comments, "The identity of the [family's] task has its theological roots in the fact that the liturgy, with the Eucharist at its center, and the sacrament of marriage are sacraments of the covenant, of ecclesial communion."[29]

29. Baldanza, *La grazia del sacramento del matrimonio,* 288-89.

"Communion" and "mission": these are the two, inseparable dimensions contained in the sacramental grace of marriage that flows from the eucharistic mystery. True to its fundamental concern, *Gaudium et Spes* situates these dimensions within the relationship between the Church and the world. Sacramental grace, nourished by the Eucharist, "shows to all both the living presence of Christ the Savior in the world and the genuine nature of the Church."[30] We will return later to this point in order to clarify the sense in which "the mission of the family" is a sacramental reality. First, however, we will pause for a moment to reflect on the problem of communion for the divorced and remarried.

Despite pressure from various cultures and theological opinions, the Holy See does not permit eucharistic communion to persons who have contracted a sacramental bond and then abandoned it to form another, non-sacramental bond. *Familiaris Consortio* recalls the theological reason behind this constant practice of the Church. While stressing that divorced persons should "not consider themselves as separated from the Church," the document affirms: "They [divorced and remarried persons] are unable to be admitted [to eucharistic communion] from the fact that their state and condition of life objectively contradict that union of love between Christ and the Church which is signified and effected by the Eucharist" (*FC* 84). A further pastoral reason is also given: If such persons "were admitted to the Eucharist, the faithful would be led into error and confusion regarding the Church's teaching about the indissolubility of marriage" (*FC* 84).

Underlying this constant discipline is the sacramental realism of the Catholic Church, which cannot overlook or obscure the intimate link between marriage and the Eucharist. As Balthasar writes, "This divine gift is offered to the world as meal and as marriage, mediating the life of the Trinity but also as a concrete, prototypical realization of earthly existence."[31] Balthasar stresses that the spousal and eucharistic relationship between Christ and the Church is not "some Idealist process hovering above" the world's conflicts; rather, it really descends to meet the most difficult human situations. Christ's gift exposes itself to all the conflicts and mistreatment that mark the destiny of the crucified Redeemer.

30. Baldanza, *La grazia del sacramento del matrimonio,* 289.
31. Balthasar, *Theo-Drama,* vol. 5: *The Last Act,* 478: "This eucharistic and spousal relationship between Christ and the Church . . . is not however, some Idealist process hovering above the abyss of this world and its resistance to God. It takes place in world-time, and so it must be seen in the deadly realism of world-time. The world, both inside and outside the Church, is always resisting being transformed into the Body of Christ."

The Church is aware of her duty to respond adequately, that is, nuptially, to the kenotic descent of Love. For her, it is not a matter of being more or less "merciful" with regard to persons in irregular situations, but of taking seriously the truth of the sacraments (the gifts of the Bridegroom) and their missionary dimension. Eucharistic communion is not only spiritual nourishment for an individual soul that has subjectively repented; within the life of the community, it is an objective sign that sacramentally expresses personal union with Christ, indeed, it is a witness to Christ in the world. Those who have divorced and remarried are in a situation that objectively contradicts the indissoluble ecclesial bond that they solemnly expressed before the community. They are unable to represent in the world the Church-Bride's unconditional "amen" to the gift of the Bridegroom in the Eucharist. Communion on the part of divorced and remarried persons would not be a genuine, personal, and ecclesial "amen" to Christ's Body and Blood, broken and shed for the salvation both of the spouses and of all mankind. While respecting the secret of conscience, the Church cannot allow sacramental communion in such cases because to do so would be — objectively — to allow a false communion that would contradict her fidelity to the Bridegroom's sacrifice.[32] Persons in irregular situations must be helped to realize that they are not excluded from the communion of the Church and to find other means of expressing their faith and their belonging to the community.

Holy Orders, Marriage, and the Sacrament of Penance

In the apostolic exhortation *Pastores Dabo Vobis,* John Paul II writes, "The priest is called to be the living image of Jesus Christ, the spouse of the Church. . . . Therefore, he is called to live out Christ's spousal love."[33] The spousal dimension of the ministerial priesthood has recently received a more explicit treatment prompted by the question of women's ordination. In *Mulieris Dignitatem,* we read: "It is *the Eucharist* above all that expresses *the redemptive act of Christ the Bridegroom towards the Church the Bride.* This is clear and unambiguous when the sacramental ministry of the Eucharist, in which the priest acts *'in persona Christi,'* is performed by a man" (*MD* 26).

32. The needed pastoral response consists, rather, in helping divorced and remarried persons to participate in the eucharistic celebration and to accept the suffering of being unable to receive communion as a form of limited "spiritual communion" marked precisely by the Lord's Cross.

33. *Pastores Dabo Vobis* 22. See also *Mulieris Dignitatem* 26.

What is interesting here is the importance given to the sacramental symbolism of man and woman in order to justify reserving the ministerial priesthood to men alone. Beyond the natural sign of masculinity, there is the sign of the initiative of the *divine* Bridegroom, which is translated into the face-to-face encounter between the masculine minister and the feminine Church. The Church-Bride responds to the minister of the Word and the sacraments by receiving the grace of her bond with the divine Bridegroom and allowing it to bear fruit in her. Since the minister is called to conform his whole life to the sacrificial and eucharistic gift of Christ the Bridegroom, there is a link between his sacramental ministry and his personal, spousal commitment, a link that underscores why these men are chosen from among those called to celibacy. All of this brings out more clearly the sacramental logic of a living, and not merely ritual, representation of the Bridegroom. The essential motivation for priestly celibacy, as distinct from consecrated virginity, is not so much the *"sequela Christi"* in the subjective sense as it is an objective belonging to the ministry of the covenant, which the priest receives in ordination, demonstrates in his life, and celebrates in the sacraments.

The connection between holy orders and marriage thus receives a new property that distinguishes it from the connection between marriage and virginity. While marriage and virginity have their complementarity as two ways of incarnating Christ's spousal love for the Church, marriage and the priesthood meet in the objectivity of the sacramental life as the two dimensions — the horizontal and the vertical, respectively — of the covenant. The priest serves as minister for the vertical gift that descends from God to fructify the spouses' covenant by means of Christ's love for the Church. Thanks to the priest's eucharistic ministry, the spouses can offer themselves to the Father in and with Christ, who gathers and enfolds them in his spousal love for the Church. The priest represents the gift of the Bridegroom both personally and sacramentally, whereas consecrated virginity and indissoluble marriage incarnate the Church-Bride's response to this gift. Thus connected by means of the priestly ministry, marriage and virginity sustain and confirm each other as the two paths of holiness that they are. In both cases, the total gift and offering of oneself, body and soul, in response to the love of Christ the Bridegroom creates a genuine ecclesial "state of life" founded on a definitive supernatural bond.[34]

Moreover, marriage and the ministerial priesthood meet and correspond

---

34. H. U. von Balthasar, *The Christian State of Life*, trans. Mary Frances McCarthy (San Francisco: Ignatius, 1983), 238ff.

in the objective, sacramental communication of the trinitarian life.[35] The sacrament of marriage expresses the reciprocal fruitfulness of the divine Persons who are present in the couple created in God's image and likeness; the sacrament of holy orders, on the other hand, gives particular expression to the gift, in Christ, of the Father, who is the origin of the entire mystery of communion in the order of nature as in the order of grace. "In the beautiful expression of St. Ignatius of Antioch, the bishop is *typos tou Patros,* he is like the living image of God the Father."[36] In representing Christ, the Head and Bridegroom, then, the episcopal and presbyteral ministry supplies the nourishment of the Word and the Bread of life that ultimately descends from the Father.

Christ has also provided a specific help for a human love affected and wounded by sin and its consequences: concupiscence, egotism, and division. Through absolution, Christ extends to the spouses the grace of repentance and reconciliation, thus renewing both the grace of their baptism and its concretization in conjugal life. The sacramental grace of reconciliation certainly includes among its effects the healing of the spouses' love, a healing that augments the couple's fruitfulness and so prepares them to share more profoundly in the trinitarian *communio personarum* given to them in eucharistic communion. The anointing of the sick also has the indirect effect of preparing for viaticum, but its specific nuptial end consists in uniting the couple's suffering of illness to Christ's paschal mystery. The fruit of this sacrament is an increase in the spiritual fruitfulness of the marriage. In fact, by facing terminal illness and accepting death the couple and the family are introduced into the infinite fruitfulness of the Lord's Cross and death.

Conclusion

The Church's entire sacramental structure expresses the joint fruitfulness of Christ the Bridegroom and the Church-Bride. Today, it is the community

---

35. Hence St. Thomas Aquinas's well-known comparison between the two sacraments: "It is, then, also like this in the spiritual life. For some propagate and conserve the spiritual life in a spiritual ministry duly, and this belongs to the sacrament of orders; and some belong to the bodily and spiritual life simultaneously, which takes place in the sacrament of matrimony where a man and woman come together to beget offspring and to rear them in divine worship" (*Summa Contra Gentiles,* Book 4, chap. 58).

36. *Catechism of the Catholic Church,* no. 1549; St. Ignatius of Antioch, *To the Trallians* 3.1; *To the Magnesians* 6.1. See M. Ouellet, "Des prêtres pour une Église-communion," *L'Église de Montréal* 25 (June 23, 1993): 643-50.

of the family that must channel this organic, spousal sacramentality into an anthropological and cultural renewal capable of generating a "civilization of love." If, in the past, the Church's sacramentality was expressed above all in the great religious orders and their apostolic and cultural activities, today the "community" that bears the torch of sacramentality is the family. As John Paul II often affirmed, "the family is the way of the Church." Today more than ever, the grace of the Redeemer must touch man in his basic human and familial relationships, so that the family, a "saved community," can become a "saving community" in turn (see *FC* 49).

CHAPTER 8

The Sacramentality of the Domestic Church

In order to consolidate the ground we have covered so far, we must complete our exploration of sacramentality with an explicit account of the family as domestic church. Vatican II's important statements on the subject inaugurated a discussion that has since produced an abundance of literature.[1] We will presuppose the scriptural and patristic testimony concerning the domestic church,[2] in order to focus instead on the theological foundations of the family's nature as a "church." Do the Magisterial and theological claims concerning the family's ecclesial character rest on a real theological foundation, or are we dealing merely with generous pastoral rhetoric lacking any sufficient conceptual basis?[3]

In order to justify this newly influential approach to the theology of the family, we propose two things: first, a systematic reflection designed to facilitate a better grasp of the ecclesial character of the sacramental couple; second, an approach to understanding ecclesial being as missionary existence in light of Balthasar's category of "theological person." This sketch should suffice to

---

1. See *Lumen Gentium* 11 and *Apostolicam Actuositatem* 11; M. Fahey, "La famille chrétienne, Église domestique à Vatican II," *Concilium* 260 (1995): 115-23; D. Tettamanzi, "La famiglia cristiana 'veluti ecclesia domestica'' nell'esortazione apostolica *Familiaris Consortio*," *La Scuola Cattolica* 111 (1983): 107-52; Tettamanzi, *La Famiglia via della Chiesa*, 2nd ed. (Milan: Massimo, 1991).

2. See O. Michel, "*Oikos, oikia*," in *Grande Lessico del Nuovo Testamento*, vol. 8 (Brescia: Paideia, 1965-1992), 337-449; D. Sartore, "La famiglia, Chiesa domestica," *Lateranum* 45 (1979): 282-303; D. Tettamanzi, "Il matrimonio e la famiglia nei Padri della Chiesa," *La Famiglia*, six articles from 1970 to 1973; S. Botero, *Per una teologia della famiglia* (Rome: Borla, 1992).

3. See G. Colombo, "La teologia della famiglia," in *Teologia sacramentaria* (Milan: Glossa, 1997), 547ff.

dispel the impression that talk of the family as "domestic church" lacks a sufficient conceptual foundation.

The Ecclesial Character of the Sacramental Couple

The latest turn in our argument so far was to highlight the paradigmatic value of the sacrament of marriage. Marriage, we have said, is not only the "most ancient sacrament," but also (in its intrinsic relation with the Eucharist) the hermeneutical key to the entire sacramental order of the New Covenant. We based our claim concerning this dimension of sacramental marriage on baptism and confirmation, which establish the Christian's radical belonging to Christ and the Church. The sacrament of marriage adds a special consecration, called the "conjugal bond," which is not only a grace that heals or perfects the couple's love, but a new ecclesial reality, an objective pneumatological bond that introduces the couple into the organic structure of the Church's sacramental being. We will return to this point below, after we have recalled a few elements pertaining to the development of the theology of the family.

The apostolic exhortation *Familiaris Consortio* contains numerous references to the "domestic church," and we can consider this frequent mention of the theme as an important step in the development of doctrine. The relevant texts can be grouped into three categories. The first includes paragraphs 21, 38, 48, and 49, which enumerate the bases that ground a discussion of the family as domestic church: through the Word, the sacraments, and the family's own unity, the family is an actualization of ecclesial communion. Paragraphs 51-54 refer to the task of evangelization, which is based on the family's participation in the Church's evangelizing mission. Finally, paragraphs 55, 59, and 61 refer to the life of the family as a domestic sanctuary where prayer and worship are offered to God. In these three categories we find a reflection, or better: an incarnation, of the chief characteristics of the Church — communion, mission, and worship — on the level of the family. As these brief indications already suggest, the family is not merely a place where the Church's pastoral work is to be "applied," but an authentic manifestation of the Church itself.

Following John Paul II, several theologians have stressed that the family is not only an "image of the Church" but an "ecclesial reality."[4] The conjugal and familial community "not only make the Church present and active, but

---

4. See A. Peelmann, "La famille comme réalité ecclésiale," *Église et Théologie* 12 (1981): 95-114.

constitute the Church herself: a 'miniature church,' of course, but a real church, a 'domestic church,' in a proper and specific sense."[5] A representative of the Eastern tradition, Paul Evdokimov, insists vigorously on this central thesis: "[The family] is not only *like* the Church; as a reality of grace, the community of the spouses is an organic part of the ecclesial community: *it is the Church.*"[6] This conviction is based on Ephesians 5:21ff., which clearly establishes the baptized spouses' participation in Christ's spousal love for the Church. It is also based on the analogy of the *communio personarum* between the Trinity and the family. As we have already noted, man created in the image of God as a "dual unity," and even as a "fruitful couple," reflects and makes present the communion and distinction of the divine Persons:

> Since it has become an "icon" in the order of the new creation through the salvific intervention of the Father and of the Son in the Spirit, the couple proclaims that the loving communion of two of the baptized is a revelation and a fruitful realization of the eternal communion of the Father and the Son in the Spirit.[7]

This participation in the communion of the Trinity is without a doubt the ultimate foundation of the family understood as an ecclesial reality. Evdokimov emphasizes the Christological and pneumatological foundation of the domestic church: "The icon of the wedding at Cana represents the wedding of the Church and of each soul with the divine Bridegroom. By virtue of the sacrament of marriage, *each couple marries Christ.* Thus in loving one another, the spouses love Christ."[8]

Evdokimov adds that, as the gift of Pentecost, the Spirit seals the "we" of the spouses and the family in a real and not merely symbolic way. *Familiaris Consortio* echoes this observation in different terms: "The Holy Spirit who is poured out in the sacramental celebration offers Christian couples the gift of a new communion of love that is the living and real image of that unique unity which makes of the Church the indivisible Mystical Body of the Lord Jesus" (*FC* 19).

Our present task, however, is to investigate the ultimate *anthropological* foundation of the ecclesial status of the couple and the family. We have dis-

---

5. L. Gendron, "Le foyer chrétien, une Église veritable?" *Revue catholique internationale Communio* 11, no. 6 (1986): 77.

6. P. Evdokimov, "Ecclesia Domestica," *L'Anneau d'Or* 107 (1962): 357.

7. Gendron, "Le foyer chrétien, une Église veritable?" 77.

8. Evdokimov, "Ecclesia Domestica," 358.

cussed baptism and the sacrament of marriage, as well as the grace of trinitarian communion in Christ and in the Holy Spirit. Turning to anthropology, the notion of the *imago Dei* as an *imago Trinitatis* certainly offers a starting point for our task, but further clarification is needed to identify the anthropological principle that unifies the being and the mission of the domestic church.[9] We can formulate the question as follows: How do we understand the sacramental couple's intrinsic and intimate belonging to the Church's communion and mission? Is the *mission* of the Christian family an extrinsic addition to its *being,* understood as communion, or does this mission consist precisely in the communional identity of the persons? Hans Urs von Balthasar proposes a notion of person that allows us the better to integrate the family's personal being and its being-communion within the Church's sacramentality:

> It is when God addresses a conscious subject, tells him who he is and what he means to the eternal God of truth and shows him the purpose of his existence — that is, imparts a distinctive and divinely authorized mission — that we can say of a conscious subject that he is a "person."[10]

Balthasar establishes a distinction between the "spiritual subject," which corresponds to what classical theology calls "person," and the "theological person," which refers to the same subject inasmuch as he has been enriched by a supernatural mission that he receives from the Word of God: " 'Person' is the 'new name' by which God addresses me (Rev 2:17) and which comes from 'the beginning of God's creation' (Rev 3:14); it always implies a task, namely, to be 'a pillar in the temple of my God' (Rev 3:12)."[11]

Christ is the archetype of the event by which the divine Word personalizes a human subject. The man Jesus is so completely assumed into the Person of the incarnate Word that, in this archetypal case, Person and Mission coincide. Christ is the One Sent by the Father to reconcile the world with God. In him, there is an ontological identity between Person and mission, founded on the a priori reality of the hypostatic union. For all other subjects, on the

9. See Botero, *Per una teologia della famiglia,* 36-67; P. Coda, "Familia y Trinidad. Reflexion teologica," in Aa.Vv., *Misterio trinitario y familia humana,* Semanas de estudios trinitarios 29 (Salamanca: Secretariado Trinitario, 1995), 195-227.

10. H. U. von Balthasar, *Theo-Drama,* vol. 3: *Dramatis Personae: Persons in Christ,* trans. Graham Harrison (San Francisco: Ignatius, 1992), 207.

11. Balthasar, *Theo-Drama,* vol. 3: *Dramatis Personae: Persons in Christ,* 208. See also M. Ouellet, "The Foundations of Christian Ethics According to Hans Urs von Balthasar," *Communio: International Catholic Review* 17 (Fall 1990): 375-401.

other hand, the relation between person and mission is a posteriori, since it is based on the divine call and on the subject's time-bound response to the mission that makes him a "person in Christ." Consequently, human persons find their theological identity "in Christ," that is, in a progressive and dramatic identification with the word-mission that defines their role in Christ's body.

This radically Christocentric understanding of person entails a corresponding ecclesial dimension. All participation in Christ's universal mission simultaneously involves a relation to the ecclesial community: "When a human being becomes a person, theologically, by being given a unique vocation and mission, he is simultaneously de-privatized, socialized, made into a locus and bearer of community."[12]

In this way, person and community ground each other without confusion or separation. As realities consisting in the integration of freedom and grace, person and community overlap and coincide. They are not constituted independently from each other; rather, they form together the *"communio sanctorum"* that is born from communion in the eucharistic body of Christ. Balthasar develops a phenomenology of persons-as-mission converging to form ecclesial communion in the image and likeness of the trinitarian circumincession.[13]

This Christocentric and ecclesial vision of the person makes for a deeper connection between an ecclesiology of communion, on the one hand, and its application to the domestic church, on the other. First of all, it allows us to express in anthropological terms the essentially missionary nature of the Church and of the family. By affirming that the person's profound identity is found "in Christ," Balthasar defines the person through his belonging to Christ, that is, through his membership in the body of Christ that is the Church. Moreover, by grounding the relation to Christ in the mission-charism to be carried out

---

12. Balthasar, *Theo-Drama*, vol. 3: *Dramatis Personae: Persons in Christ*, 271. In the context of his dramatic Mariology, Balthasar adds: "In this way there is a mutual interpenetration of the diverse missions and the persons who identify themselves with them: this is what is meant by the *communio sanctorum*. Evidently it is not only the goods and values of these persons that become common property but the persons themselves. There is an analogy here with the way Christ (and, through him, the whole triune God) becomes the 'common property' of those who share his flesh and blood and his Holy Spirit: not simply in what he *has* (his 'merits,' for instance) but in what he *is* — if we can still use words like 'property' in the realm of selflessness" (349-50).

13. We cannot present here the rich symbolic ecclesiology Balthasar develops on the basis of his theological concept of person, but refer the reader instead to his works "Who Is the Church?", in *Explorations in Theology*, vol. 2: *Spouse of the Word* (San Francisco: Ignatius, 1991), 143-91; and *The Office of Peter and the Structure of the Church*, trans. Andrée Emery (San Francisco: Ignatius, 2007), Part 2.

in the Spirit, Balthasar radically integrates the person into the community. We can therefore say not only that the person has an ecclesial dimension, but that the person is defined by an *ecclesial character.* In the context of the Eucharist, Balthasar goes so far as to say that

> the sacraments, primarily baptism into his death and Resurrection (Rom 6:3-11) and the Eucharist, which is a sharing in the one body of Christ, making us into one Body (1 Cor 10:16f.), not only give us personhood: they also fashion us into a community. Everyone who participates in the pneumatic body of Christ, shared out in the Church, not only becomes a member of the Church community: he actually acquires an intrinsically ecclesial quality.[14]

The ecclesial and missionary character, then, is not merely a dimension or quality added to a person from the outside. To the contrary, it forms the person's very identity. Conversely, persons in communion by virtue of their mission form the very identity of the Church. From this point on, it becomes theologically meaningful to attribute an ecclesial character to the family and to the family's participation in the Church's mission. The dramatic identification of person and mission lays the anthropological foundation introducing the ecclesial and missionary character of the Church into the heart of the family. By the same token, we can discard the position that sees mission as an exterior addition to the reality of the family. In the very act of a "sincere gift of self" (*Letter to Families* 11) in faith and love, the members of the community of the family and the Church actualize themselves as persons at the same time as they actualize their ecclesial mission-communion. "Theological" or "ecclesial" persons thus demonstrate their essentially relational and missionary nature. They also confirm the likeness of created persons to the uncreated Persons, as well as to the trinitarian missions that sustain both the Church-communion as *"Ecclesia de Trinitate"* and the Christian family as *"Ecclesia domestica."*[15]

14. Balthasar, *Theo-Drama,* vol. 3: *Dramatis Personae: Persons in Christ,* 281.

15. Without entering into detail, we stress that Balthasar's concept of "theological person" does not exclude those who are not visibly members of the Church. See *Theo-Drama,* vol. 3: *Dramatis Personae: Persons in Christ,* 282: "True, the New Testament does use the words 'election,' 'vocation' and 'mission' for those who are called to be ordinary members of the visible Church and those chosen for a special task within her. But the range of Jesus' eschatological work is such that he can operate directly, outside the Church; he may give grace to individual persons, and perhaps to groups, enabling them to act according to his mind; the Church must allow for this possibility."

The Family's Ecclesial Mission in Being and in Action

In the third part of *Familiaris Consortio* (17), John Paul II exhorts, "Family, become what you are!":

> And since in God's plan it has been established as an "intimate community of life and love," the family has the mission to become more and more what it is, that is to say, a community of life and love, in an effort that will find fulfillment, as will everything created and redeemed, in the Kingdom of God. (*FC* 17)

Immediately after this passage, the Holy Father proposes a way to integrate the family's manifold tasks on the basis of the love that is its essence and root:

> Looking at it in such a way as to reach its very roots, we must say that the essence and role of the family are in the final analysis specified by love. Hence the family has the mission to guard, reveal and communicate love, and this is a living reflection of and a real sharing in God's love for humanity and the love of Christ the Lord for the Church His bride. (*FC* 17)

Mission, Love, Communion

The perspective introduced in the preceding section allows us to systematize John Paul II's approach, which sees love as the foundation of the family's being and becoming, as the basis of the domestic church. The dramatic relation between person and mission, grounded in Christology and ecclesiology, points to the identification of person and love not only in a "personalistic and subjective" but also in an "ecclesial and objective" sense. The spouses actualize themselves as persons in giving themselves to the ecclesial mission entrusted to them. This mission of the domestic church is rooted above all in the act of sacramental marriage that constitutes it *(matrimonio in fieri)* — that is, in the "human act whereby spouses mutually bestow and accept each other" (*GS* 48). This reciprocal giving and receiving, which constitutes the "community of life and love" *(matrimonio in facto esse,* or the permanent sacrament), is an act of love founded on faith (between baptized persons). This act transcends the psychological dimension of feelings, sinking its roots in the spouses' will to belong to Christ in the mode of mutual conjugal self-gift. The spouses' mission "to guard, reveal, and communicate love" would have no foundation if the act constituting their community of life and love were not itself an act of love accomplished in faith and sealed by God himself.

The ecclesial character of this mutual self-gift "in Christ" is not based primarily on the sincerity of the fiancés' subjective love, but on the ecclesial faith that envelops the objective gift of their persons and culminates in the gift of the Holy Spirit (1 Cor. 7:7). This personal and objective offering "in the Lord" becomes the starting point for their conjugal mission in the dimension of being, inasmuch as their reciprocal gift founds an indissoluble conjugal bond (*res et sacramentum,* or conjugal charism). The spouses' first missionary act is thus their initial gift, which establishes the conjugal community, that is, the fact of their being bound to each other in faith. They are chosen and sent to be one flesh in Christ, and they are consecrated for this mission through the sacrament. The sacrament that comes into being through their exchange of consent confers on their bond of human love its properly ecclesial value and essentially missionary nature.[16]

The mission of the domestic church in the dimension of being and acting is based on the objectivity of the supernatural gift of Christ, who, through a charism (1 Cor. 7:7) and sacramental grace, assumes, heals, and perfects the couples' subjective and objective love. Despite the weight of an inherited juridicism whose influence is still perceptible in the conciliar texts, it is time to move beyond the essentialist exclusion of love from the constitution of sacramental marriage.[17] Such essentialism fails to take adequate account of the

16. This perspective takes up Augustine's and Aquinas's insight that the supernatural good of the sacrament surpasses its other goods, i.e., fidelity and children: "This or that may be more important to a thing in two ways, either because it is more essential or because it is more excellent. If the reason is because it is more excellent, then 'sacrament' is in every way the most important of the three marriage goods, since it belongs to marriage considered as a sacrament of grace; while the other two belong to it as an office of nature; and a perfection of grace is more excellent than a perfection of nature" (St. Thomas Aquinas, *Supplementum* q. 49 a. 3). The good of the sacrament is the "community of life and love" founded on the indissoluble conjugal bond that makes the unity of Christ and the Church visible in the "sacrament of the couple" (C. Rochetta).

17. See U. Navarrete, "Consenso matrimoniale e amore coniugale con particolare riferimento alla Cost. *Gaudium et Spes,*" in *Annali di dottrina e giurisprudenza canonica* (Vatican City: Libreria Editrice Vaticana, 1971), 203-14. Assuming an account of love as "habitus, a psychological phenomenon not subject to the direct control of the will," the author concludes that "love has no juridical relevance to the essential structure of marriage. It is a non-juridical element with respect to the conjugal bond" (214). While this position makes sense within a purely juridical framework, it becomes untenable, it seems to me, when seen from a theolog-

fact that the spouses' act of will has its concrete locus in faith. Faith informs the spouses' reciprocal gift and welcome, giving their exchange of consent the objectivity of a ministerial act of love in the name of Christ and the Church. Of course, some juridically valid marriages are barren of love experienced on an anthropological or psychological level, but this lack cannot be a norm authorizing the exclusion of love from the sacramental act that constitutes marriage. Apart from presupposing a reductive vision of love, this conception also ignores the objective gift of the Holy Spirit, who enters into the theological or ecclesial constitution of the conjugal bond.

Moving beyond this position requires a new theological approach to human love in light of an "adequate" trinitarian anthropology. Klaus Hemmerle and Hans Urs von Balthasar provide us with a set of conceptual tools for renewing the foundation of sacramental marriage that is based on the objectivity of human love. According to Balthasar, "This objective element that even inspires their common love can be called (it makes no difference) either the spirit of the loving covenant or the covenant itself as the institution transcending them both."[18] Balthasar explains that the vow of love, a mutual self-emptying in donation to the other, already bears in itself a third that transcends the subjectivity of the two spouses:

> The personal and free character of this objective *tertium quid* will, once more, be demonstrated by the possible bodily fruit of the union, the child, who is more than the sum of its parents' marriage but is the unforeseen product of their transcendental hope.[19]

In light of the intimate bond between person and mission, person and love, we understand better *Familiaris Consortio*'s insistence on love as the fundamental mission of the family:

> With love as its point of departure and making constant reference to it, the recent Synod emphasized four general tasks for the family: 1) forming a

---

ical and sacramental perspective. We cannot define the theological essence of the marriage-sacrament on the basis of the juridical minimum required for validity.

18. H. U. von Balthasar, *Explorations in Theology*, vol. 4: *Spirit and Institution*, trans. Edward T. Oakes (San Francisco: Ignatius, 1995), 219.

19. Balthasar, *Explorations in Theology*, vol. 4: *Spirit and Institution*, 222. See K. Hemmerle, "Matrimonio e famiglia in una antropologia trinitaria," *Nuova Umanità* 6, no. 31 (1984): 3-31.

community of persons; 2) serving life; 3) participating in the development of society; 4) sharing in the life and mission of the Church. (*FC* 17)

All the particular missions of the family are summed up in one fundamental mission: love. Of course, the love in question here is not limited to human sentiment and emotions, or even to the evolution of interpersonal relationships between the spouses and their children. These subjective dimensions of love are taken up into the mystery of the covenant, that is, into the love between Christ and the Church. The couple and the family, then, offer Christ and the Church a locus of sacramental incarnation, growth, and missionary service vis-à-vis a world waiting for the revelation of the children of God. In fact, the love at play in conjugal and family relationships is Christ's supernatural love for the Church; this love is entrusted to the couple and to the family to be lived, celebrated, served, and transmitted to new generations. As we read in *Familiaris Consortio:* "The Holy Spirit, who is poured forth in the celebration of the sacraments, is the living source and inexhaustible sustenance of the supernatural communion that gathers believers and links them with Christ and with each other in the unity of the Church of God" (*FC* 21).

The priority given to the formation of a community of persons among the tasks of the domestic church indicates a certain priority of being and love over the various activities that can flow from the charism and grace of marriage (procreation, education, apostolate, etc.). The family's mission consists above all in developing and cultivating the communion given in the sacrament, ensuring its expression in a life of fidelity to the Spirit of Love.[20] Each of the "natural" finalities (procreation, mutual help, etc.) is taken up into the sacramental mission that unites all the dimensions of marriage and the family in faith. The many tasks we have just mentioned ultimately proceed from the Holy Spirit, who unites the spouses in his characteristic manner, i.e., through their fruitful mutual belonging in one flesh. From this flows the demand for conjugal and familial holiness. And this sanctity means life in the Spirit who shapes their entire common life and each of their relationships, inside and outside the family, configuring them to Christ the Bridegroom, Son, and Brother.

The key to a deeper understanding of the sacramental fruitfulness of Christian marriage has already been discussed earlier in this chapter: it lies precisely in the ecclesial character both of the spouses' persons and of the couple. Through the total gift of their persons — a gift sealed by the Spirit bestowed in

---

20. For further development of this theme, see C. Rochetta, *Il sacramento della coppia* (Bologna: EDB, 1996), 255-74.

the sacramental celebration — the couple is constituted as a domestic church, becomes a dwelling place of the Holy Spirit, and is rooted in the unity of the Trinity. The point is not simply that a couple is blessed and called to holiness in a manner specific to marriage; rather, their very identity as a couple is ecclesial, inasmuch as their relationship becomes a sacrament of the objective sacramental relationship between Christ the Bridegroom and the Church-Bride. The love between Christ and the Church is poured out into the man-woman relationship and culminates in a shared fruitfulness for the enrichment of both. The Church's fruitfulness is prolonged in the family, while the family's spiritual and human fruitfulness makes the Church to grow both quantitatively and qualitatively. The mission of the domestic church is not limited to a morally "meritorious" mission following upon the spouses' solemn commitment. It consists above all in the dynamic and organic unfolding of a sacramental communion set within the objective structure of the Church. Vatican Council II reminded us that spouses have a proper "charism" amongst the people of God. This objective charism is above all the Christian conjugal bond that consecrates spouses to form a "community of life and love." This community performs a service on behalf of life and society, a mission of education and evangelization, and even an ecclesial ministry that variously incarnates the fundamental service offered by the couple to the love of Christ and the Church.

In this perspective, the mission of the domestic church comes down to this: tending toward holiness in all relationships *ad intra* and *ad extra*. What the spouses and their children accomplish on the level of action is simply an unfolding of their quality as domestic church. Because they belong to Christ and to the Church, the couple and the family seek to live their relationships in availability to Christ, the Head and Bridegroom. It is ultimately he who chooses the measure of the simultaneously supernatural and natural fruitfulness granted to the couple. It is not the couple's task to determine what the particular mission of their family should be. In an authentically Marian attitude, they allow Christ to determine their relationship with him, their relationship to one another in him, and their relationship as parents to the spiritual and bodily children they receive from the Creator Spirit, the Sanctifier.

The Model of the Holy Family, the Original Domestic Church

In the apostolic exhortation *Redemptoris Custos* (n. 7), John Paul II argues that the Holy Family is more than a model; it is the *original* domestic church. Mary and Joseph had a genuine marriage open to family that they lived out according to the law of Moses. St. Augustine defended the authentically human character of their marriage, which, though virginal, lacked none of the elements necessary for the full reality of marriage: "In Christ's parents all the goods of marriage were realized — offspring, fidelity, the sacrament: the offspring being the Lord Jesus himself; fidelity, since there was no adultery; the sacrament, since there was no divorce."[21]

Mary and Joseph said "yes" to God in faith, entrusting themselves totally to him in order to serve his will. God blessed their mutual consent beyond any possible expectation. Mary's initial "yes" to the marriage was supremely elevated by the grace of the Annunciation, which defined her maternal mission with respect to the Son of God. Joseph's "yes" to marriage was marked by that of Mary, to which he had to adapt his plans and responsibilities. Both of them consented before God to the mystery of their marital vocation, but Joseph gave his consent in dependence on Mary, welcoming God's plan for her and for their family. In this way, Joseph consented to the grace of a virginal relationship. While he had to renounce his physical fruitfulness, he was strengthened in his paternity and so enabled to carry out the mission of foster-father to Jesus.[22]

It is fairly easy to imagine how this marriage enriched Mary and Joseph as persons, who were united not only by bonds of human affection and obedience to the Mosaic law, but above all by the gift of the incarnate Word. God chose them in order to give them his only-begotten Son made flesh, so that they could give him to the world. In the daily life of their family, Mary and Joseph were taken up into Jesus' divine-human relationship with his heavenly Father: "Through the mystery of the Incarnation, Jesus, the Man-God, united in himself forever the divine Trinity with the earthly trinity."[23] In the simplest experiences of work, prayer, and conversation, Mary and Joseph were united to the Word of God made man, whom they helped to educate through the grace of a virginal fatherhood and motherhood.

The divine favor enjoyed by the Holy Family was not experienced as a privilege, but as a mission of service for the salvation of the world. It is important to stress, with John Paul II, the sacramental dimension of the relationships among the members of the Holy Family. God's self-gift to humanity in Jesus

21. St. Augustine, *De nuptiis et concupiscentia* 1.11.13 (*PL* 44.421).
22. See A. von Speyr, *Handmaid of the Lord,* trans. E. A. Nelson (San Francisco: Ignatius, 1985), chap. 7: "Mary and Joseph."
23. T. Stramare, "Formulazione di una teologia attuale della santa Famiglia," in Aa.Vv., *La Santa Famiglia nei primi XVI secoli della Chiesa. Atti del I Congresso sulla Sacra Famiglia* (Barcelona, 1994), 537.

Christ was accomplished through the authentic maternal mediation of Mary and the genuine paternal mediation of Joseph. Since the maternal mediation is more obvious, let us pause for a moment on Joseph's fatherhood:

> Inserted directly in the mystery of the Incarnation, the Family of Nazareth has its own special mystery. And in this mystery, as in the Incarnation, one finds a true fatherhood: the human form of the family of the Son of God, a true human family, formed by the divine mystery. In this family, Joseph is the father: his fatherhood is not one that derives from begetting offspring; but neither is it an "apparent" or merely "substitute" fatherhood. Rather, it is one that fully shares in authentic human fatherhood and the mission of a father in the family.[24]

John Paul II sees in this a consequence of the hypostatic union: in taking on Jesus' humanity, the Word of God also takes on his constitutive relationships, which include his relationship with his mother and, on a lower level to be sure, his relationship with his foster-father. Hence,

> together with human nature, all that is human, and especially the family — as the first dimension of man's existence in the world — is also taken up in Christ. Within this context, Joseph's human fatherhood was also "taken up" in the mystery of Christ's Incarnation. On the basis of this principle, the words which Mary spoke to the twelve-year-old Jesus in the Temple take on their full significance: "Your father and I . . . have been looking for you."[25]

We must stress Joseph's singular relation to the heavenly Father, who chose him to give a fatherly face to the human growth of his incarnate Son: "Joseph is the man with whom, in a certain sense, God the Father shared his fatherhood."[26] Between the heavenly Father and the earthly father, there was a kind of "covenant in fatherhood, in which Joseph played a role more important than that of Abraham."[27] Joseph's intimate relationship with the heavenly Father can be understood as a "model" or a "role," but in the homilies just cited, John Paul II uses the language of "covenant" and "participation" to describe it.

24. John Paul II, Apostolic Exhortation *Redemptoris Custos* 21.
25. John Paul II, *Redemptoris Custos* 21.
26. John Paul II, Homily, October 9, 1994.
27. John Paul II, Homily, March 19, 1984.

The heavenly Father gave the child Jesus to the Holy Family of Nazareth, a first step in the gift of his Son to the Church and to all mankind. He continues to give this Child to Christian families, above all through the sacrament of baptism, which generates his Son in the members of Christ's Body. Jesus thus lives in them and asks the father and mother of the family to help him grow until he reaches the full stature of the perfect man (see Eph. 4:13). The reality experienced by Joseph and Mary continues in the family, the domestic church. The daily interactions of parents with their children contain a "great mystery": the mystery of a spiritual fatherhood and motherhood with regard to their children, whom they receive from the Father as brothers and sisters of the only-begotten Son. In each of them, the heavenly Father sees his own Son and asks the parents to give a human, sacramental face to his love for the Son who lives in them. The children, for their part, sense in the fully human love of their father and mother the beating of the eternal Father's heart. In this way, they discover the mystery of the Son who is growing in them, and they learn to recognize the "gift of God" in the sacramental heart of their father and mother.[28]

The Domestic Church, Sacramentum Trinitatis *and Symbol of the Civilization of Love*

We are now close to a provisional conclusion of our reflection on the theology of marriage in its relation to the sacramentality of the Church. The spousal approach we have adopted leads naturally to the theme of the domestic church as a *sacramentum Trinitatis.* This move involves more than stressing the similarity between the trinitarian relations and the relations in the family; it also involves highlighting *the covenant between them,* that is, the sacramentality of family relationships with respect to the relations of the Trinity. An ecclesiology of the Holy Family has already shown us a way to the mystery of the heavenly Trinity through the mystery of the "earthly trinity" of Jesus, Mary, and Joseph, which already contains the incarnate Son. Moreover, the more developed understanding of the trinitarian bond of the Holy Spirit, who seals the nuptial bond between the spouses; the Christological and ecclesiological notion of person; and the anthropology of the *imago Trinitatis* are all elements of a systematic nuptial theology aimed at a deeper understanding of the sacramentality of the family with respect to the trinitarian mystery.

28. See M. Ouellet, *Divine Likeness: Toward a Trinitarian Anthropology of the Family* (Grand Rapids: Eerdmans, 2006), chap. 6: "Fathers and Mothers . . . as Your Heavenly Father."

As Klaus Hemmerle observes, "Phenomenology unveils the vocabulary of human existence, and theology reveals this existence to be trinitarian. But only active communion with the life of the triune God that is opened to us makes both him and ourselves 'eloquent in our life.'"[29] The life of the Trinity is the space into which we are introduced through baptism. Through the sacramental experience of conjugal and familial love, spouses exercise a proper participation in this mystery of unity and fruitfulness: "Through our being one as the Father and the Son are one, the world must come to faith (cf. John 17:21-23). This vocation of the *Ecclesia* is also the vocation of the 'miniature *Ecclesia*' that is the family."[30]

The domestic church accomplishes its sacramental mission by mediating Christ's love for the Church, which is to say, the Trinity's love for the world. The "material" for this mediation is the multiplicity of everyday relations that make up a family's common life, its communication, education, and service to society. The "form" of this mediation, on the other hand, is spousal, paternal, maternal, filial, and fraternal love, inasmuch as this love incarnates through words, gestures, attitudes, and sentiments the Christic form of Love. The most intimate and most exalted content of this mediation is the communion of the Trinity, given to the couple and the family through the outpouring of the Holy Spirit in the sacramental celebration of marriage (*FC* 19) and renewed in each Eucharist. If sin does not exclude the Holy Spirit from their communion, the persons and all their conjugal, parental, and familial relationships become the dwelling place of the trinitarian love in which they participate — and this love makes them fruitful. Paul VI offered a magnificent commentary on this truth:

> Through parents who love their child, in whom Christ lives, emerges the love of the Father, which is poured out over his beloved Son (cf. John 14:7-11). Through their authority, his authority is exercised; through their dedication, his Providence is revealed, as that of the Father from whom all fatherhood in heaven and on earth takes its name (Eph. 3:14-15).[31]

This insight opens the way to a deeper understanding of the participation of the spouses and the family in the Church's saving mission:

29. Hemmerle, "Matrimonio e famiglia in una antropologia trinitaria," 31.

30. Hemmerle, "Matrimonio e famiglia in una antropologia trinitaria," 30-31.

31. Paul VI, "Address to the Teams of Our Lady," *La Documentation catholique* 67, no. 1564 (1970): 504. *Familiaris Consortio* 25 takes up the same idea: "In revealing and in reliving on earth the very fatherhood of God, a man is called upon to ensure the harmonious and united development of all the members of the family."

For this reason they not only receive the love of Christ and become a saved community, but they are also called upon to communicate Christ's love to their brethren, thus becoming a saving community. In this way, while the Christian family is a fruit and sign of the supernatural fecundity of the Church, it stands also as a symbol, witness and participant of the Church's motherhood. (*FC* 49)[32]

The domestic church appears, then, as a sign and instrument of the unity of the human race with God. Just as the divine missions of Christ and the Holy Spirit extend through salvation history by means of the Church's sacraments, these missions are prolonged in the dual unity of the spouses and in the unity of the family, in which they find a privileged place of sacramental expression. When these divine missions are welcomed, lived in holiness, and transmitted to others, then the family becomes a fruitful and attractive "church in miniature." This is why the central reality of marriage is, and must increasingly become, the sacrament, i.e. the "sign" of, and "service" to, Christ's Love for the Church. Looked at from this point of view, the first mission of Christian spouses is to live their union in faith as a trinitarian mission, that is, as an authentic self-gift in Christ and in the Holy Spirit.

In order to serve the trinitarian mission of the domestic church, the spirituality of marriage and the family must undergo a theological conversion. On the basis of St. John Chrysostom's exhortation, "Make your house as a church," we must develop a genuinely "sacramental" or "iconic" sense of the family. Couples can grow spiritually only if they are aware of the mystery of their life and family relationships — all of which are indwelt by the trinitarian "great mystery" that shines forth from the spousal relationship between Christ and the Church. Such an awareness can only be the fruit of grace; it has its source in a life of prayer, charity, sacrifice, and frequent contact with the eucharistic mystery, the source and summit of all sacramentality. The holiness of spouses and of families is above all the fruit of their readiness to welcome the holiness of the Trinity, a holiness characterized by the unity founded in relations of love. Lived out in truth and authentic love, without a false spiritualism or inattention to everyday realities, spousal and familial relationships become transparent to this mystery and serve its sacramental expression and communication to the world.[33]

---

32. The text references *Lumen Gentium* 41.

33. See A. Scola, *The Nuptial Mystery*, trans. Michelle K. Borras (Grand Rapids: Eerdmans, 2005), 98: "I believe that one of the most serious temptations that besets Christians

Contemporary man is disoriented by a loss of the sense of God and of man. But by seeing and encountering the God who is Love in the trinitarian image and likeness of the domestic church, he rediscovers a concrete, human, ordinary access to the *"sacramentum magnum"* of the Church: through the holy witness of couples and families. Such families are now the "way of the Church," the symbol of the civilization of love that the Church proposes to the lost and despairing men and women of our time. The prophetic cry John Paul II uttered at the beginning of his pontificate has lost none of its timeliness:

> Man cannot live without love. He remains a being that is incomprehensible for himself, his life is senseless, if love is not revealed to him, if he does not encounter love, if he does not experience it and make it his own, if he does not participate intimately in it.[34]

In the midst of joys and difficulties and despite the contrary winds of the culture, the Christian family, evangelized and evangelizing, becomes ever more essential for bringing the gospel of Love made flesh to today's world.

---

today is spiritualism. What I mean is the often unintentional but nevertheless serious way some people have of looking at Christ's ascension as a disincarnation."

34. John Paul II, Encyclical Letter *Redemptor Hominis* 10.

PART THREE

Trinity and Nuptiality: Toward a Eucharistic
Theo-drama of the Nuptial Mystery

CHAPTER 9

The Eucharist as Trinitarian Event

Our methodological starting point is *lex orandi, lex credendi, lex theologandi*. We would like to explore further the relation between the Trinity and the Eucharist, that is, to see how God gives himself to man in the distinction of the divine Persons through the eucharistic gift of Jesus Christ. This trinitarian gift has been received, celebrated, and lived in the Church's faith since the Last Supper. It has been passed down to our own day through the various liturgical traditions that have transmitted "his rite" within forms of prayer already existing in the Jewish tradition. The Church's eucharistic and trinitarian faith has thus been fashioned by the liturgical prayer handed down by the apostles. It is from this liturgical prayer that we must begin: *lex orandi, lex credendi.*[1]

In the eucharistic mystery, through words, gestures, and silence, God gives himself to man in Jesus Christ, and man responds to the gift of God by uniting himself in his turn to Christ, the Mediator and supreme *Leitourgos* of this *admirable commercium et connubium.* Recounting this saving event and understanding it ever more deeply is the goal of theology; and comprehending the trinitarian dimension that emerges from the eucharistic celebration is the goal of our reflection. Both tasks presuppose a rereading of Scripture and the liturgy that, mindful of historical-critical research, reflects on the

1. On this topic, we refer the reader to: L. Bouyer, *Eucharist: Theology and Spirituality of the Eucharistic Prayer* (South Bend, IN: University of Notre Dame Press, 1989); C. Giraudo, *Eucharistia per la Chiesa. Prospettive teologiche sull'Eucharistia a partire dalla "lex orandi"* (Rome: Gregoriana; Brescia: Morcelliana, 1989); E. Mazza, "L'Eucaristia nei primi quattro secoli," in *Scientia Liturgica,* vol. 3: *L'Eucharistia,* ed. A. J. Chupungco (Casale Monferrato: Piemme, 1998), 22-73; D. N. Power, "Teologia della celebrazione eucaristica," in Chupungco, ed., *Scientia Liturgica,* vol. 3: *L'Eucharistia,* 334-85.

foundational events of the New Testament, the trinitarian structure of the eucharistic prayers, and the trinitarian and ecclesial communion actualized in the eucharistic celebration. While the latter belongs to the symbolic and ritual order, it nonetheless contains a historical and eschatological dimension that provides the basis for the theological realism of the Eucharist: *lex orandi, lex theologandi.*

To this we add another premise from trinitarian theology. The eucharistic gift of Jesus is rooted in his identity as the Word of the Father made flesh *(Verbum caro factum)*. The Father offers this Word in time by the power of the Spirit, prolonging in the flesh the eternal generation of the only Son. The mystery of the Eucharist-Church is the *terminus ad quem* of this event, the historical and eschatological goal of the Son's generation in time. The grace of the trinitarian life is thus poured out on the Church. This is why the Son's eternal Eucharist, shared with the Church in time, must be seen in connection with the trinitarian theophanies of Jesus' baptism in the Jordan and on the Cross. This link also becomes evident in light of the role of the Holy Spirit, who accompanies and actively mediates the entire process of the Incarnation, from Jesus' conception in Mary's womb to his death, Resurrection, and Eucharist. Indeed, the Holy Spirit does not merely actualize the sacramental economy; he also serves as the indispensable mediator of our understanding of Christ, God the Father's Word, the Word of eternal Love, who has become the body broken and the blood poured out for us. In light of the Spirit, we believe in Jesus Christ, the original Sacrament; in his eucharistic gift, which generates the Church, he is the *Sacramentum Trinitatis.*

Mindful of the essential role of the Holy Spirit, who is the living and objective memory of the trinitarian event in history, we will attempt first to glimpse through a narrative account the involvement of the divine Persons in the baptismal and eucharistic event of Jesus Christ, which is the source of the entire sacramental economy. Secondly, we will turn to the biblical and patristic notion of *mysterion* in order to highlight what is the key from which the formation of the Church's trinitarian and eucharistic faith derives. Finally, we will address the relation between transcendence and history, since this relation provides the background for the narrative of the trinitarian relations revealed in the life, passion, death, Resurrection, and Eucharist of Jesus Christ.

A Biblical and Liturgical Narrative[2]

An infant or an adult is welcomed into the Church through baptism. The sacrament of baptism is performed using the simple gesture of aspersion (or immersion), together with the words of Jesus pronounced by a minister of the Church. As he pours water over the catechumen's forehead, the minister says, "I baptize you in the name of the Father and of the Son and of the Holy Spirit." This gesture celebrated in the liturgical assembly is, and has been down through the centuries, a faithful execution of the Lord's command: "Go . . . and make disciples of all nations, baptizing them . . ." (Matt. 28:19).

The sacramental gesture accomplished *in persona Christi* fundamentally signifies a gift of Christ that communicates participation in his Sonship. This gift therefore ultimately has its source in the Father: "You are my beloved son/daughter; today I have begotten you." The Father who begets his Son from all eternity and in time prolongs his act of generation in this newborn child or adult baptized into the Church's faith. Through the sacramental gesture of the Son and the breath of the Spirit, the Father extends the gift of adoptive filiation to the Church's children, so as to enable them to participate in the eucharistic banquet, which is the pledge of the eschatological banquet. Consideration of Jesus' baptism in the Jordan and his baptism of fire on the Cross[3] will serve to introduce us to the trinitarian event of the Eucharist.

2. For a fuller understanding of the sense of theological narrative, see C. Rochetta, "Théologie narrative," in *Dictionnaire de théologie fondamentale*, ed. R. Latourelle and R. Fisichella (Montreal: Bellarmine; Paris: Éd. du Cerf, 1992), 1377-81. Narrative theology focuses on the biblical texts in order to narrate their meaning in a mode different from that of systematic or argumentative theology. As an exercise in memory, "narrative has a *performative* value that it would not be too much to call sacramental" (1380). See also Rochetta, *I sacramenti della fede*, vol. 1: *Sacramentaria biblica fondamentale*, 7th ed. (Bologna: EDB, 1998), 24-43. We must add, however, that the performative value of language is not sufficient to explain the efficacy of the sacraments. This efficacy also requires the action of the Holy Spirit, who "gives life" to the word, causing its receiver to assimilate it and so bear fruit. This pneumatological dimension is still insufficiently developed in liturgical theology. See Power, "Teologia della celebrazione eucaristica"; while affirming that the sacraments come from the Spirit in a generic sense, Power does not assign the Spirit any significant role in his theology of the liturgical celebration.

3. See P. Coda, *Uno in Cristo Gesù. Il battesimo come evento trinitario* (Rome: Città Nuova, 1996); Aa.Vv., *La Santissima Trinidad y el bautismo cristiano*, Semanas de estudios trinitarios 26 (Salamanca: Secretariado Trinitario, 1992).

The Theophany at the Jordan

At the end of his ministry, John the Baptist says, "I baptize you with water for repentance, but he who is coming after me is mightier than I, whose sandals I am not worthy to carry; he will baptize you with the Holy Spirit and with fire" (Matt. 3:11; Mark 1:8; Luke 3:16). And: "He on whom you see the Spirit descend and remain, this is he who baptizes with the Holy Spirit" (John 1:33). The synoptic narratives, which belong to the genre of the theophany, draw our attention to the trinitarian nature of the event: "When he came up out of the water, immediately he saw the heavens opened and the Spirit descending upon him like a dove; and a voice came from heaven, 'Thou art my beloved Son; with thee I am well pleased'" (Mark 1:10-11). The parallel version of Luke adds that Jesus "was praying," thus indicating the privileged place of his encounter with the Father. "With thee I am well pleased" is translated in the *Traduction Œcuménique de la Bible:* "You are my Son, today I have begotten you," with a footnote arguing that this translation is especially consonant with the evangelist's thought.[4]

This inaugural event reveals Jesus' messianic identity and the beginning of his mission. Jesus is the beloved Son, in whom the new Spirit of the messianic age rests and dwells, the Spirit that brings purification for sins and the reality of the New Covenant written on the human heart. But in order to produce its effect in believers, Jesus' baptism in water must be sealed by the baptism of fire on the Cross.[5] The Johannine account of Jesus' baptism makes the reference to the Cross explicit: to be "born anew" from on high (John 3:3, 7) means to be born from him who has been "lifted up" (John 3:14). The theophany at the Jordan thus points to the culmination of the trinitarian event in history.

---

4. *Traduction Œcuménique de la Bible. Édition intégrale* (Paris: Éd. du Cerf/SBF, 1977), note to Luke 3:22: "This formula reproduces Ps 2:7 and signifies Jesus' messianic enthronement, the beginning of his mission in the midst of the people of God. The fact that this word is pronounced by the Father makes it the revelation par excellence of Jesus' mystery."

5. In Jesus' exchange with Nicodemus (John 3:3-6), the relation between "water" and "Spirit" distinguishes John's baptism from that of Jesus. The fundamental affirmation is that only he in whom the fullness of the Spirit dwells can communicate that Spirit to others. See F. M. Braun, "Le baptême de Jésus d'après le quatrième Évangile," *Revue Thomiste* 48 (1948): 347-93; P. R. Tragan, "Battesimo e fede cristologica nel dialogo fra Gesù e Nicodemo (Gv 3, 1-21)," in *Fede e sacramenti negli scritti giovannei,* ed. P. R. Tragan (Rome: Pontificio Ateneo S. Anselmo, 1985), 47-120.

The Theophany of the Cross

The Meaning of the Event Anticipated in Jesus' Prayer at the Last Supper

The trinitarian event of the Son's generation in the flesh culminates in the unique event of the paschal triduum: Calvary, the descent into hell, and the Resurrection from the dead. John's interpretation of the event highlights the mystery of Jesus' obedience. When Jesus announces his departure to the Father and the coming of the Spirit, he says, "The ruler of this world is coming. He has no power over me; but I do as the Father has commanded me, so that the world may know that I love the Father" (John 14:30-31). Jesus' obedience is the expression of his love, that is, his Sonship.

The profound meaning of the Passion is revealed above all in Jesus' priestly prayer: "Father, the hour has come; glorify thy Son that the Son may glorify thee" (John 17:1). Immediately afterward, he explains: "I glorified thee on earth, having accomplished the work which thou gavest me to do" (John 17:4). At the end of an entire life of obedience expressing his love for the Father and the Father's love for him and for mankind, Jesus is fully aware that the final fulfillment has come. The institution of the Eucharist during the Last Supper bears witness to this:[6] "And now, Father, glorify thou me in thy own presence with the glory which I had with thee before the world was made" (John 17:5).

The meaning of the mutual glorification of Father and Son in the paschal hour becomes clear toward the end of the priestly prayer: "The glory which thou hast given me I have given to them, that they may be one even as we are one" (John 17:22). Father and Son wish to share their glory. The mutual gift of their glory is the gift of their unity in love, that is, the gift of the Spirit.[7] Jesus

---

6. As for the exegetical question of Jesus' awareness of the salvific meaning of his death, the systematic doubt raised by Bultmannian exegesis can now be regarded as obsolete. See the study of H. Schürmann, *Comment Jésus a-t-il vécu sa mort?* (Paris: Éd. du Cerf, 1977; and J. Gnilka, *Gesù di Nazareth. Annuncio e storia* (Brescia: Paideia, 1993), 360-64.

7. See Coda, *Uno in Cristo Gesù*, 149-50: "*Doxa* is the being-God that the Father does not 'deem a thing to be grasped' (see Phil. 2:7) — as the Son shows by living this attitude in his turn — but gives (stripping himself) and precisely in this way reveals and shares. It is not for nothing that, in John 17, Jesus, summarizing the mission he received from the Father, can affirm: 'And the *doxa* which thou hast given me I have given to them' (17:22). If Jesus of Nazareth is the truth of God (*Logos*, Son) revealed and contemplated, the *doxa* that radiates from him is God's life (Spirit) participated and received." See H. U. von Balthasar, *The Glory of the Lord: A Theological Aesthetics*, vol. 7: *Theology: The New Covenant*, trans. Brian McNeil (San Francisco: Ignatius, 1989), Part III, "In Laudem Gloriae," 389ff.

pronounces the great "epiclesis" in the priestly prayer, asking the Holy Spirit to come upon his sacrifice. Because of this prayer and sacrifice, the Father will make the Holy Spirit, *doxa-communio*, descend upon him and upon those who belong to him: "I in them and thou in me, that they may become perfectly one, so that the world may know that thou hast sent me and hast loved them even as thou hast loved me" (John 17:23). The granting of Jesus' prayer comes through the dramatic involvement of the three divine Persons in the Passion.

The Unfolding of the Trinitarian Theo-Drama[8] of the Redemption

At the beginning of the Passion narrative, Jesus solemnly declares the triune God's passion for sharing his glory: "Having loved his own who were in the world, he loved them to the end" (John 13:1). Although Jesus is the chief actor here, the great Protagonist of the encounter between God and sinners is precisely the Father, who delivers his only Son into their hands: "For God so loved the world that he gave his only Son" (John 3:16). "For our sake, he made him to be sin who knew no sin, so that in him we might become the righteousness of God" (2 Cor. 5:21).

From all eternity, the Son was always in agreement with this gift, this handing over (as he mentions in his prayer), but this does not prevent him from feeling the terrible consequences of that decision. During the Passion, he is overcome by an incalculable, unbearable weight of suffering, which at its extreme point obscures his filial awareness of the Father's presence: "My God, my God, why have you abandoned me?" In a certain way, the obscurity of sin enters into his relationship of love with the Father. The suffering Son painfully assumes and experiences the guilt of sinners and their distance from God. The Holy Spirit, who had always intervened and confirmed the loving union between the Father and the incarnate Son, can no longer be felt except in the form of a separation that they share and to which they consent on account of the world's sin. All three Persons thus participate in Christ's *kenosis*, though, of course, each in his way.[9]

The hour prefigured by the Exodus has now come: the hour of liberation

---

8. See H. U. von Balthasar, *Theo-Drama*, vol. 4: *The Action*, trans. Graham Harrison (San Francisco: Ignatius, 1994).

9. See H. U. von Balthasar, *Mysterium Paschale*, trans. Aidan Nichols (San Francisco: Ignatius, 2000). A first, lyrical contemplation of the paschal mystery appeared in 1945 after Balthasar had encountered Adrienne von Speyr: Balthasar, *Heart of the World*, trans. Erasmo Leiva-Merikakis (San Francisco: Ignatius, 1979).

from slavery achieved through the crossing of the Red Sea of sin and death. After Jesus tasted the vinegar, he cried, " 'It is finished'; and he bowed his head" and died (John 19:30). John shows that even in the darkness of abandonment, Jesus remains the Lord who performs the ultimate act that is his death. The giving up of his spirit is both the last free act of this obedient man and the prelude to the eucharistic gift of the Holy Spirit. In his last breath, Jesus gives his Spirit back into the hands of the Father for whom he has accomplished his mission. This is why the Father, touched to the heart by this gift, allows the pierced heart of the dead Son to become the well-spring of the paschal and sacramental fruit of the world's reconciliation with God: the New Covenant in the blood of the Lamb.

John bears witness to this: "One of the soldiers pierced his side with a spear, and at once there came out blood and water" (John 19:34). The evangelist sees this phenomenon as a sign of the gift of the Spirit (see John 4:14; 7:38-39) and of eternal life (the blood: John 6:51-55). The patristic tradition saw the same sign as a source of baptism and the Eucharist, as well as of the gift of the Spirit. Devotion to the pierced heart of Jesus extends this witness in history.[10] The believing Church, represented by Mary and John, has perceived here the "flowing spring of the Spirit" (Origen) and wrote down the memory "that you also may believe" (John 19:35). This Spirit of Father and Son precedes and establishes the witness of the apostles, raising Jesus from the dead, and bringing his redemptive work to fulfillment through the actualization of his eucharistic gift for the Church and the world.

On the evening of Easter, Jesus came into the midst of his disciples and said to them, " 'Peace be with you.' When he had said this, he showed them his hands and his side. . . . 'As the Father has sent me, even so I send you.' And when he had said this, he breathed on them, and said to them, 'Receive the Holy Spirit.' 'Sins . . . are forgiven . . .' " (John 20:19-22). The risen Lord, who has returned to the Father, establishes his Church upon the reconciling, regenerative, and unifying power of the Holy Spirit.

We thus come to the conclusion of the trinitarian event of the Lord's Pasch. It is a baptismal and eucharistic event, in which the Son is submerged by the waters of death and raised in the fire of the Spirit: "You are my beloved

---

10. See I. de la Potterie, *Il mistero del cuore trafitto. Studi biblici* (Bologna: EDB, 1988), 110-11: "The living water of the Spirit makes the blood of Jesus present in the Church. The Spirit prompts believers to unite themselves to Jesus Christ and to live in their turn the reality that the blood symbolizes, that is, Jesus' life as Son, his obedience to the Father to the point of giving his life." See also H. Rahner, "*Flumina de ventre Christi. L'esegesi patristica di Giov. 6, 37-38,*" *Biblica* 22 (1941), reprinted in H. Rahner, *L'ecclesiologia dei Padri* (Rome: Paoline, 1971), 291-394.

Son, today I have begotten you." The extreme descent to Cross and hell is reversed, so to speak; or better, this descent reveals its glory in the definitive victory of trinitarian Love in heaven. The Father receives the Son's sacrifice for all and responds with the gift of the Resurrection. The chief implication of this glorious gift is the "general absolution" of the sins that the Son confessed *pro nobis* on the Cross. But it also brings the crowning of the redemptive Incarnation, since it confirms Christ as the Son of God with power (Rom. 1:4), as the One who has become the Mediator of trinitarian life for all humanity. Because of this life, the Church receives her trinitarian and spousal identity from the eucharistic gift of Christ dead and risen.

The Eucharist: "Memorial" of the Supper and of the Cross

"For as often as you eat this bread and drink the cup, you proclaim the Lord's death until he comes" (1 Cor. 11:26). The theophany of the Cross leads to the theophany of the Eucharist. The paschal event, the center and fulfillment of human history, reaches the apex of its meaning in the eucharistic celebration. Here Jesus Christ remains present in the midst of his own under the signs of the eucharistic supper, which prolongs the Supper of the Lord: "The Lord Jesus on the night when he was betrayed took bread, and when he had given thanks, he broke it, and said, 'This is my body which is for you. Do this in remembrance of me. . . . This cup is the new covenant in my blood. Do this, as often as you drink it, in remembrance of me'" (1 Cor. 11:23-25). Although Paul is writing around the year 55, he had already received this "tradition" around the year 49.

According to the Lukan narrative, which is also very ancient, the liturgy Jesus celebrated during the Last Supper unfolds as follows: the rite of the cup, the rite of the bread, supper, the final rite of the cup.[11] Each of the three rites mentioned here is accompanied by a prayer of benediction or thanksgiving.[12] The eschatological words spoken over the cup establish the significance both of the paschal supper and of the cup ritual itself. Jesus will no longer drink

11. H. Schürmann, *Der Einsetzungsbericht Lk 22, 19-20* (Münster: Aschendorff, 1955). See also G. Mazzanti, *I Sacramenti, simbolo e teologia*, vol. 2: *Eucaristia, Battesimo e Confirmazione* (Bologna: EDB, 1998), chap. 1: "'La cena pasquale del Cristo fu la sua cena.' Radicamento storico,'" 21-61.

12. In the second century, this sequence of elements would be abbreviated in the eucharistic celebration; the supper was separated and the rites of the bread and the cup fused into one.

the "fruit of the vine" or eat the Passover until the kingdom of God is accomplished. The present, with its imminent darkness, is already placed in the light of the future, so much so that the Last Supper contains the image of the kingdom of God:[13] "In Jesus' words, this supper, whose theological meaning concerns the Passover/Pasch, acquires the value of a 'type' and becomes the model of the future supper, the eschatological banquet of the coming kingdom."[14]

"Do this in memory of me." At the Last Supper, Jesus commands that his ritual gesture be repeated and remain as a norm and model for the Church. The New Testament testifies to the essential elements of this gesture: (1) he took bread, (2) gave thanks, (3) broke it (4) and gave it to the disciples, (5) saying. . . . (6) he took the cup, (7) gave thanks (8) and gave it to the disciples, (9) saying. . . . This gesture is situated in the larger context of the Passover supper, an objective "memorial" *(zikkaron)* of the *mirabilia Dei* in the history of the Jewish people.[15] In this sense, the memorial of Jesus kept by the Church contains not only a ceaselessly renewed ritual gesture, but also and above all the sacrificial content of this gesture, which was offered on the Cross once and for all. The Letter to the Hebrews expresses the matter in the following terms:

> But when Christ had offered for all time a single sacrifice for sins, he sat down at the right hand of God, then to wait until his enemies should be made a stool for his feet. For by a single offering he has perfected for all time those who were sanctified. (Heb. 10:12-14)

The author of Hebrews then adds solemnly, "the Holy Spirit also bears witness," pointing to the fulfillment of the New Covenant: " 'I will remember

---

13. See Mazza, "L'Eucaristia nei primi quattro secoli," 22-73, here 32; also K. Rengstorf, *Il vangelo secondo Luca* (Brescia: Paideia, 1980), 410.

14. Mazza, "L'Eucaristia nei primi quattro secoli," 32. The author adds: "This means . . . that there are no further steps between the Last Supper and the coming of God's kingdom. This is an important element for a correct understanding of the sacraments" — it highlights their eschatological dimension.

15. The meaning of the Jewish *"zikkaron,"* or "memorial," "in no way means a subjective, human psychological act of returning to the past, but an objective reality destined to make some thing or some one perpetually present before God and for God himself" (L. Bouyer, *Eucharist: Theology and Spirituality of the Eucharistic Prayer,* trans. Charles Underhill Quinn [Notre Dame: University of Notre Dame Press, 1968], 103-4). See M. Thurian, *L'Eucharistie. Mémoriale du Seigneur, sacrifice d'action de grâce et d'intercession* (Neuchâtel: Delachaux et Niestlé, 1959). This aspect of memorial seems to be relatively ignored in E. Mazza, *La celebrazione eucaristica, Genesi del rito e sviluppo dell'interpretazione* (Milan: San Paolo, 1996), 16-18; see G. Mazzanti, *I sacramenti, simbolo e teologia,* vol. 2, 36.

their sins and their misdeeds no more.' Where there is forgiveness of these, there is no longer any offering for sin" (Heb. 10:15, 17-18).[16]

Through the objective memorial of the Eucharist, Jesus' priestly act, which he accomplished once and for all (Heb. 10:10), is celebrated and proclaimed by the Church:

> Paul, a servant of Jesus Christ . . . set apart for the gospel of God . . . concerning his Son, who was . . . designated Son of God in power according to the Spirit of holiness by his resurrection from the dead, Jesus Christ our Lord. (Rom. 1:1-4)

> For if the sprinkling of defiled persons with the blood of goats and bulls and with the ashes of a heifer sanctifies for the purification of the flesh, how much more shall the blood of Christ, who through the eternal Spirit offered himself without blemish to God, purify your conscience from dead works to serve the living God. (Heb. 9:13-14)

Who Offers?

> No other thought is so persistent and so penetrating in the Roman Canon as the idea that the Church offers a sacrifice to God the Father, presents it and recommends it to him, asks him to accept it, urges it upon him and gives many reasons for this, urgently and almost anxiously, as if the all-decisive question for her salvation and for that of her children were that God should accept this sacrifice of hers.[17]

How do we explain the Church's insistence here? Does the Church claim to substitute Christ as the primary offerer of the sacrament? This is not her

---

16. See footnote b to this verse in *Traduction Œcuménique de la Bible. Édition intégrale:* "This text has been used in controversy. Protestants drew from it objections to Catholic teaching, which presents the Mass as a sacrifice; Catholics responded that the Mass is not a sacrifice different from that of the Cross, rather, it is a sacrament that makes this unique sacrifice present." In fact the text from Hebrews opposes Jesus' sacrifice to those of the Old Covenant.

17. H. U. von Balthasar, "The Mass, a Sacrifice of the Church?" in *Explorations in Theology*, vol. 3: *Creator Spirit*, trans. Brian McNeil (San Francisco: Ignatius, 1993), 185-243, here 185. In the Eucharistic Canon, we find the word *"sacrificium"* four times, "victim" three times, "offer" four times, and "oblation" twice — all analogical expressions that express the same idea of offering.

intention; such a claim would be pretentious in the extreme. In reality, the Church fought to vindicate the sacramentality of the priestly minister precisely in order to affirm that it is Christ who offers the eucharistic sacrifice. The High Priest who has ascended into heaven and is seated at the Father's right hand continues to exercise his salvific and priestly mediation through the Church's various ministries, and in a particular way through the "ministerial" priesthood.

The eucharistic rite was instituted precisely in order to place at the Church's disposal the personal gift of Christ that was accomplished once and for all: "When Christ came into the world, he said, 'Sacrifices and offerings thou hast not desired, but a body hast thou prepared for me. . . . Lo, I have come to do thy will, O God'" (Heb. 10:5, 7). It is precisely by this will of God that we are sanctified, thanks to the offering that Jesus Christ made of his body once and for all.

The Church continually receives this broken body and this shed blood from the Lord; she does not fabricate them for herself. Of course, she prepares the material elements, the symbols of human labor, but the decisive, creative Word that confects their transubstantiation is pronounced by the Lord acting through his minister in the power of the Spirit. Although she receives this gift from on high as a sacrifice of purification for her sins, the Church nonetheless does not remain passive in, or extraneous to, the event being celebrated; she allows herself to be drawn into it by the Holy Spirit who springs forth from the pierced heart of Christ. In the unity of the Spirit given by Christ, and in the communion sealed by him, the Church becomes in a certain sense the offering subject in Christ and with Christ. We will return to this question in the second part of our investigation.[18]

Our trinitarian perspective encourages us to follow Balthasar in adding yet another element:

So Christ dispenses himself in the sacraments within the Church, too: "Christ is the one who baptizes through the Church, who teaches, rules, loosens, binds, offers sacrifice and sanctifies, enlivening his whole Body

18. The question has to do with the foundation of the nuptial relation that involves the Church in Christ's offering. Is the Church's participation in this offering based above all on her hierarchical structure, that is, on the participation *"in persona Christi Capitis"* enjoyed by those ordained to the ministerial priesthood? Or is this participation rooted in the spousal reality of the Church symbolized by Mary? See Balthasar, "The Mass, a Sacrifice of the Church?", as well as Part II of *The Office of Peter and the Structure of the Church,* trans. Andrée Emery (San Francisco: Ignatius, 2007).

with his divine power" (DS 3806). But Christ effects all of this with the commission and authority of the Father through the Holy Spirit they have in common. For that reason in all three Synoptic Gospels the true Lord of the table in the eucharistic banquet is the heavenly Father, who sets out for us the best he has to offer. Similarly, the precious taste of the gifts welling up within all the sacraments comes from the Holy Spirit, the Spirit of the giving Father and of the Son who lets himself be given as food and drink. It is the Spirit who enables us, when we pray the Canon of the Mass with the Church, to address all thanks and gratitude, all honor and glory, through him and with the Son to the Father.[19]

Who Is Offered?

When he is placed in our hands to be offered and consumed ("take and eat"), Christ is offering himself and inviting the Church both to offer him to the Father and to offer herself along with him. The chief reality that the Church discerns under the veil of the sacrament is the *mysterium fidei,* the body and blood of the Lord who offers himself. In giving himself, moreover, Christ ratifies the Father's act of giving him, Christ, to and for us. Both Persons, Father and Son, are united in the sacrifice. For the same reason, they glorify each other in the gift of the Son *pro nobis.* The words of Christ's minister, by confecting transubstantiation *in persona Christi* and in the power of the Spirit, also express the gift of the Father, the gift of the Son, and the gift of the Holy Spirit. These words actuate in the broken body and the shed blood the mystery hidden in God from all eternity: "You are my beloved Son, today I have begotten you." The trinitarian event of the Son's eternal generation is prolonged in the eucharistic incarnation. It becomes a real, symbolical-sacramental event in the time of the Church, in order to give eternal life to the world.

This divine gift both generates the Church and finds her already there; it renews her faith, purifies her, and sanctifies her, integrating her into Christ's obedience to the Father. Christ offers himself on the eucharistic altar, but not without including the Church as his Bride: "When Jesus saw his mother, and the disciple whom he loved standing near, he said to his mother, 'Woman, behold your son!'" (John 19:26). Jesus asked his mother to consent to his death,

---

19. H. U. von Balthasar, *Epilogue,* trans. Edward T. Oakes (San Francisco: Ignatius, 2004), 117. The author refers to Matthew 22:1-10 (the king's wedding banquet); Luke 14:15-24; and John 6 (the Father gives us the true Bread from heaven).

to renounce him and to accept the beloved disciple as a son in exchange for him. This is a dramatic moment of revelation par excellence. The incarnate Word's last word, his death, cannot fall into the void; it must be received by the woman who first received him in her faith and in her womb. If this word were not received, the "truth" of the covenant would be diminished for lack of a human response. At the eschatological hour of the supreme sacrifice, the Church is involved in the first person in Mary's faith. She gives her consent to the unique sacrifice of the divine Bridegroom in the name of all humanity.[20]

Christ the Bridegroom and the Church-Bride are thus united and made fruitful in the sacrifice, although each in a different way. The Son's offering opens and constitutes the source of all fruitfulness. The *fiat* of Mary-Church only participates in this fullness, which is divinely established, even though it does require the creature's receptive "yes." This "yes" does not add to or augment the Bridegroom's fruitfulness, but rather allows it to bear fruit in her, opening for him the space of her believing womb.[21] This participation of Mary-Church in the very event of the redemption, which began at the foot of the Cross, remains somehow present in the sacramental "mystery" of each Eucharist. It remains present in the objective faith of the Church that surrounds, includes, and at times supplements the personal faith of individual believers, both ministers and faithful.

Finally, the Son's sacrifice, to which the Woman consented in a manner appropriate to a feminine person, is received by the Father as an offering of reconciliation for the New Covenant. The Father responds with the gift of the Holy Spirit, a gift that (symbolically) already springs forth from the opened side of the dead Christ. The Spirit transforms the entire substance of Christ the Bridegroom into a eucharistic seed that is deposited in the womb of the Church-Bride to make her fruitful with and in Christ.[22] The Spirit accomplishes the miracle of the shared fruitfulness of the Bridegroom and the Bride, offering himself as the fruit of their "nuptial mystery." In this way, he allows himself to be poured out into the hearts of those participating in the sacrifice,

20. St. Thomas Aquinas understands Mary's "yes" as representing all humanity: *Summa Theologica*, IIIa, q. 30 a. 1. See also A. Scola, *The Nuptial Mystery*, trans. Michelle K. Borras (Grand Rapids: Eerdmans, 2005), 106-9: "The Nuptial Mystery and Welcoming the Other."

21. See H. U. von Balthasar, *Theo-Drama*, vol. 3: *Dramatis Personae: Persons in Christ*, trans. Graham Harrison (San Francisco: Ignatius, 1992), 306-12.

22. See H. U. von Balthasar, *Explorations in Theology*, vol. 4: *Spirit and Institution*, trans. Edward T. Oakes (San Francisco: Ignatius, 1995), 224-30. See also S. L. Mahoney, *The Analogy between the Eucharist and Marriage according to Hans Urs von Balthasar*, Dissertatio ad doctoratum (Rome: Pontificia Università Gregoriana, 1999).

who receive him as the pledge of the wedding feast of the Lamb to which the eternal King invites all mankind.

The Trinitarian Drama of the Eucharistic Celebration

The eternal exchange of gifts between the divine Persons is prolonged in the salvific economy (which involves mankind, creation, and the Church) through the event of Christ's Incarnation that culminates in the paschal mystery. The celebration of the Eucharist is the real symbol (sacrament) of this trinitarian exchange of uncreated and created gifts. In each Eucharist, the Father gives a gift to the incarnate Son and the Son to the Father in the unity of the Holy Spirit; this gift-giving involves the Church and the world from within. A glance at the general structure of the liturgy, beginning — again, narratively — with a concrete example, i.e., the solemnity of the Lord's Annunciation, will help us to see this point.

The beginning of the celebration immediately identifies the partners of the covenant: the triune God and sinful man. The Sign of the Cross and the *Confiteor* are preceded by the entrance antiphon: "The Lord said, as he entered the world: Behold, I come to do your will, O God." This text makes us aware of the Word's attitude of readiness before his incarnation: the obedience that is consonant with his generation. The opening prayer asks that we become "participants in his divine nature."

The liturgy of the Word prepares the assembly to receive the gift of the Word made flesh. The first reading recalls the prophecy of Isaiah 7:14, which contains the quintessence of the Old Testament promise: "Behold, a virgin shall conceive and bear a son, and shall call his name Immanuel." The second reading, from the Letter to the Hebrews, explains the sacrificial finality of the Son's obedience: "And by that will we have been sanctified through the offering of the body of Jesus Christ once for all" (Heb. 10:10). Finally, the Gospel of the Annunciation brings out the role of the three divine Persons: "Hail, full of grace, the Lord is with you!" (Luke 1:28); "Behold, you will conceive in your womb and bear a son. . . . He will be great, and will be called the Son of the Most High" (Luke 1:31-32); "The Holy Spirit will come upon you, and the power of the Most High will overshadow you; therefore the child to be born will be called holy, the Son of God" (Luke 1:35). After the angel has pointed to Elizabeth's pregnancy as an additional piece of evidence, indeed, as the supreme sign of God's respect for his rational and free creature, Mary says, "Behold, I am the handmaid of the Lord; let it be to me according to your word" (Luke

1:38). Mary's act of faith, which is the essential core of the Church's entire creed, concludes the trinitarian dialogue regarding the mystery of the Incarnation that represents the center and goal of human history.

In the symbolic offering of bread and wine, the Church gathers all intentions, her own and those of the world, together with all her goods, her work, and her suffering. These things destined for the sacrificial altar are gifts intended by the Creator for the incarnate Son, the Redeemer and Lord of the universe. The Son receives the gifts and, through the ordained minister, pronounces the decisive words over them: "This is my body, given for you"; he then takes the cup, saying, "This is the chalice of my blood, the blood of the new and eternal Covenant, which is poured out for you." Jesus thus takes our "symbolic" body (the bread) and makes it become his "real," substantial Body. He receives our gift, which comes from the Father, to bless and consecrate it with the gift of his body and blood, thus "symbolically" binding our body to his body, our being to his being.[23] The manner in which this event occurs is so profound and mysterious that we cannot adequately express it with our earthly categories. The Holy Spirit, who "specializes" in union within distinction, is its artisan and permanent mediator. This is why the prayer following the eucharistic conversion becomes the shared prayer of the Head and the Body, the Bridegroom and the Bride. It is a prayer of praise, thanksgiving, and intercession, which culminates in the *amen* to the Glory of the Trinity — extending into the Our Father, which is prayed together with the Son in the Spirit, that is, within the Holy Trinity.[24]

As it is celebrated in the Church's faith, the prodigious gesture of the Son immolated, dead, and risen culminates in the Pentecostal moment of the eucharistic liturgy: holy Communion. The Son's return or ascension to the Father in the obedience of love, together with all our goods, intentions, and sufferings,

---

23. We note that the mystery of transubstantiation does not cancel out the rich physicality of bread and wine, whose "accidents" remain unaltered, whereas their "substance" becomes the true body and blood of Christ. Approaching the question symbolically (that is, "theologically," which is not opposed to "ontologically"), we can say that our body, which is represented by these elements, is united to the Lord's body in a way analogous to that in which the "accidents" of bread and wine are "subjected" to the body of Christ. This eucharistic relation to the Lord, which is rooted in baptism, constitutes our personal Christian identity. It is precisely through the Eucharist that Christ makes the Church his Body, conferring on her her deepest identity.

24. Orthodox theology helps us to perceive the trinitarian drama of the eucharistic action, particularly its movement toward the Father. See B. Bobrinskoy, *Le Mystère de la Trinité* (Paris: Éd. du Cerf, 1986), 185: "The 'Our Father,' together with communion, is precisely the culmination of the eucharistic mystery, where the Church establishes herself in a filial attitude."

is blessed anew by the Father with the supreme gift of the Holy Spirit, the quintessence of trinitarian communion. The consecratory *epiclesis* over the gifts that we have offered to Christ is followed by the Pentecostal *epiclesis* over the community that Christ offers to the Father. The Father responds with the gift of the Spirit poured into the hearts of those participating in the liturgy. In distributing the Bread from heaven, he also gives the Spirit who makes us taste and assimilate that Bread with the new, spiritual identity consisting in our sanctified persons and our formation of "one Body" in Christ. This Pentecostal gift bursts forth superabundantly in its character as Person-Gift, or Person-*Communion,* while also bestowing his created-uncreated gifts of faith, hope, and charity, which are the pledge of eternal life. The post-communion ends: "By the power of his Resurrection may we come to eternal joy." *Ite, missa est:* the final, trinitarian blessing leads to mission, so that all might know and receive the gift of God.

Like the theophanies of the Jordan and of the Cross, then, the sacramental event of the Eucharist represents heaven's opening, the descent of the incarnate Word, Christ's ascension with the prize of the redemption, and the outpouring of the Holy Spirit of Father and Son: in short, a trinitarian drama, an exchange of gifts between the divine Persons accomplished in the Church's liturgical mystery. In the eucharistic celebration, Christ does not die again, his sacrifice is not repeated or even renewed. Nevertheless, while remaining unique, his sacrifice is sacramentally represented for us (in mystery) so that, in faith, we might become contemporaries of the paschal mystery and participants in the communion of the Trinity.

Though belonging to the order sacramental signs, then, the Eucharist is nonetheless the Father's eschatological Word, which literally places the life, death, and Resurrection of his Son into our hands. This sacramental event extends the theo-drama of the Cross into human history. Or, from the reverse perspective, the Eucharist draws human history into the eschatological center of gravity that is Christ's death and Resurrection. In either case, the Father truly offers his eternal Word not only in the eternity of his immortal life, but also in the temporality of our sacramental signs. He thus extends his trinitarian communion, through the event of the Incarnation and Easter, all the way into the eucharistic meal and the concrete, daily reality of our present life in the flesh. This gift especially involves the Holy Spirit, who is the agent of Christ's Incarnation and Resurrection, as well as of his "memorial" in the Church's Eucharist.

Precisely in its trinitarian character, the event of the Resurrection represents the supreme seal of total reciprocity between the Father and the Son made flesh — a seal impressed in the now reconciled and glorified *caro pec-*

cati. Consequently, Christ's glorified flesh becomes the source of the Spirit; in other words, it becomes eucharistically fruitful. His flesh is no longer subject to the laws of time and space because it now belongs to the eschatological world of eternal life. The Risen One did not, however, lose his capacity to express himself in the temporal world. Quite to the contrary! He has attained the supreme level of self-expression through his personal (eucharistic) body, and this extends even through his new, ecclesial body as well. The narratives of the post-Easter appearances offer a concrete demonstration of this point. For forty days, Christ revealed that he could give himself and be personally encountered in his concrete, familiar presence through verbal ("Mary!" "Rabbouni!") or sacramental signs (Emmaus). "It is the Lord!" exclaims John from the boat, at the invitation of the man standing on the shore. This is why the forty days after the Resurrection are essential for introducing the Church into the sacramental economy.[25]

We can conclude this narrative, biblical-sacramental account by recalling the intuition with which we began our reflection: the three divine Persons are dramatically involved in the gift of the incarnate Son, which is the original eucharistic sacrament. This gift of love is accomplished once and for all in Christ's paschal mystery, even as the manner of this accomplishment leaves room for the Holy Spirit to reveal its trinitarian and eschatological fruitfulness in the time of the Church and through the economy of the sacraments of the New Covenant. The Church and the other sacraments derive from the Eucharist,[26] the source of eternal life that sprang forth from Christ's side in order to heal and glorify human history, lifting it up into the communion of the Trinity.

The Biblical and Patristic Notion of *Mysterion*

The narration of the divine Persons' involvement in Jesus' life and death enables us to grasp the sacrament of the Eucharist as a prolongation of the mystery of the Incarnation of Jesus Christ, itself the original sacrament of the Trinity in history. Christ's paschal baptism leads to the dramatic theophany of the Eucharist: "Today I have begotten you" as the firstborn of a multitude of brethren. In him and in the power of the Holy Spirit, these brethren are

---

25. See H. U. von Balthasar, *A Theology of History* (San Francisco: Ignatius-Communio Books, 1994); also G. Mazzanti, *I sacramenti, simbolo e teologia*, vol. 1: *Introduzione generale* (Bologna: EDB, 1997), 150-51.

26. See G. Mazzanti, *I sacramenti, simbolo e teologia*, vol. 2, 17-18.

called to be his Body and Bride, that is, the Church. The eucharistic Trinity makes the Church.

Our task now is to reflect on the foundations of this biblical-liturgical narrative, in order to arrive at a better understanding of the trinitarian logic of the sacramental economy in general and of the Eucharist in particular. The encounter between the triune God and the community of believers unfolds in the sphere of Christ's Word and gestures, which the Church keeps, proclaims, and actualizes in the power of the Holy Spirit. We must identify the theological categories that have marked the Church's understanding of the sacraments. This means identifying above all the root and foundation of that understanding: the biblical-patristic notion of *mysterion.*

We know that in the Old and the New Testament, *mysterion* does not have the technical meaning that it would later receive in the twelfth century.[27] The formulation of the Scholastic definition of sacrament as an efficacious sign of grace *(signum efficax gratiae)* presupposed a long development involving a semantic shift from the notion of "mystery," understood in the broad sense as a historical saving event, to that of "sacrament," understood in the strict sense as a means of grace. Our chief aim in tracing this evolution is to identify the central, most general notion, from which the Eucharist (understood as a trinitarian and liturgical event) derives. Our investigation will focus, then, on the trinitarian dimension of the *mysterion* and on its link with the eucharistic *anamnesis,* which is the fundamental structure of the Christian sacraments.[28] Contemporary sacramental theology, in fact, will need to rediscover the biblical and patristic notion of *mysterion* if it wishes to advance beyond Scholasticism's more instrumental approach and so recover a more symbolic and anthropological sense of the sacraments while also doing justice to the Church's sacramental tradition.[29]

27. See G. Colombo, "Dove va la teologia sacramentaria?" in *Teologia sacramentaria* (Milan: Glossa, 1997), 37ff.

28. See R. Schulte, "I singoli sacramenti come articolazione del sacramento radicale," in *Mysterium Salutis,* vol. 8 (Brescia: Queriniana, 1975), 51-189; J. Ratzinger, "De la Cène de Jésus au sacrement de l'Église," in *L'eucharistie, pain nouveau pour un monde rompue* (Paris: Communio-Fayard, 1981), 35-51.

29. We recall G. Colombo's critique of K. Rahner, who radically rejected O. Casel's "mysteric approach" and privileged fundamental theology over historical investigation in his approach to the sacraments: "Rahner's theological move was to reject almost unexamined O. Casel's theory of 'mystery,' even though historians would judge it to be an authentic and fruitful contribution to the renewal of sacramental theology in our century" (*Teologia sacramentaria* [Milan: Glossa, 1997], 73). See also J. Betz, "Eucharistie," in *Sacramentum Mundi,* vol. 1 (Freiburg i.B., 1967), 1226-32; A. Gerken, *Theologie der Eucharistie* (Munich, 1973), 166-68.

The Mysterion *in the Scriptures*[30]

We will begin with a brief allusion to the Old Testament. At the root of the term *mysterion* is an idea familiar to Israel from the time of the prophets: that of the revelation of God's secrets. This use of the term figures in Wisdom 6:22, which presents the origin of nature and of wisdom as a revelation hidden yet open to all, initiated and non-initiated alike. Possession of this revelation is not the result of human effort; it is rather a gift God grants to man in response to the latter's invocation (see also Wis. 8:19–9:18). The text of Daniel 2:27-30, 46-48 is even more significant: Here the term "mysterion" takes on the fundamental meaning of "eschatological secret," or the mysterious proclamation of events that God has determined for the future. These secrets have either a soteriological (the world to come, the goal of the plan of salvation) or a theological (God's intimate being) bearing.

The Witness of the Gospels

Whereas the term *mysterion* is widely used before the New Testament,[31] it is found only once in the synoptic Gospels, in Mark 4:11 and its two parallels, Matthew 13:11 and Luke 8:10. In each case, *mysterion* refers to the coming of God's kingdom in Jesus: "To you has been given the secret of the kingdom of God" (Mark 4:11). In the Gospel of Mark, with its emphasis on the "messianic secret," the *mysterion* is Jesus himself. His eschatological irruption into history is a gift from on high demanding a decision of faith.

"To you it has been given to know the secrets of the kingdom of heaven" (Matt. 13:11; Luke 8:10). Here the secrets are in the plural: mysteries, and the knowledge of them is communicated. Matthew and Luke bring out the hidden, enigmatic nature of the parables and of their connection with the "mysteries."

30. See G. Bornkamm, "Mysterion," in *Grande Lessico del Nuovo Testamento,* vol. 7 (Brescia: Paideia, 1971), 645-716; Schulte, "I singoli sacramenti come articolazione del sacramento radicale," 89-97; L. Bouyer, *The Christian Mystery: From Pagan Myth to Christian Mysticism,* trans. Illtyd Trethowan (Edinburgh: T&T Clark, 1989), 5-130; C. Rochetta, *Sacramentaria fondamentale. Dal "mysterion" al "sacramentum"* (Bologna: EDB, 1990), 191-243; R. Penna, *Il "mysterion" paolino. Traiettoria e costituzione* (Brescia: Paideia, 1978).

31. R. E. Brown, "The Pre-Christian Concept of 'Mystery,'" *Catholic Biblical Quarterly* 20 (1958): 417-43; Brown, "The Semitic Background of the New Testament 'mysterion,'" *Biblica* 39 (1958): 426-48. The term was used above all in the apocalyptic and mystical literature of extra-biblical Judaism; see Bornkamm, "Mysterion," 686.

The revelation of the *mysteria*, which Jesus communicates to his own, is a pure gift of God. The plural is most likely a reference to the (plural) "plans of God" hidden in the Old Testament but now fulfilled by Jesus. Both uses allude to the fulfillment of Old Testament prophecies (Matt. 2:17-23; 3:3; Luke 24:26).

The Fourth Gospel

According to Jean Daniélou, "The Gospel of John is conceived as a sort of paschal catechesis. It shows the baptized the sense in which the sacraments they received during the Easter vigil are divine events that continue the *mirabilia* of Yahweh, both at the time of the Exodus and at the time of the Passion and Resurrection of Jesus."[32]

It is well known that the Fourth Gospel is rich with sacramental symbols and allusions. Cana, the bread of life, the washing of the disciples' feet, the pierced side of the crucified Christ, etc. all have a sacramental meaning, as the consistent exegesis of the patristic and mystical tradition attests. But, as Rochetta points out, there is an even deeper level in play here: The entire trajectory of Jesus' earthly story, which begins with his coming from the Father into the world and ends with his return from the world to the Father, reveals a sacramental character. The Fourth Gospel presents Jesus' existence as a great Passover: Jesus is the one who comes among us from the Father and who returns from the world to the Father after he has accomplished the work *(ergon)* that was entrusted to him; this is the meaning of Jesus' Pasch (John 13:1).[33]

The sacramental meaning of Jesus' existence thus finds its place within his movement of descent and re-ascent, a movement that is especially apparent in the bread of life discourse: "It was not Moses who gave you the bread from heaven; my Father gives you the true bread from heaven. For the bread of God is that which comes down from heaven, and gives life to the world" (John 6:32-33). At the end of this discourse, which is often referred to as a hard saying, Jesus asks them, "Do you take offense at this? Then what if you were to see the Son of man ascending to where he was before? It is the spirit that gives life, the flesh is of no avail; the words that I have spoken to you are spirit and life" (John 6:61-63). Although John never uses the term *mysterion,* the Fourth

32. J. Daniélou, *Sacramentum futuri* (Paris: Beauchesne, 1950), 139.

33. Rochetta, *Sacramentaria fondamentale,* 187. See also V. Pasquetto, *Incarnazione e comunione con Dio. La venuta di Gesù nel mondo e il suo ritorno al luogo di origine secondo il IV Vangelo* (Rome: Teresianum, 1982); O. Cullmann, *Les Sacrements dans l'évangile johannique, la vie de Jésus et le culte de l'Église primitive* (Paris: PUF, 1951).

Gospel is more explicit than the Synoptics about the trinitarian dimension of the mystery opened to humanity through Christ's Incarnation.

This trinitarian dimension appears, for example, in Jesus' way of referring to his disciples as those whom the Father has given him:

> All that the Father gives me will come to me; and him who comes to me I will not cast out. For I have come down from heaven, not to do my own will, but the will of him who sent me. (John 6:37-38)

> My sheep hear my voice, and I know them, and they follow me; and I give them eternal life, and they shall never perish, and no one shall snatch them out of my hand. My Father, who has given them to me, is greater than all, and no one is able to snatch them out of the Father's hand. I and the Father are one. (John 10:27-30)

> And this is the will of him who sent me, that I should lose nothing of all that he has given me, but raise it up at the last day. (John 6:39)

For John, God's presence is no longer bound to the Temple but to the person of the glorified Jesus. The sacraments that he entrusts to the Christian community flow from the paschal mystery and "take the place of the miracles Jesus worked during the time of the Incarnation."[34] As an expression of the power of the Spirit whom the Risen One bestows on the Church, the sacraments enable believers to live the life that he, Jesus, came to bring to the world and anticipate the time of the eschaton (John 20:21-23). The sacraments could not be a source of eternal life before Jesus' re-ascension to the Father, "for as yet the Spirit had not been given" (John 7:39).

The Pauline Letters

We find the term *mysterion* used about twenty times in the Pauline epistles. We limit ourselves to recalling the main passages. "But we impart a secret and hidden wisdom of God, which God decreed before the ages for our glorification" (1 Cor. 2:7). Paul is speaking here of his preaching, whose goal is to unveil God's "hidden wisdom," a term corresponding to the phrase "testimony" or "secret" of God used in 1 Corinthians 2:1. The central content of this "mystery" is given in the

---

34. Cullmann, *Les Sacrements dans l'évangile johannique*, 85.

event of Christ's Pasch, into whose understanding only the Spirit can introduce us (1 Cor. 2:10). *The mystery appears, then, in the very person of its Author:* "The mystery hidden for ages and generations but now made manifest to his saints. To them God chose to make known how great among the Gentiles are the riches of the glory of this mystery, *which is Christ in you, the hope of glory*" (Col. 1:26-27).

This passage highlights the historical-salvific dimension of the *mysterion,* and thus fittingly culminates in an eschatological claim concerning Christ, the hope of glory. Our passage follows Paul's hymn to Christ as Head of the whole cosmos:

> He is the image of the invisible God. . . . For . . . all things were created through him and for him. . . . For in him all the fullness of God was pleased to dwell, and through him to reconcile to himself all things, whether on earth or in heaven, making peace by the blood of his cross. (Col. 1:15-16, 19-20)

Such is the horizon of the mystery of Christ in us, the Christ for whom and in view of whom we were created, not least in order to be reconciled through the blood of his Cross.

Another important passage occurs in the Letter to the Ephesians: "For he has made known to us in all wisdom and insight the mystery of his will, according to his purpose which he set forth in Christ as a plan for the fullness of time, to unite all things in him, things in heaven and things on earth" (Eph. 1:9-10). This text is part of the great initial *berakah* of Ephesians 1:3-14, a hymn of blessing that recounts the major stages of God's saving plan and sets them within a trinitarian pattern. The pattern has its origin in the Father, becomes visible in the Son, and is accomplished in the Spirit for the sake of men, whether Jew or pagan. Christ represents the center and the decisive fulfillment of this great plan: "The *mysterion* is manifested in him as a gathering of all beings, visible and invisible, under his Lordship, so that they can be transfigured and brought to the Father in the power of the Spirit."[35] The

---

35. Rochetta, *Sacramentaria fondamentale,* 200. See Schulte, "I singoli sacramenti come articolazione del sacramento radicale," 179: "The type of *anamnesis* characteristic of the sacraments is incomparable, since it represents the *mysterion* that is already accomplished, yet is also still to be accomplished with a view to God's *eschata.* . . . The sacrament involves precisely the offering and acceptance of a co-participation in this 'recapitulation' *(anakephalaiosis),* which gathers up all the effects produced in the individual sharer in the sacramental event, as well as in the Church: the community of believers intent on proclaiming and celebrating God's mighty deeds to the glory of God the Father."

entire letter develops the same grand theme: Christ, regenerating humanity in his blood, gathers all things — the cosmos and history — into unity under his authority and leads them to God the Father in the Spirit. The conclusion of the First Letter to the Corinthians re-echoes this great vision of Christ, whom it shows handing over the kingdom to the Father after having subjected all things to himself (1 Cor. 15:24-28).

We find another relevant passage in Ephesians 3, where Paul writes:

> To me . . . this grace was given, to preach to the Gentiles the unsearchable riches of Christ, and to make all men see what is the plan of the mystery hidden for ages in God who created all things; that through the church the manifold wisdom of God might now be made known to the principalities and powers in the heavenly places. (Eph. 3:8-10)

This passage adds some new elements to the picture: Paul's reference to the *"oikonomia"* of the mystery, which he connects here both with God the Creator, and with the Church, through whose means the *mysterion* is manifested in the "today" of history. This reference is filled out in another familiar passage, Ephesians 5:32: "This is a great mystery, and I mean in reference to Christ and the Church." The majority of exegetes see in this "great mystery" a direct reference to the spousal relationship between Christ and the Church, which Genesis 2:24 had foretold and which Christian marriage must not only imitate but sacramentally reproduce.[36] For Paul, the profound meaning of the man-woman relationship is rooted in the *Christian mysterion,* thanks to the awareness of the New Covenant that is inaugurated by the paschal event and that gives rise to the Church, the Bride of Christ.

The semantic variations we find in the Pauline literature demonstrate the polyvalent use of the term *mysterion.* The *mystery of God,* the *mystery of Christ,* or the *economy of the mystery* all refer to complementary aspects of the same event. The first expression chiefly indicates the Author and Origin of the plan of salvation; the second concerns the One who revealed and accomplished the hidden plan in himself; the third portrays the plan's progressive actualization in history and recalls its stages, which, by God's design, find their fullness in the *eschaton* of Christ and its unfolding in the "already and not yet" of the Church.

For all the variety of its nuances, the meaning of the term *mysterion* remains fairly constant in the New Testament. Its classical meaning (a "hidden

---

36. K. H. Fleckenstein, *"Questo mistero è grande." Il matrimonio in Ef 5, 21-33* (Rome: Città Nuova, 1996).

reality") grounds its extension to designate God's salvific action in the depths of history and, finally, to refer to the reality of God's total plan, which reaches from eternity to the "today" in which the Church awaits the final *parousia*. The motive force of this *mysterion* is divine love, which prepared the whole plan in the secret of eternity, but has revealed it in Christ and now allows its unfolding until the end in the Church.[37]

The Trinitarian Drama of the *Mysterion*

The texts we have examined so far present the *mysterion* as the open manifestation "in Christ" of the triune God's loving plan in salvation history. Basing ourselves on these passages, we are now ready to undertake an exploration of their deeper meaning in light of a trinitarian theology inspired by St. Paul and St. John. The following reflection develops C. Rochetta's trinitarian approach to sacramental theology using resources drawn from the Christocentric and trinitarian theology of von Balthasar.[38] Taking our inspiration from the title of one of Balthasar's works, we will try to understand the "whole" in terms of the "fragment": Christ, who unveils the trinitarian logic of the *mysterion*.[39]

1. Everything (created reality, humanity, the actualization of redemption, and the gift of grace) has its origin in the Father and his free and benevolent choice of love. Everything that proceeds from the Father-Creator (in unity with the two other Persons of the Holy Trinity) is a free, gratuitous, and superabundant gift of love oriented toward the incarnate Son (Col. 1:16); all is created "for him" (Col. 1:16; John 6:37-39; Heb. 1:2).[40]

---

37. See John Paul II, *Man and Woman He Created Them: A Theology of the Body*, trans. Michael Waldstein (Boston: Pauline Books and Media, 2006) [= *TOB*], 487-91.

38. See Rochetta, *Sacramentaria fondamentale*, 393: "The New Testament notion of 'mysterion' (and consequently of 'sacrament') has a trinitarian pattern both in its 'descending' and in its 'ascending' phase: Everything comes from the Father through the Son in the Spirit, and everything returns to the Father through the Son in the Spirit. The formula 'from, through, in, to' (*a Patre, per Filium eius, Jesum Christum, in Spiritu Sancto, ad Patrem*) perfectly summarizes the movement of the 'mysterion,' from its beginning (*exitus a Deo*) to its fulfillment (*redditus ad Deum*). Because the liturgy reflects and re-presents the 'mysterion,' it has an essentially trinitarian structure. This structure is visible both in its doxological form and in its individual acts, including the sacraments." See also C. Vagaggini, *Il senso teologico della liturgia* (Rome: Paoline, 1965), 202-9; M. Ouellet, "Christocentrisme trinitaire," *Anthropotes* 16, no. 2 (2000): 305-24.

39. H. U. von Balthasar, *A Theological Anthropology* (Eugene, OR: Wipf and Stock, 2010) [the original German title is *Das Ganze im Fragment*, "The Whole in the Fragment" — Trans.].

40. Schulte, "I singoli sacramenti come articolazione del sacramento radicale," 153:

2. The incarnate Son receives this entire gift with the same gratitude with which he receives the Father's divine nature. For Christ, the superabundant gift of "all things" placed in his hands by the Father (John 6:37; 10:27-30; 17:2ff.) is a grace and a mission, that is, an opportunity to express in a creaturely medium his uncreated filial love for the Father. He performs this expression precisely by offering himself for the Incarnation (Heb. 10:5-10), taking the lost creature up into his obedience of love, and returning with it, now transformed into the Bride purified in his blood (John 14:31; Phil. 2:6-11; Eph. 5:25-26), to the Father.

3. Everything culminates in the "Gift" of the Holy Spirit, the eternal seal of trinitarian Love who becomes the seal of the reconciled creature's unity with God the Father in Christ. While the Holy Spirit already collaborates in creation and redemption, he is nonetheless not yet given "in Person" before the trinitarian event of Christ's Resurrection. This historical and eschatological event marks the inbreaking of the kingdom, that is, the glorification of humanity and of the cosmos in the power of the Holy Spirit, "that God may be all in all" (1 Cor. 15:28). The Spirit proceeds from the Father and the Son who died and was raised; he is poured into our hearts, where he glorifies the Father and the Son through the theological life of believers. He thus infinitely confirms the reciprocal love between the Father and the incarnate Son, while he introduces all men into this infinite exchange of Love. The Eucharist is the sacramental mediation par excellence of the gift of the Spirit, through whom man participates in the trinitarian exchange. Such is the mystery of "Christ in you, the hope of glory!" (Col. 1:27).[41]

Mysterion *and* Sacramentum *in the Writings of the Church Fathers*[42]

The evolution of the terms *mysterion* and *sacramentum* in the Fathers is rather complex. Broadly speaking, however, we can say that it is characterized by a

---

"Creatures exist through the Logos, that is, they are elements lovingly offered and pronounced by God in virtue of his personal relationship with his Logos."

41. See *Eucharistic Prayer II:* "Humbly we pray that, partaking of the Body and Blood of Christ, we may be gathered into one by the Holy Spirit." As Colombo comments in the spirit of the *Catechism* of Pius X, "The sacraments are efficacious signs of grace, that is, they signify and confer grace; but grace, as we learn from theological analysis, is the created aspect in man of the uncreated gift, which is the Holy Spirit. So to speak of 'grace' means to speak above all of the gift of the Holy Spirit" (*Teologia sacramentaria,* 107).

42. In addition to Bornkamm, "Mysterion," 706-16, see E. Ruffini, "Sacramentalità ed economia sacramentale negli scritti dei Padri della Chiesa," in E. Ruffini and E. Lodi, "*Mys-*

semantic shift from the biblical concept of *mysterion* ("salvific event") to the notion of *mysterion* current in the Greek cultural matrix: "mystery-truth." The appearance of the "mystery-rite" in the fourth century, although in harmony with the biblical *mysterion,* was insufficient to halt the growing division between these two fundamental meanings. In what follows, we present a few aspects of the question that help explain the evolution of the concept and its identification with, or translation as, "*sacramentum.*"

The *Mysterion*-Event in the First Three Centuries

Ignatius of Antioch (d. 107) qualifies Mary's virginity, her birth-giving, and Jesus' death on the Cross as "three mysteries" *(tria mysteria).* As Rochetta explains, "the first form in which *mysterion* is used is a 'retrospective' one: it designates the salvific events of Christ's life, understood as facts in which the unique '*mysterion tou theou*' is revealed and accomplished."[43]

In opposition to the Gnostic dualism of the second century, Irenaeus of Lyons (d. 202) worked out an entire theology of history centered on the idea of the "recapitulation" of all things in Christ. History — stretching from the creation of the world to the moment of the Incarnation and the birth of the Church — appears to Irenaeus as an event of revelation (*Adversus Haereses* 3.20.2; 4.6.6) through which God communicates himself to man and man is made capable of participating in God's life (4.20.6-7). Although Irenaeus refrains from using the term "*mysterion*" so as to avoid confusing the sacraments with the Gnostic "mysteries," his sacramental theology is clearly patterned on the reality underlying the use of the term in Pauline theology.[44] Irenaeus writes:

> When, however, the Word of God became flesh, he confirmed both these [man's image and likeness to God] for he both showed forth the image truly, since he became himself what was his image; and he re-established the similitude after a sure manner, by assimilating man to the invisible Father through means of the visible Word. (5.16.2)[45]

---

terion" e "*sacramentum.*" *La sacramentalità negli scritti dei Padri e nei testi liturgici primitivi* (Bologna: EDB, 1987), 59-204; also Rochetta, *Sacramentaria fondamentale,* 246-85.

43. Rochetta, *Sacramentaria fondamentale,* 246.

44. Rochetta, *Sacramentaria fondamentale,* 248. See also J. Daniélou, "S. Irénée et les origines de la théologie de l'histoire," *Recherches de Science Religieuse* 34 (1947): 227-31.

45. St. Irenaeus of Lyons, *Against Heresies,* reprint of vol. 1 of the *Ante-Nicene Fathers* (Ex Fontibus, 2010).

The theology of Alexandria initiates a semantic shift whereby *"myste-rion"* eventually comes to mean "the hidden truths of Christianity." We already glimpse this shift in Clement of Alexandria, but the tendency receives a strong philosophical and mystical accent in Origen (d. 254). For Origen, the whole of sensible reality is *"mysterion,"* the "real symbol" or "imitation and participation in the reality expressed" in it.[46] On Origen's account, the rites of the Christian religion are mysteries having their source in the great Mystery. They are partic-ular modes of participation in the Word-Sacrament according to its threefold manifestation: in the Incarnation [in the man Jesus], in the Scripture, and in the Church. Balthasar explains Origen's understanding of the sacramental efficacy of the Logos made flesh in the following passage:

> The Savior's humanity is the source of all salvation. According to Origen, the hypostatic union is the exemplary cause of every union pleasing to God (*C. Cels.* 3, 28). There is more: we would never have known God in himself if he had not become incarnate (*In Io. com.* 10, 4). His "hidden, ineffable, invisible" presence only becomes nearness for us through Christ (*In Ps. com.* 118, 169); but through him, God becomes "tangible," "read-able," as if he were flesh (*In Matth.* 1, 18; *C. Cels.* 4, 15). . . . Consequently, the touch by which Jesus healed was, like his miracles, the symbol of a more spiritual touch; the healing power his touch communicated to the eyes of the blind (*In Matth. com.* 16, 9) was the sign of an interior healing: "And more as a matter to be understood by the mind than to be perceived by the senses, Jesus touched the leper, to cleanse him, as I think, in a twofold sense — freeing him not only, as the multitude heard, from the visible leprosy by visible contact, but also from that other leprosy, by his truly divine touch." (*C. Cels.* 1, 48)[47]

The second, sensible manifestation of the Logos is the "mystical body," the Church:

> If the "mystical body" is not pure metaphor, if this communion of saints is truly incarnate, and if, moreover, this body is nonetheless distinct from every other body because it is the body of Christ — if these two condi-tions meet, then we must touch this body as we would touch the flesh of

---

46. Rochetta, *Sacramentaria fondamentale*, 250. See also H. U. von Balthasar, *Parole et mystère chez Origène* (Paris: Éd. du Cerf, 1957).

47. Balthasar, *Parole et mystère chez Origène*, 99-100.

Christ. Origen in fact compares baptism to direct contact with the Savior's humanity (*In Lev. hom.* 4, 8): through him, we are "sanctified and joined to the body of the Church." (*In Rom. com.* 8, 5)[48]

Despite Origen's symbolical realism, Ruffini is right to note that his sacramental theology stresses less revelation-as-event than revelation-as-teaching: "The actualization of the mystery no longer follows the old pattern: mystery-decree, mystery-event, mystery-eschatology. Rather, it follows a new pattern: mystery-truth hidden in God, mystery-truth gradually revealed in history, mystery-truth and eschatological vision."[49]

These witnesses authorize our conclusion that in the second century the term *mysterion* (and the plural, *mysteria*) was predominately used in the sense of "*actio salutaris Dei.*" In the third century, on the other hand, with the exception of Irenaeus, the term tends to become a synonym for knowledge and doctrine.

The *Mysterion*-Rite in the Greek Tradition (Fourth and Fifth Centuries)

By the fourth century, when the Christian community had finally emerged victorious in the Roman world, it no longer had reason to fear the influence of the mystery cults and could assimilate certain of their elements without endangering its own identity. Athanasius (d. 373), followed by the Cappadocians, Basil (d. 379), Gregory of Nazianzen (d. 390), and Gregory of Nyssa (d. 394), ordered their sacramental theology around the notion of the "*oikonomia* of salvation." Now, this economy was primarily a matter of mystery and symbol, since it appeared as the inbreaking of divine reality into the reality of this world and the consequent elevation of the realities of this world to heaven. In Gregory of Nyssa's sermon on the baptism of Christ, we read:

> The bread again is at first common bread, but when the sacramental action consecrates it, it is called, and becomes, the Body of Christ. So with the sacramental oil; so with the wine: though before the benediction they are of little value, each of them, after the sanctification bestowed by the Spirit, has its several operations. The same power of the word, again, also

48. Balthasar, *Parole et mystère chez Origène*, 109.
49. Ruffini, "Sacramentalità ed economia sacramentale," 88.

makes the priest venerable and honorable, separated, by the new blessing bestowed upon him, from his community with the mass of men. While but yesterday he was one of the mass, one of the people, he is suddenly rendered a guide, a president, a teacher of righteousness, an instructor in hidden mysteries.[50]

The *mysterion* figures in this passage as the reality of salvation hidden under the sacramental "symbol."

Among the Greek Fathers, John Chrysostom (d. 407) best represents the use of the term *mysterion* in relation to worship. Among the 200 times the term appears in his writings, about 160 indicate the "cultic mystery," which can refer either to baptism or (more often) to the Eucharist.[51] Generally speaking, the *mysterion* is an unknown, mysterious, and, therefore, terrible reality; it always implicitly includes some kind of knowledge bound to faith:

And in another sense, too, a mystery is so called: because we do not behold the things which we see, but some things we see and others we believe. For such is the nature of our Mysteries. I, for instance, feel differently upon these subjects from an unbeliever. I hear, "Christ was crucified"; and forthwith I admire his loving-kindness unto men: the other hears, and esteems it weakness. . . . He hearing of a laver, counts it merely as water: but I behold not simply the thing which is seen, but the purification of the soul, which is by the Spirit.[52]

John Chrysostom, then, regards the *mysterion* as a hidden reality that finds a new, living expression in the Church's liturgical action. In Homily 82 on the Gospel of Matthew, Chrysostom sees the sacramental mysteries (in first place the Eucharist) as a commemorative "symbol" that makes present the

50. Gregory of Nyssa, *In diem luminum sive In baptismum Christi: PG* 46.581. ["On the Baptism of Christ: A Sermon for the Day of the Lights," trans. Henry Austin Wilson (http://www.ewtn.com/library/PATRISTC/PII5-17.TXT)].

51. See E. Mazza, *La mistagogia. Una teologia della liturgia in epoca patristica* (Rome: CLV, 1988).

52. St. John Chrysostom, *In Epistulum primam ad Corinthios Homilia* 7.1, cited in Rochetta, *Sacramentaria fondamentale,* 256 [Homily 7 on 1 Corinthians, trans. Talbot W. Chambers (http://www.newadvent.org/fathers/220107.htm)]. We note that Chrysostom is one of the chief sources of O. Casel's theology of the mysteries. See "Das Mysteriengedächtnis der Messliturgie," *Jahrbuch für Liturgiewissenschaft* 6 (1929): 113-204; "Neue Zeugnisse für das Kultmysterium," *Jahrbuch für Liturgiewissenschaft* 12 (1935): 99-171.

mystery of Christ's Pasch, reactualizing its vital power in the "today" of believers' lives. In his celebrated mystagogical catecheses, Cyril of Jerusalem (d. 386), like Theodore of Mopsuestia (d. 429) after him, prolongs Chrysostom's approach along analogous lines. At the end of the fourth century, the sacramental rites are directly and habitually designated by the term "*mysteria.*" As Rochetta notes, "The mystery is any sacred reality or ritual action that hiddenly points to something other than itself. The accent is placed on the hidden, 'mysteric' element of the sacred reality or ritual action."[53]

This approach also accentuated reverential awe in liturgical celebration, an attitude that found an extreme expression in Pseudo-Dionysius (d. 520).

The *Mysterion-Sacramentum* in the Latin Tradition

In the Latin language, *sacramentum* is a technical term for the soldier's oath of fidelity. How, then, was this word chosen to translate *mysterion?* "Originally, *sacramentum* referred to an act of consecration, of initiation; in other words, it had the same meaning as *mysterion,*"[54] that is, a sacred reality. Tertullian was the first to adopt this term for expressing Christian realities such as the Creed, the *regula fidei* to which the Christian committed himself in baptism. Among the many instances of the term in Tertullian, scholars distinguish two fundamental meanings: in eighty-four cases, it refers to the "*iuramentum*" (military obligation, consecration, rite of initiation); in fifty other cases, the term is taken in the Greek sense of "*mysterion,*" where it has the essential meaning of a secret or hidden reality.

Both senses of the term were retained in the later tradition. Cyprian (d. 258) gives the term a markedly juridical cast, whereas Hilary of Poitiers (d. 367) frequently uses it to refer to the liturgical rites. St. Ambrose (d. 397) recovers the New Testament tradition, with its Pauline emphasis on *mysterion* as a reality of salvation history. The *mysterion* continues in the Church "*in mysterio,*" that is, in ritual action. For Ambrose, *sacramentum* also refers to the totality of salvation history, especially to the events of the Old Testament. The visible sign-character of the *mysterium* seems to be the dimension that gives his use of the term *sacramentum* its distinctive note. The *sacramentum ritualis* is the presence of the *mysterium* under a visible form. The Holy Spirit works within it and causes it to effect grace. Thus the waters of baptism, to

---

53. Rochetta, *Sacramentaria fondamentale*, 258-59.
54. Bornkamm, "Mysterion," 714.

take one example, derive their efficacy from the descent of the Spirit upon them, which communicates to them the power of sanctification. In the end, Ambrose's is a theology of the economy of salvation. The "mystery-sacrament" is the *actio Dei,* which appears as a salvific history involving the Church as an integral part; the "sacramental rites" of our present time have their place within this history.

St. Augustine (d. 430) marks a very important step in the development of sacramental theology. Its characteristic feature was a set of distinctions forged by theological controversy, whose effect was to narrow Ambrose's broader historical-salvific vision. Augustine's use of *sacramentum,* which is more frequent than *mysterium* in his work, chiefly has to do with ritual. As C. Couturier has shown, Augustine uses the term *sacramentum* in a threefold sense: as rite, symbol, and truth.[55] As rite, it refers to the sacred signs such as baptism, the Eucharist, etc.; as symbol, it refers to the allegorical sense of Scripture as a whole, which is founded on the relation of promise and fulfillment between the Old and the New Testament; as truth, it designates the foundational mysteries of Christianity, including the Trinity and the Incarnation.

Under the influence of his struggle against the Donatist heresy, Augustine develops the distinction between *sacramentum* and *virtus sacramenti, signum et res,* in order to justify the non-repeatable character of the baptismal sign (form), even in the case of those who have lost unity with Christ's Church. This is a fundamental distinction that often reappears in other, non-polemical contexts. What is the sacrament for Augustine? "The *sacramentum is* a *sacrum signum* [sacred sign]" (*De Civitate Dei* 10.5), a *"visibile verbum"* [visible word] (*In Johannis Evangelium Tractatus* 80.3). In *De Doctrina Christiana,* Augustine works out a general theory of the "sign," which he describes as a "reality that, beyond what it presents to the senses, makes us think of something other than itself."[56] Two things are required: a similitude between the sacramental sign and the reality it indicates, and also a word. Both together constitute the sacrament: "Take away the word, and the water is neither more nor less than water. The word is added to the element, and there results the sacrament."[57]

Concretely, the *res sacramenti* is "what happens in the soul" (*In Epis-*

55. C. Couturier, "*Sacramentum* et *Mysterium* dans l'oeuvre de St. Augustin," in *Études Augustiniennes,* ed. H. Rondet (Paris: Aubier-Montaigne, 1953), 163-332, here 181-83 and 256-62.

56. *"Res, praeter speciem quam ingerit sensibus, aliud aliquid ex se faciens in cogitationem venire"* (2.1.1).

57. Translation of this and the following excerpt taken from St. Augustine, *Tractates on the Gospel of John,* trans. John Gibb, from *Nicene and Post-Nicene Fathers,* First Series, vol. 7 (http://www.newadvent.org/fathers/1701080.htm).

tulam Johannis ad Parthos Tractatus 6.3.11): faith, the paschal event (8.14.15), grace (9.10.11). In order to show the Donatists that they possessed the *sacramentum* but not the *res*, Augustine sought to clarify his thought using the category of *sphragis*, of *consignatio* or *sigillum*: Supposing it is validly celebrated, baptism confers a "mark" (which can be neither repeated nor erased), a mark analogous to the image impressed on a coin or to a *"militiae character."* Thanks to these distinctions, then, Augustine gave the decisive push forward in the development of the notion of sacramental "character."

The value of the sacramental act is assured by the divine Word, which confers efficacy on the action that is celebrated. Like baptism, the eucharistic mystery is also accomplished by the divine word. In the sacramental act, Christ himself, and not the human minister as such, is the agent. Of course, Christ is the *Christus totus*, the Head with his body, Christ in his Church. This is why heretics, while they have the *"signum sacramenti,"* do not have the *"res sacramenti"*: since they are not in communion with the Church, they are not in communion with Christ and his grace. Augustine also explains that sacramental efficacy does not depend on the moral condition of the minister but rather on Christ himself: "There was to be a certain peculiarity in Christ, such that, although many ministers, be they righteous or unrighteous, should baptize, the virtue of baptism would be attributed to Him alone. . . . Paul may baptize, yet this is He that baptizes; Judas may baptize, still this is He that baptizes" (*In Johannis Evangelium Tractatus* 6.7).

These Augustinian distinctions filtered down to the following era through St. Leo the Great (d. 461) and St. Gregory the Great (d. 604), two important contributors to sacramental theology. Leo employed the terms *mysterium* and *sacramentum* as synonyms, stressing the *"hodie"* (today) of the liturgical rites with respect to the paschal mystery. For his part, Gregory distinguished "ever more clearly between 'sacrament' and 'mystery,' attributing the function of sanctifying to the first alone (or nearly alone) and referring the second to the hidden reality beyond the sign."[58]

The Meaning of a Semantic Evolution

During the first two centuries of the Christian era, the use of the term *mysterion* among the Greek Fathers conformed to the New Testament, where *mysterion* means the divine plan realized by God through the course of history

---

58. Rochetta, *Sacramentaria fondamentale*, 277.

in Christ and in the Church. Around the same time, the school of Alexandria introduced a new use of the term to mean an obscure truth or a truth to be believed. While for a time opposition to the pagan mysteries led the Fathers to hearken back to the classical sense of "hidden reality," or to *mysterion* in its Pauline meaning, by the fourth century the term was increasingly used to refer to the sacramental rites.

The Latin Fathers used *sacramentum* to translate *mysterion* in the sense of oath or baptismal consecration (Tertullian). Later, St. Augustine decisively marked Western theology by interpreting *sacramentum* using the notion of *"sacrum signum,"* or sacred sign. The post-Augustinian development increasingly identified *sacramentum* with the sign or visible form, and *mysterion* with the invisible reality *(res invisibilis)*.

Although far from complete, our investigation of the history of sacramental theology has enabled us at least in principle to identify a shift from the original meaning of sacramentality as "economy" to a more "functional" construal of this sacramentality, a shift whose key factor was the interpretation of the "*mysterion*-rite" as the sacred sign of an invisible reality. Moreover, the separation between "mystery-as-event" and "mystery-as-truth" gradually led to a dissociation of the celebration of the sacraments from the history of salvation: "The mystery celebrated is no longer understood as a real insertion or participation in the mystery as event, but merely as the enjoyment of the fruits produced by the latter."[59]

The result of this trend was an impoverished understanding of the causal relationship between God's salvific action and history. Indeed, this impoverishment ultimately affected the very notion of history itself. History came to be seen merely as a place where God's action — whether revelatory or "economic" — takes place: God's action is situated within history but does not actually make history.

The challenge currently facing sacramental theology, and above all eucharistic theology, is to rediscover the event-character of the *mysterion* and to express its intrinsic relationship with the salvation history that is actuated in the sacramental *anamnesis*. The question at stake here, then, concerns what we could call "God's history bound to human history,"[60] particularly as it affects our main topic, namely, the sacramental event:

59. Ruffini, "Sacramentalità ed economia sacramentale," 203. Ruffini continues: "Though rapid and brief, this sketch suffices to demonstrate the vast complexity of the process set in motion by an initial semantic modification of the term 'mystery.' This change led to various dissociations, the most relevant being the dissociation of revelation from dispensation" (204).

60. Schulte, "I singoli sacramenti come articolazione del sacramento radicale," 137.

At stake is precisely the *anamnetic character* of the sacramental event, which, though of course calling for theological reflection, must embody the full amplitude both of the historical fact of the Crucifixion and of the presence of the *mysterion* here and now in the ecclesial event. The same holds true for the eschatological dimension.[61]

This insight suggests the importance of further reflection to show how the eucharistic celebration can be understood as the Church's insertion into the intra-trinitarian exchange through the actualization of Christ's paschal sacrifice by the Spirit.[62] This approach calls for treatment of the question concerning the immanent Trinity and its economic manifestation in the paschal and eucharistic mystery of Jesus Christ. Once this fundamental question has been clarified, we can go on to the second part of our study, where we analyze the relation between the Trinity and nuptiality in the Eucharist.

The Trinity in History and the Eucharist

The elements that have come to light through our study of the biblical and patristic notion of *mysterion* can serve as the basis for a systematic reflection on the Eucharist. The divine Persons' gift to man in Christ prompts the question concerning the relation between history and transcendence, time and eternity, and between the salvific act accomplished once and for all and its many actualizations in the Church's eucharistic celebrations throughout history. We can ask three intrinsically interrelated questions here: First, how can the event of Christ be considered as "trinitarian history," that is, as an unfolding of the trinitarian "mystery" within time? Second, how can such a co-penetration of history and transcendence in the Incarnation of the Word be shared with human beings through the sacramental sacrifice of the Eucharist? Finally, what is

---

61. Schulte, "I singoli sacramenti come articolazione del sacramento radicale," 137.

62. See Schulte, "I singoli sacramenti come articolazione del sacramento radicale," 178: "It should be clear that the integrity of the sacramental event requires the participants — God, the Church, the individual man — to make themselves 'present' in a conscious manner. They do this by representing themselves and their 'path' of life before God, so as to enter with their *whole* (historically affirmed and configured) being into the *mysterion*, in other words, so as to participate in it. Now, the *anamnesis* aims precisely at this goal. For God (and for Christ), the *anamnesis* means the chance to offer, and to offer as a path of grace, the *mysterion* as (already) realized and revealed. This happens insofar as the *mysterion* takes concrete shape as a present reality, imparted *now* as gift for the future and for the eschatological state."

the Holy Spirit's role in linking the unique event of Christ, who was crucified, died, and was raised, with his eucharistic presence in human history? These questions demand a theological reflection that goes beyond the metaphysical approach to history and transcendence traditionally deployed to tackle the relationship between the uniqueness of Christ's sacrifice and the multiplicity of eucharistic celebrations.[63]

The Trinity in History: Jesus Christ, the One and Only Priest of the New Covenant[64]

Our reflection takes its inspiration from the Letter to the Hebrews, which presents Jesus as the High Priest of the New Covenant: "We have such a high priest, one who is seated at the right hand of the throne of the Majesty in heaven, a minister in the sanctuary and the true tent which is set up not by men but by the Lord" (Heb. 8:1-2). The priestly mediation of Christ, who "through the eternal Spirit offered himself without blemish to God" (Heb. 9:14), reestablishes communion between humanity and the Trinity: "Although he was a Son, he learned obedience through what he suffered; and being made perfect he became the source of eternal salvation to all who obey him, being designated by God a high priest after the order of Melchisedek" (Heb. 5:8-10).

The unsurpassable mediation of the High Priest has its roots in the ontological constitution of the incarnate Word, who is both true God and true man. He is installed as the sole Mediator between God and humanity through the historical-eschatological event of the Incarnation. The Letter to the Hebrews sheds light on Christ's appointment as high priest by recalling his obedience,

63. It may be helpful to note a pertinent remark of Klaus Hemmerle regarding the "historical lack of a Christian ontology" capable of correcting the intellectualistic drift of the modern account of revelation: "The most distinctive elements of the Christian claim did not renew in any lasting way our prior comprehension of the meaning of being. Indeed, they did not even spark the development of a genuinely Christian ontology. In short, the specifically Christian did not penetrate either the 'schools' or the general mental atmosphere, and it did not shape the subsequent history of thought" (*Tesi di ontologia trinitaria* [Rome: Città Nuova, 1996], 37).

64. For further study of the themes of this section, see: Balthasar, *A Theology of History*; B. Forte, *Trinità come storia. Saggio sul Dio cristiano*, Simbolica ecclesiale 4, 5th ed. (Milan: San Paolo, 1993); Mazzanti, *I sacramenti, simbolo e teologia*, vol. 1, 107-51; Mazzanti, *I sacramenti, simbolo e teologia*, vol. 2, 63-162; G. Leblond, *L'Agneau de la Pâque éternelle* (Paris: Desclée, 1987), 37-87 and 109-36; K. Hemmerle, *Partire dall'unità. La Trinità come stile di vita e forma di pensiero* (Rome: Città Nuova, 1998).

by which he was made "perfect" and so became the cause of eternal salvation — that is, the original sacrament of salvation. Our main interest here is the manner in which the Son of God "became man," which by implication is also the manner in which the man Jesus, the Mediator of the covenant, "becomes God":

> In his scandalous identity as the unique subject of divine and human history, which both find their accomplishment in him, Jesus Christ is the *covenant in person*. He is less the "hypostatic" meeting-point of two symmetrical natures than the subject of two conditions, two completely diverse and incomparable histories, whose meeting takes the form of a dynamic, relational interplay in him. This dynamic and disconcerting encounter is both the opening of one world to the other and the subversion of the human world by God's world.[65]

The covenantal history described by Bruno Forte in this passage is nothing other than the hypostatic union seen as founding the covenant between human and trinitarian history. Theologians agree that the hypostatic union grounds the theandric and salvific value of Jesus' gestures and mysteries. Nevertheless, for centuries theology held to an abstract metaphysical view of the union of the divine and human natures in the one Person of the Logos. The unique and unsurpassable dignity of Christ, the High Priest, was thought to rest almost exclusively on his divine Person rather than on what this Person had accomplished in history. Excluded from theological reflection, historicity could play no role in explaining the salvific value of Jesus' gestures and mysteries. We owe the rediscovery of the historical dimension to Casel's vision of the real presence of Christ's "mysteries" in the Church's liturgical action.[66] The initial resistance to Casel's approach mainly took the form of metaphysical objections to the possibility of repeating a historical event. The later rejection of a "theology of the mysteries" by Rahner and his disciples reflected their fundamental ontology and its one-sided stress on God's transcendental self-communication in Christ to the detriment of the concrete, historical dimension of his mysteries.

65. B. Forte, *Gesù di Nazareth, storia di Dio, Dio della storia* (Rome: Paoline, 1981), 189.
66. See S. Marsili, *Eucharistia, teologia e storia della celebrazione*, 2nd ed. (Casale Monferrato: Marietti, 1989), 56: "The real reason behind the hostility and apprehension Casel provoked was that his return to the 'mystery' caused a genuine crisis not for faith in the reality of the sacrament, but rather for the theology of the sacraments and of the Eucharist *in specie*, as transmitted by post-Tridentine theology."

The salvific value of Christ's acts depends not only on the fact that they proceed from a divine Person but also on the fact that, in himself, Jesus Christ is the history of the covenant between the Trinity and humanity. This covenant history intimately binds, without confusion or separation, the divine gift and the reception of the gift "in Christ." Jesus' entire life (prayer, work, preaching, Passion, sacrifice, death, etc.) reveals and communicates in theandrically enacted history the intra-trinitarian life of the Father and the Son in the Holy Spirit. As Rochetta notes, "The Father responds to Jesus' act of filial obedience by raising the Crucified One from the dead and glorifying him at his right hand as the *Kyrios,* giving him 'a name that is above every other name' (Phil. 2:9-11)."[67] The total incarnation of the Word thus culminates in his exaltation at the Father's right hand together with the Bride acquired by his paschal sacrifice. What was accomplished historically by Jesus' obedience is thus taken up into glory: It is the gift and response that contains the "yes" of God and of all humanity to the new and eternal Covenant.

Christ the Priest is the original sacrament of salvation, inasmuch as he incarnates the trinitarian event that is now open to all men in his human life, itself sealed and glorified in his death and Resurrection. Jesus is truly the Christ, the One anointed with the Spirit, the "Covenant in person," as Bruno Forte, echoing Hans Urs von Balthasar, puts it. His entire life, from his birth to his paschal fulfillment, is a marriage between the transcendent God and historical man, a historical and eschatological wedding. Jesus' entire history is thus a mediation of trinitarian history for humanity: a descending and ascending mediation that assures the reciprocal inter-penetration of history and transcendence.[68] It is precisely Christ's hypostatic union, which is historically realized, unfolded, and fulfilled through and in the grace of the Holy Spirit, that opens the world of the intra-trinitarian relations to those of man. In the event of Christ's Pasch, the reciprocal Love of the Father and the incarnate Son, mediated and ratified by the Holy Spirit, is accomplished and revealed as trinitarian history in human history. At the same time, the history of humanity, fallen into estrangement from God through sin, is taken up and transfigured within trinitarian history. The recapitulating grace of the dead and risen High

---

67. Rochetta, *Sacramentaria fondamentale,* 398. Rochetta's approach could be completed by an integration of the pneumatological aspect within a broader trinitarian framework.

68. Hemmerle, *Tesi di ontologia trinitaria,* 47: "Jesus Christ proclaims and brings the kingdom of God, and in him the kingdom comes to encounter us; between us and God there is thus a radical, unreserved communication. In Jesus, God himself shares all that is ours and all that is his. He does not exclude anything of himself from the gift that he makes to us in Jesus Christ; nothing of ourselves is left outside the history that becomes the very history of God."

Priest consists precisely in reconciling sinners with God and offering them a real participation in the exchange of love governing the relations between the divine Persons.

Time and eternity, history and transcendence are not mutually exclusive; to the contrary, they meet in Jesus Christ, the High Priest of the New Covenant.[69] He has opened the temple of the Trinity to humanity's worship and has transformed human history into a liturgy of trinitarian glorification. His pierced heart, the meeting point of all the mysteries, is the source from which eternal life springs up for human history.

Christ the Priest's Descending and Ascending Mediation in the Eucharist

The focal point of the integration of human history into that of the Trinity is the Church's liturgy, in which the trinitarian exchange attains its highest expression in the temporal sphere of sacramental language. This suggests the need to grasp the meaning of the liturgy and to clarify the nature of Christ's priestly mediation in the eucharistic mystery. "Are the mysteries of salvation *really* present at the heart of the liturgy when they are symbolically reproduced in sacramental worship?"[70] This question was the object of the lively debate generated by the publication of Odo Casel's work on the theology of the mysteries. Casel strongly affirmed the presence of Christ's "mysteries" in the liturgy, but failed to introduce the necessary theological qualifications and to clarify the difference between these mysteries and those of the pagan world.

---

69. We heartily recommend Balthasar's essay on the theology of history, which offers an original account of the harmony between time and eternity in Christ: "Now it is his receptivity to everything that comes to him from the Father that is the basis of *time* and *temporality* as these terms apply to the Son in his creaturely form of existence. This receptivity is the very constitution of his being, by which it is perpetually open to receive his mission from the Father. This temporal constitution is so far from contradicting his eternal being as Son that it is what directly, intelligibly and appropriately reveals that eternal being in this world. It is precisely *because* the Son is eternal that he assumes temporality as his form of expression when he appears in the world, elevating it so as to make of it a precise, suitable, perfectly fitting utterance of his eternal being as Son" (*A Theology of History*, 33-34).

70. Leblond, *L'Agneau de la Pâque éternelle*, 109. See Vagaggini, *Il senso teologico della liturgia*, 201: "When we speak of Christ's presence and action in his Church, we can be tempted to conceive of them as an ensemble of facts that took place once for all during Jesus' earthly life but that no longer belong to the present except in the purely psychological sphere of knowledge and affection."

His intuition was nonetheless correct, and it provided new resources for understanding that the Church's Eucharist contains not only the effects of Christ's Passion, but makes the Passion itself present to the Church's faith.

The basic question requiring deeper exploration here concerns the contemporaneity of Christ and the assembly during the sacramental event. Does he become our contemporary through the celebration? Or better: Do we somehow become contemporaries of his sacrifice? How do we understand his eucharistic presence, especially in its sacrificial dimension? Is it an effect produced at a distance from the theandric action accomplished by the Word, which transcends time and whose universal validity belongs solely to heaven? Or are we dealing with the transferal of our historical moment into the unique, eschatological event accomplished by the incarnate Word at the center of world history? Does the irreversible character of time permit such a transferal? More concretely, whose presence is that of Christ in the Eucharist? Is it the presence only of the sacrificed Christ, or does it include the Risen One as well? In sum, are the concrete and particular mysteries of Jesus' life and the paschal mysteries of Christ dead and risen irrevocably over and done with, or do they remain in a certain way open and accessible to all times?

All these questions are recapitulated in the question concerning Christ's presence in the Eucharist, which also determines which sort of communion with him the Eucharist effects. Before exploring the theo-dramatic character of this presence, we recall Trent's clear affirmation of the sacrificial value of the Eucharist. The decree on the sacrifice of the Mass (twenty-third session, 1562) reads as follows:

> He, then, our Lord and God, was once and for all to offer himself to God the Father by his death on the altar of the Cross (cf. Heb 7:27) to accomplish *for them* [there] an everlasting redemption. But, because his priesthood was not to end with his death (cf. Heb 7:24), at the Last Supper, "on the night when he was betrayed" (1 Cor 11:23), in order to leave to his beloved Spouse the Church a visible sacrifice (as the nature of man demands) — by which the bloody <sacrifice> that he was once for all to accomplish on the Cross would be re-presented, its memory perpetuated until the end of the world, and its salutary power applied for the forgiveness of the sins that we daily commit . . . he offered his body and blood under the species of bread and wine to God the Father.[71]

71. Denz 1740; see *Catechism of the Catholic Church*, 1366.

The Council of Trent clearly safeguarded the sacrificial character of the Eucharist in response to Protestantism, which one-sidedly stressed the uniqueness of Christ's sacrifice to the detriment of the sacramental realism of the Eucharist. While the Tridentine text indicates the difference between the bloody (Cross) and unbloody (Eucharist) modes of the sacrifice, it leaves open space for theology to explain the presence of the unique sacrifice of Calvary in the Church's eucharistic celebrations. The Council speaks of the "institution of the sacrifice of the Mass," which is the foundation of the sacrificial character of the Eucharist:

> Declaring himself constituted a priest forever according to the order of Melchizedek (cf. Ps 110:4; Heb 5:6; 7:17), he offered his body and blood under the species of bread and wine to God the Father, and, under the same signs, gave them to partake of to the disciples (whom he then established as priests of the New Covenant) and ordered them and their successors in the priesthood to offer, saying: "Do this in remembrance of me," etc. (Lk 22:19; 1 Cor 11:24), as the Catholic Church has always understood and taught.[72]

Having recalled these articles of faith, we can go on to pursue a deeper understanding of the manner in which Christ's unique sacrificial offering becomes present in the eucharistic celebration. For Johannes Betz, "The response can only be the following: it does not become present in an absolute sense, of itself, but rather in a relative sense, in symbol." According to Betz, the Eucharistic symbol owes its distinctive character to the fact that "Jesus himself conferred on the supper a new meaning: the presence of his action on the Cross." In the Church's Eucharist, then, "the Glorified One brings about this signification and saturates it with an unprecedented ontological density." Obviously this happens "not only in the participants' believing consciousness, but objectively, in the sacramental event." Not only because it is the Logos who

---

72. Denz 1740; see *Catechism of the Catholic Church*, 1366. See R. Tremblay, "A proposito della presenza sacrificale di Cristo nell'Eucharistia," in *Gesù Cristo Speranza del mondo*, ed. I. Sanna (Rome: PUL-Mursia, 2000), 509: "In order for this sacrifice to be prolonged in the Eucharist, the presence of the same Priest and the same victim is required. The Council [of Trent] refers to the eternal nature of Jesus' priesthood and to the permanence of the immolation that derives from it. The bond between the sacrifice of the Eucharist and the sacrifice of the Cross must therefore be forged in eternity. We must stress that the double offering of the Mass and the Cross nonetheless forms a single sacrifice, in the sense that we are simply dealing with two different ways of expressing the same immolation."

is acting, but because Jesus' human decisions themselves reach into eternity, which "contemporaneously embraces all the moments of past time."[73]

Basing ourselves on Betz's — still overly formal — position, we will now seek to unfold the trinitarian dimension of Christ's sacramental presence:

That which is made present in the Church's sacraments is this living dialectic of love between the Son who, in the eternal Spirit (Heb. 9:14), gives himself unceasingly by giving his Spirit (to the Father and to men); and the Father, who, because of the Son's obedience of love (Heb. 5:7), ceaselessly hears him by transfiguring him in the Spirit, making him Spirit.[74]

Christ's priesthood, which makes him sacramentally present in the Eucharist, is precisely this dramatic exchange between heaven and earth that integrates human history within the circle of the trinitarian relations. The High Priest who obeys and suffers, dies and is raised, ceaselessly intercedes at the right hand of the Father, to whom he presents his own sacrifice, so that the Holy Spirit may be communicated to redeemed humanity for the consummation of the eschatological wedding feast. Through the exercise of his eschatological and sacramental priesthood, God's eternal life is continually descending to Earth, and the broken and tragic history of humanity is continually being fully taken up and received into the "womb" of our trinitarian "native land."

A theological understanding of the sacrificial offering of the eucharistic Christ requires that we keep in mind two inseparable, but often neglected, truths: Christ's Resurrection and the gift of the Holy Spirit. This is because the Resurrection, accomplished by the Father in the power of the Holy Spirit, involves the glorification of Christ's life and his death, that is, of the sacrificial offering that "was" received and heard then and "always" is so now.[75] Christ

73. J. Betz, "L'Eucharistia mistero centrale," in *Mysterium Salutis,* vol. 8 (Brescia: Queriniana, 1977), 346-47.

74. Leblond, *L'Agneau de la Pâque éternelle,* 121. Leblond continues: "In this way, it is not only Christ's interior *disposition* that, as Fr. Vagaggini says, remains in glory and in some way creates the continuity between the saving act of the Cross and the sacraments lived throughout time. Rather, it is truly *this unique act,* accomplished once and for all, which is *always 'in act'* in glory and can thus be made present in the sacraments. Since the moment of his death, *Christ has never 'come out of' this unique act;* it is the act by which he was brought to perfection (Heb. 5:9), that is, constituted as the eternal, ever actual Pasch of salvation" (122-23).

75. Betz, "L'Eucharistia mistero centrale," 229-387, here 340: "The authors of the Letter to the Hebrews (10:5-10) and John (3:16; 12:27) already understand the Incarnation as the beginning of the sacrifice. In particular, the Resurrection, being a moment within the act of

does not leave this offering behind once it has been received and sealed, since he has now completely "passed over" into the eternally living sphere of the trinitarian exchange. It would be more correct to say that Christ is always in the process of "passing over" from this world to the Father, since his Pasch is not entirely completed until the final *parousia,* when the definitive Passover will be achieved — through him, with him, and in him — for his entire ecclesial and cosmic body. In all of this, the Risen One also shows himself precisely as the Mediator of the New Covenant, who draws all to himself through the gift of his eucharistic body, human history's eschatological center of gravity. This eucharistic body constitutes the fundamental unity of his ecclesial body and builds up the progressively unfolding unity of the *Christus totus* in the communion of the One Spirit.[76]

Taken in its profound meaning, the Resurrection is chiefly a salvific and spousal event.[77] It is the glorification of the Word made flesh and of his descent into the abyss of our *caro peccati,* the descent that ends in man's ascension to God's right hand for the eschatological wedding feast. The Resurrection seals the inscription of Jesus' divine filiation in his eucharistic flesh enabling the gift of the Holy Spirit to pour forth from it and so to guarantee the divinization of all the brothers and sisters of the Only-Begotten.[78]

---

the Cross, is the confirmation and acceptance of this sacrifice on the part of God." See also Mazzanti, *I sacramenti, simbolo e teologia,* vol. 1, 128-29: "In rising from the dead, Christ also plunged his earthly existence into the divine permanence; he made his past rise together with his body, inserting it into the perennial dimension of Life, of absolute presence. . . . His past has not disappeared, it is not in vain; it, too, has been transformed, just like his body, which continues to live in the eternal duration of the life without end. Christ's historical past shaped, identified, and permeated his body, which — as this historical body that he made his own — now lives risen with him. The historical and earthly experience of the risen Christ rises, too, never to die again, like the permanent event of the Risen One himself, in whose life and glory it participates."

76. Mazzanti, *I sacramenti, simbolo e teologia,* vol. 1, 130 n. 55: "All of this plays a fundamental role in the theology of the sacraments: They are a real encounter with the Risen One, who has raised up with him his historical past, his human lived reality; if this were not the case, the sacraments would be empty ritual, vain memory, sterile nostalgia, useless choreography."

77. The spousal meaning of the Resurrection will be developed further on in this work.

78. Following his monumental *Résurrection, mystère de salut,* F. X. Durwell explored the sacrificial dimension of the Eucharist from an eschatological perspective. R. Tremblay writes, "We are not dealing with an addition to the paschal mystery, or with a 'reproduction,' or a 'renewal,' or an indefinite multiplication, or a reiteration, or a re-actualization of the redemptive sacrifice. Rather, we are dealing with the sacrifice itself, insofar as it stands forth to disclose itself within the Church and, through her, in the world" ("A proposito della presenza sacrificale di Cristo nell'Eucaristia," 514). See F. X. Durwell, *L'eucharistie, sacrement pascal*

At this point in our reflection, we must register a criticism of the post-conciliar tendency to shift the Eucharist's sacrificial action almost exclusively to the side of the Church. Whereas post-Tridentine theology stressed the real presence of Christ's unique sacrifice in the Mass, contemporary theology risks emptying Christ's sacrificial action of meaning by its one-sided emphasis on the Church's prayer and action. Edward J. Kilmartin, following Cesare Giraudo, affirms that "the *transitus* of Christ himself is recalled but is not represented objectively and sacramentally to the assembly in the Eucharistic Prayer, for the Eucharistic Prayer is prayer of the Church."[79] This position seeks a more adequate integration of the ecclesial and pneumatological dimensions of the Eucharist, but fails to express its Christological dimension. Indeed, it empties the celebration of its theo-dramatic character. The Church becomes the main actor, and Kilmartin's emphasis on the Holy Spirit's actualization of Christ's presence to the Church and the Church's presence to Christ minimizes the action Christ himself performs in each celebration. When we examine this reduction more closely, we find that it is rooted in an overly extrinsic connection between the event of the Resurrection and the gift of the Spirit.

Even granting that the Holy Spirit accomplishes both Christ's Resurrection and the eucharistic *anamnesis,* this fact does not render Christ's gift irrelevant, but crowns it with the manifestation of its superabundant fruitfulness. While the pneumatological and eschatological aspect of Christ's Resurrection makes possible the concrete actuation of his "mystery" within the sacramental dimension of the Church, it does not follow that the Church becomes the main actor, as if the celebration were a kind of ecclesial self-realization. The Church has no power over the Risen One except for the power he conferred in his command, "Do this in memory of me." The Church is and remains the handmaid, who owes everything to her Master and who receives herself from the gift of the Bridegroom's eucharistic Body, which is what raises her to the dignity of the Bride. Of course, even in her receptivity, the Church is also active: she *allows* herself to be inspired, gathered, and governed by the Spirit of the Risen One, the Spirit communicated to her through the memorial of the sacrifice of the Cross. It is precisely the Spirit who has the power

(Paris: Éd. du Cerf, 1980); see also G. Martelet, *Résurrection, eucharistie et genèse de l'homme* (Paris: Desclée, 1972).

79. Kilmartin continues, "Sacramental celebrations are acts of the Church in which the Church manifests and realizes itself as body of Christ, of which Christ is the head and in which the Holy Spirit is the mediation of the presence of Christ to the Church and the Church to Christ." E. J. Kilmartin, *The Eucharist in the West: History and Theology* (Collegeville, MN: Liturgical Press, 1998), 370.

of recalling, actualizing, and universalizing Christ's gift. We will return to this point further on.

Seen in light of Christ's sacrificial Passover, the sacrament of the Eucharist appears above all as a free manifestation of the Risen One himself. In the mighty working of the Spirit, the Risen Lord comes to encounter the Church with the power of his death and of his entire, now glorified history.[80] As Vatican Council II affirmed, "We ought to believe that the Holy Spirit in a manner known only to God offers to every man the possibility of being associated with this paschal mystery" (*GS* 22). This contact is established "sacramentally" by the Church acting within the believing community that eucharistically receives its Master and Bridegroom. As a "sacramental" Bride, the Church is permanently constituted by the gift of the water, the bread, and the blood (the sacraments) that flow from the pierced heart of the "Lamb of the eternal Pasch."[81] The Church's identity emerges from the eucharistic Pasch, the permanent *kenosis* of Christ, who, in giving his eucharistic Spirit, draws her into his gift to the world. We now understand more clearly how the faithful participate in Christ's history, which unfolds trinitarian history in time: This history is open, offered, and even communicated to believers through the faith of the Church.

The Gift of the Spirit, Seal, Memory, and Fruitfulness of the Mysterion

The third question we address here concerns the role of the Holy Spirit in the eucharistic self-communication of the Trinity. Christ offered himself to the Father "through the eternal Spirit" (Heb. 9:14), waiting to be liberated by him from death and humiliation (Heb. 5:7-10). As the High Priest of the New Covenant, Jesus Christ wished to abandon himself and his destiny completely to the Father and to the love of the Spirit, leaving to them both the fruit of his human action and the extension and spread of his work. In the moment of "separation" at the end of his sacrifice, he entrusts himself to the Father, while allowing the Spirit to continue his work.[82]

In dying, Christ causes the Spirit to come forth from himself in the form

---

80. On this subject, see G. Mazzanti, "I 'quaranta giorni' del Risorto tra i suoi: paradigma dell'economia sacramentale e dell'eschaton realizzato," in *I sacramenti, simbolo e teologia*, vol. 1, 150-51. The reader will notice Mazzanti's debt to Balthasar here.

81. The title of Leblond's *L'Agneau de la Pâque éternelle.*

82. See H. U. von Balthasar, *Theo-Logic*, vol. 2: *Truth of God*, trans. Adrian J. Walker (San Francisco: Ignatius, 2004), 244ff.; Mazzanti, *I sacramenti, simbolo e teologia*, vol. 1, 131ff.

of gift: "When Jesus had received the vinegar, he said, 'It is finished'; and he bowed his head and gave up his spirit" (John 19:30). He not only expires, emitting his last breath; he hands over and gives his Spirit. According to the Gospel of John, Christ is glorified even in his death: His death coincides with the act of giving the Spirit. His glorification in death is precisely the seal of trinitarian love in his flesh. This glorification means the accomplishment of the mystery of the Father: "You are my Son, today I have begotten you" (Ps. 2:7; Heb. 5:5). It also means the accomplishment of the incarnate Son's obedience: "A [personal and ecclesial] body you have prepared for me. . . . Lo, I have come to do your will, O God" (Ps. 40:6-8; Heb. 10:5-7). Finally, it means the reciprocal granting of prayers by Father and Son, that is, their dramatic unity in the Spirit of love, who is now free to bring the saving work to its final fulfillment: "The Father and I are one" (John 10:30); we have "become one" in the glory of the Holy Spirit at the heart of the covenant with the created world. The culmination of trinitarian history is thus the culmination of salvation history. This history is to find its completion, after the pattern of Christ's rising, in the general resurrection of the dead. At that point, God will conclude the adventure of human history by manifesting his glory in Christ's final *parousia.*

Anthropologically speaking, the locus of human history's culmination in trinitarian history is the obedience of faith wrought in us when the Holy Spirit joins our sinful freedom to Christ's deed on our behalf. By means of this work, the Spirit reseals in us through faith what was first sealed in Christ's death and Resurrection. In the words of Klaus Hemmerle: "By giving us his Son, in making him take on our flesh, in giving him to answer in our place, obedient unto death, God did not do something *to* us: he did something *for* us, so that we, in and through him, might become capable of doing 'the same.'" The possibility of this "ethical" identification is based on the eucharistic identity by whose means "unconditional love, the Holy Spirit, is given to us with this finality: that through him, and that *sus-tained* by the Son, we may become able to give the response that this [love] *con-tains.*"[83]

In this sense, the universalization of salvation is the Spirit's task: it is he who *universalizes* Christ's individual and historical existence, revealing its normative validity for every individual human existence in history. According to Balthasar, the Spirit interprets "the life of Jesus . . . giving it the form and the

83. Hemmerle, *Tesi di ontologia trinitaria,* 47: "If God is triune and as such has his history in our history, then our basic situation of being human, our thinking and our being — in fact, all of being — undergoes a change, a con-version. This change surpasses every measure of 'traditional' human thought about God, about man himself, about the world, and about being" (48).

force of an unfailingly valid norm. In doing so, he does not issue a further, new revelation; he only exposes the full depth of what has been completed, giving it a dimension which is new for the world: a total relevance to every moment of history."[84] This is why it is the Spirit who is the agent of the sacraments, the actualizing mediation by which the whole (the *Totus Christus*) becomes accessible in the fragment (the sacramental symbol). The Holy Spirit is the ultimate object and subject of the exchange between the Father and the incarnate Son, precisely as the Spirit of the Covenant who makes human history into trinitarian history — that is, a history of salvation.

The Spirit's universalizing or unifying action consists above all in *anamnesis,* or the remembrance of Christ's work: "But the Counselor, the Holy Spirit, whom the Father will send in my name, he will teach you all things, and bring to your remembrance all that I have said to you" (John 14:26). Following Gustave Martelet, Giorgio Mazzanti stresses that the Holy Spirit's "activity of remembering . . . belongs to another order than any more or less mechanical recollection (M. Légaut)."[85] *Anamnesis* is not a mere "re-evocation," but a powerful "glorification," which makes Christ sacramentally present to the believer and leads the believer into communion with him. "He will glorify me, for he will take what is mine and declare it to you. All that the Father has is mine; therefore I said that he will take what is mine and declare it to you" (John 16:14-15).

This eucharistic and eschatological *anamnesis* of the Spirit brings to inter-penetration the time of concrete man — of the Church — and the time of the triune God. As Mazzanti writes:

> Only the Spirit-Memory (who is already the loving, mnemonic bond of love between Father and Son) holds together the "time" of the relational event of the trinitarian Persons, the "historical" time of the Risen One, and ecclesial and cosmic time. Only he brings about a continual exchange among these "times." There is thus a perennial communication, a continual perichoresis, of "times": from *intra-trinitarian* "time" to *historical and economic* time to *ecclesial and cosmic* time, all thanks to the active presence of the Spirit. The Christ of John's Gospel entrusts himself totally

84. Balthasar, *A Theology of History,* 82; see Mazzanti, *I sacramenti, simbolo e teologia,* vol. 1, 137ff.

85. Mazzanti, *I sacramenti, simbolo e teologia,* vol. 2, 113, citing G. Martelet, *Résurrection, eucharistie et genèse de l'homme. Chemins théologiques d'un renouveau chrétien* (Paris: Desclée, 1972), 191. The reference is to Marcel Légaut, *Introduction à l'intelligence du passé et de l'avenir du christianisme* (Paris: Aubier, 1970), 27.

to "this" Spirit, handing over "his" future for the salvific future of every man and woman.[86]

The Spirit's remembering is thus Christological, in the sense that it glorifies the total Christ by inserting the entire arc of his human adventure into trinitarian history. The Spirit's memory is in fact *trinitarian memory*. It eucharistically "recapitulates" human history. Not by undoing the proper consistency of creation, but by "super-creating" it by the power of the same Spirit. As Durwell puts it:

> In order to make the risen Christ present, the Spirit does not need to abolish the bread, the fruit of the earth and of human labor. It is mistaken to say, "What is on the altar is no longer bread, just the false appearances of bread." The Spirit does not put an end to the first creation, but leads it to its fullness. The only thing that breaks faith with creation is sin, whereas the Spirit transforms creation by enriching it, by "super-creating" it. He changes the bread and wine by making them bread and wine on a qualitatively higher level: the sacrament of the eschatological table.[87]

The foregoing helps us better understand the sense in which sinful human freedom's encounter with Christ at the heart of the eucharistic exchange between the divine Persons is anything but a threat. To the contrary, it reinforces, saves, and affirms the proper consistency of liberated human freedom.[88]

In conclusion, we recall the inseparability and complementarity of Christ's Resurrection and the gift of the Spirit within the event of the Eucharist, the *culmens et fons* of the Church's entire fruitful activity. The Resurrection is the signature of the (trinitarian) Name of God in the immolated and glorified flesh of Christ; the gift of the Holy Spirit is the communication of this Name to all the members of his body through communion in his paschal sacrifice. The outpouring of the Holy Spirit in the Church's Eucharist thus seals in human

---

86. Mazzanti, *I sacramenti, simbolo e teologia*, vol. 2, 111.

87. F. X. Durwell, *Lo Spirito Santo alla luce del mistero pasquale* (Rome: Paoline, 1985), 120. Durwell works out in some detail the pneumatological realism of transubstantiation hinted at earlier. This realism theologically and symbolically links our body to the body of Christ through the permanence of the eucharistic species.

88. See R. Carelli, *La libertà colpevole. Perdono e peccato nella teologia di Hans Urs von Balthasar* (Milan: Glossa, 1999). We will return to this topic below, where we will highlight the importance of the criteria governing Carelli's thesis on the relation between grace and freedom in Balthasar.

hearts the intra-trinitarian reciprocity, which then bears fruit — a fruit that is itself — within human relations. This *"mysterion"* of the covenant between God and humanity is now on its way toward the final *parousia,* when the Son, after having subjected all things, will subject himself to the Father, so that God may be all in all (1 Cor. 15:24-28).

This glimpse of the final destiny of cosmos and creation in the glory of the Trinity suggests a way of extending our theo-dramatic vision of the eucharistic mystery to the other sacraments. Seen in this light, in fact, the whole human reality of birth, growth, nourishment, healing, fatherhood, and covenant turns out to be sustained by a Christological and trinitarian "mystery" that confers an infinite meaning on our everyday life. Every situation of human life, even the most humble and hidden, has a connection with the flowing source of trinitarian Being. Here again, the reversal of meaning accomplished in Christ's Pasch bursts upon us with explosive force. The life of Jesus filled the empty jars of human life to overflowing with living water. Christ's death reversed the tragic meaning of human death, transforming it into a source of eternal life. Once again, it is not the episodes of human life that determine the meaning of the sacraments; it is the episodes of Christ's life that open trinitarian history in order that every episode of human life can participate in it as in its abyssally profound archetype. The Christological situations, then, are what give divine content to the human symbols that were prepared from all eternity to bear the "mystery."

Concretely, the birth of a child is a memory and a prophecy of the birth of the Son of God in eternity and in time. Baptism reveals the link between the "mystery" and the "symbol," making man participate in eternal filiation, "in Christ." In a similar way, a human wedding is the symbol of the "wedding feast of the Lamb"; Christ's paschal and eucharistic supper with the Church permits us a foretaste of this wedding feast here below, in this intermediate time before the final *parousia.*

CHAPTER 10

The Spousal Mystery of the Eucharist

So far we have presented the relation between the Trinity and the Eucharist from "above," that is, in light of the mystery revealed in Scripture. Although this approach is of fundamental importance, it does not of itself suffice to account for the spousal mystery of the Eucharist. In order to do justice to this sponsality, we must highlight the role of the human partner in the gift of God, with particular emphasis on faith's response to the trinitarian gift of the Eucharist. To that end, we propose a change of perspective in the present chapter, which will reflect on how the Eucharist relates to the Trinity from "below," that is, from an anthropological and ecclesial point of view. We will approach this goal in three stages: first, we will take stock of the data provided by the witness of faith in the Christian tradition; second, we will engage critically with the contemporary literature on "symbol and sacrament"; finally, we will offer our own contribution to reflection on the ecclesial Bride's participation in the sacrifice of the Mass.

The Trinitarian Gift of Christ the Bridegroom for the Church-Bride[1]

God's anger strikes him instead of the countless sinners, shattering him as by lightning and distributing him among them; thus God the Father,

---

1. The following section, comprising the first part of this chapter ("The Trinitarian Gift of Christ the Bridegroom for the Church-Bride"), reproduces, with slight modifications, an article previously published as "Trinity and Eucharist: A Covenantal Mystery," *Communio: International Catholic Review* 27 (Summer 2000): 262-83; translated by David L. Schindler Jr.

in the Holy Spirit, creates the Son's Eucharist. Only the Eucharist really completes the Incarnation.[2]

The Church owes her existence to the final act of Jesus, who, on the night before he died, left his disciples not only the memory of his sacrifice, but the command to re-enact this gesture: "Do this in memory of me." The Church scrupulously obeys the command she received from the Lord, because the Eucharist is the "summit toward which all of the Church's activity strives, and at the same time the source from which she draws all of her virtue."[3] Now, the Eucharist, source and summit of the life of the Church, refers in its origin, its structure, and its end to the mystery of the Trinity. That is why John Paul II placed the celebration of the Great Jubilee of the Year 2000 under the sign of the *glorification of the Trinity* by inviting all the faithful to *a particularly Eucharistic year,* because the "Savior, who took flesh in Mary's womb twenty centuries ago, continues to offer himself to humanity as the source of divine life."[4]

We propose here to explore the mysterious interrelationship between the Incarnation and the Eucharist. Is there in fact a genuine continuity between the trinitarian act of the Cross and that of the Mass, between the sacrificed body of Jesus Christ and his eucharistic body, scattered to the four winds? Or, in other words, can we speak of a eucharistic kenosis of the incarnate Word and even of a kenosis of the Trinity[5] in the Eucharist? What role do the Holy Spirit and the Resurrection play in this continuity/discontinuity? To be sure, we will be able only to touch on such questions in this essay, but we do so in the hope that we may illuminate the intimate bond that connects these mysteries.

Because Jesus instituted the Eucharist in order to establish the New Covenant, this latter will form the guiding thread for our study. We will begin by recalling the faith of the Church, the trinitarian structure of which has

---

2. Hans Urs von Balthasar, *Theo-Drama,* vol. 4, *The Action,* trans. Graham Harrison (San Francisco: Ignatius, 1994), 348.

3. Vatican II, Constitution on the Sacred Liturgy, *Sacrosanctum Concilium* 10.

4. John Paul II, *Tertio Millennio Adveniente* 55.

5. The expression is used by Hans Urs von Balthasar but not admitted by all theologians. It means that the Son does not empty himself of his divinity by becoming man as far as death on the Cross without expressing the mystery of the Father, whose Image and Word he is. Correlatively (and analogically), the Father cannot beget the Son without "emptying" himself in the very act of giving himself eternally to the Son in the Spirit. The trinitarian kenosis signifies the self-detachment within God that is revealed in the Son's kenosis on earth. See Balthasar, *Theo-Drama,* vol. 4: *The Action,* 319-32 ("The Cross and the Trinity").

emerged historically from her liturgical prayer. The *lex orandi, lex credendi,* indeed, offers a sure foundation, which presupposes the Holy Spirit's "theology in act." Next, through a consideration of the account of Jesus' priestly prayer in John's Gospel and the kerygma of the Resurrection in St. Paul, we will see that the trinitarian structure of the covenant springs from Scripture itself. Finally, in light of the nuptial symbolism of covenant, which can be drawn from many sources in the tradition, we will offer a more systematic interpretation of the eucharistic link between the Trinity and the Church. In order to justify our method, these three steps will be prefaced by a brief look at the contemporary problematic of the relationship between the Eucharist, the Trinity, and the Church.

"The Eucharist Makes the Church"

Several years ago, the common declaration that emerged from an ecumenical dialogue group between Orthodox and Catholics gave evidence of a renewed awareness of the intimate relationship between the Trinity, the Eucharist, and the Church. "The eucharistic celebration, taken as a whole, makes present the trinitarian mystery of the Church."[6] This succinct formulation felicitously expresses an ancient tradition. We owe the rediscovery of this ancient tradition to Fr. Henri de Lubac, who crystallized the thought of the Fathers in an expression that has become famous: "*L'Eucharistie fait l'Église* — the Eucharist makes the Church."[7] The ecumenical *rapprochement* with Orthodoxy depends in large part on the common exploration of the trinitarian link between the Eucharist and the Church, of which the Fathers of the Church had a much more vivid sense than we, and which has now returned to the center of the *intellectus fidei,* thanks to the liturgical and patristic renewal that was inaugurated at Vatican Council II.

The great pioneer of the contemporary "return to the Christian sources" has shown that, in the Fathers, Christ's sacramental body, which from the beginning was called the *Corpus mysticum,* was the source of the ecclesial

---

6. Common Orthodox-Catholic Declaration, cited by P. MacPartlan, *Sacrament of Salvation* (Edinburgh: T&T Clark, 1995), 71.

7. H. de Lubac, *Corpus Mysticum: The Eucharist and the Church in the Middle Ages,* trans. Gemma Simmonds et al. (South Bend, IN: University of Notre Dame Press, 2006), 88. Paul MacPartlan has shown the richness of this expression in his comparative study of the ecclesiastical and eucharistic thinking of Henri de Lubac and John Zizioulas: *The Eucharist Makes the Church* (Edinburgh: T&T Clark, 1993).

body, called the *Corpus verum*. This linguistic inversion, which strikes us as odd, did not in any respect attenuate the reality of Christ's substantial gift in the Eucharist. "Nourished by the body and blood of the Savior, his faithful thus all 'drink of the one Spirit,' who truly makes them into one single body. Literally speaking, therefore, the Eucharist makes the Church. It makes of it an inner reality."[8] The evolution of the ideas and *thought patterns* during the Middle Ages, which occurred through the influence of Beranger's eucharistic heresy, unfortunately brought about an inversion of this ancient order, for the benefit of a metaphysical affirmation of the real presence, but to the detriment of the vital bond between the sacramental body, which had become the *Corpus verum*, and the ecclesial body, which had become the *Corpus mysticum*. The expression "*Corpus mysticum*," however, in this context, no longer retained all of the symbolic realism it had for the Fathers.[9]

One of the most fundamental tasks of theology today is to open access once again not only to the metaphysical realism of medieval theology but also to the Fathers' symbolic realism, which professed in an integral manner the mutual relation between the eucharistic body of Christ and his ecclesial body on the basis of the biblical symbolism of the body and marriage. In this respect, renewal of the *intellectus fidei* requires the implementation of the principles offered in the encyclical *Fides et Ratio,* in particular the need for a realistic epistemology rooted in the historical aspect of knowledge and, thus, rooted in tradition. Indeed, the encyclical underscores the importance of a "rediscovery of the determining role of this tradition for a right approach to knowledge. The appeal to tradition is not a mere remembrance of the past; it involves rather the recognition of a cultural heritage . . . [which enables us] today to develop for the future an original, new, and constructive mode of thinking."[10] If this epistemological principle is valid for philosophy, it is *a fortiori* valid for a theology of the Eucharist and of the Church, which is demonstrated in an exemplary fashion by Fr. de Lubac.[11]

---

8. De Lubac, *Corpus Mysticum,* 88.

9. "[L]ater theologians . . . thought that in this case *mystical* was more aptly opposed to *natural*. . . . In itself, this was no mistake; because once the expression was acquired, it is clear that this opposition immediately presented itself, in the way that the *mystical* sense of Scripture is opposed to the *literal* sense. But a temptation developed here, in the case of the Church, precisely as in that of Scripture: the temptation of no longer seeing anything in this metaphor except the metaphor itself, and of considering 'mystical' as a watering-down of 'real' or of 'true.' To a greater or lesser extent, many fell victim to it" (de Lubac, *Corpus Mysticum,* 248-49).

10. John Paul II, *Fides et Ratio* 85.

11. "Ontological symbolism holds in the history of Christian thought — and in Chris-

Contemporary efforts to take a symbolic approach to eucharistic theology have not yet, on the whole, attained a satisfactory balance precisely because the witness of the sacramentary tradition has not been sufficiently integrated by the conceptual systems inherited from modern thought. These latter remain stamped by the rationalist or irrationalist tendencies of modernity and postmodernity. Karl Rahner's symbolic theology *(Theologie des Symbols)*, for example, applied to the relationship between the Eucharist and the Church, places too strong an emphasis on the Church which makes the Eucharist and not enough on the Eucharist as the source of the mystery of the Church;[12] the theology of Louis Marie Chauvet, moreover, although it has a trinitarian structure, is too dependent on the Heideggerian critique of onto-theology; hence, his thought betrays an ethical turn that is no longer able adequately to integrate the realism of the presence and the common action of Christ and the Spirit at the heart of the eucharistic event.[13] These systematic efforts nevertheless open up the way toward a development that would affirm to an ever greater extent both the legitimacy and the necessity of a properly theological and sacramental symbolics, in order to provide an understanding of the eucharistic faith that is more in line with the Church's great tradition.

Our intention in the following pages is not to determine and assess the state of symbolic theology in relation to the Eucharist;[14] nor to enumerate the new philosophical questions raised by the eucharistic mystery;[15] we wish merely to offer a reflection on the covenant between the Trinity and the Church, which occurs in the celebration of the Eucharist. The questions raised above invite us to contemplate the mystery of the contemporaneity of Jesus

---

tian thought itself — too important a place to remain unknown or neglected with impunity — particularly in sacramental theology" (de Lubac, *Corpus Mysticum*, 256).

12. See K. Rahner, *Schriften zur Theologie*, vol. 4: *Zur Theologie des Symbols* (Einsiedeln: Benziger, 1960), 275-311; K. Rahner, *The Church and the Sacraments*, trans. W. J. O'Hara (Freiburg: Herder, 1963); for a criticism, see G. Colombo, "Dove va la teologia sacramentaria," and "Teologia sacramentaria e teologia fondamentale," both in *Teologia sacramentaria* (Milan: Glossa, 1997), 4-86; A. Bozzolo, *La teologia sacramentaria dopo Rahner* (Rome: Las-Roma, 1999).

13. L. M. Chauvet, *Symbole et Sacrement. Une relecture sacramentelle de l'existence chrétienne* (Paris: Éd. du Cerf, 1987). For a criticism, see G. Lafont, "Recensione di L.-M. Chauvet, Symbole et sacrement," *Ecclesia orans* 5 (1988): 231-35; Y. Labbé, "Réceptions théologiques de la 'post-modernité,'" *Revue des Sciences Philosophiques et Théologiques* 72 (1988): 397-462.

14. See G. Colombo, *I sacramenti, simbolo e teologia*, vol. 1: *Introduzione generale*; vol. 2: *Eucaristia, Battesimo e Confermazione* (Bologna: EDB, 1997-1998).

15. See J.-L. Marion, *God without Being*, trans. Thomas A. Carlson (Chicago: University of Chicago Press, 2012).

Christ not only with the Church of the third Christian millennium, but with the Church of every age. This unique man will remain with the Church until the end of time in a manner that is authentically human, which we ought to understand in the light of the new eucharistic presence that he acquired through his resurrection from the dead. Nothing less than the whole trinitarian mystery is needed to bring about the continuity/discontinuity of the Incarnation in the Eucharist, which allows the Church, Body of Christ and Bride of the Lamb, to experience the Whole in the fragment.

"This Cup Is the New Covenant in My Blood"

"Before the feast of the Passover, when Jesus knew that his hour had come to depart out of this world to the Father, having loved his own who were in the world, he loved them to the end" (John 13:1). After this solemn exordium, St. John the Evangelist recounts the gesture of the washing of the feet, which explains the meaning of the sacrament that the apostle Paul and the synoptic evangelists recount in terms of the institution of a rite: "The Lord Jesus on the night when he was betrayed took bread, and when he had given thanks, he broke it, and said, 'This is my body which is for you. Do this in remembrance of me.' In the same way also the cup, after supper, saying, 'This cup is the new covenant in my blood. Do this, as often as you drink it, in remembrance of me'" (1 Cor. 11:23-25).

This final symbolic and solemn act of the Lord, which may indeed be read as a last testament, ritually anticipated the bloody sacrifice that was to take place the following day upon the Cross. Here, Jesus revealed his most profound identity, "knowing that the Father had given all things into his hands and that he had come from God and was going to God" (John 13:3); the words of the gospel take for granted that Jesus knew the ultimate meaning of his mission and the eschatological significance of his gesture; the synoptic Gospels bear witness to this as well: "I tell you I shall not drink again of this fruit of the vine until that day when I drink it new with you in my Father's kingdom" (Matt. 26:29). Disregarding the objections raised by a certain Bultmannian form of biblical criticism, the Church's scriptural testimony affirms that, at the moment he instituted the Eucharist, Jesus was aware of having been sent into the world in order to seal the new and eternal Covenant between God and his people.[16]

---

16. See Chapter 9, note 6, above regarding overcoming the systematic doubt raised by Bultmannian exegesis regarding Jesus' consciousness of his mission.

This is proven by the Scriptures and by the way they have been continuously interpreted by the tradition, which quite early on made explicit the trinitarian structure of the Eucharist.

The early Church, in effect, testifies to the divine identity of Jesus through the trinitarian structure of the liturgy and especially of the eucharistic prayer. St. Justin provides one of the first testimonies: "There is then brought to the president of the brethren bread and a cup of wine mixed with water; and he taking them, gives praise and glory to the Father of the universe, through the name of the Son and of the Holy Ghost, and offers thanks at considerable length for our being counted worthy to receive these things at His hands."[17] Later, the Apostolic Constitutions of the third century likewise preserve the same structure, with an insistence on the epiclesis: "Send down upon this sacrifice your Holy Spirit, the witness of the Lord Jesus' sufferings, that he may show this bread to be the body of your Christ, and the cup to be the blood of your Christ."[18]

In the preface to his eucology, Serapion takes up once again this same trinitarian perspective. Doing so, however, he insists in a particular way on the involvement of the faithful in this mystery, which has been called an epiclesis upon the community: "We beg that you make us living men. Give us the spirit of light, that we might know you, who are true, and the one whom you have sent, Jesus Christ. Give us the Holy Spirit, that we might speak and express your ineffable mysteries." The awareness of sharing in a singular communion with the Trinity is confirmed in the passage that follows this text, in which the prayer that Jesus instituted is raised powerfully to the Father: "May the Lord Jesus Christ speak in us with the Holy Spirit; may he celebrate you through us. For you are beyond every principality, power, might, and lordship, you are beyond any name that is spoken, not only in this century but in the century to come."[19]

If we take into account the differences concerning the epiclesis, the analysis of the Church's early liturgical traditions reveals that the literary structure of the anaphora corresponds to the trinitarian economy of salvation. We give thanks to God the Father *(eucharistia)* in recalling the gift of Jesus Christ *(anamnesis)* that the Holy Spirit makes present in the Church's offering *(epiclesis)*. "The tradition of the Churches of Antioch, Jerusalem, and Syria have a clear trinitarian structure"; "the tradition of the Church of Alexandria (as well

17. St. Justin, *First Apology* 65.3-4, trans. Marcus Dods and George Reith, from *Ante-Nicene Fathers*, vol. 1 (http://www.newadvent.org/fathers/0126.htm).

18. *The Apostolic Constitutions* 8.12, trans. James Donaldson, from *Ante-Nicene Fathers*, vol. 7 (http://www.newadvent.org/fathers/07158.htm).

19. *The Eucology of Serapion*, cited in A. Hamman, "L'Eucharistie," *Ichthus* 9 (Paris: Desclée, 1964), 45.

as the Roman Canon) expresses in a different way the same truth, namely, that the Holy Spirit is the agent of the consecration."[20] Amidst the diversity of the traditions that accentuate here the words of the priest in the name of Christ or there the action of the Holy Spirit, "the whole sacramental celebration is founded on two affirmations: it is Christ who acts and he does so by means of the Holy Spirit *(epiclesis)*."[21]

Arguing against the Gnostics, St. Irenaeus of Lyon, for his part, places the emphasis on the realism of the flesh and blood of Jesus Christ, "the new oblation of the new covenant; which the Church receiving from the apostles, offers to God throughout all the world, to him who gives us as the means of subsistence the first-fruits of his own gifts in the New Testament." It is through the sovereign name of Jesus Christ, of which the Father is twice the author, that the Church offers her sacrifice to the almighty God, a sacrifice that is pure and holy like the incense in the book of Revelation, symbolizing the prayer of the saints (Rev. 5:8).[22]

Let us add the testimony of the most famous doctor of the fourth century Syrian Church, St. Ephraim, who expresses the realism of the eucharistic consecration in trinitarian terms that are still close to Jewish categories: "Jesus our Lord took the bread in his hands — in the beginning it was only bread — blessed it, made the sign of the cross upon it, consecrated it in the name of the Father and in the name of the Holy Spirit, broke it, and distributed the pieces to his disciples; in his most merciful goodness, he called the bread his living body and filled it with himself and with the Holy Spirit; stretching out his hands, he gave his disciples the bread that his right hand had consecrated."[23] St. Ephraim, justly called "the cither of the Holy Spirit," underscores more than anyone else the realism of the gift of the Holy Spirit that makes possible the most intimate communion between God and man: "Take it and eat it with faith, do not be afraid, for it is my body, and he who eats it with faith, eats along with it the fire of the Holy Spirit. . . . *Take it and eat it, all of you,* and through it, eat the Holy Spirit; for it is truly my body, and he who eats it will have eternal life."[24]

In this context, we cannot ignore St. Augustine, who is more inclined to develop the relationship between the eucharistic body and the mystical body

20. M. M. Garijo Guembe, "Epiclesis y Trinidad. Estudio històrico y sistematico," *Eucaristia y Trinidad* 24 (1989): 115-47, here 144-45. See also L. Bouyer, *Eucharist: Theology and Spirituality of the Eucharistic Prayer* (South Bend, IN: University of Notre Dame Press, 1989).

21. Garijo Guembe, "Epiclesis y Trinidad," 146.

22. St. Irenaeus of Lyons, *Adversus haereses* 4.17-18: *PG* 7.1019-29.

23. St. Ephraim, *Mimré 4: On the Passion;* cited by Hamman, "L'Eucharistie," 97-98.

24. St. Ephraim, *Mimré 4: On the Passion;* cited by Hamman, "L'Eucharistie," 98.

of Christ. The formula "The Eucharist makes the Church" is a particularly fitting expression of his thought. Indeed, the bishop of Hippo repeatedly draws attention to the mystical union of Christ and the Church on the basis of the eucharistic unity of the whole Christ, Head and Body. He emphasizes the need for unity by reference precisely to the nuptial symbol of two in one flesh and in one body: "You who have life in him, you become a single flesh with him. This sacrament does not entrust us with the body of Christ so that we may be divided. The Apostle affirms that this truth was announced in the Scriptures: *the two shall be one flesh. This is a great mystery, I mean that it refers to Christ and the Church* (Eph 5:31-32). In another place, speaking of the same Eucharist, he says: *All of us form one bread, one body.*"[25]

In his commentary on John's Gospel, the great Latin doctor takes up the same Pauline analogy of Christ-Bridegroom, Church-Bride and connects it with Eve's birth from the side of Adam: "As Adam slept, Eve was formed from his side; as Christ died, the lance pierced his side so that the mysteries could pour forth, from which the Church was born."[26] St. Augustine therefore inserts the Eucharist, the sacrifice of the covenant, into the heart of the spousal union between Christ and the Church. Christ leaves his heavenly Father in order to cleave to his bride the Church and become one flesh with her.

According to the way it was understood from the beginning, the mystery of the New Covenant thus extends even to the sacrificial realism of the Cross and the Eucharist; Christ, the Bridegroom immolated and offered in communion, gives birth to the Church-Bride from his pierced side and unites himself to her in a single eucharistic flesh. This nuptial mystery is consummated by the epiclesis upon the gifts and upon the community, which indissolubly unites redeemed humanity, in the Holy Spirit, to her divine Bridegroom through the body and the blood of Christ. Such is the faith the Church has always professed, which the *Catechism of the Catholic Church* has reiterated in reference to the Council of Trent: "At the last supper, 'on the night when he was betrayed' [1 Cor. 11:23], he wanted to leave to his beloved spouse the Church a visible sacrifice (as the nature of man demands) by which the bloody sacrifice which he was to accomplish once for all on the cross would be re-presented, its memory perpetuated until the end of the world."[27]

25. St. Augustine, *Sermon on the Sacrament of the Altar, Addressed to Neophytes* (*PL* 2.406); Augustine's authorship of this sermon is contested. Cited in Hamman, "L'Eucharistie," 245.

26. St. Augustine, *Commentary on the Gospel of John* 9.10.

27. *Catechism of the Catholic Church*, 1366, citing the Council of Trent, Denzinger-Schönmetzer, *Enchiridion Symbolorum* (1965) [hereafter Denz], 1740.

These several testimonies offer a good illustration of the central object of the Church's faith concerning the memorial of Jesus Christ in the Eucharist. The celebration of the Eucharist "is properly the paramount act of faith of the whole Church. Presented with the total and unique object of her faith, the 'mystery,' the Church in the Mass grasps it or rather surrenders to it."[28] Through the celebration of the mystery of the New Covenant, the Church is introduced by the Holy Spirit into Christ's sacrifice to the Father for the salvation of the world. She becomes contemporaneous with the trinitarian act of her founder, which fulfills the Jewish *berakah* and institutes a new rite of communion for the Church of every age. We must now develop Jesus' intention by returning to Scripture in order to grasp at its source the first theological reflection on the trinitarian gift of the Eucharist and thus the permanent actuality of the mystery of the Incarnation.

"I Have Given Them the Glory That You Have Given Me"

The faith to which the Church's tradition bears witness is bathed in the light of Scripture, above all in the perspectives that John and Paul offer, which most explicitly present a trinitarian understanding of the mystery of the Church and the Eucharist. Here, we will take up very briefly the meaning of the priestly prayer Jesus utters at the moment he offers himself as a sacrifice and, then, the Pauline vision of the saving power of the Resurrection, which crowns the mystery of the covenant.

When Christ prepares to surrender himself into the hands of sinners in order to be put to death, he makes sure beforehand to surrender himself into the hands of the apostles, so that they may be the witnesses and custodians of his total and eschatological gift. But even before he proceeds to the act of eucharistic self-giving, Jesus addresses himself to the Father in prayer, in order to thank the Father for having brought him to this supreme hour of love: "Father, the hour has come; glorify your Son, so that your Son may glorify you and that, according to the power you have given him over all flesh, he may give eternal life to those whom you have given him!" (John 17:1-2). Here, Jesus reveals the very essence of his priestly existence: his love for the Father ("so that your Son may glorify you") and his will to reveal the Father's love to sinners ("glorify your Son"). He places himself in the Father's hands in order to be glorified by him, that is, in order to be

28. Bouyer, *Eucharist,* 469.

surrendered, out of love, into the hands of sinners, so that he can bring them eternal life.

This prayer for glorification expresses the prophetic awareness Jesus had in relation to the final fulfillment of his sacrifice for the remission of sins. Being the one sent by the Father to fulfill the Scriptures, he is not only willing to sacrifice himself but also to allow himself to be sacrificed by the Father, who surrenders him into the hands of sinners (John 3:16) so that the Father's love for sinners might be revealed and made once again accessible to them. By allowing himself to be immolated, out of the pure obedience of love, the Son thus reveals his personal, filial relationship to the Father and assumes into this relationship both the sinful world in need of redemption and the testimony of the trinitarian God: "And this is the testimony, that God gave us eternal life, and this life is in his Son. He who has the Son has life; he who has not the Son of God has not life" (1 John 5:11-12).

Just a word here about the evil of sin, which offends God and has to be assumed and overcome for the love of the covenant: "The estrangement of the sinful No is overtaken and encompassed by the free-will, obedient estrangement of the divine Yes. God's anger at the rejection of divine love encounters a divine love (the Son's) that exposes itself to this anger, disarms it and literally deprives it of its object."[29] Against the interpretations that would try to play down the scandal of the Cross, Balthasar emphasizes that Christ is accused of the world's sin *(Stellvertretung)*[30] so that he can drink its cup to the dregs and, thereby, bring about a true reconciliation between the world and God. The mutual glorification of the Father and the Son thus passes through the darkest night of divine abandonment; but its fruit is the gift of glory that shines out at the end of the priestly prayer: "That they may all be one; even as thou, Father, art in me, and I in thee, that they also may be in us, so that the world may believe that thou hast sent me. The glory which thou hast given me I have given to them, that they may be one even as we are one" (John 17:21-22).[31]

I have given them the glory that you have given me. In Gregory of Nyssa's eyes, the gift of unity and the gift of glory are one and the same thing, that is, the gift of the Holy Spirit: "Now, the bond of this unity is glory. The fact that glory is the name of the Holy Spirit, no one who has examined the issue would be able to deny, if he has considered these words of the Lord: *The glory you*

---

29. Balthasar, *Theo-Drama*, vol. 4: *The Action*, 349.

30. On this notion, see the article of A. Espezel, "Le mystère pascal au coeur de la médiation du Christ," *Communio: Revue catholique international* 17, no. 2-3 (1997): 101-11.

31. "These are the thoughts which the Last Supper was to convey to the first Christians, and which were to impregnate their later eucharistic celebrations" (Bouyer, *Eucharist*, 97).

have given me, I have given to them. In effect, he gave them this glory when he said to them: *Receive the Holy Spirit.*"[32] The same author returns to this point elsewhere in even more explicit terms: "And the Spirit is called glory, as Christ says to the Father in another place: 'Glorify me with the glory which I had from the beginning before the world was, with thee. . . .' Nothing existed before all ages except the Father, the Son, and the Holy Spirit." This glory was therefore the Spirit, "and so Christ says in the passage previously quoted, 'The glory which thou hast given me, I have given them,' so that through it" — through the Spirit — "they may be made one with me, and through me with thee."[33]

Indeed, Jesus' priestly prayer culminates in the petition for the gift of trinitarian unity; this unity is the glory of God insofar as the gift from the Father to the Son and from the Son to the Father is confirmed by the Spirit of their communion, the Spirit of glory. Eusebius of Caesarea, for his part, affirms: "Thus the Father and the Son are one through the glory they share, and by giving to his followers a part in their glory, God has found them worthy even of this union itself."[34] The Eucharist is the privileged place of this gift because it is the Holy Spirit's role, according to St. John, to recall the work and the Person of Jesus, and in particular the memory of his eucharistic deed: "But the Counselor, the Holy Spirit, whom the Father will send in my name, he will teach you all things, and bring to your remembrance all that I have said to you" (John 14:26).

The mystery of the Incarnation thus comes to completion in the Eucharist, in the moment that the communion in Jesus' paschal sacrifice brings the inner unity of the divine Persons into the hearts of believers. This trinitarian unity becomes not only open and accessible to them, but truly communicated and received in communion: "that the love with which thou hast loved me may be in them, and I in them" (John 17:26). The Eucharist is in this way inscribed into the sacramental logic of the Incarnation.[35] It is instituted not only in memory of the Incarnation, for lack of something better, but in order to con-

---

32. Gregory of Nyssa, *Homily 15 on the Song of Songs.*

33. Gregory of Nyssa, *Treatise on the Text: "Then the Son himself shall be subject"* (PG 44.1316-21), cited by H. de Lubac, *Catholicism: Christ and the Common Destiny of Man,* trans. Lancelot Sheppard and Elizabeth Englund (San Francisco: Ignatius, 1988), 403. See also Gregory of Nazianzus, *Fourth Theological Oration* 5 (PG 36.108).

34. Eusebius of Caesarea, *The Sacerdotal Prayer,* in *On the Theology of the Church,* book 3, chaps. 18-19 (PG 24.1042-43); cited by de Lubac, *Catholicism,* 397.

35. A. Scola, "La logica dell'incarnazione come logica sacramentale. Avvenimento ecclesiale e libertà umana," in *Wer ist die Kirche? Symposion zum 10. Todesjahr von Hans Urs von Balthasar* (Einsiedeln: Johannes Verlag, 1999), 99-135.

tinue and "fulfill" *("accomplir")* the Incarnation through the sacramental economy of the Holy Spirit in the Church. From this perspective, the sacrament of the Eucharist is in a certain way the pneumatological and ecclesiological modality of the Incarnation. It gives the most concrete and the most universal expression to the mystery of the covenant between the Trinity and humanity. Thus, from the ecumenical perspective of the Second Vatican Council, the universal Church appears as a "mystery of communion," as "a people brought into unity from the unity of the Father, the Son, and the Holy Spirit."[36]

A new appreciation of the gift of the three divine Persons in the eucharistic memorial will perhaps allow us a better understanding of the trinitarian logic of this continuation and fulfillment. Jesus takes the bread, blesses it, breaks it, and hands it over, saying: "Take and eat it, this is my body." In carrying out this deed and in uttering these words, Jesus gives himself, as the Son of the Father, to the very end of love. This is why he was sent, and he pours the whole of his substance into the elements that he chooses, in order to remain concretely present among his disciples. Jesus does not merely celebrate the Jewish Passover with his disciples; he institutes "his" memorial: "Do this in memory of me." His prophetic act, in conjunction with the Word, creates a new order of things (*berit:* set of conditions): that is, it gives rise to the New Covenant, which brings the first to completion.

Jesus' eucharistic deed, which he expresses in the first person as a gift that is altogether his own, is not for all of that any less an act of obedience. Jesus carries out the Father's will for his life and his death. Balthasar writes: "It is the Father who gives his Son's Body for the world through the unitive mediation of the Spirit; this Body is given up through divine love more than through the world's hatred."[37] The greatest sacrifice thus falls to the Father, who hands his Son into the hands of sinners. "God so loved the world that he gave his only Son" (John 3:16). He takes the bread from heaven, blesses it, breaks it, and distributes it so that his Son's executioners might have life in abundance. Jesus' words are thus, above all, the words of the Father, who, in giving his Son to sinners, gives in fact himself. What appears to be his "wrath" is ultimately only an economic modality of his absolute gift. And this gift is offered with such perfect consent from the Son that, in reciprocally "glorifying" each other, the Father and the Son even give the "communion of glory" that unites them: the Spirit of Truth.

36. *Lumen Gentium* 4; *Unitatis Redintegratio* 2.
37. H. U. von Balthasar, *Theo-Drama*, vol. 5: *The Last Act*, trans. Graham Harrison (San Francisco: Ignatius, 1998), 477.

That is why the Eucharist must in the end be just as much an act and a word of the Holy Spirit. "In all three Synoptic Gospels," writes Balthasar, "the true Lord of the table in the eucharistic banquet is the heavenly Father, who sets out for us the best he has to offer. Similarly, the precious taste of the gifts welling up within all the sacraments comes from the Holy Spirit, the Spirit of the giving Father and of the Son who lets himself be given as food and drink. It is the Spirit who enables us, when we pray the Canon of the Mass with the Church, to address all thanks and gratitude, all honor and glory, through him and with the Son to the Father."[38] The Spirit gives flavor to the gift. He makes it truly assimilable through faith and thus gives it a saving power "for us" in making it present on the altar and in the heart of the liturgical assembly.

The activity proper to the Spirit is to universalize the eucharistic gift from the Father and the Son for us and to incorporate us into it — or, rather, to incorporate us into the dead and resurrected Christ by giving us a communion in his offering, which the Father was pleased to accept. This is what accounts for the central role of the epiclesis; the Spirit is called upon the gifts and upon the community, in order to bring to completion "in us" the Gift of the Father and the Son, who sanctify us by sharing their "communion" with us. The Spirit thus continues to carry out in the Church the work of glorification that he began in Christ, in the supreme sacramental hour of the Cross, when Jesus let out his last breath "for us," surrendering his Spirit into the hands of the Father.[39] John sees the whole sacramental economy as flowing forth from the supreme gift of "the Spirit, of water and blood," which confirms in the flesh of the incarnate Word the Truth of the God of the Covenant.

"Designated Son of God in Power according to the Spirit of Holiness"

John's Gospel views the gift of glory in relation to the very event of the Incarnation and the Cross. In St. Paul, the gift of glory passes through the kenosis and the Resurrection: "And being found in human form he humbled himself and

38. H. U. von Balthasar, *Epilogue*, trans. Edward T. Oakes (San Francisco: Ignatius, 2004), 117.

39. "*The giving up of the Spirit is his greatest gift; he gives it by renouncing it.* Only through the departing of this Soul *(Anima)* is Christ's Spirit freed and handed over because of his willingness to remain thirsty, joined with the soul/blood in order to issue, 'together' with it, from the pierced side of the dead Christ (in the Gospel of John, in fact, living water means the Spirit: Jn 7:37-39; 3:4-10)" (G. Mazzanti, *I sacramenti, simbolo e teologia*, vol. 2: *Eucaristia, Battesimo e Confermazione* [Bologna: EDB, 1998], 109).

became obedient unto death, even death on a cross. Therefore God has highly exalted him and bestowed on him the name which is above every name, that at the name of Jesus *every knee should bow,* in heaven and on earth and under the earth, and *every tongue confess* that Jesus Christ is Lord, to the glory of God the Father" (Phil. 2:8-11). This liturgical proclamation is taken up more kerygmatically at the beginning of the Letter to the Romans: "The gospel concerning his Son, who was descended from David according to the flesh and designated Son of God in power according to the Spirit of holiness by his resurrection from the dead, Jesus Christ our Lord" (Rom. 1:3-4); and again from a soteriological perspective in the First Letter to the Corinthians: "If Christ has not been raised, then our preaching is in vain and your faith is in vain" (1 Cor. 15:14).

The kerygmatic formula of Romans 1:4, with its trinitarian structure, links the resurrection of Christ with the power of the Spirit of holiness. The formula of the Letter to the Philippians, without mentioning the Spirit (unless we see a reference to him at the beginning of the chapter), nevertheless connects the gift of the Name to the raising up of Jesus as Lord, which corresponds to the resurrection brought about by the power of the Spirit: "If the Spirit of him who raised Jesus from the dead dwells in you, he who raised Christ Jesus from the dead will give life to our mortal bodies also through his Spirit, who dwells in you" (Rom. 8:11). By resurrecting Christ from the dead, the Spirit does not force him back into the limitations of a temporal and spatial body; rather, he glorifies his flesh in a way that is inconceivable to us, but which becomes accessible and even familiar through the eucharistic miracle: "It is sown a physical *(psychikon)* body, it is raised a spiritual body. If there is a physical body, there is also a spiritual body. Thus it is written, 'The first *man* Adam *became a living being*'; the last Adam became a life-giving spirit" (1 Cor. 15:44-45). The flesh of Christ was not left behind like so much useless and outgrown matter; on the contrary, it is preserved as precious, that is, it is transfigured, universalized, and raised from the experiential sphere of our senses so that it may participate in the glorious sphere of the Spirit and faith.

It is important in this context to underscore the trinitarian meaning of the Resurrection, which is inseparable from its soteriological significance. We cannot reduce it, as has so often been the practice, to a mere apologetical function. The Resurrection is the core of all the mysteries; the Trinity, the Incarnation, the covenant, and the Eucharist all stand or fall with the Resurrection, because it is the seal of the Trinity on the union of the partners of the covenant. By raising, through the power of the Holy Spirit, the one who was crucified, God in effect definitively revealed his trinitarian identity and man's vocation to eternal life. More precisely, he reveals that One of the Trinity has become man and that, in this man, *all* men are called to become God through participation.[40] Now, the trinitarian identity of Jesus, true God and true man, is fully manifest when the Holy Spirit raises him from the dead, confirming that he is the Son whose sacrifice was pleasing to the Father. The Resurrection therefore confirms that God the Father has a consubstantial and eternally begotten Son who has taken on flesh in the power of the Holy Spirit in order to save humanity.

The role of Christ's resurrection in the faith of the Church is thus not a secondary matter. It is not an extrinsic confirmation of the divinity of Christ, whose theandric deeds would in any event have had the power to transcend time and space and extend their effects in the sacraments. The resurrection is the seal of the Trinity on the covenant. The covenant, which was established in the Person of the incarnate Word and sealed in blood on the cross, receives its confirmation when the Holy Spirit raises him from the dead. The inbreaking of the Holy Spirit in the flesh of Christ, who transforms this flesh into a spiritual body and a life-giving spirit, is the proof of the success of the covenant, the proof of the fecundity of the covenant, which is the outpouring of the same Holy Spirit. That is why it falls to the Holy Spirit to "confirm" the fecundity of the Sole Mediator of the New Covenant, through the Eucharist that makes the Church, by making her into the Body of Christ and the Bride of the Lamb.

What the Spirit of Truth confirms in eternity, namely, the consubstantial Love between the Father and Son, he comes to confirm in the economy by designating Christ the Son of God with power through the resurrection from the dead; Jesus is thus "confirmed" as Christ, that is, as the Sole Mediator of the New Covenant, the source of the life-giving Spirit poured out over all flesh. This confirmation is poured out over the Church at Pentecost, in which the apostles receive the Holy Spirit, the Witness *par excellence* of the Love of the Trinity, who communicates to the apostles his light and his power in order that they themselves might become witnesses of the resurrected Savior and ministers of the New Covenant.

"This Is a Great Mystery"

At the climax of the high prayer of the anaphora, after the recitation of the memorial, the Church places the following exclamation in the mouth of the priest: "Let us proclaim the mystery of faith." This cry of jubilation refers to

---

40. The Fathers often repeated the axiom: "God has become man so that man may become God."

the event that is right at that moment occurring: namely, the conversion of the elements that represent the life and work of man into the body and blood of Christ through the power of the Holy Spirit. What this conversion means is the great passage of the world to God, which occurs through Christ's paschal mystery. This event is the mystery of the New Covenant, the nuptial encounter between Christ the Bridegroom and the Church his Bride, who was born from his pierced side. Through the power of the blessing, or the epiclesis, upon the eucharistic species, the living Christ, whose death we proclaim until he comes again, is joined to the ecclesial community as his body and his spouse. "This is a great mystery," exclaims Paul the apostle, as referring sacramental marriage to the union of Christ and the Church.

"It is thus a single body, a single person, a single Christ, the head with his members, who is raised up to heaven, and in his gratitude he cries out, as he presents the Church in her glory to God: 'Here is bone of my bone and flesh of my flesh!' And revealing that he and she are joined together in a genuine per-. sonal unity, he says again: 'and they shall be two in one flesh.' "[41] Fr. de Lubac used this beautiful text from Rupert to conclude his study on the Eucharist and the Church in the middle ages. The text captures beautifully the symbolism of the body and the wedding feast, which is a common possession shared by the tradition. In this text, we see the rejoicing of the New Adam who gives thanks for "the personal unity" (is this not the Holy Spirit?) to the Father who joins him to his Body and Bride.

St. Ambrose sees in the Eucharist the "wedding gift" that Christ makes to his spouse, and in communion he sees the kiss of Love. And Cabasilas can with justice observe: " 'This is a great mystery' (Eph. 5:32) says the blessed Paul in exalting this union. This is the much celebrated wedding feast in which the most holy Bridegroom leads the Church to the marriage ceremony like a betrothed virgin (cf. 2 Cor. 11:2). Here, Christ feeds the choir that surrounds him and that is why among all his mysteries we are flesh of his flesh and bone of his bones (Gen. 2:23)."[42]

In this same vein, Pope John Paul II indicates the parallel between the text from Genesis 2:24 and Ephesians 5:32, by underscoring that Christ's gift to the Church is not only a redeeming love but a properly spousal love. It is the love of the divine Bridegroom who sacrifices himself for his Bride in order to sanctify her, "that he might present the church to himself in splendor, without spot or wrinkle or any such thing, that she might be holy and without blemish"

---

41. Rupert of Deutz, *De divinis officiis* 1.2.11 (*PL* 170.43).
42. Cabasilas, *Life in Christ* 4.30.

(Eph. 5:27). What characterizes spousal love is the desire for reciprocity. The reciprocity between Christ and the Church can be perfect because the Lord himself, through his eucharistic gift, expands his Bride's capacity to love: consider Mary, the New Eve, at the foot of the Cross in which the nuptial symbol finds its full realization. Moreover, the pope concludes, "The expressions referring to care for the body, and above all for its *nourishment,* to *providing food for it,* suggest to a number of Scripture scholars a reference *to the Eucharist,* with which *Christ, in his spousal love, 'feeds' the Church.*"[43]

Hans Urs von Balthasar, in turn, takes up this nuptial symbolism, which was familiar to the Fathers:

> The primeval unity lies in the fact that *the Church was fashioned out of Christ just as Eve was fashioned out of Adam:* She flowed from the pierced side of the Lord on the cross, where he slept the sleep of death inflicted on him by the powers of evil. In this sleep of mortal suffering, he cleansed the Church "that he might present [her] to himself . . . in all her glory, not having spot or wrinkle or any such thing" (Eph 5:27). As man, he allowed himself to fall into the sleep of death so that, as God, he might derive from this death the mystery of fruitfulness by which he would create for himself his Bride, the Church. Thus the Church is, yet is not, Christ himself — his body and his spouse. "He who loves his own wife, loves himself. For no one ever hated his own flesh; on the contrary, he nourishes and cherishes it, as Christ also does the Church (because we are members of his body . . .)" (Eph 5:29-30). We are not speaking here of an individual physical body, but rather of the whole fruitfulness of the "seed" (1 Jn 3:9) of God "ingrafted" (Jas 1:21), in the ecstasy of suffering on the cross, into the spiritual/physical body of the Church and of all those in the Church who are ready to receive it.[44]

"This is a great mystery" — because of the miracle of transubstantiation, which makes the Church the Body of Christ and the Bride of the Lamb. This nuptial mystery infinitely multiplies the dignity of the human partner and at the same time confirms the importance of his body, his history, and his rootedness in the cosmos. But its supreme grandeur lies in the humility of the

43. John Paul II, *Man and Woman He Created Them: A Theology of the Body,* trans. Michael Waldstein (Boston: Pauline Books and Media, 2006) [= *TOB*], 486.

44. H. U. von Balthasar, *The Christian State of Life,* trans. Sr. Mary Frances McCarthy (San Francisco: Ignatius, 1983), 233-34.

divine partner, who in each instance humbles himself to the utmost in order to espouse his fallen but redeemed creature, through his Son "in agony until the end of time" (Easter). Indeed, the eucharistic mystery contains not only an effect of Christ's passion, but the very act of his passion-death-resurrection. This act, which was placed by God "once and for all" (Heb. 10:10) at the center of human history, transcends the linear time that we experience and confers upon the *kairos* of the faith an eschatological covenantal structure. This trinitarian act breaks into the history of the Church as Jesus broke into the place where the disciples were gathered on Easter evening, showing to Thomas the holes in his hands and the wound in his side and solemnly declaring: "Blessed are those who have not seen and yet believe" (John 20:29).

The permanence of the wounds in the body of the resurrected Christ gives symbolic expression to the permanence of Christ's historical and eschatological sacrificial deed, which remains forever accessible through the liturgical act of the Church. Such a permanence is possible by virtue of the Resurrection. For the Resurrection is the crowning of the Incarnation; it is not its cancellation, but its confirmation, or indeed its glorification. This glorification is the work of the Holy Spirit, who thus places the final seal of the Trinity on the flesh and blood of Christ. This body that is glorified in the Spirit is in effect the supreme testimony of trinitarian Love. For the resurrection of Christ is the Father's answer to the Son's love unto death; it bears witness to the fact that God did not only reconcile himself to the world through the crucified Son but that he gave himself up as absolute Love. In allowing the Spirit to descend upon the apostolic Church in prayer with Mary, the Father gives witness to his fruitfulness, which extends even to the glorified flesh of the Son, and with the Son *(Filioque)* he sends the ultimate fruit of their eternal communion. The Church, the covenantal mystery and mystery of communion, is nourished at the spring of the Eucharist on the *Donum Dei*.

God is Love. And it is in the eucharistic kenosis of Jesus Christ that this Love is handed over to the world. The Father and the Holy Spirit have no less a part than he does in this kenosis. For in raising Jesus from the dead, and in distributing his sacramental body and blood, they do not eliminate his kenosis, but glorify and confirm it; this kenosis incarnates the most profound inner mode of being of the Trinity: "How could God have hidden himself more humbly than behind a piece of bread and a few drops of wine, how could he have better taught us divine humility and nobility than in this hiddenness?"[45]

---

45. H. U. von Balthasar, *Eucharistie. Gabe der Liebe* (= *Antwort des Glaubens*, 44) (Freiburg, i.Br.: IBK, 1986), 12.

The foremost dream of this humble love is to bring all of humanity into communion with his divinity, with his ineffable quality of being absolute and vulnerable Gift, in the spousal and kenotic modality *par excellence:* the Eucharist. The whole of the Church's testimony springs from this Gift of Love and her entire incarnate spirituality drinks from this spring of glory that Jesus never allows to run dry, "so that the love with which thou hast loved me may be in them, and I in them" (John 17:26).

Welcoming an Incomparable "Present"

The path that we have followed has brought us to the affirmation of a kenotic continuity between the Incarnation and the Eucharist, the mystery of the covenant. This continuity is possible by virtue of the Holy Spirit, who glorifies Christ and makes his humanity available for the mystery of the marriage between the Trinity and the Church in the Eucharist. Having placed ourselves resolutely within the perspective of the faith, we have underscored the continuity and the eschatological contemporaneity of the Word made flesh in the Eucharist. Our age is, by contrast, inclined to underscore the discontinuity because of the mediation of the ritual and because of a theology of symbol that is still too dependent on modern rationalism.[46]

A simple re-reading of Scripture in the Spirit of the tradition has allowed us to recover the witness of the two-thousand-year-old faith of the Church and has given us the freedom to contemplate the eucharistic mystery, which is accessible to faith alone, as the Gift of the Whole in the fragment — God the Bridegroom, the Church-Bride, and the wedding feast of "the Lamb of the eternal Passover"[47] — which can already be savored in the *sobria ebrietas* of the Spirit, in the hope of final consummation. This is the reason for the authentic jubilation of the Church in the beginning of the third Christian millennium. The Church does not celebrate merely a gift received from a tradition that is buried in the past; rather, it joyously receives an incomparable "Present," a veritable "wedding gift" that comes from the future and that already transports her into the Kingdom of God.

This incarnate Love gives itself unreservedly to the immaculate faith of

---

46. "Never before has theological thinking been so imperiously called to produce its own logic, a radically theo-logic (which precisely does *not* mean 'dialectical theology')" (Jean-Luc Marion, "Le présent et le don," in Aa.Vv., *L'Eucharistie, pain nouveau pour un monde rompu* [Paris: Communio-Fayard, 1981], 129).

47. G. Leblond, *L'Agneau de la Pâque éternelle* (Paris: Desclée de Brouwer, 1987).

Mary, who is always present within the Church's prayer so that the Church, as a bride or a poor handmaid, may receive the kenotic form of the gift that God chose in order to express his own superabundance of glory, even while remaining familiar, almost ordinary, in his seeking correspondence and reciprocity: Take and eat, this is my body; take and drink, this is my blood. "If I then, your Lord and Teacher, have washed your feet, you also ought to wash one another's feet" (John 13:14). That is why the Trinity's Church humbles herself in the ecstasy of adoration and the kenosis of service, so that the Kingdom may come, on earth as it is in heaven. *Adoro te devote latens Deitas, quae sub his figuris vere latitas.*[48] "The Spirit and the Bride say: 'Come!' May he who hears say: 'Come!' And may he who is thirsty draw near, may he who desires receive the water of life without price" (Rev. 22:17).

Symbol and Sacrament in a Trinitarian Perspective

Having offered a substantial account of the Church's eucharistic faith in the first part of this chapter, we are now ready to engage critically with new approaches to eucharistic theology based on the notion of symbol. Many contemporary theologians argue that the Eucharist, together with the sacramental economy in general, is better understood as a "mediation" and "symbol" of man's encounter with God, rather than merely as a "means" or "instrument" of salvation. Now, this sacramental encounter in faith occurs within a ritual language belonging specifically to the symbolic order.[49] We must accordingly reflect now both on symbolical and sacramental language and on its ontological and theological significance as a mediation of the covenant between God and man in Christ.[50]

Our treatment of symbol and sacrament will refer to two authors who have developed a fundamental sacramental theology in a symbolic key: Giorgio Mazzanti and Louis-Marie Chauvet. Dialogue with Mazzanti's "symbolic-nuptial" and Chauvet's "symbolic-paschal" approach will clarify our own

---

48. "I adore you with devotion O my hidden God, who truly veils himself in these forms" (St. Thomas Aquinas).

49. L. M. Chauvet, *Les sacrements. Parole de Dieu au risque du corps* (Paris: Les Éditions Ouvrières, 1993); Chauvet, *Symbole et Sacrement. Une relecture sacramentelle de l'existence chrétienne* (Paris: Éd. du Cerf, 1987). See also Mazzanti, *I sacramenti, simbolo e teologia*, vol. 1: *Introduzione generale* (Bologna: EDB, 1997).

50. For an introduction to the relation between symbol and theology, see P. Miquel, *Petit traité de théologie symbolique* (Paris: Éd. du Cerf, 1987).

approach, which we can call "trinitarian and nuptial." We hope to arrive in this way at a "dramatic" retrieval of eucharistic logic, one that integrates the "realism" of the Scholastics and the "symbolism" of contemporary theology.

Let us begin, then, with a preliminary note on the history and definition of the symbol. Depending on the age, the symbol has been considered either as a privileged instrument of knowledge and identity or as a poor instrument of primitive peoples, children, and the uneducated. The symbol, whose use was so frequent among the ancient peoples of the Middle East, subsequently became an object of contempt for Greek rationalism, only to reemerge during the Middle Ages with its lapidaries, bestiaries, and heraldry. During the Enlightenment, the symbol then gave way to allegory, before recovering its proper place with Romanticism, only to suffer a new eclipse during the positivist era. Our own age, which is marked by a culture of the image and an attraction for the esoteric, is restoring the symbol to its rights of citizenship.[51]

From an etymological perspective,

> the *symbolon* is a sign of recognition, an object separated into two halves and entrusted to two associates. Each of them then had to keep his respective part and hand it down to his descendants. The idea was that once the two complementary halves were re-united, their exact fit would enable their respective possessors to recognize each another and to vouch for the bonds established by the earlier pact.[52]

The word "symbol" has the same root as the Greek *symbolē*, which means "summary" or "condensation." Both of these etymologies apply nicely to the Creed, the "Symbol" of the Apostles that is both a summary of Christian doctrine and a formula by which Christians can be recognized.

Giorgio Mazzanti's Symbolic-Nuptial Approach

The interest of Giorgio Mazzanti's work lies in its rich offering of symbolically, anthropologically, and theologically suggestive insights. Mazzanti writes within the sacramental horizon of Balthasar's theological aesthetics while developing his own distinctive approach inspired by profound study of symbol. He interprets the symbol (from the Greek *sym-ballein*, to bind or hold to-

---

51. See Miquel, *Petit traité de théologie symbolique*, 7.
52. E. Ortigues, *Le Discours et le Symbole* (Paris: Aubier, 1977), 60.

gether) in a vital existential key that overcomes the intellectualist and reductive approach of modernity. Mazzanti thus presents the anthropological and existential nature of the symbol as a "duality in dynamic tension":[53]

> The symbol is not so much a matter of *aliquid stat pro aliquo* (U. Eco), yet neither is it merely the case that *per symbolum aliquid aliud fit, per symbolum opposita unum fiunt* (M. Trevi). Nor is it enough to say that the symbol "stands for" (as a function of) the other. The point is that *aliquid stat AD aliud;* or even *aliquid stat IN aliud.* What unites the various significations of "symbol," then, is the fundamental meaning of "becoming one FROM and IN two." The symbol is what holds two dimensions in tension, in relation. In the symbol, a thing finds itself *in* the other, and this "in" should be understood both as a movement towards and as a resting in; an aspect of the one is present in the other, and so the one tends toward the other and both call for each other reciprocally.[54]

The symbol is thus essentially communional: It unites in reciprocity, keeping both elements distinct but without separation. Now, the human being's relation to the symbol is neither accidental nor fortuitous, neither occasional nor casual, for "man's constitutive nature is itself symbolic":

> If the symbol is in fact the tension between two realities, a co-respondence, a reciprocal pointing of two realities to each other within the same reality/condition — if it is "one composed from and in two" — then man is already in himself a symbolic tension/reality. . . . He himself is the field of a continual and structural symbolic tension; he experiences a twofold constitution within himself (e.g., his breath: inhaling and exhaling; the beating of his heart: diastole and systole; his day: waking and sleeping).

---

53. Mazzanti, *I sacramenti, simbolo e teologia,* vol. 1, 39-54: "The symbol . . . appears first of all as a bond, as something that links two dimensions of one and the same reality, or two realities" (44ff.). Mazzanti refers to various descriptions of the complex symbolic world: sign, image, metaphor, allegory. He also stresses that the powerful symbols of blood and water (life) contain a link with the reality symbolized that is not merely external but intrinsic. See M. Girard, *Les Symboles dans la Bible* (Montreal: Bellarmin; Paris: Éd. du Cerf, 1991), 29-99.

54. Mazzanti, *I sacramenti, simbolo e teologia,* vol. 1, 51. "This relation, this conjoint bond, is not the fruit of an intellectual operation. . . . It happens in the real/concrete. It is contact with blood that allows us to experience life. It is contact with water that makes us feel/experience its dynamism and its symbolic reality. . . . Symbolic experience demands immersion in factual reality. There is no symbol apart from its actual occurrence" (52).

In sum, man knows by his own experience what it means to be "one from and in two."[55]

On the basis of these premises, Mazzanti goes on to develop a phenomenology of symbolic corporeity as the locus of the dynamic relation between the "I" and the body, between the I-body and the world/universe, and between my person and other persons. For example, human verbal or gestural expression, situated in time through repetition, binds man and woman in a relationship of mutual "symbolic" knowledge — not only conceptual knowledge, then, but real, affective knowledge saturated with the entire density of the language of sexuality. The model of knowledge informing Mazzanti's approach is "dialogue," the reciprocity between subject and object, rather than modernity's rigid distinction between the autonomous thinking subject and the object that is represented or dominated by it.[56]

One of the anthropological fruits of Mazzanti's analysis is what he calls the "paradigm of the nuptial symbol": "It seems to us that if the basis of the symbol is the 'duality' of reality, and if the symbol is 'one from and in two,' then nuptiality, even more than the meal, is the symbol that is most comprehensive and most expressive of man's nature and destiny."[57]

Now, if we ask what enables the symbolic event, what effectively establishes the bond between two parties, Mazzanti maintains that we cannot simply point to some determinate "background" (historical, geographical, or cultural); "this background can constitute the horizon or framework of the symbolic experience, but cannot constitute its inner dynamic": "Even the dialogical symbol presupposes a more original Symbol. There must be something

---

55. Mazzanti, *I sacramenti, simbolo e teologia*, vol. 1, 56.

56. In this epistemological context (*I sacramenti, simbolo e teologia*, vol. 1, 68-69), Mazzanti refers to Balthasar and Gadamer, who offer a model of the subject-object relation that goes beyond their rigid modern opposition. See H. U. von Balthasar, *Theo-Logic*, vol. 1: *Truth of the World*, trans. Adrian J. Walker (San Francisco: Ignatius, 2000); the first "sketch" was written in 1947. G. Gadamer, *The Beginning of Philosophy*, trans. Rod Coltman (New York: Continuum, 1998): "For the Greeks, the essence of knowledge is the dialogue and not the mastery of objects comprehended as proceeding from an autonomous subjectivity, that victory of modern science that has even in a certain sense led to the end of metaphysics" (70).

57. Mazzanti, *I sacramenti, simbolo e teologia*, vol. 1, 95-96 n.: "The act of eating finally leads to the elimination of the symbolic tension; the person who takes in food consumes it by assimilating it. The tension remains, however, in the nuptial relation of spouses. Even so, the spouses celebrate their wedding with a banquet/nuptial meal. This is why nuptial symbolism includes that of the meal, not vice versa." See Balthasar, *Theo-Drama*, vol. 5: *The Last Act*, 470-87 ("Meal and Marriage").

that allows this dialogue to be, that permits it. There is, as it were, a symbolizing and translating Spirit that binds together both the various aspects of the real and the various persons involved."[58] According to Mazzanti, then, *the true structure of the symbol* is not dual but triadic. Beyond the two focal points of the symbol, there is a power impelling the transition from one to the other and so enabling the two to tend toward each other.

The itinerary of Mazzanti's symbolic-anthropological account leads to Christ, who is the "Symbol of symbols," that is, the fulfillment of all possible bonds between flesh and spirit, man and woman, individual and community, time and eternity, heaven and earth, etc. Christ binds the Trinity and society in his flesh, which was fashioned by the *Pneuma* precisely for the sacramental communication of the trinitarian symbol, i.e., the Holy Spirit, to humanity.[59] The Cross marks the culmination of this formation and communication, when in obedience Jesus breathes forth the Spirit with his own last vital breath. This event is the source of the symbolic sacramental order, which Mazzanti interprets by means of the nuptial symbol. That said, Mazzanti does not penetrate to the nuptial core that would give his new approach its decisive systematic capstone. As a result, he does not draw on nuptiality either to ask or to answer the question of the sacraments as acts of Christ and the Church.

Mazzanti's anthropologically detailed and theologically grounded vision of the symbol and of symbolics gives him a key to explaining the "eucharistic symbol" and the "nuptial symbolics of the Eucharist."[60] He bases this explanation on two things: the realism we find in the symbolic density of Christ's gesture at the Last Supper; and the mnemonic task of the Holy Spirit, who efficaciously accomplishes the universalization and reception of the eucharistic symbol, thus making Christ's death and resurrection to be present. Despite certain limits due to the fluidity of the symbol and to the novelty of his symbolic approach, Mazzanti successfully produces a reformulation of the traditional

---

58. Mazzanti, *I sacramenti, simbolo e teologia*, vol. 1, 81: "The Spirit accomplishes all this by activating the 'spirit' of man, his symbolic perception and experience."

59. Mazzanti, *I sacramenti, simbolo e teologia*, vol. 1, 94: "Basing ourselves on the 'personal' and 'relational' revelation of Christ, that is, on the 'economic' Trinity, we can also think of the Trinity as the perfect integration between symbol and rite: between (i) the relation among the trinitarian Persons as a dynamic happening (which is symbolic: the Persons tend toward, and are turned to face, one another) and (ii) their relation as a reality already complete because eternally achieved and maintained (ritual: persons give themselves to one another)."

60. Mazzanti, *I sacramenti, simbolo e teologia*, vol. 2, 63-99 (chap. 2, "Eucharistic Symbolics").

doctrine that, without losing its substance, stands both in harmony with contemporary sensibilities and in continuity with patristic tradition.

The weak point in Mazzanti's first book lay in his choice of a symbolic pneumatology that more or less ignores an important dimension of the nuptial symbolism of the Incarnation and the intra-trinitarian life: the dimension of fruitfulness. This weakness appears in Mazzanti's way of "skimming over" the mystery of the hypostatic union without pausing to ponder its properly nuptial dimension, which is brought about precisely by the Holy Spirit.[61] Mazzanti went on to correct this lacuna in his second book, which also draws on the gift of trinitarian fruitfulness communicated in the Eucharist to offer an account of the *nuptial symbol,* together with the *nuptial symbolism* flowing from it, in light of fecundity. Having realized the "symbolic" richness of Balthasar's work, Mazzanti comes close to its inner core, though his approach to the nuptial symbol and the mystery of the Trinity reflects his own distinctive accents.[62] But Mazzanti consistently pursues his project to the end, opening new possibilities not only for an enrichment of sacramental theology, but also for a renewal of theology as such.

A complete presentation would require an examination of Mazzanti's third book, which provides resources for setting the dramatic, historical, and symbolical character of the sacraments even more firmly on the foundation of a *nuptial theology.*[63] We would find in this work an approach even closer to, and more in harmony with, Balthasar's. Balthasar's move is to present a Christological *analogia sponsalis,* which is transformed, so to speak, into a *trinitarian katalogical fruitfulness* through the espoused creature's association

61. It is surprising that Mazzanti does not make explicit use of the nuptial symbol in his Christological and pneumatological treatment of the question; see Mazzanti, *I sacramenti, simbolo e teologia,* vol. 1, 113-27 (chap. 2, "Christ: The Symbol Par Excellence").

62. Mazzanti felicitously reprises the patristic language concerning the Spirit as the "eternal bond and intra-trinitarian kiss." Yet he goes on to conclude: "Hence the real/global symbol that is Christ, effected through the Spirit, opens onto the same symbol-Spirit; and the latter, who already mediates the eternal generation of the Son from the Father, opens the Christ-symbol to man" (*I sacramenti, simbolo e teologia,* vol. 1, 127); "the Spirit is the Father's womb, the space and the deepest recess of his being, from which the Word is generated" (178). In my opinion, it is not an entirely correct formulation of the order of the processions in God to say that the Holy Spirit "is mediation" for the begetting of the Word or that he is the "womb" from which the Word is begotten. This claim obscures the nuptial dimension of the Holy Spirit and of the entire Trinity, inasmuch as it overlooks the Spirit's identity as the fruit of the mutual consubstantiality of Father and Son.

63. G. Mazzanti, *Teologia sponsale e sacramento delle nozze. Simbolo e simbolismo nuziale* (Bologna: EDB, 2001).

with the eternal event of Love who becomes flesh.[64] The consequence is an intimate and inseparable involvement of Christ and the Church in this spousal dimension. We will return to a consideration of the sacramental implications of Balthasar's thought after having briefly presented Chauvet's more systematic work of symbolic sacramental theology.

The Symbolic-Paschal Approach of Louis-Marie Chauvet: Exposition and Critique

Louis-Marie Chauvet's account of the sacraments presupposes his rejection of classical onto-theology and follows in the footsteps of Heidegger's herme-neutic of language as symbol.[65] The fruit of a long and gradual development, Chauvet's work finds a simple, pastorally accessible expression in his book *Les sacrements.*[66] Chauvet's analysis in this work focuses on the symbol as a symbolic exchange between "subjects" rather than as an informative sign. The symbol is the mediation of mutual recognition. The structure of symbolic language has a giver and a receiver, who responds with an "obligatory" return-gift, and the entire interchange occurs within a shared "universe" of meaning (culture, tradition, rites, etc.) to which both are "subject."[67]

The structure of the symbol is trinitarian rather than merely dual. On the anthropological level, it functions differently from performative or informative language, in which values, utility, economy, etc. play a role. Symbolic language does not affect the value of the things "said" or "exchanged" as such, but rather concerns the active communication by which subjects recognize one another as subjects. Small talk about the weather over breakfast, for example, means

64. See the last part of Balthasar's *Epilogue,* which synthetically develops this approach. See Mazzanti, *Teologia sponsale e sacramento delle nozze,* 205ff., 247.

65. M. Heidegger, *On the Way to Language* (New York: HarperCollins, 1982); and the lecture entitled "Die Sprache," 1950.

66. Chauvet, *Les Sacrements.*

67. Chauvet, *Les Sacrements,* 31: "In order for the subject to come into being and maintain himself as a subject, he must build reality into a 'world,' that is, into a meaningful whole in which each element, whether material (tree, wind, house) or social (family relationships, clothing, food, work, or leisure), is integrated into a system of *knowledge* (of the world and of society), of acknowledgment (code of courtesy, mystical and ritual code of relationships to divinities or to ancestors) and of *ethical action* (values with a normative function that dictate behavior). It is always with this always-already constructed world that the child and the adult have to do, and not with brute physical things. Through this process, the universe and its events form a coherent whole, which we call the 'symbolic order.'"

next to nothing on the level of information, but it can reveal a great deal about the subjects' level of willingness to communicate.

For Chauvet, sacramental language is properly symbolic: it does not signify informative content but rather the event of communication between God and man.[68] The sacrament is the mediation of mutual recognition; it is the constitutive event of Christian identity as a relational one inscribed in bodily existence. This constitution of identity demands a passage through symbolic logic, that is, the mediation of the symbol. Such mediation, in fact, establishes distance in order to represent the subjects' gift and return-gift, thus grounding the possibility of their incarnate communion.

The triadic structure of the sacramental symbol appears in the indirect character of the return-gift; its return to God passes through the ethical, thereby including the ecclesial and historical dimension as well. The gift received from God — the gift of Jesus Christ in the Scriptures — is immediately offered back (dispossession) with the sacrifice proper to the Church, the body of Christ. This sacrificial response accomplished in the Holy Spirit necessarily embraces the real existence toward which sacramental logic — as a paschal logic — tends. The structure of the sacrament thus involves a threefold referent: God who gives, the sacramental symbol, and the return-gift through the ethical.

Chauvet bases the trinitarian theology underpinning his account on the paschal mystery, which he reads in a broad and integrated way that contrasts with the medieval tendency to focus on the Incarnation as an instrument of grace. The sacraments are a symbolic language rooted in Christ, the original sacrament. As the Word made flesh unto death on the Cross, Christ reveals God's "humanity," that is, the paradoxical fact of his extreme nearness precisely in his symbolic "distance" in the mystery of death in solidarity with sinners.

Chauvet lays his pneumatological groundwork, on the other hand, in the illocutionary and perlocutionary role of the Holy Spirit, who is not a new object of discussion but rather the "third" who creates the common horizon of the subjects in communication.[69] The Spirit is free and liberating; he obliges the subjects to convert to sacramental logic, to go beyond the sacrament into

---

68. Chauvet, *Les Sacrements*, 92: "The sign is situated on the side of 'saying something about something,' that is, on the side of the transmission of information or of knowledge; the symbol, on the other hand, is on the side of 'speaking to someone,' that is, of communication with a subject acknowledged and affirmed as subject."

69. Chauvet, *Les Sacrements*, 181-82: "To return to the linguistic terms we used earlier, we can say that his [the Holy Spirit's] function is less 'locutionary' (the content of statements about God) than 'illocutionary' (the work that he carries out regarding the truth of Christians' relationship with God and one another) and 'perlocutionary' (their witness of life)."

real life, where worship becomes existential as opposed to merely ritual. Without this movement, the faithful would remain in the "imaginary" register of immediate "reification" — under the illusion, in other words, of direct communication with God, either without mediation or with a mediation interpreted as a "hold on God" (idolatry). The conversion to symbol is an ethical process that makes the truth of the sacrament.

In its account of the Eucharist, Chauvet's sacramental theology highlights the action of the Holy Spirit as the "agent of God's 'somatization': he gives a body to the Word." The Eucharistic Prayer eloquently expresses the Spirit's role in effecting "the threefold body of Christ": the historical body ("conceived by the Holy Spirit"), the eucharistic body (the first epiclesis), and ecclesial body (the second epiclesis). Chauvet adds that this "somatization" consists in "inscribing the very difference of God into the body of humanity," so that the Spirit is above all "the one who accomplishes God's 'hiddenness' in Christ, in the flesh of humanity."[70] God thus conceals himself in humanity, giving it the chance to emerge as a sacramental "place" (the Church) where he continues to take flesh and to grow until "mature manhood, to the measure of the stature of the fullness of Christ" (Eph. 4:13).

Many critics have found fault with Chauvet's vision of the sacraments, either on theological grounds or on account of his anthropological and philosophical assumptions. In our opinion, his work lacks a trinitarian foundation; his doctrine of symbol is still too dependent on its Heideggerian matrix and he misses the chance to subject his borrowed categories to the conversion needed to adapt them for use in theology. Chauvet presents us, then, with an "anthropological theology," which rationally establishes in advance the system of categories into which the sacraments must be inserted in order to receive their full intelligibility. While acknowledging the richness and correctness of Chauvet's analysis on particular points, we cannot help thinking that he somehow succumbs to the temptation to reduce the Word of God to the laws of human language. To be sure, he himself is aware of the limits of his approach, yet he ultimately remains within an anthropocentric conceptual horizon.[71]

To take just one example, Chauvet one-sidedly stresses the symbol's func-

---

70. Chauvet, *Les Sacrements*, 182-83.

71. See G. Colombo, "La 'conversione postmoderna' della teologia sacramentaria. L'opera di L.-M. Chauvet," in *Teologia sacramentaria*, 392-404: "In particular, I share the fear that the Christian sacraments will lose their character, that they will dissolve into a 'rituality' whose only goal is to exemplify man's being rather than to reveal God's action in Jesus Christ" (397). See also P. Gisel, "Du symbolique au symbole ou du symbole au symbolique? Remarques intempestives," *Recherches de Science Religieuse* 73 (1987): 357-69.

tions of "distancing" and "pointing beyond itself," but fails to emphasize as vigorously as he ought the fact that these functions are determined above all "theologically," that is, by the real presence of Christ's gift, and not "anthropologically," by a rational logic of mediation. The reason why Christ's presence in the Eucharist points to an ethical return-gift is not to be found in the logic of "symbol," but in a "theological" content: the fact that Christ humbles himself to wash his disciples' feet, the fact that they materially assimilate him precisely in the extreme form of kenotic love. Chauvet's approach remains overly determined "from below," that is, by the laws of language. It is underdetermined by the theological content that transcends language and its laws, even as it enters into them.

On the other hand, Chauvet's way of exhibiting the coherence of the sacraments does not follow a trinitarian logic, but rather gives the impression of juxtaposing Christology and Pneumatology. This explains why he can slide, so to speak, from a Christological grounding of the institution of the sacraments to a pneumatological annulment of this same institution, as if Christ and the Spirit were working in opposite directions. His insistence on the "somatization" of God's "difference" in the corporeal sphere does not adequately explain the sense in which Eucharist fulfills the Incarnation. Chauvet's insistence on discontinuity threatens the dimension of continuity, that is, the incarnational realism of the Eucharist.[72] Furthermore, even though he systematically incorporates the Church as an institution, and acknowledges her intrinsic involvement in the sacramental-symbolic order, Chauvet does not present her in her spousal role: The Church never rises beyond the level of a "symbolic" necessity, grounded in the fact that faith involves *"renunciation of the immediacy* of vision, of knowing, and consent to the mediation of the Church."[73] In sum, Chauvet's view of the sacraments lacks a pneumatological and trinitarian Christology deep enough to ground the sacramental order within the economic relationship of the three Persons in light of the paschal mystery reread in a nuptial key.[74]

---

72. Chauvet concludes his proposal by adding a catechetical motif that, in my opinion, illustrates this danger: "God's action in the sacraments is of course real, but its reality is entirely of a spiritual (we should say 'pneumatic') nature that resists all demonstration and is opposed to all 'reification'" (*Les Sacrements*, 184).

73. Chauvet, *Les Sacrements*, 42-43: "You cannot have access to the recognition of the risen Jesus unless you renounce seeing/touching/finding him immediately by means of cogent proofs"; Chauvet deduces this law from the disciples' encounter with Christ at Emmaus and makes it the starting point of faith and thus of the Church's mediation. Regarding his trinitarian approach, see Chauvet, *Les Sacrements*, 169-85, especially 180-85.

74. See Chauvet, *Symbole et Sacrement*, chap. 13, where the author presents his un-

*Toward a Deeper Trinitarian and Spousal
Understanding of the Eucharist*

From an Anthropological-Linguistic to a Theological Symbolics

Basing ourselves on the insights gained in our critique of the two above-mentioned approaches, we can now delve more deeply into theological symbolics. Taking Balthasar's *Theo-Drama* as our compass, we can move in two different directions. The first of these is an ontological symbolics that situates the symbolical function of man and of language within the horizon of being and the transcendentals. "Symbolical" communication does not necessarily require the elimination of metaphysics. A "meta-anthropological" approach that does not confine itself to the "meta-physical" provides a way of drawing out the triadic structure of the human being by showing the reciprocal reference of subject and object within the horizon of being as love. It is precisely the adoption of love as the supreme foundational element in the ontological and symbolical order that allows us to clarify the basic hermeneutical principle of human language. If the act of communication between subjects truly exists, it is because there is the "gift" of being, which an infant experiences from the first moment of consciousness as good, true, and beautiful. According to Hans Urs von Balthasar, this original experience of the child who is awakened to himself by his mother's smile embodies the paradigmatic meaning of human language as an event of love that points beyond to the totality of Being. Balthasar offered an initial sketch of such a meta-anthropology, the inaugural act of a trinitarian ontology, in 1947, and re-published the text without modification in 1985 as the first volume of *Theo-Logic: Truth of the World.*[75]

---

derlying theological option in fairly radical terms under the title "The Sacraments, Symbolic Figures of God's Hiddenness" (501-57). His approach to overcoming onto-theology, and his sense of its implications, seem to be more in line with Protestant than with Catholic thought: "In the domain of the symbol, the God-man relation is conceived according to the framework of otherness, a framework that 'surpasses' the dualistic nature-grace dichotomy undergirding classical onto-theology. This new framework requires that 'God,' on the one hand, and our relationship to him, on the other, are both expressed in the mode of openness" (555).

75. Balthasar, *Theo-Logic*, vol. 1: *Truth of the World*. In the introduction to this work, Balthasar warns against the danger of a reductive understanding of God's self-revelation that divides it into a "transcendental revelation" related to the universal openness of the Holy Spirit, and a "categorical revelation" related to revelation's Christological dimension: "Rather, Christ's Holy Spirit, working in a mysterious way, universalizes Christ's historical, risen reality as the *universale concretum,* thereby enabling its radiance to penetrate 'to the ends of the earth'" (11). See also his *A Theology of History* (San Francisco: Ignatius-Communio Books, 1994).

The second direction in which we propose to advance our exploration is theological, in that it involves reflection on the language of God, who assumes the sketch of meaning that we call human language and fills it with the Word made flesh even to the point of shedding his blood and becoming eucharistic food. Needless to say, this super-determination of human language far exceeds the linguistic sphere and its intrinsic possibilities, relying, as it does, on possibilities made available by the logic of trinitarian love. This logic appropriates everything in order to express itself in the most adequate way, taking up the word, or silence, or even flesh *("Verbum caro factum")* to the point of identification with the sin of the world:

> Now, this consideration shows that faith, looking upward *(ana)* from the fleshly exposition of God in Christ *(anō)*, and recognizing its adequacy, understands that this exposition cannot be grasped as what it claims to be unless it is read from above downward *(kata)*. God exposits himself from above; it is not the man Jesus who explains God from below. The Johannine Jesus constantly expresses this (Jn 3:11-13; 3:32f.; 6:46; 7:29; 8:23, 55).[76]

This approach offers us a way of working out a nuptial account of the relation between sacramental language as God's self-communication and the spousal mystery of the Church; a nuptial account, then, of the intrinsically dramatic relationship between revelation and faith. Such an account prolongs the trajectory of our earlier considerations regarding the *"mysterion,"* while incorporating the historical and eschatological horizons opened by Christ's gift made universally available in the Holy Spirit — all on the basis of the trinitarian and spousal logic of the paschal mystery. In this way, we can attain a deeper theo-dramatic integration whose key move is a more vigorous accentuation of the pole of faith. The insufficiency of the approaches we have encountered thus far stems from their failure to integrate faith as a constitutive principle of the sacramental order.

Sergio Ubbiali proposes a systematic reflection along similar lines, but he opts for a transcendental approach à la Rahner that results in an insufficient presentation of the trinitarian logic of the sacramental drama and, a fortiori, of its spousal hermeneutic. For Ubbiali, "self-determination specifies the act

---

76. H. U. von Balthasar, *Theo-Logic*, vol. 2: *Truth of God*, trans. Adrian J. Walker (San Francisco: Ignatius, 2004), 313. The entire second half of this work offers an analysis of human language as it is taken up, intensified, and surpassed within the katalogical analogy of the divine Word who becomes flesh; see Part IV: "Kata-logical Aspects" (171-218) and Part V: "The Word Was Made Flesh" (219-361).

of truth's manifestation and thus becomes the 'ecclesial' act par excellence to the extent that it takes on the form of witness."[77] Ubbiali's approach reconnects the drama of sacramental action to the historical and symbolic character of ecclesial mediation, which touches the believing subject from within by means of concrete, liturgical forms that become part of his personal salvation history. The event of the sacrament and the self-determination of freedom reinforce each other and express their intrinsic mutuality through the mediation of the Church's witness. In our opinion, Ubbiali's approach, while very good at raising the issue of the intrinsic relation between the sacramental event and human freedom, fails to offer a satisfactory answer to the question. This failure reflects, in turn, the lack of a trinitarian anthropology based on the pneumatologically established nuptial bond between Christ and Mary-Church.

The Holy Spirit and the Church's "Nuptial" Faith

It follows that a renewed appreciation of the sacraments as saturated, unifying symbols and a rediscovery of their role as privileged places of dramatic communication with God require a valorization of the spousal act of faith, unfortunately neglected in almost all treatments of the subject. Many authors speak of the sacraments as symbols yet are led to overlook their spousal significance by the assumption that faith remains extrinsic to the sacraments' constitution.[78] In view of this situation, we need to stress more than just the necessity of maintaining an intrinsic relationship between revelation and faith. Above all, we need to stress the necessity of doing theology on the basis of faith. It is not enough to engage in a more or less rational reflection on the data of revelation using a reason aware of its historical and linguistic determination. We must refine our appreciation of the epistemological conditions of possibility for theology, the "science of faith," in light of the mediation of the Holy Spirit, who is faith's transcendental "Subject."

At the basis of the sacramental economy is the event of the Word made

---

77. S. Ubbiali, "Il sacramento cristiano e l'agire libero dell'uomo. Per una 'drammatica' dell'azione sacramentale," in *Gesù Cristo, Unico Salvatore del Mondo, Pane per la Nuova Vita. Convegno Teologico in preparazione del XLVII Congresso Eucaristico Internazionale* (Rome: PUL, April 27-28, 2000), 157; Ubbiali, "Il sacramento cristiano," in *Celebrare il mistero di Cristo*, vol. 2: *La celebrazione dei sacramenti* (Rome: Edizioni Liturgiche, 1996), 13-28; "Il sacramento e la fede," *La Scuola Cattolica* 127 (1999): 313-44.

78. On the subject of the link between grace and faith, see G. Colombo, "Grazia e libertà nell'atto di fede," in *La ragione teologica* (Milan: Glossa, 1995), 143-58.

flesh, the Word who remains in the flesh in order to draw carnal man into the inner dialogue of the Trinity. The goal of the Incarnation is the gratuitous incorporation of man, along with his entire expressive repertoire, into the exchange between the divine Persons. Man the symbol, man the *imago Dei,* finds his relational identity *(similitudo)* in Christ the Symbol, who binds the entire creation to the divine Persons' history of eternal love. The man-woman symbol, full of nuptial meaning, thus becomes the privileged "language" for God to express to humanity and in human terms[79] the intimacy he desires, to speak it as his creature's predestination "in Christ" to attain the dignity of the holy and immaculate Bride.

One of the deficits of sacramental theology is its lack of the symbol that is the Holy Spirit, the "poet" of the living bond between Christ and the Church. This poet does not compose in a realm beyond ordinary sacramental language but precisely at the heart of it. Through the simplest symbols of bread, wine, water, the Holy Spirit allows us to glimpse the beauty and the eternal density that fill daily life as the place in which the "real" encounter, the "immediate" appropriation of the gift of the Risen One, takes place. The sacraments of faith are not primarily symbols that establish a distance in order to connect us with a level "other" than that of being. The sacraments of faith give God in Christ. This gift takes place through symbolic expression without being canceled by it; to the contrary, it makes use of this symbolic expression and converts it into an epiphany of the "Whole in the fragment."[80] The challenge of a renewed sacramental theology is to integrate reflection on the symbol without losing the substance of the Gift made flesh, who has established a total proximity to believers of all times through the bond of the Holy Spirit.

It is not enough, then, to replace the "productionist" model of Scholasticism with the "symbolical" model favored by contemporary theology. A further step is necessary, one requiring explicit reference to the horizon of meaning and the act of appropriation that makes the new model meaningful for, and attractive to, the human person. A presentation of this horizon in spousal terms would have to exhibit the interior urgency and beauty of faith's "yes" to the event to which we are convoked (*ec-clesia,* con-vocation).[81] The sacramental encounter with Christ is not merely a "categorical" complement of the "transcendental"

---

79. The Song of Songs, at the center of the Bible, thus turns out to be a key to reading the entire nuptial story of God and chosen humanity; see L. A. Schökel, *I nomi dell'amore. Simboli matrimoniali nella Bibbia* (Casale Monferrato: Piemme, 1997).

80. The original German title of H. U. von Balthasar, *A Theological Anthropology.*

81. In the following chapter, we will return to the trinitiarian horizon that confers a sacramental meaning and significance on all of human existence.

communication already accomplished in the soul. Kantian categories such as these reveal their inadequacy by their tendency to relativize the concrete sacramental event. The Eucharist is not accessory to Christian identity; rather, it constitutes this identity, which cannot be abstracted from its source. The reevaluation of sacramental practice and the crisis of sacramental theology thus require a renewed pneumatological integration that sacrifices neither the realism of the tradition nor the anthropological symbolism of contemporary thought.

What follows are some reflections that, though still fragmentary, will serve to lead us to the heart of this question.[82] Through the dynamism of faith, human history becomes the history of accomplished salvation. Faith is the indispensable mediation of the Gift of God. The Word was made flesh through Mary's faith, and this faith was a work of the Holy Spirit. From the beginning, faith is the *"forma sponsalis"* of the reception of God's Word among men. But in order to find the ultimate root of the spousal form of faith, we must ascend to the Person of the Holy Spirit as the intra-trinitarian fruit of the mutual gift of the Father and the Son. Existing from all eternity as the subjective-objective ecstasy of Love, that is, as Person-Gift, the Holy Spirit appears in the economy of salvation as the mediator and agent of the reception of the divine Gift. The same Spirit who eternally receives the Word of Love from the Father likewise receives him in the womb of Mary and of the Church. The Holy Spirit thus reinforces the human faith of Mary and of the Church until it becomes the "divine" faith of the Woman who receives the Word of God into her heart before she receives him in her womb (St. Augustine).

In order to understand this spousal mediation of the Holy Spirit in the event of the Eucharist, we must be attentive to the gift of the Spirit who accomplishes the Incarnation and the paschal mystery as a mystery of the covenant. The paschal gift of the Holy Spirit is given for two ends: the eschatological and sacramental completion of the Word and the communication of the spousal attitude by which the "sacramentalized" divine Word is received. This takes place on the Cross, where the divine Word and the faith of Mary-Church meet "nuptially" within the mediation of the Spirit breathed forth by the dying Christt. This original correspondence, *in actu primo redemptionis*, between gift and reception in the Holy Spirit, constitutes the trinitarian structure of the sacramental drama and is the foundation of the Church's participation in Christ's redemptive sacrifice.

---

82. For further exploration of the link between the Holy Spirit and the sacraments, see Balthasar, *Theo-Logic*, vol. 3: *Spirit of Truth*, trans. Graham Harrison (San Francisco: Ignatius, 2005), 335-52; also Mazzanti, *I sacramenti, simbolo e teologia*, vol. 1, 170-200.

An allusion to the mystery of Holy Saturday in this context can help us resist the temptation to impose human symbolism on the nuptial gift of God in the eucharistic Christ. Christ's descent into hell provides, in fact, the eschatological background that allows the Holy Spirit to measure the abyss of the Word of God and to lead fallen human logic to its absolute limit. As Adrienne von Speyr stresses, no one can rationally appropriate the mystery of Holy Saturday.[83] Only the Holy Spirit can cross the abyss carrying human reason with him, inviting it to a Pasch of faith that passes from human logic to a divine logic of absolute Love. Indeed, the Holy Spirit returns from the abyss with the Risen One, having overcome with him the human contradictions of sin and death in the flesh. From now on, this victory of trinitarian Love contains not only the gift of the Risen One but also a new, properly pneumatological method for binding the divine Whole to human history: the sacraments. This new form of encounter with God in the sacraments requires a "new," purely spousal faith, the faith of the Church, which remained always present in Mary from the moment of the Annunciation, through her presence at the foot of the Cross, to Pentecost. This nuptial faith grounded in the "bond of the Spirit" is not an achievement from below but rather a gift from above that nonetheless perfectly respects the human freedom involved in the sacramental event. More: it is the ever-new gift of the Holy Spirit, which strengthens the Church-Bride, and therefore human freedom, enabling its permanent welcome, in act and eucharistically, of the transcendent Word made flesh, who descended into the abyss and re-ascended to the right hand of the Father.

The Church's spousal faith flows, then, from a Marian grace enabling her to entrust herself totally to Christ and so to let him fashion her in the humility and hiddenness of the Risen One's sacramental signs. Just as the sacramental economy marks a new, "pneumatological" stage in the kenosis of trinitarian Love, faith's nuptial response involves a dramatic "more" with respect to the theo-dramatic "ever more" of the Word made flesh. Indeed, Christ's will to bind himself to bread and wine in the modality of his body handed over and his blood poured out marks another step in his loving self-abasement in service of the Church. The nuptial gift of the Eucharist thus heightens the dramatic character of the Church's encounter with the Risen

83. See M. Ouellet, "Adrienne von Speyr et le Samedi Saint de la théologie," in *Adrienne von Speyr und ihre spirituelle Theologie* (Einsiedeln: Johannes Verlag, 2002). See H. U. von Balthasar, *First Glance at Adrienne von Speyr*, trans. Antje Lawry and Sergia Englund (San Francisco: Ignatius, 1981); A. von Speyr, *Das Wort und die Mystik*, vol. 2: *Objektive Mystik* (Einsiedeln: Johannes Verlag, 1970); Aa.Vv., *La missione ecclesiale di Adrienne von Speyr. Atti del II Colloquio Internazionale del pensiero Cristiano* (Milan: Jaca Book, 1986).

One. In its symbolic and kenotic form, the Eucharist demands of believers a greater personal and ecclesial commitment to the ethical and missionary demands of the Word made flesh. It is not the human forms of mediation, with their logic of "distancing" and of "communion in the symbol," that determine the ethical demands placed on us by the sacraments of faith. Faith is not, as Chauvet takes it, the renunciation of an illusory immediacy for the sake of a mediation that is simultaneously established and annulled in the "sacramental symbols." Faith is precisely the act of being taken up into the *immediacy God established in the flesh,* the act of being seized and driven by the Holy Spirit in the footsteps of the One who was crucified and risen. The ethical demand of the existential return-gift proceeds immediately from the Christological and trinitarian content of the sacraments, which faith receives in the Holy Spirit as a spousal imperative: the Bride must correspond to this kenotic love with kenotic love in turn.

The Lord who humbled himself to wash his disciples' feet did more than give them a moral example to imitate; he freed the Holy Spirit to keep his, Christ's, deed ever alive, to surround the disciples on every side, and to attract them through the glorious fascination of this kenotic gift of love. Christ's deed is not confined to the past; it remains alive in each Eucharist thanks to the universalizing mediation of the Holy Spirit, who safeguards the concreteness of Christ's flesh and of his gestures within the symbols of the sacramental celebration. We thus see more clearly how the gift of Christ the Bridegroom, glorified by the Holy Spirit, carries in itself the grace of the Bride's reception of the gift, thus enabling the eucharistic "one flesh" to reveal the existential "one Spirit" of Love.

In the perennial contemporaneity of the Holy Spirit, then, the Church-Bride is always receiving the deed that the Lord enacts for her here and now. The substantial and symbolic realism of the Eucharist does not exist to give the Church license to exploit a past that can be taken for granted because already safely possessed. The "pneumatological" realism set forth here consists precisely in the ever-renewed vitality and contemporaneity of the dramatic event of Christ the Bridegroom's gift to the Church-Bride. The Fathers of the Church realized the deep significance of the blood and water that flowed from the side of the crucified Christ, which they described as the permanent source of the Church's sacraments. Patristic reflection went so far as to see the sacraments as the actualization of the eschatological event of Cross and Resurrection for the sake of the Church wending her pilgrim way through time. The Eucharist makes the Church. The sacramental symbols maintain the concrete presence of the Risen One in the Church, through the epiclesis over the sacred species and over the community. By the same token, they preserve the Church in the existential attitude of the Bride who is always listening to the Word and always open to the Holy Spirit charged with constituting her as Christ's Body and Bride.

This pneumatological approach enables us to see more clearly the sense in which the sacraments are acts of Christ the Bridegroom *for* the Church and *with* the Church-Bride. The first thing to strike us is the Church's contemporaneity with Christ. This contemporaneity comes about precisely through faith in the sacraments, which link the eschatological gift of Christ the Bridegroom to the Church on pilgrimage in time. The Holy Spirit maintains "in his Person" the spousal bond established once and for all on the Cross, while making it fruitful through the eucharistic "one flesh." This nuptial union means that the event of the Word of Christ and his pierced heart never ceases to generate the Church as the Bride of the Lamb who was slain.[84]

In celebrating the Eucharist, then, the Church remains conscious that she owes herself entirely to the fruitfulness of her Bridegroom. She expresses her faith in the privileged form of profoundly grateful obedience; the eucharistic celebration affords her a means of acknowledging day by day her own identity as a fruit of the Bridegroom's eucharistic gift. Although her faith plays a real role in the celebration, it does not "determine" the conditions of her self-realization as the Lord's Bride. To the contrary, it is the eucharistic gift instituted by Christ that determines her and keeps her ever faithful to her dependence as the Lord's humble handmaid. Even when she is led to make a contribution of her own, for example by adapting the celebration of the Eucharist and the other sacraments to the historical and cultural circumstances of different peoples, the Church remains subject to Christ's Spirit. The Church's respect for Christ's ever-actual initiative expresses her faith in the concrete, historical, and eschatological gift of Christ's Spirit, who comes to meet her in time and who establishes her in her spousal identity.

In the next section, we go on to consider the most specific form of the Church-Bride's participation in the Bridegroom's fruitfulness within the context of his eucharistic offering. The trinitarian and spousal logic of the eucharistic Pasch intrinsically requires the Bride's participation in the Bridegroom's suffering love, which is to say: in the fruitfulness of his divine-human sacrifice. Jesus' words on the Cross are decisive in this regard, in that they disclose to his mother Mary the horizon of her spiritual motherhood. The mother of Jesus becomes the mother of the Church and of all humanity: "'Woman, behold

---

84. See I. de la Potterie, *Il mistero del cuore trafitto. Studi biblici* (Bologna: EDB, 1988).

your son!' And he said to the disciple, 'Behold, your mother!' And from that hour the disciple took her to his own home" (John 19:26-27).[85]

Is the Mass a Sacrifice of the Church?

The spousal approach we have been developing here raises a number of questions regarding the relation between the Eucharist and the Trinity, the most important of which undoubtedly concerns the Eucharist as a sacrifice of the Church. Can we say that within the drama of the Eucharist there is something like a sacrifice of the Church alongside the unique sacrifice accomplished once and for all by Christ? What meaning can we assign to the Church's cultic sacrifice, which the Council of Trent declared to be a *verum et proprium sacrificium* (true and proper sacrifice)?[86] The ecumenical significance of these questions is obvious, since the Reformers consistently criticized the Church for claiming to add "her" own contribution to Christ's exclusive sacrifice. Balthasar observes:

> The real point of the protest is directed, not so much against the first paradox — that the unique historical event of the Cross as such should be able to receive a continuously new act of being made present again (re-presentation) through all the ages — as against the second paradox: that the absolute uniqueness of the one who offers this sacrifice, Jesus Christ, should be doubled in these acts of representation by the sacrificing Church, which perhaps goes so far here as to take the place of the first offerer.[87]

In order to respond to the question raised here, we propose to take our lead from Balthasar, who offers what remains the most complete, most speculatively and spiritually rich account of the issues involved. We begin with a few preliminary anthropological and pneumatological data that will help us glimpse something of the depth of his proposal.

---

85. For a further exploration of the spousal bond between Christ and the Church in the eucharistic celebration, see H. U. von Balthasar, "The Mass, a Sacrifice of the Church?" in *Explorations in Theology*, vol. 3: *Creator Spirit*, trans. Brian McNeil (San Francisco: Ignatius, 1993), 185-243.

86. Denz 1753.

87. H. U. von Balthasar, "The Mass, a Sacrifice of the Church?" 187. See G. Bätzing, *Die Eucharistie als Opfer der Kirche* (Einsiedeln: Johannes Verlag, 1986).

Anthropological and Ecclesiological Presuppositions in the Light of Pneumatology[88]

Balthasar's daring argument that the man-woman relation provides the most adequate image for describing the unfathomable mystery of the Trinity and its involvement in the world has not failed to generate a reaction among theologians.[89] Balthasar sets up his account of the connection between the Spirit and the Church's institutional element in terms of the I-thou relation, especially in the form of man and woman, the paradigm, for Balthasar, of the personal relationship that can occur only within an irreducible difference. The man-woman relation, then, is the key to a suggestive (though, as with all analogies, fragmentary and incomplete) analogy based on the reciprocity of "disposing" and "letting dispose," of "doing" and "letting be done," of "being" and "letting be," of gift and reception, within the miracle of a permanent fruitfulness.[90]

By the very nature of the case, reflection on the human person and his capacity for speech and action obliges us to begin with a discussion of freedom. Every human act, originating as it does in a self-disclosing freedom, is always generative, in that it brings something new into existence. Man's freedom is his greatest mystery, which we cannot deduce from circumstances; it emerges when a person goes out of himself toward another in order to encounter another freedom.[91]

At this point in our reflection, we need to introduce the spousal relation between man and woman and to stress their free and sovereign decision for mutual self-entrustment. A *third factor* emerges from this reciprocity, which Balthasar describes as follows:

> The personal coming together of the two self-emptying partners is only possible in terms of the third factor, which — long before the arrival of a

---

88. For the following synthesis, see P. Martinelli, "Il rapporto tra Carisma e Istituzione," *Rivista internazionale di teologia e cultura: Communio* 167-168 (September-December 1999): 147-63.

89. See Balthasar, *Theo-Logic*, vol. 3: *Spirit of Truth*, 105-64.

90. On sponsality as a dominant theme in Balthasar's theology that runs through his anthropology, his Christology, his ecclesiology, and even his trinitarian theology, see C. Kaiser, *Theologie der Ehe. Der Beitrag Hans Urs von Balthasars* (Würzburg: Echter, 1997). We should also mention C. Giuliodori's comparative study of this question in *Intelligenza del maschile e del femminile. Problemi e propettive nella rilettura di von Balthasar e P. Evdokimov* (Rome: Città Nuova, 1991). Also A. von Speyr, *Theologie der Geschlechter* (Einsiedeln: Johannes, 1969).

91. See H. U. von Balthasar, *Explorations in Theology*, vol. 4: *Spirit and Institution*, trans. Edward T. Oakes (San Francisco: Ignatius, 1995), 214.

child — is that objective of the meeting of their two freedoms. And that third term is their marriage vows, in which each one affirms the freedom of the other, handing over each one's mystery to the other. We call this "objective" because it is more than the juxtaposition of their two subjectivities — although it is also their creative product, their will to become one (to belong to one another). This is a will that is placed over and between them, because neither one of them can claim for himself or herself the unity that arises from their mutual affirmations.[92]

In the very act of their definitive mutual self-entrustment, Balthasar argues, two freedoms are obliged to acknowledge the presence of a third that is more than the two of them added together. Moreover, this third constitutes the rule of their reciprocity, to which the future birth of a child will bear fruitful witness.

Whereas human experience can offer only a fragile intuition, continually threatened by weakness and sin, to prove the truth of this claim, Christian revelation exhibits it as a fully achieved archetype. Basing himself on St. Paul's spousal theology and eucharistic thought, Balthasar explains the eternal covenant between God and man by means of the spousal relationship uniting Christ and the Church — a relationship essentially constituted by Christ's eucharistic self-gift to his Bride.[93] In this sense, the institution of the Eucharist is the center of the Christ-Church relation, since it is here that Christ gives himself completely and irrevocably in total freedom.[94]

At the same time, Balthasar remains conscious that the very logic of the spousal analogy requires an adequate correspondence on the part of the receiving subject if the gift is to be given.[95] It is just here that the theological person (and mission) of Mary clearly enters the scene to embody the requisite response in all its perfection. Docile to the Holy Spirit, Mary offers the "yes"

92. Balthasar, *Explorations in Theology,* vol. 4: *Spirit and Institution,* 218-19.

93. Balthasar remarks that the Church is simultaneously before and after the eucharistic mystery; she is before it as what Christ came to save with his blood, and after it insofar as Christ's gift of himself on the Cross enables her, at last, to become what she is meant to be; see *Explorations in Theology,* vol. 4: *Spirit and Institution,* 224-25.

94. See H. U. von Balthasar, *Mysterium Paschale,* trans. Aidan Nichols (San Francisco: Ignatius, 2000), 95-100; *Eucharistie, Gabe der Liebe;* "The Mystery of the Eucharist," in *New Elucidations,* trans. Mary Theresilde Skerry (San Francisco: Ignatius, 1986), 111-26; "The Holy Church and the Eucharistic Sacrifice," *Communio: International Catholic Review* 12, no. 2 (Summer 1985): 139-45.

95. See H. U. von Balthasar, *The Glory of the Lord: A Theological Aesthetics,* vol. 7: *The New Covenant,* trans. Brian McNeil (San Francisco: Ignatius, 1989), 77-114.

by which she enables the Incarnation and accompanies her Son's mission in perfect accord even to the point of his eucharistic gift on the Cross. The perfect reciprocity between Christ's eucharistic self-donation and the receptivity of Mary-Church enables the institution of the Eucharist to be the efficacious sign of the irrevocable and indissoluble character of God's gift to men.

The foregoing allows us to glimpse the emergence of the two factors that jointly constitute the germ of Balthasar's entire ecclesiology: on the one hand, the institutional element that attests to the irrevocability of Christ's gift to the Church; on the other hand, the perfect, fruitful reception of this gift by a feminine, indeed, Marian subject.

The logic of sponsality makes it possible to explain the function of the (essentially sacramental) institution in terms of its role in guaranteeing, within the ecclesial body, the permanence and contemporaneity of the deed by which Christ the Bridegroom gives his life for his Bride. Drawing both on the thought of Adrienne von Speyr and on the ecclesiology of Louis Bouyer, Balthasar affirms, "The institution guarantees the perpetual presence of Christ the Bridegroom for the Church, his Bride."[96] Thus, "the abiding structure of offices in the Church (the 'institution') means that we are guaranteed the possibility of participating in the original event at any and every time."[97]

At this point, Balthasar introduces Peter, the key figure who symbolizes institutional office in the Church. Peter can take over the objective mission of the institution only to the extent that he knows himself as an "inadequate" sinner who must therefore rely on the immaculate subjectivity of the Church that finds its personal embodiment in Mary. The holiness that Peter communicates within the institution is not subjective, but objective; in order to administer the institution he needs a kind of "loan," so to speak, from the subjective holiness of the immaculate Church. Balthasar sees here the ultimate reason why the subjective "Marian principle" precedes the so-called "Petrine principle" of the Church.[98]

---

96. H. U. von Balthasar, *Theo-Drama*, vol. 3: *Dramatis Personae: Persons in Christ*, trans. Graham Harrison (San Francisco: Ignatius, 1992), 354.

97. Balthasar, *Theo-Drama*, vol. 3: *Dramatis Personae: Persons in Christ*, 355. Regarding the contemporaneity of Christ involved in sacramental logic, see Scola, "La logica dell'incarnazione come logica sacramentale," 99-135.

98. Balthasar, *Theo-Logic*, vol. 3: *Spirit of Truth*, 312-18.

Contemporary Responses to the Question
Regarding the Church's Sacrifice

Leaving aside the first of the two above-mentioned paradoxes — the unique sacrifice of Christ and its sacramental multiplication in time — let us pause to consider the second: the unique oblation of Christ is the true and proper oblation of the Church in the liturgical actualization of the *mysterion*. In order to explain his own account of this thesis, Balthasar refers to the work of Odo Casel, Max Thurian, and Louis Bouyer on the Eucharist as the true and proper sacrifice of the Church.

Balthasar notes that "Odo Casel's intuitive synoptic view of God's salvific act in the focal points 'Cross-resurrection' and 'liturgy' gives a central answer to our question."[99] Casel stresses the priority of the cultic reality over every subjective act that receives and accompanies its unfolding: "Christ posits his salvific work anew in the liturgy of the Church. This work is accomplished also without us, in a wholly subjective manner."[100] Casel's account also makes room for the Church's subjectivity:

> Christ living in time made his sacrifice alone on the cross; Christ raised up by the Spirit makes the sacrifice together with his Church which he has purified with the blood from his own side, and thus won her for himself.... The Church, not yet brought to her completion, is drawn into this sacrifice of his; as he sacrificed for her, she now takes an active part in his sacrifice, makes it her own.[101]

The Church's participation in Christ's offering, her co-offering with him, contains several aspects that must be carefully distinguished. "'[T]he Church through the priests' ministry'[102] carries out the mystery and so offers her bridegroom's sacrifice,"[103] since Christ's act is the *causa principalis* in the *causa instrumentalis*. Casel makes much of the indissoluble connection between the mystery of the *corpus mysticum*, on the one hand, and the mystical nuptiality of Christ and the Church, on the other. The Christ-Church bond is the "original mystery," while marriage is merely its derived image;

99. Balthasar, "The Mass, a Sacrifice of the Church?" 194.
100. O. Casel, *Das christliche Kultmysterium,* ed. P. Burkhard Neunheuser (1960), 189. Quoted in Balthasar, "The Mass, a Sacrifice of the Church?" 195.
101. O. Casel, *The Mystery of Christian Worship* (New York: Crossroad, 1999), 13.
102. *"Sacerdotum ministerio"*; see Denz 1743.
103. Casel, *The Mystery of Christian Worship,* 22.

the Lord's self-donation in the cultic mystery is *the* "spousal gift," indeed, it *is* marriage itself.[104]

Although Casel's teaching harmonizes with numerous texts from the Fathers, especially Augustine,[105] Balthasar raises a question regarding the mode of the *identity* of the sacrifice between Head and Body, Bridegroom and Bride. The sacrifice of the Head does not become the sacrifice of the Church solely through the priestly ministry; it likewise becomes the Bride's sacrifice through a more personal participation in the sacrifice on her part. This participation is the context in which the Church does what Casel's intuition attributes to her: "Yet the Church still wants to give testimony of her love . . . she will be doing, not merely taking something. For this, again, she has the mysteries and in them she can express her love."[106] But, Balthasar insists, "Who or what is this *Ekklēsia* that can dare to take all this upon herself?"[107] Note the allusion to his article, "Who Is the Church?", which offers a thorough pneumatological and trinitarian account of the Church-Bride's personhood vis-à-vis Christ.

Max Thurian complements Casel's theory with an account of the question informed by Scripture as a whole. Avoiding the risks of the comparative religions approach, Thurian highlights the biblical notion of memorial *(zikkaron)*, showing how the various strands of the Old Testament converge on the eschatological fulfillment brought by the Messiah. He concludes by affirming that the Eucharist is a sacrifice:

> It is the sacramental *presence of the sacrifice of the Cross,* through the power of the Holy Spirit and of the Word. It is the liturgical offering [or presentation] that the Church makes of this sacrifice of the Son before the Father, in thanksgiving for all his acts of blessing and in the petition that he may grant these afresh. It is *participation by the Church* in the intercession that

104. Casel, *The Mystery of Christian Worship,* 26, 29; see Balthasar, "The Mass, a Sacrifice of the Church?" 199.

105. St. Augustine, *De Civitate Dei* 10.20 (PL 41.298): *"Ipse offerens, ipse et oblatio. Cujus rei sacramentum quotidianum esse voluit Ecclesiae sacrificium: quae com ipsius capitis corpus est, se ipsam per ipsum dixit offerre"; De Civitate Dei* 10.6 (PL 41.284): *". . . efficitur ut tota ipsa redempta civitas . . . universale sacrificium offeratur Deo per sacerdotum magnum. . . . Quod etiam sacramento altaris fidelibus noto frequentat Ecclesia, ubi ei demonstratur, quod in ea re quam offert, ipsa offeratur."*

106. Casel, *The Mystery of Christian Worship,* 29-30.

107. H. U. von Balthasar, "The Mass, a Sacrifice of the Church?" 203; "Who Is the Church?" in *Explorations in Theology,* vol. 2: *Spouse of the Word* (San Francisco: Ignatius, 1991), 143-91.

the Son makes to the Father in the Holy Spirit, that he may bring salvation to all men and that the kingdom may come in glory. It is the *self-offering* of the Church to the Father, in unity with the sacrifice and the intercession of the Son, as her highest adoration and her perfect consecration in the Holy Spirit.[108]

For Balthasar, Max Thurian provides a counterweight to Casel's theology: "Here, it is (on the basis of the Old Covenant) the covenant between God and the people, their mutual gift of self — God's gift in the word, the people's gift in the reply of praise and sacrifice — that comes first and is then fulfilled in the sacrifice of Christ."[109] Louis Bouyer goes even further than Thurian by highlighting the astonishing continuity between the *berakoth* of the synagogue and the seder, on the one hand, and the *eulogia*-Eucharist of early Christianity, on the other. The entire Old Testament economy is recapitulated in Christ, who is both God's perfect Word to the world and the perfect representative of humanity and its response to God. We thus begin to see in outline the biblical pattern of sacrifice, whose fulfillment is inscribed within the inner dynamic of the memorial remembrance of salvation history:

> [T]he Cross is effectively redemptive for mankind only insofar as men associate themselves with it through the eucharistic eating of his flesh and blood. The life-giving Spirit will become their own spirit only insofar as they will adhere by faith to the Word who proposes that flesh and blood to them, i.e., insofar as they make the very "eucharist" of the Son their own. . . . And insofar as we ourselves, in this faith, are thus associated with the unique salvific oblation, we become one sole offering with Christ. Thus we can offer our own bodies, with his and in his, as a living and true sacrifice, giving to the Father, through the grace of the Son and in the communication of the Spirit, the "reasonable" worship which he expects from us.[110]

Despite the impressive scripturally based "Evangelical-Catholic consensus" concerning "the Eucharist . . . as the sacrifice, not only of the Lord,

---

108. M. Thurian, *L'Eucharistie. Mémorial du Seigneur, sacrifice d'action de grâce et d'intercession* (Neuchâtel: Delachaux et Niestlé, 1959), 223; quoted in Balthasar, "The Mass, a Sacrifice of the Church?" 201-11.

109. Balthasar, "The Mass, a Sacrifice of the Church?" 211.

110. Bouyer, *Eucharist*, 465-66.

but also of the Church,"[111] Balthasar remains dissatisfied with the conceptual framework in which the unity of the sacrifice is expressed:

> If we were to . . . avoid this dilemma, then we should need at the same time to demand the absolute *prius* of the deed of suffering of the Son of God on the Cross (and in an introductory manner in the Cenacle), but in such a way that this *prius* would include from the very outset (*in actu primo*), and not merely subsequently, an element of fellowship, with the possibility of maintaining the antithetical character of this while avoiding the danger of dissolving the outlines into a mystical or democratic identity.[112]

In order to resolve this dilemma, Balthasar turns to the Johannine literature.

The Johannine Contribution

"The only justification of the *offerimus* that can be maintained with integrity to the very end" can be found in "the Gospel of love," in the sphere of absolute love that "truly has 'seen,' i.e., understood 'the glory of the Only-begotten of the Father, full of grace and truth'; and in this 'understanding' also lies the knowledge of how one is to respond to this absolute love that 'goes up to the end' (Jn 13:1)."[113] Using the language of symbols, the Gospel of John shows how "the answer to the offer love makes is then a part of this offer itself: this guarantees that the answer, too, is absolute, exact love, an aspect of the word of love itself."[114]

Balthasar continues by noting that "The best point of entry into the Johannine-eucharistic thought is the episode of the foot-washing, which gives us (so to speak) an anatomy of the Eucharist from John's point of view, and it cannot possibly be accidental that this episode stands in the Fourth Gospel in place of the institution narrative that the three others have."[115] Keeping in mind John's indirect and existential style, "One could understand the farewell discourses in their totality as a gift that permits us to look into the eucharistic heart of Jesus, but one will certainly not be wrong in interpreting the act of

111. Balthasar, "The Mass, a Sacrifice of the Church?" 214.
112. Balthasar, "The Mass, a Sacrifice of the Church?" 215-16.
113. Balthasar, "The Mass, a Sacrifice of the Church?" 216.
114. Balthasar, "The Mass, a Sacrifice of the Church?" 216.
115. Balthasar, "The Mass, a Sacrifice of the Church?" 218; see O. Cullmann, *Les Sacrements dans l'Évangile johannique* (Paris: PUF, 1951).

washing the disciples' feet in particular as something directly transparent to the eucharistic event."[116]

At the center of the scene we find Jesus' dialogue with Peter: "Peter must utter his Yes *in persona Ecclesiae* in a state of nonunderstanding, in pure obedience, indeed, more than this, in the confusion of an elemental shrinking back in terror." Why? Precisely because Jesus is instituting a new order of eucharistic communion with himself, overturning "the total religious order of values of the natural man . . . the *homo religiosus*." For the moment, all that is required is to "let this happen": "What Peter must choose (in a state of nonunderstanding) is that the Master who is loved above all things should suffer for him (since this is the situation of foot-washing)."[117]

"[F]ar beyond what he considered his own greatest possible sacrificial endeavors," then, Peter must give his assent to "something that is the *sacrifice of the Lord*."[118] John situates Peter's "yes" within the Church's ministerial contribution to Christ's sacrifice: "It is . . . significant that precisely Peter, who wanted to be there with his 'sacrifice' (and 'all the disciples said the same' Mt 26:35), will not be present on Golgotha . . . and that no kind of identity whatsoever is established between his 'sacrifice' and the sacrifice of the Lord."[119]

Thus, while Peter's contribution as the personification of the ministerial, "official Church" is introduced into the heart of the sacrifice thanks to the threefold humiliation corresponding to his threefold denial (John 21:15-17), it remains subjected to the "superiority of love to the Church's office."[120] Balthasar notes:

the Johannine mystery of being in agreement with the sacrifice of the Lord is, in its central dimension, a feminine mystery: Adrienne von Speyr, in her meditations on the Gospel of John, was no doubt the first to see this as a whole and to disclose it as the "mystery of the three Marys": Mary of Bethany (Jn 12:1-8), the mother Mary (Jn 19:25-27), and Mary of Magdala (Jn 20:11-18). In all three it is one single attitude that is demanded, and this is determined and formed each time alone through the sacrificial attitude of the Lord.[121]

116. Balthasar, "The Mass, a Sacrifice of the Church?" 218.
117. Balthasar, "The Mass, a Sacrifice of the Church?" 220-21.
118. Balthasar, "The Mass, a Sacrifice of the Church?" 223.
119. Balthasar, "The Mass, a Sacrifice of the Church?" 223-24.
120. Balthasar, "The Mass, a Sacrifice of the Church?" 224.
121. Balthasar, "The Mass, a Sacrifice of the Church?" 224. Citing Adrienne von Speyr, *John*, vol. 4: *The Birth of the Church: Meditations on John 18–21*, trans. David Kipp (San Francisco: Ignatius, 1991).

Mary of Bethany, the "contemplative" (Luke 10:38-42) who anoints Jesus, embodies the acceptance by which love consents to the Lord's destiny without even knowing the significance of her gesture: "She has anointed me for my burial":

> The Yes spoken by Mary of Bethany was a Yes to the death on the Cross, the anointing of the suffering Messiah-Servant of the Lord for his decisive office; an anointing he does not receive from God, since he always possesses this from the outset, but which he receives from the "Church": from the Church that listens to the Word of God, believes and loves, the Church whose gesture is the expression of her faith and her love.[122]

Balthasar then turns to Mary Magdalene: "At the other end of the *triduum mortis* stands Magdalen at the grave: as the representative of the sinners who are redeemed by the Cross, she is the pure, purified eros for the 'Bridegroom of blood,' whom she seeks blindly in tears and in the yawning emptiness of the tomb."[123] Then: *"Mary!" "Rabboni!"* And yet: "Do not hold me, for I have not yet ascended to the Father; but go to my brethren . . ." (John 20:16-17). Balthasar comments:

> The Paschal embrace is held open in such a way that there is space within it for absolute love: a "sacrifice" of permitting Jesus to withdraw to the Father, an agreement with the movement of the Resurrection itself, with his coming from the realm of the dead and his rising up to the heavenly realm, the single, solitary movement of Christ — but a movement that wishes to be accompanied by the agreement of those who love and who have been redeemed: *personam Ecclesiae gerens.*[124]

This is the "post-Easter, transfigured form of the sacrifice," in which "renunciation" is filled by the gift of self to the brethren in whom one meets the Lord.

Finally, the culmination: "the Mother of the Son at the Cross. She does nothing and says nothing, she is only there. And the dying Son disposes over her, so thoroughly that he foists another son on her and gives her to this son as mother. She is not asked," because she is always in agreement with her Son.[125]

---

122. Balthasar, "The Mass, a Sacrifice of the Church?" 225.
123. Balthasar, "The Mass, a Sacrifice of the Church?" 225.
124. Balthasar, "The Mass, a Sacrifice of the Church?" 226.
125. Balthasar, "The Mass, a Sacrifice of the Church?" 226.

Her entire life had been a *sequela* whose very logic had required moments of incomprehension and "rejection." Within that same logic, she now lives the moment of the greatest conformity with him: the moment of supreme "abandonment": "'As the Father has abandoned me, so I am now abandoning you.' This is the 'sword piercing right through the heart' . . . [at] the moment when the divine human heart would be pierced through on the Cross."[126]

In commenting on the first of the solutions to the problem of the Church's sacrifice discussed above, Balthasar argues that Casel's mystical and symbolic approach reveals a triple distinction:

> 1) We have the presence of "the Church of those who love" *in actu primo redemptionis* . . . so that the Church plays her role, not first in the form of the cult mystery, but already in the historical redemption. 2) This role is feminine, not only initially, but all the way: it does not change subsequently into a masculine-active cooperation in the activity (the cooperation of the Body with the Head in an identity of sacrifice) but remains, as the fundamental action of the *Ekklēsia,* in the act of permitting the Head and Bridegroom to work and in receiving him. 3) The primary antithesis of Creator and creature is preserved through this antithesis, despite all the unity of Bridegroom and Bride, Head and Body.[127]

As for the second solution, which draws on the Old Covenant (Thurian, Bouyer), Balthasar notes that the idea of the Church's sacrifice is specific to the New Testament and goes beyond an undifferentiated consent to the fulfillment of God's will in the framework of the covenant:

> Here, the subject must accept that it is another, God and man at one and the same time, who suffers this night to the full for him. But this agreement has theological significance only when it is given in love, and here in a love that counts in God's eyes, a love that has a divine form, is shaped by the (incarnate) Word and has been made ready to give answer.[128]

But how does the participation of the Church of love become a part of the *mysterium* of the Mass? If it is true that not only the effects of the sacri-

---

126. Balthasar, "The Mass, a Sacrifice of the Church?" 228.
127. Balthasar, "The Mass, a Sacrifice of the Church?" 228.
128. Balthasar, "The Mass, a Sacrifice of the Church?" 229: "Agreement on the part of sinners is theologically irrelevant: that is the egotistic joy that someone else is willing to suffer the punishment I have deserved."

fice but the "event itself" becomes present "in an 'unbloody' manner," that is, "ministerially," how are we to understand the sacrificial "time" of the Bride that simultaneously accompanies it? Here is Balthasar's own answer:

> This is why it is *necessary* at all costs for the elemental experience also to be communicated that I, the one redeemed — but also (in the contemporaneity) precisely now and again and again the one to be redeemed — make it known by my presence at the sacrifice of Christ that *I will this death,* in the ecclesial-feminine sense, that I am in agreement with this death. . . . We must — not as sinners, but in the Spirit of the Bride-Church — share in experiencing the absolute pain that we must allow the Beloved to keep his own will to die a vicarious death. The sword must penetrate us at this thought.[129]

At the same time, Balthasar is equally keen to maintain the distinction between the sacrifice of Christ and that of the Church within the same historical and ministerial event. He points out that the Son of God's voluntary humiliation for love of the Father does more than merely establish an abyss of difference between his sacrifice and ours. In addition, it lays the foundation for our believing "yes" to his self-humiliation: "Christ obeys the Father in pure love, but we obey the Son's will to obedience. This is where the true *subalternatio* lies, already *in actu primo redemptionis;* and the Johannine theology endeavors to make this clear to us from all aspects."[130] But the logic of the Lord's sacrifice is precisely to draw his own into his action. In order fully to accomplish his self-gift and to allow himself to be "consumed" by man, he "needs a mouth that can eat him and drink him. . . . This makes the mouth that consumes him an essential part of the sacrifice of the Lord."[131]

Reflecting further on this logic, Balthasar observes:

> And yet, their "sacrifice" is not addressed ultimately to him but, through him and in him, *to the Father.* Here we must look once again at the mystery of the three Marys. Common to all three is the fact that they *allow* the Son *to leave,* to take his way that leads, through the darkness of hell, back to the Father. . . . He is to have his own will, which, however, is the will of the Father.[132]

129. Balthasar, "The Mass, a Sacrifice of the Church?" 232-33.
130. Balthasar, "The Mass, a Sacrifice of the Church?" 233.
131. Balthasar, "The Mass, a Sacrifice of the Church?" 234.
132. Balthasar, "The Mass, a Sacrifice of the Church?" 236.

They release him into his movement toward the Father:

> We grasp here the deepest theological sense of the *clementissime Pater*, *"of-ferimus tibi . . ."* *"hostiam immaculatam"* . . . and thus grasp what *eucharistia* means for the Church: thanksgiving to the Father for the departure of the Son and thanksgiving that we are permitted to let him depart. His departure is his Eucharist, and we bless the Father for this Eucharist of his.[133]

Now, the crowning moment of this entire theology arrives when "Mariology is affirmed, in the spirit of the Constitution *Lumen Gentium,* as the final piece and the heart of ecclesiology."[134] Balthasar adds:

> For all that has been said contained a hidden presupposition all the time: that the perfect *fiat* of the *Ecclesia,* the perfectly loving agreement with the sacrifice of the Bridegroom, does exist somewhere in reality. . . . [H]ow could a sinner be capable of playing this role, which demands spotless love? The disposition he would have to portray would necessarily always be something high above him, an ideal that had not been realized, so that it would not be possible anywhere for the Church to play the role assigned to her in Christ's sacrifice in keeping with what was expected. This is why the dogma of the Immaculate Conception of Mary is a strict postulate of ecclesiology, and this precisely in the sense in which it is expounded by the Church's Magisterium: as a grace coming from the Cross of Christ, as true redemption, but, for the sake of the work of Christ, as anticipated redemption. If the Church were "glorious, holy, spotless without stain or wrinkle" (Eph 5:26f.) *only* in an eschatological sense, then there would be no ultimate basis for what has been written in these pages.[135]

The Church, whose personal center is Mary, is the perfect recipient of the Bridegroom's perfect gift.[136] In Mary, there is "an identity of communion and offering in sacrifice and also the identity of the sacrifice of Christ and

---

133. Balthasar, "The Mass, a Sacrifice of the Church?" 236.
134. Balthasar, "The Mass, a Sacrifice of the Church?" 238-39.
135. Balthasar, "The Mass, a Sacrifice of the Church?" 239.
136. See Balthasar, "The Mass, a Sacrifice of the Church?" 239: "We have mentioned . . . the patristic-scholastic view that Christ himself consumed the eucharistic species at the Last Supper, above all because only he is able to be both the perfect giver and the perfect receiver. This strange and . . . biblically scarcely justifiable idea becomes redundant if the Church that has her personal center in Mary is the perfect receiver."

the sacrifice of oneself."[137] This idea serves as the archetype of the eucharistic disposition or intention. Balthasar remarks on the ecumenical significance of this approach: "Strangely enough, the genuine Protestant concern to free the eucharistic sacrifice of Christ from alien encrustations — whether these are mystical or of an Old Testament kind — can be guaranteed best by means of a radically considered Mariology."[138]

As Balthasar observes in conclusion:

> But it is ultimately only through the working of the *Holy Spirit* that one can understand the unity in antithesis between Christ and the Church. Man and wife are one flesh, but Christ and the Church are one spirit in the mystery of the Eucharist. The Body of the Lord is what the Spirit gives us in order to pour into us the Spirit of the Lord; and he is what we give back, in order to share in the Spirit of the Lord, who is a Spirit of the gift of self to the Father. "The one who cleaves to the Lord is one Spirit with him" (1 Cor 6:17), but through the Body and in the Body, to the extent that [it] has become an instrument and a gift of the Spirit.[139]

In this eucharistic relation, the symbol consisting in the man-woman relation is "both fulfilled . . . and transcended into the Spirit, without thereby being disembodied, as something that stands on its own without any analogy to it, since it is the high point of the unique paths God's revelation takes with man."[140] It is the Spirit who creates the eucharistic unity of Christ and the Church. In other words, it is in himself, i.e., in the gift of himself united to the Lord's eucharistic flesh, that he guarantees the encounter between Bridegroom and Bride in the single sacrifice of the "nuptial mystery."

In this mystery of communion, at this meeting point of ministry and love, it is impossible to separate the contribution of the institutional Church from that of the Church of love, not even with respect to their origin: "Everything comes from the Son, everything comes from the Spirit, everything is bestowed by the Father through them both. Peter is in Mary, and Mary, as the most obedient of all, is under Peter, because she is under everything that is established by the Son."[141]

As Balthasar recalls in *Theo-Logic*, this is the condition enabling the prolongation of Christ's sacrifice in the Eucharist celebrated by the Church:

137. Balthasar, "The Mass, a Sacrifice of the Church?" 240.
138. Balthasar, "The Mass, a Sacrifice of the Church?" 240.
139. Balthasar, "The Mass, a Sacrifice of the Church?" 241.
140. Balthasar, "The Mass, a Sacrifice of the Church?" 241.
141. Balthasar, "The Mass, a Sacrifice of the Church?" 242-43.

In utter love Mary surrenders what is most her own, her offspring, in his self-sacrifice for the world's sin: only in this way does her perfect subjective holiness become a precondition enabling Christ's sacrifice and his Eucharist to become a single, perfect sacrifice in the exercise of the hierarchical priesthood. The Son performs the sacrifice, and the Mother-Ecclesia, in perfect love, allows it to happen.[142]

Conclusion

Is the Mass a sacrifice of the Church? Our answer to this question has drawn on a theological symbolics based on the drama of revelation, which by its very nature exhibits a pattern of Word-and-response whose archetype appears in Mary's immaculate "yes." The Word of God encounters *in actu primo redemptionis* the ecclesial and feminine "yes" of Mary. Far from being a sacrifice "added" to Christ's sacrifice, her "yes" is the immaculate Church's consent to the unique sacrifice of the Bridegroom, who desires and includes precisely this "yes" of love.

Balthasar's Johannine account of the response of the Church of love integrates both the Petrine principle of ministry and the Marian principle of love, which jointly enable the simultaneous achievement of the vertical, spousal gift of Christ and the authentic reception and participation of the ministerial and feminine ecclesial Bride. In the eucharistic "one flesh," that is, in the unity of Christ's sacrifice, the immaculate Church acts as a discreet and humble *partner*, while fully respecting the abiding distinction between the creature and the Creator. Finally, it is the Holy Spirit's mediation that makes possible both the minister's objective, sacramental action and the feminine and subjective attitude of the Bride, both of whom "let it," that is, Christ's oblation of love for sinners, "be done" (*Geschehenlassen*).

The ecumenical potential of this approach lies in its ability to maintain the distinction between Christ's absolute gift and the Church's reception of it, while rereading the Church's *verum et proprium sacrificium* as a requirement of Christ's own spousal love, which from the beginning desires the nuptial consent of the Church.[143] The Eucharist is the fruit and the pledge of the shared fruitfulness of the Bridegroom and the Bride.

---

142. Balthasar, *Theo-Logic*, vol. 3: *Spirit of Truth*, 314.
143. Cf. Bätzing, *Die Eucharistie als Opfer der Kirche*, 130ff.

CHAPTER 11

Toward a Nuptial Trinitarian Anthropology

In this final chapter of the book, we conclude our reflection by exploring some of the anthropological and sacramental implications of the trinitarian and spousal approach that we sketched in the chapters preceding it. Revealed in Jesus Christ and actualized in the Eucharist, the theo-drama invites man to share God's engagement in the world by serving the glory of trinitarian communion in history. Since the Church is "in Christ like a sacrament or as a sign and instrument both of a very closely knit union with God and of the unity of the whole human race" (*LG* 1), our final task must be to draw out the trinitarian anthropology that has implicitly underlain our work, while indicating something of its ultimate horizon of meaning and of its sacramental significance.[1]

Balthasar highlights the anthropological implications of the "theo-drama" when he writes that "The *communio eucharistica* becomes — 'analytically,' as it were — the *communio sanctorum*."[2] He summarizes his approach in volume 4 of *Theo-Drama:*[3]

---

1. For further study of the themes of this chapter see, beyond the authors already cited, K. Hemmerle, *Partire dall'unità. La Trinità come stile di vita e forma di pensiero* (Rome: Città Nuova, 1998); G. Greshake, *Der dreieine Gott. Eine trinitarische Theologie* (Fribourg, Basel, Vienna: Herder, 1997); J. Ratzinger, *The Spirit of the Liturgy,* trans. John Saward (San Francisco: Ignatius, 2000); E. Cambòn, *Trinità, modello sociale* (Rome: Città Nuova, 1999); G. Biffi, *Canto nuziale* (Milan: Jaca Book, 2000).

2. H. U. von Balthasar, *Theo-Drama,* vol. 2: *Dramatis Personae: Man in God,* trans. Graham Harrison (San Francisco: Ignatius, 1990), 410.

3. A more detailed development can be found in *Theo-Drama,* vol. 4: *The Action,* trans. Graham Harrison (San Francisco: Ignatius, 1994), "The Dramatic Dimensions of the Eucharist," 389-406, and "The Dramatic Dimension of the Communion of Saints," 406-23.

So the "communion of saints" can only be created on the basis of the principle of the good "in Person"; and here we cannot posit any hiatus between the action of the Holy Spirit and that of the Son who eucharistically gives himself to all (and behind whom stands and works the Primal Giver, the Father). In the foreground there is the fellowship *(koinonia)* with the Trinity as such, which is the result of grace; this, as Origen concludes from 1 John 1:3-4, produces the community of believers.[4] Augustine deduces from this that the Spirit who sustains the unity of Father and Son is "somehow" the unifying principle of the *communio sanctorum*.[5] Here we must not forget, however, that the Spirit is the Spirit of the self-giving Son and that the prototype of the unifying love between believers is the entire love of the Trinity.[6] Paul himself lists all three Divine Persons as giving the different gifts of the Spirit that characterize the Church's unity (1 Cor 12:4-6).[7]

The foundation of the communion of saints in the Trinity will serve as a starting point for our reflection on the core of trinitarian anthropology, a reflection that will prepare us, in turn, for a deeper understanding of the ultimate meaning of Christian existence. In pursuing this task, then, we will make use of the key intuitions of what we can now call the eucharistic and spousal model of sacramental theology. We hope to demonstrate in this way the extent to which eucharistic faith involves the whole of Christian existence in the theo-drama of salvation history, that is, in the *mysterion* of the new and eternal Covenant. Against this backdrop, the man-woman symbol, understood as *imago Dei* and reread eucharistically in light of the spousal symbol of Christ and the Church and of the trinitarian mystery, offers us a new paradigm not only for a different way of doing sacramental theology, but also for a Christian hermeneutic of existence.[8] What does it mean for man to be taken up eucha-

4. Origen, *In Leviticum Homilia* 4.4.

5. *"Ideo societas unitatis Ecclesiae Dei . . . tamquam proprium est Spiritus Sancti, Patre sane et Filio cooperantibus, quia societas est quodammodo Patris et Filii ipse Spiritus Sanctus,"* St. Augustine, *Serm.* 71.20 (*PL* 38.463).

6. St. Bonaventure, *In Primum Librum Sententiarum* 1, d. 14, a. 2 q. 1; 1, d. 10, a. 1 q. 3 (Quaracchi I, 249, 199)

7. Balthasar, *Theo-Drama,* vol. 4: *The Action,* 408-9.

8. John Paul II, *Man and Woman He Created Them: A Theology of the Body,* trans. Michael Waldstein (Boston: Pauline Books and Media, 2006) [= *TOB*], 511: "All the sacraments of the New Covenant find their prototype in some way in marriage as the primordial sacrament." A footnote in the Italian text clarifies: "The 'prototypical' character of marriage is based on the fact that . . . the sacrament of marriage 'synthetically' expresses the spousal love of Christ and the Church, to which all the sacraments are efficaciously related." Although this paradigmatic

ristically into the exchange of "gifts" between the divine Persons? What does it mean for God to be involved in human history to the extreme point of his paschal and eucharistic kenosis?

The Eucharistic and Nuptial Meaning of Existence

Let us attempt, then, to clarify the meaning of human existence in light of the Eucharist, rather than trying to grasp the meaning of the Eucharist within some *a priori* anthropological and symbolical horizon. It is worth recalling that our fundamental presupposition is Christocentric: It is Christ who defines man, not man who must define Christ. It is the situations experienced by Christ that confer sacramental value on human life from above, not the situations experienced by man that determine the significance of sacramental grace from below.[9] Our question, then, concerns the anthropological consequences that follow from what Christ did when, in offering his own body (Heb. 10:5-10), he assumed all of man and all men and women into his eucharistic and paschal oblation to the Father. In order to answer this question, we must keep in mind the content of Chapter 9: biblical-liturgical narrative and, above all, the trinitarian drama of the *"mysterion."*

The Eucharistic and Spousal Paradigm

The reversal of perspective that has guided us from the beginning has its source in the paschal and eucharistic mystery insofar as it is both trinitarian and spousal, that is, insofar as it is the historical enactment of the covenant. The meaning of human existence flows from this mystery and is illumined by the event that takes place in the paschal and eucharistic Christ: "You are my beloved Son, today I have begotten you." As we have already noted, Christ's paschal baptism in the fire of trinitarian love culminates in his eucharistic kenosis-exaltation, which, in turn, generates the Church as his Body and

---

character does not deprive the Eucharist of its pride of place in the sacramental order — a preeminence founded on the substantial presence of the Lord's body and blood — marriage does add a symbolic complement in whose light we grasp the nuptial meaning of the Eucharist. Hence the intimate bond between the two sacraments.

9. Of course, the shift in accent from one perspective to the other does not annul the value or even the necessity of approaching sacramental theology from an ascending, anthropological perspective as well.

Bride. The continuity between the Incarnation and the Eucharist means that the Father unceasingly sends his incarnate Word in the power of the Holy Spirit to generate the Church, the holy Bride who listens and responds to the Word of God in faith. This Word made eucharistic flesh in the womb of faith joins his ecclesial Body and Bride to the offering performed once and for all by the eschatological Bridegroom. It follows that through its communion in the immolated and glorified body of the paschal Lamb the ecclesial body (*Corpus mysticum*) participates in the eucharistic and spousal dimension of the New Covenant. It is this participation that gives Christian life its ultimate meaning.

Now, in order to grasp the eucharistic and spousal significance of human existence, let us first recapitulate our earlier discussion of the theological drama of the Eucharist. As the above-mentioned reversal implies, it is the Eucharist that gives meaning to human existence and not vice versa. By analogy, it is not the man-woman relation that gives meaning to the Christ-Church relation, but rather the latter that gives meaning to the former. What bearing does the Eucharist have, then, on the theological meaning of human existence? Matthew 22:1-14 offers us an initial clue: "The kingdom of heaven may be compared to a king who gave a marriage feast for his son, and he sent his servants to call those who were invited to the marriage feast; but they would not come." The emblematic motif of the wedding feast contains an eschatological meaning, one concerning God's plan for salvation history. God prepares a wedding feast for his Son, which he invites all to enter wearing their wedding garment, that is, with faith. The Father demonstrates his love for his only Son by offering him an additional created gift: a created bride. Unfortunately, the promised bride, that is, humanity, fails to ratify the Father's love for the Son by refusing to give herself in return. Mankind falls into sin and disgrace, leaving the "paradise" of trinitarian love to pursue its own affairs. Indeed, it disregards the invitation to the feast and even kills the messengers charged with relaying it.

The Son does not abandon his promised bride to the miserable fate of those excluded from the feast. In virtue of his eternal consent to the shared work of the Trinity, he sacrifices himself for her salvation, purifying her in the bath of regeneration and presenting her to himself as a holy and immaculate bride (Eph. 5:26-27; Col. 1:22; 2 Cor. 11:2; Rev. 19:7-8). Christ's sacrifice, which he offered in the eternal Spirit (Heb. 9:14), thus turns the situation of condemnation and perdition into one of salvation. The proof of this transformation is precisely his Resurrection from the dead, which reveals the Father's response to the Son's sacrifice, that is, his glorification of the Son, and thus seals the victory of the New Covenant with the confirmation and fruitfulness of the Holy Spirit. This trinitarian exchange is the source of the original sacrament of Christ the Bridegroom and the Church-Bride, who are indissolubly united by the intra-trinitarian bond of the Holy Spirit. But this fruitful bond of the new and eternal Covenant also contains the sacraments, which, springing from the Lord's pierced heart, constitute the Church-Bride. The Church receives herself in the Holy Spirit from the nuptial and ever-actual gift of the eucharistic Bridegroom.

The Holy Spirit figures here, then, as the "confirmation" of trinitarian love in the glorified and eucharistic flesh of Christ, in that he seals once and for all Christ's immolation for his Bride and assures the universal extension of the sacramental economy. The sacrament of the Eucharist, the source and summit of all the Church's activity (*Sacrosanctum Concilium* 10), is intimately linked with all the other sacraments; it celebrates and actualizes the nuptial encounter of the Bridegroom and the Bride: "Christ indeed always associates the Church with himself in this great work wherein God is perfectly glorified and men are sanctified. The Church is his beloved Bride who calls to her Lord, and through him offers worship to the Eternal Father" (*SC* 7).

The Ultimate Meaning of Human Existence in a Trinitarian and Spousal Perspective

Man Fashioned in the Image and Likeness of God through Sacramental Grace

"Today I have begotten you"; "this is my body, given up for you"; "your sins are forgiven"; "Holy Father, keep [my disciples] in thy name, which thou hast given me, that they may be one, even as we are one" (John 17:11); "Father, I desire that they also, whom thou hast given me, may be with me where I am, to behold my glory which thou hast given me in thy love for me before the foundation of the world" (John 17:24).[10] Scripture preserves these words of Christ, as so many definitions of the human being. They are therefore much more than the framework in which human existence receives a "Christian"

---

10. "I give them eternal life, and they shall never perish, and no one shall snatch them out of my hand. My Father, who has given them to me, is greater than all, and no one is able to snatch them out of the Father's hand. I and the Father are one" (John 10:28-30); see also John 6:37; 17:2.

meaning. They generate life and holiness; they communicate the "form" for which human existence was conceived from the beginning, the form of eucharistic and, therefore, of sacramental existence. Historical man is like a lump of clay (Gen. 2:7, 22-23) destined to be molded by Christ's grace and so to become, in the power of the Holy Spirit, a sacrament of trinitarian Love (Gen. 1:27-28; Eph. 5:21-32).

From baptism to the anointing of the sick, along with the intermediate stages: confirmation, the Eucharist, penance, marriage, and holy orders, man receives the "Christic form" to which he was predestined from before the world was made. This "filial-fraternal-spousal" form, which the Holy Spirit sculpts in human subjects according to the nuptial model of Christ and the Church, reflects the glory of the Trinity in the *imago Dei*. Even more, this form incarnates the divine "likeness" in the "image," descending from on high through the eucharistic mediation of the incarnate Word and spreading its rays in the seven sacraments. This form proceeds essentially from the Father through the archetype of spousal charity, that is, Christ and the Church and so — by means of the eucharistic and paschal gift of the Holy Spirit — comes to shape man and woman called to participate in the divine nature (2 Pet. 1:4). John Paul II reminded us that "marriage and virginity or celibacy are two ways of expressing and living the one mystery of the covenant of God with His people" (*FC* 16). They are the two ways in which the "eucharistic and spousal" form brings to fulfillment the vocation to love inscribed in the human person by virtue of his creation in the image of the God who is Love (*FC* 11).[11]

As the foregoing suggests, the Holy Spirit confers divine likeness on man and woman through the sacraments of Christ and the Church. By virtue of the sacraments, the integration of man and woman into the trintarian life takes on a concrete, fleshly form. Indeed, the sacraments stamp them with the features of Christ and the Church, features that reflect both the sacramental "characters" they receive and the particular charisms the Holy Spirit confers on them for the service of the community.[12] Man (i.e., both men and women)

11. "Christian revelation recognizes two specific ways of realizing the vocation of the human person in its entirety, to love: marriage and virginity or celibacy. Either one is, in its own proper form, an actuation of the most profound truth of man, of his being 'created in the image of God'" (*FC* 11); "In spite of having renounced physical fecundity, the celibate person becomes spiritually fruitful, the father and mother of many, cooperating in the realization of the family according to God's plan" (*FC* 16).

12. This is the place to mention the multiplicity of personal vocations, whether common or individual, which enrich the basic pattern of the states of life with particular gifts for the

thus receives his "true form," his "theological person in Christ,"[13] his "personal and ecclesial identity" precisely through the sacraments, which incorporate him at the same into Christ's mission. Sacramental grace is always also a mission. To receive sacramental "gifts" means to receive oneself from grace; but it also means to be directly incorporated into God's dramatic engagement for the world's salvation.

When, in fact, redeemed man *(anima ecclesiastica)* finds himself nuptially taken up "into Christ" through the Church's Eucharist, he receives even more than the response to his heart's deepest desire *(desiderium naturale visionis);* he also really participates in the expression of the Father and Son's Love for the world. By sharing with others the gift he has received — that is, himself, eucharistically transformed — he participates through mission in the mode of being revealed in the Trinity's openness to the world. This means that Christian existence not only tends toward its proper fulfillment in God, but also that in the wake of Christ's eucharistic kenosis it is drawn into God's descent, into his commitment for the world. Human existence thus becomes properly "theo-dramatic," that is, an authentic extension of Christ's mission. This insight brings us to the ultimate consequence of our eucharistic anthropology: the participation of man, trans-united to the eucharistic body of Christ, in the Father's gift to the Son and the Son's gift to the Father in the unity of the Holy Spirit.[14]

Saved through the Fire of Trinitarian Love

The Book of Daniel's well-known story of Shadrach, Meshach, and Abednego (Daniel 3) presents us with a metaphor for the mystery of the human person

---

service of ecclesial communion, *sacramentum Trinitatis.* See H. U. von Balthasar, *The Christian State of Life,* trans. Mary Frances McCarthy (San Francisco: Ignatius, 1983), 345-87.

13. On Balthasar's account, man is a (natural) "subject" who is called to become a theological "person in Christ" (grace), receiving in faith and carrying out in obedience the mission for which he has been predestined in the body of Christ that is the Church; see H. U. von Balthasar, *Theo-Drama,* vol. 3: *Dramatis Personae: Persons in Christ,* trans. Graham Harrison (San Francisco: Ignatius, 1992), 202-8, 245-50, 271-82. See also M. Ouellet, *L'Existence comme mission. L'anthropologie théologique de Hans Urs von Balthasar* (Rome: PUG, 1983), 56-81.

14. The sacramental approach presented here focuses on the ecclesial form of grace, without denying that "the range of Jesus' eschatological work is such that he can operate directly, outside the Church; he may give grace to individual persons, and perhaps to groups, enabling them to act according to his mind; the Church must allow for this possibility" (Balthasar, *Theo-Drama,* vol. 3: *Dramatis Personae: Persons in Christ,* 282).

taken up in and with Christ into the furnace of trinitarian Love. The three Israelites were thrown into the fiery furnace on account of their refusal to adore the golden statue erected by King Nebuchadnezzar. Thanks to the miraculous intervention of the angel of the Lord, they were protected from the fire and praised God from the midst of the flames without suffering any harm.

Predestined to the *Gloria Dei*, man is called to praise his Lord with all his being, learning to walk freely amid the flames of eternal Love.[15] The passage to the fullness of this glory cannot occur without a genuine baptism of fire in the Holy Spirit. The Spirit banishes sin and its concomitant effects, making the human being fully transparent to Love, because now caught up in the event of the trinitarian processions in both a receptive and an active mode. That is to say, man is involved in the exchange between the divine Persons. The Eucharist marks the earthly inauguration of this participation in God's eternal life. The Eucharist, in fact, sacramentally associates the Church, in a feminine manner proper to her bridal identity, with the sacrificial offering of the divine Bridegroom. In faith, then, the Church participates in Christ's eucharistic sacrifice, thereby receiving the Holy Spirit of the Father and the Son — the Spirit who is trinitarian communion in the ecclesial community. This is why the Church, united to Christ as her Head and Bridegroom, is raised up to the dignity of a sacramental subject of the trinitarian life. She finds herself elevated, in other words, to the status of a holy Bride of the Most High, with all the "spousal rights" entitling her to participate fruitfully in the overflowing life of the trinitarian relations. Clearly, each member of the community benefits from this elevation in the form of a richer, more meaningful life that overflows into adoration, active service, and illumination for the glory of God and the salvation of the world.

Called to glorify God in his body, man glimpses the ultimate meaning of his existence in the unveiling of this intra-trinitarian horizon. He realizes that the fulfillment of his destiny exceeds even the framework of human history saved by Christ; it occurs above all within the framework of a trinitarian history whose specific note is the mutual glorification of the divine Persons. Man thus discovers his ultimate end in being given by the Father to the Son as a bride. At the same time, he realizes that the Son receives him with an infinite gratitude, in order to save him and return him to the Father as a holy spouse. Finally, in the Spirit of the Father (John 15:26) and of the Son, he learns that God's fruitfulness becomes his, in the nuptial mystery of Christ the Bridegroom and the Church-Bride.

---

15. "Set me as a seal upon your heart, as a seal upon your arm; for love is strong as death, jealousy is cruel as the grave. Its flashes are flashes of fire, a most vehement flame" (Song 8:6).

At the Service of the Beatitude of the Trinity

The trinitarian and spousal theology that we have presented here ultimately requires a change of horizon for theological anthropology. The shared, reciprocal commitment of the divine Persons in the history of the covenant between God and humanity opens a new horizon of gratuity and meaning for Christian and human life. If it is true that man, the *imago Dei*, is the "object" of the exchange between the divine Persons; and if it is true that he is called through faith to be, in a certain sense, the "subject" of the exchange of uncreated love between those same Persons, then the horizon of his limited, tormented, apparently banal and insignificant existence, opens onto the infinite. In this reversal of perspective, we suddenly realize that it is not just man who seeks his beatitude in God, but that God himself desires to share his beatitude with man. Consequently, while God means something to man, it is also the case that man means something to God. God has staked his glory on man's destiny. If theocentric trinitarianism is correct, then the human person's participation in sacramentality cannot be confined to his service of God's love for humanity; above all, human existence attains the real summit of its sacramental engagement by expressing God's Love for God.

This claim implies a radical shift in (though not a simple break with) our habitual way of understanding man's final end. St. Thomas rightly describes man's beatitude as a created, participated reality,[16] but he has little to say about the "trinitarian" character of the divine beatitude in which man shares. Now, God's beatitude is nothing other than his Being-as-Love, that is to say, his "Co-Being" in the eternal joy of the substantial exchange between the three divine Persons. The creature is predestined in Christ "to the praise of his glorious grace" (Eph. 1:6), that is, to receive the grace of being, and of becoming ever more, a nuptial mystery grafted onto the mutual glorification of the divine Persons: "for through him we both have access in one Spirit to the Father" (Eph. 2:18).

Man's final end, then, turns out to consist less in the attainment of his own beatitude than in the service of the beatitude of the Trinity. Man's true

---

16. St. Thomas Aquinas, *Summa Theologica*, Ia IIae, q. 3 a. 1: "In the first sense, then, man's last end is the uncreated good, namely, God, who alone by his infinite goodness can perfectly satisfy man's will. But in the second way, man's last end is something created, existing in him, and this is nothing else than the attainment or enjoyment of the last end. Now the last end is called happiness. If, therefore, we consider man's happiness in its cause or object, then it is something uncreated; but if we consider it as to the very essence of happiness, then it is something created."

beatitude is achieved above all in *the service of God* and only secondarily in the accomplishment of the *desiderium naturale visionis*. The perspective of desire ultimately remains anthropocentric, whereas the perspective of service takes up the Augustinian and Thomistic restless heart *(cor inquietum)* into the reversal envisaged by the "principle and foundation" of St. Ignatius of Loyola's *Spiritual Exercises:* "Man is created to praise, reverence, and serve God our Lord, and by this means to save his soul."[17] Balthasar boldly develops the theocentric and trinitarian turn that still remains implicit in St. Ignatius's theology. His anthropology offers an alternative both to medieval cosmo-centrism and modern anthropocentrism: the third way of trinitarian Love.[18]

Balthasar does not merely consider man's beatitude against the backdrop of the common works of the divine Persons *ad extra*. His account is trinitarian in a deeper sense, in that it places beatitude within the horizon of the exchange *between the divine Persons*. At first glance, this change of perspective may seem insignificant, but upon closer consideration it confers an utterly new and unexpected meaning on the entirety of human existence. In the light of the Eucharist, the generative principle of the *communio sanctorum*, the whole of human existence thus receives its full sacramental value. Human life, woven through to its core by faith, hope, and charity, enters fully into ecclesial communion:

> The entire development [of the expression *"communio sanctorum"*] shows increasingly that the shared communion of the Church's members results not only from the fact of sharing in the Church's common goods, distributed by the Holy Spirit; what individuals themselves do, as a result of this participation in Christ's freely bestowed love, also enters into the exchange. Thus Christ's *pro nobis* perfects his members' ability to *be* and *act* on behalf of others.[19]

Participation in trinitarian Love thus coincides with committed engagement in the communion-mission of the Church.

The foregoing implies that the loving unity of Christian communities, which is to say: their giving and receiving, their "being with and for others,"

---

17. Ignatius of Loyola, *The Spiritual Exercises of St. Ignatius,* trans. Louis Puhl (New York, Toronto: Random House, 2000).

18. See H. U. von Balthasar, *Love Alone Is Credible,* trans. D. C. Schindler (San Francisco: Ignatius, 2004). This slim volume offers a summary of Balthasar's entire "theological aesthetics." His trilogy is like a symphony unfolding this master theme in three movements and reaching its culmination in a final fugue, that is, the *Epilogue.*

19. Balthasar, *Theo-Drama,* vol. 4: *The Action,* 418-19.

becomes the heart of the Church's mission. Over against the whole utilitarian thrust of the prevailing anthropocentric culture, we must remember that what makes the Church is not organization, but rather the love that springs from the Eucharist. The world is drawn by the gravitational pull of the Trinity at the center of the Church-sacrament, which attracts precisely through the witness of Christians' mutual love (John 13:35). As if that were not enough, trinitarian love broadens the horizon of sacramentality even further, inviting the ecclesial community and all of its members to play their role, and to live their lives, within the relations between the divine Persons. It is already a great deal — indeed, unimaginably so — to participate in the gift that God makes to the world; but it is infinitely more to participate in God's gift to God.[20] Regarding the theological virtues that define and shape the ways in which man responds to grace, Balthasar writes:

> Ultimately, they constitute the act that gives back to God what he awaits from man; above all, this is God himself, but he assumes man too. "When God gives himself to the soul with free will full of grace, the soul does the same by the power of her will, which is the more free and generous, the more it is united to God: in God, it gives God to God himself." (John of the Cross, *Flame*, 3:78)[21]

There can be nothing more beautiful, greater, or more beatifying than this "service," nothing beyond this ultimate meaning of human existence: *"Id quo majus cogitari nequit."*

Doxology, Missionary Fruitfulness, and the Theo-Logic of Nuptiality

The sacramental and trinitarian anthropology that has emerged here at the end of our work has three main characteristics: It is doxological, theo-dramatic, and (in particular) eucharistic and nuptial. This anthropology is doxological in that it deeply roots the direction and pattern of human life in the sacraments of Christian initiation, thus giving the exercise of the theological virtues of faith, hope, and charity a new prominence to the service of God's glory. The

---

20. H. U. von Balthasar, *Explorations in Theology*, vol. 3: *Creator Spirit*, trans. Brian McNeil (San Francisco: Ignatius, 1993), 46; the citation is from St. John of the Cross, "The Living Flame of Love," strophe 3, verse 5-6.
21. Balthasar, *Explorations in Theology*, vol. 3: *Creator Spirit*, 46.

triad of faith, hope, and charity structures man's daily life in function of the divine glory. This glory is not reserved for the end of the world, but is already present at the heart of human history. "The glory of God is man fully alive," said St. Irenaeus, "and the life of man is the vision of God." A doxological anthropology, then, establishes an essential relationship of correspondence between the always prior Love of God and a Marian availability to "keep" God's mighty works, meditating on them in the heart of the Church. Mary's *Magnificat* is thus the distinguishing trait of a doxological anthropology, one that reveals its theocentric and trinitarian axis.

A sacramental and trinitarian anthropology also contains a theo-dramatic dimension, since it involves man in God's dramatic engagement for the world:

> Since the Church, as Bride and Body of Christ, shares in the "merits" of her Head's entire life and suffering, she is one with him in becoming the world's "sacrament of salvation." (And here her external activity — evangelizing and pressing for the removal of injustices in the distribution of goods or racial discrimination or the repression of classes or peoples — must not be underplayed simply because of the paramount importance, on the basis of the communion of saints, of her visible, representative ["on-behalf"] activity.)[22]

Man's theo-dramatic engagement in the trinitarian communion brings with it a multiplicity of aspects, which include contemplation, action, and passion to the point of vicarious substitution for the salvation of others: "even if I am to be poured as a libation upon the sacrificial offering of your faith, I am glad and rejoice with you all" (Phil. 2:17ff.).

Engagement with Christ involves the apostle and the Church in the self-communication of the life of the Trinity. The appropriation of grace is always a matter of self-dispossession for the sake of others. This essentially paschal dispossession always takes place under the sign of spiritual fruitfulness. It is also a constant theme running throughout all the states of life. Demanding as they do the total gift of self, both Christian marriage and consecrated virginity, when chosen and lived in Christ, become, according to the measure of the gift of Christ and of the Spirit, "fruitful sacramental relationships." Through them we glimpse the way in which likeness to the Trinity is incorporated into the *imago Dei* through participation in the unity, fidelity, and fruitfulness of the

---

22. Balthasar, *Theo-Drama*, vol. 4: *The Action*, 422.

spousal relation between Christ and the Church. As this insight suggests, the spiritual fruitfulness of the communion of saints is not only a sign of belonging to the Church, but also the mark of the essentially nuptial and missionary nature of Christian existence itself.

In sum, then, we have a doxological anthropology for a contemplative acknowledgment of God's glory; a theo-dramatic anthropology for ecclesial engagement in the divine missions of the Word and of the Spirit in the world; and a eucharistic and nuptial anthropology for the service of God in all the dimensions of his mystery, both within the Trinity and in the history of salvation. If the Church is a sacrament of the trinitarian *communio personarum,* it is the Eucharist that gives her this status by maintaining the doxological, theo-dramatic and beatifying tension of God's kenotic and glorious love. The Eucharist pours into the heart of the Christian community the very Love of God: the power that throws everything off balance, yet that is the most neglected by the logic of this world. The evangelist of Love passionately proclaims that "faith conquers the world." Faith in Love brings the missing fullness of meaning that the disoriented men and women of our time desire and that only Christ can unveil. Christ crucified and glorified is precisely the nuptial encounter of all the needs of love: the "need" of God, the needs of the Church, and the needs of man who thirsts for the water of life.

The Theological and Pastoral Importance of the Nuptial Eucharistic Model

We remarked at the beginning that the classical definition of the sacraments handed down by the Scholastic tradition is in the midst of a crisis that remains unresolved either pastorally or theologically. When the sacraments are understood as "means of grace" or "signs effecting what they signify," they can no longer penetrate to the symbolic-experiential core of Christian existence or even speak to the conceptual horizon of contemporary man. Although a theological renewal has begun to redress this problem, it has not yet attained a mature synthesis capable of garnering any broad consensus. The needed synthesis would enable us to link the traditional understanding of the sacraments as efficacious acts of Christ with the aspect that contemporary sacramental theology means to stress in speaking of the "sacraments of the Church": their character as "personal encounter" (Schillebeeckx) and "symbolic language" (Chauvet, Mazzanti, Ricoeur). Generally speaking, these new developments depend on the "anthropological turn" of Karl Rahner, whose argument, reflecting as it does his new approach to fundamental theology, fails to convince on the level of sacramental theology as such.[23] Moreover, Rahner's "transcendental" approach tends to an excessive relativization of the "categorical" manifestations of God's grace (the sacraments in the strict sense) in the name of the Holy Spirit's universal "transcendental" self-communication.

The import of the theological alternative proposed in this work already becomes apparent in its disclosure of the horizon of meaning represented by trinitarian anthropology. It would be interesting to demonstrate the applicability of the "eucharistic nuptial" model to all the other sacraments. For in fact the mystery of the covenant between Christ and the Church in the Eucharist spreads its glow over all the other sacraments, which in turn find in the Eucharist the source and summit of the entire sacramental order.[24] One example is sufficient to illustrate this point: baptism, which can be seen as the Bride's bath of purification (Eph. 5:26) or as Christ's gesture/word that generates new children in the power of the Holy Spirit while including the maternal contribution of the ecclesial Bride. As we have already observed, the Eucharist is the wedding feast in which almost of itself the symbol of food opens to the nuptial encounter; holy orders is constituted by the gesture of the laying on of hands, which communicates the Holy Spirit of the Bridegroom, along with the specific capacity to represent him vis-à-vis the Bride. One could continue in this vein with all the remaining sacraments, all of which find their original principle in this spousal relationship between Christ and the Church.[25]

23. "But insofar as the church is the continuation of God's self-offer in Jesus Christ in whom he has the final, victorious and salvific word in the dialogue between God and the world, the church is an efficacious sign" (Karl Rahner, *Foundations of Christian Faith: An Introduction to the Idea of Christianity*, trans. William V. Dych [New York: Seabury, 1978], 412). G. Colombo responds: "Isn't the sacrament, which establishes the Church in this position, the thing that provides her most absolute guarantee and her most compelling justification? Can we entirely ignore the fact that the sacraments, though of course sacraments of the Church, are nonetheless first *'sacramenta Dei'*"? (G. Colombo, "Teologia sacramentaria e teologia fondamentale," in *Teologia sacramentaria* [Milan: Glossa, 1997], 76). See also J. Moignt, "Les sacrements de Dieu," *Recherches de Science Religieuse* 75 (1987): 163-70.

24. We note the difference between the spousal model and Aquinas's sacramental model, which is based on the natural needs of man and on the fundamental situations of his existence: birth, growth, purification, social initiation, food, death, cultic office. The spousal model reinterprets these anthropological situations within the Christocentric horizon of the covenant, which forms the decisive matrix of the sacraments. This is why we see a shift from physical efficient causality to interpersonal causality, from the category of efficacy to the category of sacramental fruitfulness.

25. The systematic development of the spousal model is the aim of Part II of the present work.

The nuptial eucharistic model, taken as a hermeneutical key to the sacraments, offers a "theo-logical"[26] or "Christocentric" alternative to the prevailing "anthropocentric" approach to sacramental theology. In conclusion, we will indicate a few points that suggest the theological and pastoral importance of this spousal and eucharistic model.

1. The first point to stress is simply our trinitarian and spousal starting point itself. As we have noted, the contemporary "anthropological turn" has failed to provide an adequate account of the Christ-Church relation present in the sacraments. By contrast, the spousal model looks to the trinitarian mystery revealed in Scripture in order to draw out of it both the nuptial logic of the paschal mystery and the Church's bridal involvement in the fruitfulness of the incarnate Word.

2. On the one hand, the nuptial eucharistic model reaffirms the traditional understanding of the Church's dependence on the sacraments (which expresses her ever-renewed dependence on Christ in the here and now). On the other hand, it highlights her "spousal" role (through faith) in the gift of Christ's grace to all men. The Church, then, is not reduced to the status of a "separated instrument" with respect to the "conjoined instrument" *(instrumentum coniunctum)* that the Thomistic perspective sees in Christ's humanity.

3. The spousal model highlights the Church's submission to Christ (Eph. 5:21-32), throwing into relief the dramatic and co-constitutive character of her faith, which, through the Holy Spirit, defines the essential condition of her identity as Christ's fruitful Bride. The Church's fruitfulness consists in her availability to let Christ's fruitfulness fructify passively and actively in her. She adds nothing from the outside, no independent achievement of her own of the sort that, as we know, is vigorously contested in ecumenical discussions.[27]

4. This model gives us resources for understanding the synergetic relation between Christ and the Church as the highest form of conjunction (in abiding distinction) while also safeguarding the infinite difference between

26. Our approach owes a great deal to Hans Urs von Balthasar, who demonstrated the dangers and insufficiencies of Rahner's anthropocentric approach. See the famous polemic in which Balthasar accuses Rahner of dissolving the specifically Christian into anthropology: *The Moment of Christian Witness,* trans. Richard Beckley (San Francisco: Ignatius, 1994). The theological aesthetics expounded in Balthasar's trilogy *(The Glory of the Lord, Theo-Drama,* and *Theo-Logic)* represents an enormous effort to "show" the irreducible singularity of the Christian "form" (Christ, the Church, the sacraments) in response to every tendency to absorb the scandalous particularity of Christianity into the "rational" framework of modern man.

27. See H. U. von Balthasar, "The Mass, a Sacrifice of the Church?" in *Explorations in Theology,* vol. 3: *Creator Spirit.*

the divine Creator and the creature. By clarifying the spousal nature of the relationship between Christ and the Church, we can grasp the efficacy of sacramental grace in terms of a *shared fruitfulness* of Christ and the Church while maintaining the Church's total dependence on Christ at the same time.

5. In this context, the presence of Mary immaculate at the foot of the Cross and on Pentecost takes on a supreme theological importance. In the Holy Spirit received from the crucified and risen Christ, Mary immaculate, who is the new Eve, the Bride of the Lamb and Mother of the Church, participates in the universal bestowal of grace on humanity. We can thus recuperate the contemporary development that sees the sacraments as "sacraments of the Church" and "sacraments of faith," without obscuring the fact that the participation involved here is completely derived, that is, received and answered in the power of the Holy Spirit.[28]

6. The nuptial eucharistic model represents a development in that it furnishes resources for a richer, that is, a more biblical, personalist, and symbolic account of the participation of the *imago Dei,* that is, man and woman, in God's sacramental engagement in history.[29] The sacrament of marriage and the sacramentality of the family thus receive new light and strength for their mission of incarnating in a proper, theologically grounded way the Church's sacramental mission in the world.

7. All of this entails an enriched understanding of trinitarian anthropology culminating in a full appreciation of the ultimate meaning of human and Christian existence as service of God's glory.

Despite their importance, these seven points do not set forth all the advantages, much less all the limits, of our approach. A complete presentation of our thesis would require further studies in both positive and systematic theology. Nevertheless, we have at least offered a first broad sketch of an alternative both to the traditional hylomorphic account and to the contemporary subjectivist approach.

28. Balthasar, "The Mass, a Sacrifice of the Church?" 240-42.

29. See C. Rochetta, *I sacramenti della fede,* vol. 2: *Sacramentaria biblica speciale,* 7th ed. (Bologna: EDB, 1998), 285ff., 359ff.

The Drama of the Eucharist and the Nuptial Mystery

Christ's nuptial mystery attains its supreme expression in the celebration of the Eucharist:

> All the more in that Christ's pierced side, from which blood and water flow, at the same time marks . . . *the birth of a Bride* endowed with a beauty like the Bridegroom's and inaugurates the *spousal covenant* in which the Bridegroom's very own Body and Blood are entrusted to the Church-Bride, so that Bridegroom and Bride become "one flesh" (cf. Matt. 19:6) and so one Mystical Body.[1]

Jesus Christ has instituted the sacrament of the Eucharist as a way of guaranteeing that the mutual "knowledge" and "recognition" of Bridegroom and Bride will remain an ever-fresh event throughout history. Christ's aim, then, is to assure the co-presence of their reciprocal gift and vital communion through the gift of his body and blood of the New Covenant. The eucharistic "one flesh," sealed in the blood of the Cross and offered to all generations in the eucharistic celebration, thus brings the nuptial mystery of Christ and the Church to its fulfillment. What was instituted during the Last Supper in the presence of the Apostles and then accomplished once and for all on the Cross in the presence of the immaculate Bride, culminates in the eucharistic Pentecost in which the Church-Bride receives the overflowing abundance of trinitarian fruitfulness.[2]

---

1. A. M. Triacca, "Il sangue di Cristo: Mistero di alleanza nella vita coniugale," in *Il mistero del sangue di Cristo e l'esperienza cristiana,* ed. A. M. Triacca (Rome: Centro Studi Sanguis Christi, 1987), 385-417, here 393.

2. See H. U. von Balthasar, *Explorations in Theology,* vol. 2: *Spouse of the Word* (San

The fulfillment of Christ's nuptial mystery, then, displays an entirely eucharistic stamp. The Eucharist releases the entire fruitfulness that is contained in Christ's unique sacrifice and shared with his immaculate Bride. In the face-to-face encounter between Mary and the crucified Jesus, the Holy Spirit seals the unity of the shared nuptial sacrifice and attests its infinite fruitfulness in the form of the ecclesial offspring that Bridegroom and Bride generate "together" — without, of course, cancelling the infinite difference between Creator and creature. We find the same face-to-face encounter between Bridegroom and Bride in each Eucharist, when the Holy Spirit generates and sanctifies the children of God and of the Church through Mary's faith, shared with believers, and through the ministry of the priest. The eucharistic gift of the Bridegroom is thus entrusted to, and shared with, the pilgrim Church in need of purification as she awaits the day of full communion in the wedding feast of the Lamb.

Of course, this nuptial fruitfulness of the Eucharist presupposes a continual purification of sins, a purification that the crucified and risen body of the Lord places concretely at the disposal of the Church-Bride. As Adrienne von Speyr writes, "[t]he first [crucified] body gathered the total confession into itself, but the second offers itself as pure forgiveness. . . . It perpetually offers absolution from within itself: indeed, it gives itself in absolution just as it gives itself in the Eucharist."[3]

In welcoming this absolution and in receiving communion, the ecclesial Bride is renewed in the faith of the covenant. Holy communion is the nuptial moment par excellence, the moment of fidelity strengthened in the Spirit of the Lord. This is where the thirst of God and the thirst of man — a thirst for intimacy, unity, and fruitfulness — meet. Here, too, we find the root of the happiness and ecclesial vitality of the conjugal covenant, which is interiorly shaped by, and continually receives life from, this mystery.

We have good reasons, then, for claiming that the nuptial mystery, at

---

Francisco: Ignatius, 1991), 190: "Thus it is evident that the self-outpouring in death and Resurrection of God's incarnate Word into the Church is truly the pouring forth of the trinitarian life externally. The virginal man Christ is only (as Hamann most profoundly defined) the generative organ *(instrumentum coniunctum)* of the eternally generating Godhead and the central organ in that it belongs to him alone to make himself (in the Eucharist) a seed and, at the same time — beyond any analogy with the way in which man and the Creator cooperate — to pour out his Spirit into what is produced, through his joint spiration with God the Father." See also S. Mahoney, *The Analogy between the Eucharist and Marriage according to Hans Urs von Balthasar, Dissertatio ad doctoratum* (Rome: Pontificia Università Gregoriana, 1999).

3. Adrienne von Speyr, *Confession,* trans. Douglas W. Stott (San Francisco: Ignatius, 1985), 58.

once trinitarian and eucharistic, opens the most promising theological horizon, not only for renewing the approach of sacramental theology, but also for responding to contemporary man's crisis of meaning. The human person no longer knows who he is; he is in the throes of a profound identity crisis brought on by his deafness to God's Word — the same Word who reveals to him that he is created in the image and likeness of the God who is Love. Created to love, man finds himself in an authentic gift of himself (see *GS* 24), for which he finds support in the eucharistic and nuptial grace of the risen Lord bestowed on all by the Holy Spirit and by the Church, *Sponsa Verbi*. The men and women of today can find here a chance to emerge from a sea of contradictions; they can catch their breath and commit themselves to saving humanity through the family, the "domestic church" that is sustained by all the other Christian vocations to love.

Despite the intuitive and still fragmentary character of our work, it is our hope that the approach developed here can better engage contemporary pastoral and theological problems. Its biblically-based spirit of affirmation and enthusiasm corresponds to the fundamental orientation of the encyclical *Deus Caritas Est:*

> The Eucharist draws us into Jesus' act of self-oblation. More than just statically receiving the incarnate *Logos,* we enter into the very dynamic of his self-giving. The imagery of marriage between God and Israel is now realized in a way previously inconceivable: it had meant standing in God's presence, but now it becomes union with God through sharing in Jesus' self-gift, sharing in his body and blood. (*DCE* 13)

The promotion of the nuptial symbol to its rightful dignity as a hermeneutical principle of sacramental theology offers a way of injecting new vigor into theology as a whole while countering the present confusion with a genuine response to the culture's most urgent needs. In conclusion, it is worth lending our ear once again to two voices that harmonize nicely with the perspective we have sought to develop in the present work. The first is Giorgio Mazzanti:

> The entire foregoing discussion helps us realize that sacramentality and symbolics are connected with the life, the existence, of man. But we also realize that each of the symbols or sacraments is connected with all the others. They are connected as so many expressions of a profound, original, and constitutive comm-union of God with the whole man, and as so many moments in a single drama. And the issue on which the drama turns is

this: the full realization of the symbolic nature of man's being within the supreme symbolics of trinitarian love.[4]

Our second voice, Giacomo Biffi, concurs:

> The Church's identity consists in the fact that she is humanity retrieved, transformed, and elevated to a co-principle of salvific life by her Bridegroom, the crucified and risen Lord, acting through the Holy Spirit. In the same way, theology is human thought that has welcomed the divinizing embrace of the Logos in the act of faith and has emerged transfigured and in possession of a supernatural acuity and inventiveness.[5]

We can only hope that the suggestions offered here can stimulate new theological and pastoral approaches that will make their influence powerfully felt in a contemporary culture crucified by the dictatorship of relativism, yet still open to a spiritual rebirth in the power of the Spirit of the risen Lord.

"Let us rejoice and exalt and give him the glory, for the marriage of the Lamb has come, and his Bride has made herself ready: it was granted her to be clothed with fine linen, bright and pure. . . . Blessed are those who are invited to the marriage supper of the Lamb!" (Rev. 19:7-9).

4. G. Mazzanti, *I sacramenti, simbolo e teologia*, vol. 1: *Introduzione generale* (Bologna: EDB, 1997), 200. See also chap. 4 of that book, "Lo Sposo-Agnello trafitto e la sua Sposa-Donna nelle doglie del parto," 191-94.

5. G. Biffi, *Canto nuziale* (Milan: Jaca Book, 2000), 125.

Bibliography

MAGISTERIUM OF THE CHURCH

Reference

Barberi, P., and D. Tettamanzi, eds., *Matrimonio e famiglia nel magistero della Chiesa. I Documenti dal concilio di Firenze a Giovanni Paolo II* (Milan: Massimo, 1986).

Catechism of the Catholic Church, revised 2nd edition (New York-London: Doubleday, 1997) [= CCC].

Denzinger, Heinrich, and Peter Hünermann, *Enchiridion Symbolorum: A Compendium of Creeds, Definitions, and Declarations of the Catholic Church,* Latin-English edition (San Francisco: Ignatius, 2012) [= Denz].

Enchiridion Vaticanum — Documenti ufficiali della Santa Sede, vols. 1-22 (1962-2004), official text and Italian translation (Bologna: EDB, 1966-2004) [= EnV].

Magisterial Texts in Chronological Order

Innocent III (1198-1208), Letter *Eius exemplo* to the Archbishop of Tarragona, profession of faith prescibed for the Waldensians (1208) (Denz 790-97).

Ecumenical Council of Constance (1414-1418), *Error of John Wyclif* (1415) (Denz 1151-95).

———, Bull *Inter cunctas* (1418) (Denz 1247-79).

Ecumenical Council of Florence (1438-1445), Bull *Esultate Deo* on union with the Armenians (1439) (Denz 1310-28).

Ecumenical Council of Trent (1545-1563), Decree *Ad consummationem* on the sacraments (seventh session, 1547) (Denz 1600-1630).

———, Doctrine and canons on communion under both species and the communion of children (twenty-first session, 1562) (Denz 1725-34).

———, Doctrine and canons on the sacrifice of the Mass (twenty-second session, 1562) (Denz 1730-60).

———, Doctrine and canons on the sacrament of marriage (twenty-fourth session, 1563) (Denz 1797-1816).

Pius X (1903-1914), Decree *Lamentabili* (1907) (Denz 3401-66).

Pius XI (1922-1939), Encyclical *Casti Connubii* (Denz 3700-3724).

Pius XII (1939-1958), Encyclical *Sacra Virginitas* (Denz 3911-12).

Vatican Council II, Constitution on the Sacred Liturgy *Sacrosanctum Concilium* (*EnV* 1.14-95).

————, Dogmatic Constitution on the Church *Lumen Gentium* (*EnV* 1.118-263).

————, Pastoral Constitution on the Church in the Modern World *Gaudium et Spes* (*EnV* 1.770-965).

————, Decree on the Apostolate of Lay People *Apostolicam Actuositatem* (*EnV* 1.518-77).

————, Decree on Ecumenism *Unitatis Redintegratio* (*EnV* 1.286-326).

Paul VI, "Address to the Teams of Our Lady," *La Documentation catholique* 67 (1970), n. 1564.

John Paul II, Address to the Members of the Teams of Our Lady Movement, September 23, 1982. [Translated as John Paul II, "God's Gift of Life and Love: Marriage and the Eucharist," *Communio: International Catholic Review* 41 (Summer 2014), 462-71.]

————, Apostolic Exhortation *Familiaris Consortio* (1981).

————, Apostolic Exhortation *Mulieris Dignitatem* (1988).

————, Apostolic Exhortation *Novo Millennio Ineunte* (2001).

————, Apostolic Exhortation *Pastores Dabo Vobis* (1992).

————, Apostolic Exhortation *Redemptoris Custos* (1989).

————, Apostolic Exhortation *Tertio Millennio Adveniente* (1994).

————, Comments following Recitation of the Holy Rosary, St. Patrick's Cathedral, New York, October 7, 1995.

————, Encyclical *Dives in Misericordia* (1980).

————, Encyclical *Dominum et Vivificantem* (1996).

————, Encyclical *Fides et ratio* (1998).

————, Encyclical *Redemptor Hominis* (1979).

————, Homily, March 19, 1984.

————, Homily, October 9, 1994.

————, *Letter to Families* (1994).

————, *Man and Woman He Created Them: A Theology of the Body*, trans. Michael Waldstein (Boston: Pauline Books and Media, 2006) [= *TOB*]; Italian edition: *Uomo e donna lo creò. Catechesi sull'amore umano*, 4th edition (Rome: Città Nuova–Libreria Editrice Vaticana, 1995).

Benedict XVI, Encyclical *Deus Caritas Est* (2005).

————, Post-Synodal Apostolic Exhortation *Sacramentum Caritatis* (2007).

Fathers of the Church

Reference

Corpus Scriptorum Ecclesiasticorum Latinorum (Wn 1866-) [= *CSEL*].

Migne, J.-P., ed., *Patrologiae Cursus Completus, Series Greca* (Paris: Migne, 1857-) [= *PG*].

————, *Patrologiae Cursus Completus, Series Latina* (Paris, Migne, 1841-) [= *PL*].

Bibliography

Fathers in Chronological Order

Ignatius of Antioch (d. 107), *Epistula ad Magnesios* (PG 5.758-78).

―――, *Epistula ad Thrallianos* (PG 5.778-800).

Justin Martyr (ca. 100-165), *Apologia prima pro Christianis* (PG 6.327-440).

Irenaeus of Lyons (ca. 130-200), *Adversus haereses* (PG 7.433-1118).

Tertullian (ca. 160-220), *Ad Martyres* (PL 1.619-28).

―――, *De Baptismo* (PL 1.1197-1224).

Origen (ca. 185-254), *Contra Celsum* (PG 11.637-1632).

―――, *In Leviticum Homilia IV* (PG 12.434-46).

―――, *Commentaria in Evangelium secundum Matthaeum* (PG 13.829-1800).

―――, *Commentaria in Evangelium secundum Johannem* (PG 14.21-830).

―――, *In Psalmum 118* (PG 12.1588).

Cyprian of Carthage (200/210-258), *Testimoniorum ad Quirinum* (CSEL 3/1.35).

―――, *De Ecclesiae catholicae unitate* (CSEL 3/1.224).

Eusebius of Caesarea (ca. 265-340), *De Ecclesiastica theologia* (PG 24.827-1046).

Ephrem the Syrian (306-373), *Mimré 4: On the Passion,* in *Sancti Ephraem syri hymni et sermones I* (Malines: Lamy, 1882).

Cyril of Jerusalem (ca. 313-387), *Catechesis mystagogica* on the Body and Blood of Christ (PG 33.1097A-1099A).

Gregory of Nyssa (ca. 335-394), *In diem luminum sive in baptismum Christi* (PG 46.577-600).

―――, *In Canticum canticorum Homilia XV* (PG 44.1087-1120).

―――, *In illud, quando sibi subjicierit omnia, tunc ipse quoque Filius subjicietur ei qui sibi omnia subjecit* (PG 44.1303-26).

Gregory Nazianzen (330-389/390), *Oratio teologica quarta* (PG 36.103-34).

Ambrose (339-397), *Expositio Evangelii secundum Lucam* (PL 15.1527-1850).

―――, *Epistola XIX* (PL 16.982-94).

―――, *De Mysteriis* (PL 16.389-410).

John Chrysostom (ca. 350-407), *In Epistolam primam ad Corinthios Homilia I* (PG 61.11-18).

―――, *In Matthaeum Homilia LXXXII* (PG 58.737-46).

Augustine of Hippo (354-430), *Confessionum Libri* (PL 32.659-868).

―――, *De Bono Conjugali* (PL 40.374-96).

―――, *De Civitate Dei* (PL 41.13-804).

―――, *De Doctrina Christiana* (PL 34.15-122).

―――, *De Natura et Gratia* (PL 44.247-90).

―――, *De Nuptiis et Concupiscentia* (PL 44.413-74).

―――, *In Epistulam Johannis ad Parthos Tractatus* (PL 35.1977-2062).

―――, *In Johannis Evangelium Tractatus* (PL 35.1379-1976).

―――, *Sermo III, De Sacramento altaris ad infantes* (PL 46.826-28).

―――, *Sermo LXXI* (PL 38.445-67).

Theodore of Mopsuestia (ca. 350-428), *Les homélies catéchétiques de Theodore de Mopsueste,* ed. R. Tonneau (Vatican City: Biblioteca Apostolica Vaticana, 1949).

General Bibliography

Aa.Vv. [various authors], *Amore e stabilità nel matrimonio* (Rome: Università Gregoriana Editrice, 1976).

————, *Eucaristia y Trinidad* (Salamanca: Secretariado Trinitario, 1990).

————, *Evangelizzazione e matrimonio* (Naples: D'Auria, 1975).

————, *Il matrimonio cristiano* (Turin: LDC, 1978).

————, *Il matrimonio cristiano, SILTC* 51 (1980).

————, *La missione ecclesiale di Adrienne von Speyr. Atti del II Colloquio Internationale del pensiero cristiano* (Milan: Jaca Book, 1986).

————, La *sacramentalità del matrimonio e la spiritualità coniugale e familiare* (Turin-Leumann: LDC, 1989).

————, *La Santisima Trinidad y el bautismo cristiano,* Semanas de "Estudios Trinitarios" 26 (Salamanca: Secretariado Trinitario, 1992).

————, *L'Eucharistie, pain nouveau pour un monde rompu* (Paris: Communio-Fayard, 1981).

————, *Matrimonio e famiglia in Italia* (Naples: Dehoniane, 1977).

————, *Realtà e valori del sacramento del matrimonio* (Rome: LAS, 1976).

————, "Tout récapituler dans le Christ. Propos de l'ouvrage de J. Dupuis, vers une théologie chrétienne du pluralisme religieux?" *Revue Thomiste* (October-December 1998): 591-630.

————, *Trinité et Liturgie. Conférences de Saint Serge, XXX semaines d'études liturgiques,* Paris (June 28–July 1, 1983).

Adnès, P., "La fonction sotériologique des sacrements," *Studia missionaria* 30 (1981): 89-111.

————, *Le mariage* (Tournai: Desclée, 1963).

————, "Mariage et vie chrétienne," in *Dictionnaire de spiritualité,* vol. 10, 355-88.

Alfaro, J., "Cristo sacramento de Diós Padre. La iglesia, sacramento de Cristo glorificando," *Gregorianum* 58 (1967): 5-28.

Ambrosanio, A., "Matrimonio ed Eucaristia," *Asprenas* 22 (1975): 203-19.

Auer, J., "Allgemeine Sakramentenlehre," in *Kleine katholische Dogmatik,* vol. 6: *Das Mysterium der Eucharistie* (Regensburg: Pustet, 1980). ["A General Doctrine of the Sacraments," in J. Auer and J. Ratzinger, *A General Doctrine of the Sacraments and the Mystery of the Eucharist,* Dogmatic Theology series, vol. 6, trans. Erasmo Leiva-Merikakis (Washington, D.C.: CUA Press, 1996)].

————, "Il sacramento del matrimonio," in *I Sacramenti della Chiesa, Piccola dogmatica cattolica,* vol. 7, ed. C. Molari (Assisi: Cittadella, 1989), 285-385.

————, *The Church: The Universal Sacrament of Salvation,* Dogmatic Theology series, vol. 8, trans. Michael Waldstein (Washington, D.C.: CUA Press, 1993).

Aymans, W., "Die Sakramentalität christlicher Ehe in ekklesiologisch-kanonischer Sicht," in *Treirer theologische Zeitschrift* 83 (1974): 321-38.

Baldanza, G., "Il matrimonio come sacramento permanente," in Aa.Vv., *Realtà e valori del sacramento del matrimonio* (Rome: LAS, 1976), 81-102.

————, *La grazia del sacramento del matrimonio. Contributo per la riflessione teologica* (Rome: CLV Liturgiche, 1993).

————, "La grazia sacramentale al concilio di Trento. Contributo per uno studio storico-critico," *EphLit* 97 (1983): 83-140.

Baltensweiler, H., *Die Ehe im Neuen Testament: Exegetische Untersuchungen über Ehe, Ehelosigkeit und Ehescheidung* (Zurich: Zwingli, 1967).

Balthasar, H. U. von, *Bernanos: An Ecclesial Existence* (San Francisco: Ignatius-Communio, 1996).

————, *The Christian State of Life*, trans. Mary Frances McCarthy (San Francisco: Ignatius, 1983).

————, "The Council of the Holy Spirit," *Communio: International Catholic Review* 17, no. 4 (Winter 1990): 595-611.

————, *Epilogue*, trans. Edward T. Oakes (San Francisco: Ignatius, 2004).

————, *Explorations in Theology*, vol. 2: *Spouse of the Word* (San Francisco: Ignatius, 1991).

————, *Explorations in Theology*, vol. 3: *Creator Spirit*, trans. Brian McNeil (San Francisco: Ignatius, 1993).

————, *Explorations in Theology*, vol. 4: *Spirit and Institution*, trans. Edward T. Oakes (San Francisco: Ignatius, 1995).

————, *Explorations in Theology*, vol. 5: *Man Is Created*, trans. Adrian Walker (San Francisco: Ignatius, 2014).

————, *Eucharistie: Gabe der Liebe* (= *Antwort des Glaubens*, 44) (Freiburg, i.Br.: IBK, 1986).

————, *First Glance at Adrienne von Speyr*, trans. Antye Lawry and Sergia Englund (San Francisco: Ignatius, 1981).

————, *The Glory of the Lord: A Theological Aesthetics*, vol. 1: *Seeing the Form*, trans. Erasmo Leiva-Merikakis (New York: Crossroad; San Francisco: Ignatius, 1982).

————, *The Glory of the Lord: A Theological Aesthetics*, vol. 6: *Theology: The Old Covenant*, trans. Brian McNeil (San Francisco: Ignatius, 1991).

————, *The Glory of the Lord: A Theological Aesthetics*, vol. 7: *Theology: The New Covenant*, trans. Brian McNeil (San Francisco: Ignatius, 1989).

————, *Heart of the World*, trans. Erasmo Leiva-Merikakis (San Francisco: Ignatius, 1979).

————, "The Holy Church and the Eucharistic Sacrifice," *Communio: International Catholic Review* 12, no. 2 (Summer 1985): 139-45.

————, *Love Alone Is Credible*, trans. D. C. Schindler (San Francisco: Ignatius, 2004).

————, *The Moment of Christian Witness*, trans. Richard Beckley (San Francisco: Communio-Ignatius, 1994).

————, *Mysterium Paschale*, trans. Aidan Nichols (San Francisco: Ignatius, 2000).

————, *My Work: In Retrospect* (San Francisco: Communio-Ignatius, 1993).

————, *New Elucidations*, trans. Mary Theresilde Skerry (San Francisco: Ignatius, 1986).

————, *The Office of Peter and the Structure of the Church*, trans. Andrée Emery (San Francisco: Ignatius, 2007).

————, *Parole et Mystère chez Origène* (Paris: Éd. du Cerf, 1957).

————, *Theo-Drama*, vol. 2: *Dramatis Personae: Man in God*, trans. Graham Harrison (San Francisco: Ignatius, 1990).

————, *Theo-Drama*, vol. 3: *Dramatis Personae: Persons in Christ,* trans. Graham Harrison (San Francisco: Ignatius, 1992).

————, *Theo-Drama*, vol. 4: *The Action,* trans. Graham Harrison (San Francisco: Ignatius, 1994).

————, *Theo-Drama*, vol. 5: *The Last Act,* trans. Graham Harrison (San Francisco: Ignatius, 1998).

————, *Theo-Logic,* vol. 1: *Truth of the World,* trans. Adrian J. Walker (San Francisco: Ignatius, 2000).

————, *Theo-Logic,* vol. 2: *Truth of God,* trans. Adrian J. Walker (San Francisco: Ignatius, 2004).

————, *Theo-Logic,* vol. 3: *The Spirit of Truth,* trans. Graham Harrison (San Francisco: Ignatius, 2005).

————, *A Theological Anthropology* (Eugene, OR: Wipf and Stock, 2010).

————, *A Theology of History* (San Francisco: Ignatius-Communio Books, 1994).

Barth, K., *On Marriage* (Philadelphia: Fortress Press, 1968).

Bätzing, G., *Die Eucharistie als Opfer der Kirche* (Einsiedeln: Johannes, 1986).

Beeck, F. J. van, *Grounded in Love: Sacramental Theology in an Ecumenical Perspective* (London, 1982).

Béraudy, R., "Sacrement de mariage et culture contemporaine," in *Questions et perspectives* (Paris: Desclée, 1985).

Berger, M., "La famille aujourd'hui. État des lieux," *La Pensée Catholique* 275 (January-February 1995): 9-27.

Betz, J., "Eucharistie," in *Sacramentum Mundi,* vol. 1 (Freiburg i.B., 1967).

————, "L'Eucaristia mistero centrale," in *Mysterium Salutis,* vol. 8 (Brescia: Queriniana, 1975).

Biffi, G., *Canto nuziale* (Milan: Jaca Book, 2000).

Blanquet, J., *La sagrada familia, icono de la Trinidad* (Barcelona: Hijos de la Sagrada familia, 1996).

Bobrinskoy, B., "Eucharisties d'Orient et d'Occident," in *Semaine liturgique de l'Institut Saint Serge,* vol. 2 (Paris: Éd. du Cerf, 1970), 197-240.

————, *Le mystère de la Trinité* (Paris: Éd. du Cerf, 1986).

Bonaventure of Bagnoregio. *In Primum Librum Sententiarum* (Quaracchi, 1882).

Bonetti, R., ed., *Cristo Sposo della Chiesa. Sorgente e modello della spiritualità coniugale e familiare* (Rome: Città Nuova, 1997).

————, *Il matrimonio in Cristo è matrimonio nello Spirito* (Rome: Città Nuova, 1998).

————, *Verginità e Matrimonio. Due parabole dell'Unico Amore, Percorsi pastorali* (Milan: Ancora, 1998).

Bornkamm, G., "Mysterion," in *Grande Lessico del Nuovo Testamento,* vol. 7 (Brescia: Paideia, 1971).

Borobio, D., and A. Borobio, *La Celebración en la Iglesia,* vol. 1 (Salamanca: Sígueme, 1985).

Botero, S., *Per una teologia della famiglia* (Rome: Borla, 1992).

Bourassa, F., *Questions de théologie trinitaire* (Rome: PUG, 1970).

Bouyer, L., *The Christian Mystery: From Pagan Myth to Christian Mysticism,* trans. Illtyd Trethowan (Edinburgh: T&T Clark, 1989).

————, *Eucharist: Theology and Spirituality of the Eucharistic Prayer* (South Bend, IN: University of Notre Dame Press, 1989).

————, *Rite and Man: Natural Sacredness and Christian Liturgy*, trans. M. Joseph Costelloe (South Bend, IN: University of Notre Dame Press, 1963).

Bozzolo, A., *La teologia sacramentaria dopo Rahner. Il dibattito e i problemi* (Rome: LAS, 1999).

Braun, F. M., "Le baptême de Jésus d'après le quatrième Évangile," *Revue Thomiste* 48 (1948): 347-93.

Bro, B., *Faut-il encore pratiquer? L'homme et les sacrements* (Paris: Éd. du Cerf, 1967).

Brown, R. E., "The Pre-Christian Concept of 'Mystery,'" *Catholic Biblical Quarterly* 20 (1958): 417-43.

————, "The Semitic Background of the New Testament 'Mysterion,'" *Biblica* 39 (1958): 426-48.

Bruaire, C., *L'Être et l'Esprit* (Paris: PUF, 1983).

Brueggemann, W., *Genesis*, Interpretation (Atlanta: John Knox Press, 1982).

Cabasilas, Nicholas, *La vie en Christ* [Life in Christ], 4.30, *Sources Chrétiennes* no. 355 (Paris: Éd. du Cerf, 1989).

Caffarra, C., "Le lien entre mariage-réalité de la création et mariage-sacrement," *Esprit et Vie* 88 (1978): 353-84.

Cambier, J., "Le grand mystère concernant le Christ et l'Église, Ep 5, 22-32," *Biblica* 47 (1966): 43-90.

Cambòn, E., *Trinità, modello sociale* (Rome: Città Nuova, 1999).

Camelot, P.-T., "Le Christ, sacrement de Dieu," in *L'Homme Devant Dieu. Mélanges offerts au Père Henri de Lubac. Exégèse et patristique* (Paris: Aubier, 1963).

Carelli, R., *La libertà colpevole. Perdono e peccato nella teologia di Hans Urs von Balthasar* (Milan: Glossa, 1999).

Carpin, A., *Il sacramento del matrimonio nella teologia medievale. Da Isidoro di Siviglia a Tommaso d'Aquino* (Bologna: ESD, 1991).

————, "Sacramentalità del matrimonio. Riferimenti scritturistici e patristici," *Sacra Doctrina* 2 (March-April) (Bologna: ESD, 1997).

Cascioli, R., *Il complotto demografico. Il nuovo colonialismo delle grandi potenze economiche e delle organizzazioni umanitarie per sottomettere i poveri del mondo* (Casale Monferrato: Piemme, 1996).

Casel, O., "Das Mysteriengedächtnis der Messliturgie," *JLWm* 6 (1929): 113-204.

————, *The Mystery of Christian Worship* (New York: Crossroad, 1999).

————, "Neue Zeugnisse für das Kultmysterium," *JLWm* 12 (1935): 99-171.

Cassirer, E., *La philosophie des formes symboliques* (Paris: Éditions de Minuit, 1972).

Castilla y Cortazar, B., "La Trinidad como familia. Analogia humana de la procesiones divinas," *Annales Theologici* 10 (1996): 371-416.

Chantraine, G., *Uomo e Donna* (Parma: CUSL, 1986).

Charlier, J. P., *Le signe de Cana. Essai de théologie johannique* (Brussels: La pensée catholique; Paris: Office Général du Livre, 1959).

Chauvet, L.-M., *Les sacrements. Parole de Dieu au risque du corps* (Paris: Les Éditions Ouvrières, 1993).

————, *Linguaggio e simbolo. Saggio sui sacramenti* (Turin, Leumann: LDC, 1982).

————, *Symbole et Sacrement. Une relecture sacramentelle de l'existence chrétienne* (Paris: Éd. du Cerf, 1987).

Coda, P., *Dio Uno e Trino* (Rome: Paoline, 1993).

————, "Familia y Trinidad. Reflexion teologica," in Aa.Vv., *Misterio trinitario y familia humana,* Semanas de estudios trinitarios 29 (Salamanca: Secretariado Trinitario, 1995), 195-227.

————, *Uno in Cristo Gesù. Il battesimo come evento trinitario* (Rome: Città Nuova, 1996).

Colombo, G., *La ragione teologica* (Milan: Glossa, 1995).

————, *Teologia sacramentaria* (Milan: Glossa, 1997).

Coppens, J., *La connaissance du bien et du mal et le péché du Paradis* (Louvain, Bruges, Paris: Desclée de Brouwer, 1948).

Corecco E., "Il sacramento del matrimonio. Cardine della constitutione della Chiesa," *Rivista internazionale di teologia e cultura Communio* 51 (1980): 96-122.

————, "L'Inseparabilità tra contratto matrimoniale e sacramento alla luce del principio scolastico *Gratia perficit, non destruit naturam," Rivista internazionale di teologia e cultura Communio* 16 (1974): 1010-23.

Courth, F., *Die Sakramente* (Freiburg, Basel, Vienna: Herder, 1995).

Couturier, C., "*Sacramentum* et *Mysterium* dans l'œuvre de st. Augustin," in *Études augustiniennes,* ed. H. Rondet (Paris: Aubier-Montaigne, 1953).

Cullmann, O., *La Foi et le culte de l'Église primitive* (Neuchâtel: Delachaux & Niestlé, 1963).

————, *Les sacrements dans l'évangile johannique, la vie de Jésus et le culte de l'Église primitive* (Paris: PUF, 1951).

Dacquino, P., *Storia del matrimonio cristiano alla luce della bibbia,* vol. 1: *La celebrazione del matrimonio;* vol. 2: *Inseparabilità e monogamia* (Turin, Leumann: LDC, 1988-1989).

Da Crispino, M., *Il matrimonio cristiano* (Turin: Marietti, 1976).

Daniélou, J., *Sacramentum futuri* (Paris: Beauchesne, 1950).

————, "St Irénée et les origines de la théologie de l'histoire," *Recherches de Science Religieuse* 34 (1947).

Danneels, G., "Les ministres du sacrement de mariage," in *Mariage et sacrement de mariage,* ed. P. de Locht (Paris: Centurion, 1970).

de la Potterie, I., *Il mistero del cuore trafitto. Studi biblici* (Bologna: EDB, 1988).

————, "L'exégèse biblique, science de la foi," in *L'exégèse chrétienne aujourd'hui,* ed. C. Barthe (Paris: Fayard, 2000).

————, "Le nozze messianiche e il matrimonio cristiano," in "Lo Sposo e la Sposa," *Parola, Spirito e Vita* 13 (1986): 87-104.

————, *Marie dans le mystère de l'Alliance* (Paris: Desclée de Brouwer, 1985).

de Lubac, H., *Catholicism: Christ and the Common Destiny of Man,* trans. Lancelot C. Sheppard and Elizabeth Englund (San Francisco: Ignatius, 1988).

————, *Corpus Mysticum: The Eucharist and the Church in the Middle Ages,* trans. Gemma Simmonds et al. (South Bend, IN: University of Notre Dame Press, 2006).

————, "La Révélation divine," in *Œuvres complètes,* vol. 4 (Paris: Éd. du Cerf, 2006).

————, *Scripture in the Tradition* (New York: Crossroad, 2001).

Denis, H., *Le mariage, un sacrement pour les croyants?* (Paris: Éd. du Cerf, 1990).

Bibliography

————, "Les sacrements dans la vie de l'Église," *La Maison Dieu* 93 (1968): 39-59.

————, *Sacrements, sources de vie* (Paris, 1982).

di Marco, A., "Mysterium hoc magnum est . . . Ep 5, 32," *Laurentianum* 14 (1973): 43-80.

————, "Teologia della famiglia," *Rivista Biblica* 31 (1983): 189-209.

Dizard, J. E., and H. Gadlin, *La famiglia minima. Forme della vita familiare moderna* (Milan: Angeli, 1996).

Doms, H., *Vom Sinn und Zweck der Ehe* (Breslau: Ostdeutsche Verlagsanstalt, 1935).

Durand, G., *L'imagination symbolique* (Paris: PUF, 1964).

Durwell, F. X., *L'Eucharistie, sacrement pascal* (Paris: Éd. du Cerf, 1980).

————, *Lo Spirito Santo alla luce del mistero pasquale* (Rome: Paoline, 1985).

Duss von Werdt, J., "Sacramentalità del matrimonio," in *Mysterium Salutis,* vol. 8 (Brescia: Queriniana, 1975), 422-49.

Duval, A., *Des sacrements au Concile de Trente* (Paris: Éd. du Cerf, 1985).

Elliott, P. J., *What God Has Joined . . . : The Sacramentality of Marriage* (New York: Alba House, 1990).

Espezel, A., "Le mystère pascal au cœur de la médiation du Christ," *Communio: Revue catholique internationale* 17, no. 2-3 (1997): 101-11.

Evdokimov, P., "Ecclesia Domestica," *L'Anneau d'Or* 107 (1962): 357.

————, *The Sacrament of Love* (Crestwood, NY: St. Vladimir's Seminary Press, 2011).

Fahey, M., "La famille chrétienne, Église domestique à Vatican II," *Concilium* 260 (1995): 115-23.

Fleckenstein, K. H., *"Questo mistero è grande": Il matrimonio in Ef 5, 21-33* (Rome: Città Nuova, 1996).

Forconi, C., *Antropologia cristiana come fondamento dell'unità e dell'indissolubilità del patto matrimoniale* (Rome: PUG, 1996).

Forte, B., *Gesù di Nazaret, storia di Dio, Dio della storia* (Rome: Paoline, 1981).

————, *Trinità come storia. Saggio sul Dio cristiano,* Simbolica ecclesiale 4 (Milan: San Paolo, 1993).

Gadamer, H.-G., *The Beginning of Philosophy,* trans. Rod Coltman (New York: Continuum, 1998).

Garcia de Haro, R., *Marriage and the Family in the Documents of the Magisterium: A Course in the Theology of Marriage,* trans. William E. May (San Francisco: Ignatius, 1993).

Garcia Peredes, J. C. R., *Teologia fundamental de los sacramentos* (Madrid: Paulinas, 1991).

Garijo Guembe, M., "Epiclesis y Trinidad. Estudio histórico y sistematico," *Eucaristia y Trinidad* 24 (1989): 115-47.

Gendron, L., "La famille: reflet de la communion trinitaire," in Aa.Vv., *La famille chrétienne dans le monde d'aujourd'hui* (Montreal: Bellarmin, 1995).

————, "Le foyer chrétien, une Église véritable?" *Communio: Revue catholique internationale* 11, no. 6 (1986): 77.

Genn, F., *Trinität und Amt nach Augustinus* (Einsiedeln: Johannes Verlag, 1986).

Gerken, A., *Theologie der Eucharistie* (Munich: Kösel, 1973).

Gherardini, B., "Il magistero e l'esortazione apostolica Familiaris Consortio," *Divinitas* 26 (1986): 446-57.

Gil Hellìn, F., *Il matrimonio e la vita conjugale* (Vatican City: Libreria Editrice Vaticana, 1996).

Girard, M., *Les symboles dans la Bible* (Montreal: Bellarmin; Paris: Éd. du Cerf, 1991).

Giraudo, C., *Eucaristia per la Chiesa. Prospettive teologiche sull'Eucaristia a partire dalla "lex orandi"* (Rome: Gregoriana; Brescia: Morcelliana, 1989).

Gisel, P., "Du symbolique au symbole ou du symbole au symbolique? Remarques intempestives," *Recherches de Science Religieuse* 73 (1987): 357-69.

Giuliodori, C., *Intelligenza del maschile e del femminile. Problemi e prospettive nella rilettura di von Balthasar e P. Evdokimov* (Rome: Città Nuova, 1991).

———, "La sponsalità di Cristo e della Chiesa a fondamento della vita nello Spirito della coppia cristiana," in *Cristo Sposo della Chiesa Sposa*, ed. R. Bonetti (Rome: Città Nuova, 1997).

Gnilka, J., *Der Epheserbrief. Auslegung* (Freiburg: Herder, 1971).

———, *Gesù di Nazaret. Annuncio e storia* (Brescia: Paideia, 1993).

Godefroy, L., G. Le Bras, et al., "Mariage," in *Dictionnaire de théologie catholique*, ed. A. Vacant et al. (Paris, 1955-1957), vol. 9/2, 2044-2335.

Goffi, T., ed., *Nuova enciclopedia del matrimonio,* revised edition (Brescia: Queriniana, 1988).

Gorce, D., "Mariage et perfection chrétienne d'après saint Jean Chrysostome," *Études Carmélitaines* 21 (1936): 245-84.

Grelot, P., *Le couple humain dans l'Écriture* (Paris: Éd. du Cerf, 1962).

Greshake, G., *Der dreieine Gott. Eine trinitarische Theologie* (Freiburg, Basel, Vienna: Herder, 1997).

Hamman, A., "La liturgie baptismale," in *Mysterium Salutis,* vol. 5: *Dieu et la révélation de la Trinité* (Paris: Cerf, 1970), 189-95.

———, "L'Eucharistie." *Ichthus* 9 (Paris: Desclée, 1964).

Heidegger, M., *On the Way to Language* (New York: HarperCollins, 1982).

Hemmerle, K., "Matrimonio e famiglia in una antropologia trinitaria," *Nuova Umanità* 6, no. 31 (1984): 3-31.

———, *Partire dall'unità. La Trinità come stile di vita e forma di pensiero* (Rome: Città Nuova, 1998).

———, *Tesi di ontologia trinitaria. Per un rinnovamento del pensiero cristiano* (Rome: Città Nuova, 1996) [original German, 1976].

Hinschberger, R., "Image et ressemblance dans la tradition sacerdotale," *Recherches de Science Religieuse* 59 (1985).

Hünermann, P., *Reflexionen zum Sakramentenbegriff des II. Vatikanums. Glaube im Prozeß*, ed. E. Klinger and K. Wittstadt (Freiburg, 1984).

Iacobone, P., *Mysterium Trinitatis. Dogma e Iconografia nell'Italia medievale* (Rome: PUG, 1997).

Ignatius of Loyola, *The Spiritual Exercises of St. Ignatius,* trans. Louis J. Puhl (New York: Random House, 2000).

Infante, R., "Lo sposo e la sposa. Contributo per l'ecclesiologia del quarto Vangelo," *Rivista di Teologia* 37 (1996): 451-81.

International Theological Commission, Propositions on the Doctrine of Christian Marriage (1977).

Bibliography

Jedin, H., and K. Reinhardt, *Ehe, Sakrament in der Kirche des Herrn* (Berlin: Morus-Verlag, 1971).

John of the Cross, "Living Flame of Love," in *Collected Works of St. John of the Cross*, trans. Kieran Kavanaugh and Otilio Rodriguez (Washington, DC: Institute of Carmelite Studies, 1991).

Jüngel, E., "Die Kirche als Sakrament?" *Zeitschrift für Theologie und Kirche* 80 (1983): 432-57.

Kaiser, C., *Theologie der Ehe. Der Beitrag Hans Urs von Balthasars* (Würzburg: Echter, 1997).

Kasper, W., *Le Dieu des Chrétiens* (Paris: Éd. du Cerf, 1985).

————, *Glaube und Geschichte* (Mainz: Matthias Grünewald Verlag, 1970).

————, *The God of Jesus Christ*, new edition (London, New York: T&T Clark, 2012).

————, *Jesus the Christ*, revised edition (London: Bloomsbury; New York: T&T Clark, 2011).

————, *Theology of Christian Marriage* (New York: Crossroad, 1983).

Kerber, W., "Ehe," in *Philosophisches Wörterbuch*, ed. W. Brugger (Freiburg: Herder, 1988), 73-74.

Kilmartin, E. J., *The Eucharist in the West: History and Theology* (Collegeville, MN: Liturgical Press, 1998).

Koch, G., "Die Ehe," in *Sakramentenlehre II* (Graz: Styria, 1991), 244-98.

Kuhn, P., "I sacramenti della Chiesa. Un settenario," in *Incontrare Cristo nei sacramenti. Sussidio teologico per una pastorale sacramentaria*, ed. H. Luthe (Cinisello Balsamo: Paoline, 1988).

Kunzler, M., "Die dogmatische Lehre von der gottlichen Unveränderlichkeit und die trinitarischen Doxologien im liturgischen Gebet der byzantinischen Kirche — Eine Gegenüberstellung," *Theologie und Glaube* 80 (1990): 22-35.

Labbé, Y., "Réceptions théologiques de la 'post-modernité,'" *Revue des Sciences Philosophiques et Théologiques* 72 (1988): 397-462.

Ladaria, L. F., *Il Dio vivo e vero* (Casale Monferrato: Piemme, 1999).

Lafont, G., "Recensione di L.-M. Chauvet. Symbole et sacrement," *Ecclesia orans* 5 (1988): 231-35.

Leblond, G., *L'Agneau de la Pâque éternelle* (Paris: Desclée de Brouwer, 1987).

Le Bras, G., "Le lien entre mariage-réalité de création et mariage sacrement," *Esprit et Vie* (1978): 353-64, 369-84.

Légaut, M., *Introduction à l'intelligence du passé et de l'avenir du christianisme* (Paris: Aubier, 1970).

le Guillou, M.-J., "La Sacramentalité de l'Église," *La Maison Dieu* 93 (1968).

Lehmann, K., "Sacramentalité," in International Theological Commission, *Problèmes doctrinaux du mariage chrétien* (Louvain-la-Neuve, 1979), 180-217.

————, "Zur Sakramentalität der Ehe," in *Ehe und Ehescheidung. Diskussion unter Christen* (Munich: Kösel, 1972), 57-65.

Lies, L., *Sakramententheologie. Eine personale Sicht* (Graz, 1990).

————, "Trinitätvergessenheit gegenwärtiger Sakramententheologie?" *Zeitschrift für Theologie und Kirche* 105 (1983): 290-314, 415-29.

Ligier, L., *Il matrimonio. Questioni teologiche e pastorali* (Rome: Città Nuova, 1988).

Lopez Martin, J., "Funciòn didascalica de la liturgia en el Misterio trinitario segùn el Missale Romanum y el Ordo penitentiae," *Estudios Trinitarios* 12 (1979): 3-52.

Magrassi, M., *Vivere l'Eucaristia*, 7th edition (Noci: La Scala, 1985).

Mahoney, S. L., *The Analogy between the Eucharist and Marriage according to Hans Urs von Balthasar, Dissertatio ad doctoratum* (Rome: Pontificia Università Gregoriana, 1999) (*excerpta ex dissertatione* [Rome, 2000], 80).

Maistriaux, R., *Matrimonio, via alla santità* (Milan: Paoline, 1968).

Marchesi, G., *La cristologia trinitaria di Hans Urs von Balthasar* (Brescia: Queriniana, 1997).

Marengo, G., "Creazione, alleanza, sacramentalità del matrimonio," *Anthropotes* 1 (1992): 27-39.

Marini, E., *La SS. Trinità nei Sacramenti della Chiesa*, 2nd edition (Rome: Scuola Salesiana del libro, 1949).

Marion, J.-L., *Étant donné. Essai d'une phénoménologie de la donation*, 2nd edition (Paris: PUF, 1997).

——, *God without Being: Hors Texte*, 2nd edition, trans. Thomas A. Carlson (Chicago: University of Chicago Press, 2012).

——, "Le présent et le don," in Aa.Vv., *L'Eucharistie, pain nouveau pour un monde rompu* (Paris: Communio-Fayard, 1981).

Marsili, S., *Eucaristia, teologia e storia della celebrazione*, 2nd edition (Casale Monferrato: Marietti, 1989).

Martelet, G., *Genesi dell'uomo nuovo* (Brescia: Queriniana, 1976).

——, "Mariage, amour et sacrement," *Nouvelle Revue Théologique* 95 (1963): 577-97.

——, *Résurrection, eucharistie et genèse de l'homme* (Paris: Desclée, 1972).

——, "Seize thèses de christologie sur le sacrement de mariage," *La Documentation catholique* 75, no. 1744 (1978): 571-75.

Martimort, A. G., ed., *I segni della nuova alleanza* (Rome: Paoline, 1962).

——, *L'Église en prière*, vol. 3: *Les sacrements*, revised edition (Paris, Tournai: Desclée, 1984).

Martin, F., "Male and Female He Created Them: A Summary of the Teaching of Genesis Chapter One," *Communio: International Catholic Review* 20, no. 2 (1993): 240-65.

Martinelli, P., "Il rapporto tra Carisma e Istituzione," *Rivista internazionale di Teologia e Cultura, Communio* 167-68 (September-December 1999): 147-63.

Martinéz Peque, M., *Lo Spirito Santo e il matrimonio* (Rome: EDR, 1993).

Mattheeuws, A., *Les "dons" du mariage. Recherche de théologie morale et sacramentelle* (Brussels: Culture et Vérité, 1996).

——, *Union et procréation. Développements de la doctrine des fins du mariage* (Paris: Éd. du Cerf, 1989).

Mazza, E., *L'Action eucharistique. Origine, développement, interprétation* (Paris: Éd. du Cerf, 1999).

——, *La mistagogia. Una teologia della liturgia in epoca patristica* (Rome: CLV, 1988).

——, "L'Eucaristia nei primi quattro secoli," in *Scientia Liturgica*, vol. 3: *L'Eucaristia*, ed. A. J. Chupungco (Casale Monferrato: Piemme, 1998).

Mazzanti, G., *I sacramenti, simbolo e teologia*, vol. 1: *Introduzione generale;* vol. 2: *Eucaristia, Battesimo e Confermazione* (Bologna: EDB, 1997-1998).

—————, *Teologia sponsale e sacramento delle nozze. Simbolo e simbolismo nuziale* (Bologna: EDB, 2001).

McDermot, C., *The Tridentine Canon on the Sacramentality of Marriage* (Rome: PUG, 1978).

McPartlan, P., *The Eucharist Makes the Church* (Edinburgh: T&T Clark, 1993).

—————, *Sacrament of Salvation* (Edinburgh: T&T Clark, 1995).

Meyendorff, J., *Marriage: An Orthodox Perspective* (Crestwood, NY: St. Vladimir's Seminary Press, 1975).

Michel, O., "Oikos, oikia," in vol. 8 of *Grande Lessico del Nuovo Testamento,* ed. G. Friedrich et al. (Brescia: Paideia, 1965-1992).

Milano, A., *Persona in teologia* (Rome: EDR, 1996).

Miquel, P., *Petit traité de théologie symbolique* (Paris: Éd. du Cerf, 1987).

Miralles, A., *Il Matrimonio. Teologia e vita* (Cinisello Balsamo, Milan: San Paolo, 1996).

Moingt, J., "Les sacrements de Dieu," *Recherches de Science Religieuse* 75 (1987): 163-70.

Molinski, W., "Ehe," in *Sacramentum Mundi*, vol. 1 (Freiburg: Herder, 1967), 961-98.

Moltmann, J., *Trinità e Regno di Dio* (Brescia: Queriniana, 1983).

Mondin, B., *Dizionario enciclopedico del pensiero di San Tommaso d'Aquino* (Bologna: ESD, 1991).

Morandé Court, P., "L'actualité de Gaudium et Spes et la mission de l'Église, à l'heure de changements qui font époque et de nouveaux défis," in *Gaudium et Spes, Bilan de trente années,* Lorette 95 (Vatican City: Pontifical Council for the Laity, 1996), Revue 39, 56-70.

Mosso, D., *Vivere i sacramenti* (Cinisello Balsamo: Paoline, 1992).

Mühlen, H., *Una mistica persona* (Rome: Città Nuova, 1968).

Navarrete, U., "Consenso matrimoniale e amore coniugale con particolare riferimento alla Cost. Gaudium et Spes," in *Annali di dottrina e giurisprudenza canonica* (Vatican City: Libreria Editrice Vaticana, 1971), 203-14.

Nicolas, J.-H., *Synthèse dogmatique. De la Trinité à la Trinité* (Fribourg: Éd. Universitaires, 1986), "L'Église et les sacrements" and "Le sacrement de mariage," 623-1158.

Nicolau, M., *Teologia del segno sacramentale* (Rome: Paoline, 1971).

O'Neill, C., *Meeting Christ in the Sacraments* (New York: Alba House, 1964).

O'Riordan, J., *Evoluzione della teologia del matrimonio da Leone XIII ai nostri giorni* (Assisi: Cittadella, 1974).

Ortigues, E., *Le Discours et le Symbole* (Paris: Aubier, 1977).

Osborne, K. B., *Sacramental Theology: A General Introduction* (New York: Paulist Press, 1988).

Otmar Meuffels, H., *Kommunikative Sakramenten Theologie* (Freiburg, Basel, Vienna: Herder, 1995).

Ouellet, M., "Adrienne von Speyr et le Samedi Saint de la théologie," in *Adrienne von Speyr und ihre spirituelle Theologie* (Einsiedeln: Johannes, 2002).

—————, "Christocentrisme trinitaire," *Anthropotes* 16, no. 2 (2000): 305-24.

—————, *Divine Likeness: Toward a Trinitarian Anthropology of the Family* (Grand Rapids: Eerdmans, 2006).

—————, *L'existence comme mission. L'anthropologie théologique de Hans Urs von Balthasar* (Rome: PUG, 1983).

————, "The Foundations of Christian Ethics according to Hans Urs von Balthasar," *Communio: International Catholic Review* 17, no. 3 (1990): 375-401.

————, "Hans Urs von Balthasar et la métaphysique. Esquisse de sa contribution à partir d'Épilogue," *Path* 5, no. 2 (2006): 473-83.

————, "Marriage and the Family within the Sacramentality of the Church," *Communio: International Catholic Review* 41, no. 2 (Summer 2014): 226-44.

————, "Priestly Ministry at the Service of Ecclesial Communion," *Communio: International Catholic Review* 23, no. 4 (Winter 1996): 677-87.

————, "Theological Perspectives on Marriage," *Communio: International Catholic Review* 31, no. 3 (Fall 2004): 419-33.

————, "Trinity and Eucharist: A Covenantal Mystery," *Communio: International Catholic Review* 27, no. 2 (Summer 2000): 262-83.

————, *La vocazione cristiana al matrimonio e alla famiglia nella missione della Chiesa* (Rome: L.U.P., 2005).

Padilha, T., and R. Padilha, "Mariage et famille dans le Magistère pontifical après Vatican II," in Pontifical Council for the Laity, *Gaudium et Spes, Bilan de trente années,* Lorette 95 (Vatican City: Pontifical Council for the Laity, 1996).

Pasquetto, V., *Incarnazione e comunione con Dio. La venuta di Gesù nel mondo e il suo ritorno al luogo di origine secondo il IV Vangelo* (Rome: Teresianum, 1982).

Peelmann, A., "La famille comme réalité ecclésiale," *Église et Théologie* 12 (1981): 95-114.

Penna, R., *Il "mysterion" paolino. Traiettoria e costituzione* (Brescia: Paideia, 1978).

————, *Lettera agli Efesini. Introduzione, versione, commento* (Bologna: EDB, 1988).

Pesch, O. H., "Ehe im Blick des Glaubens," in *Christlicher Glaube in moderner Gesellschaft* (Freiburg i. Br.: Herder, 1981), 8-43.

Pompei, A., "Saggio bibliografico sulla recente teologia del matrimonio," in *Evangelizzazione e matrimonio,* ed. S. Cipriani (Naples: PFTIM, 1975), 244-63.

Pontifical Council for the Family, *Familia et Vita* 1, no. 2 (1996).

Power, D. N., "Teologia della celebrazione eucaristica," in *Scientia Liturgica,* vol. 3: *L'Eucaristia,* ed. A. J. Chupungco (Casale Monferrato: Piemme, 1988).

————, *The Eucharistic Mystery* (New York: Crossroad, 1995).

Przywara, E., *Christentum gemäss Johannes* (Nurnberg, 1954).

————, *L'uomo. Antropologia tipologica* (Milan: Fabbri, 1968).

Rahner, H., "Flumina de ventre Christi. L'esegesi patristica di Giov. 6,37-38," *Biblica* 22 (1941), reprinted in Rahner, *L'ecclesiologia dei Padri* (Rome: Paoline, 1971).

Rahner, K., *The Church and the Sacraments,* trans. W. J. O'Hara (Freiburg: Herder, 1963).

————, "Die Ehe als Sakrament," in *Schriften zur Theologie,* vol. 8 (Einsiedeln, Zurich, Cologne: Benziger, 1967), 519-40.

————, *Foundations of Christian Faith: An Introduction to the Idea of Christianity,* trans. William V. Dych (New York: Seabury, 1978).

————, *Kirche als Sakrament* (Freiburg: Herder, 1960).

————, "Marriage as a Sacrament," *Theology Digest* (1969): 4-8.

————, "Zur Theologie des Symbols," in *Cor Jesu,* vol. 1 (Rome, 1959).

Ratzinger, J., "Biblical Interpretation in Crisis," in Aa.Vv., *Biblical Interpretation in Crisis: The Ratzinger Conference on Bible and Church* (Grand Rapids: Eerdmans, 1989).

————, *Collected Works: Theology of the Liturgy* (San Francisco: Ignatius, 2014).

Bibliography

————, "Le concept de sacrement," *Nova et Vetera* 87, no. 2 (2012): 133-52.

————, "De la Cène de Jésus au sacrement de l'Église," in Aa.Vv., *L'eucharistie, pain nouveau pour un monde rompu* (Paris: Communio-Fayard, 1981), 35-51.

————, "Matrimonio e famiglia nel piano di Dio," in Aa.Vv., *La Familiaris Consortio* (Vatican City: Libreria Editrice Vaticana, 1982), 77-88.

————, *The Nature and Mission of Theology: Essays to Orient Theology in Today's Debates*, trans. Adrian Walker (San Francisco: Ignatius, 1995).

————, Preface to the Italian edition of H. Luthe, ed., *Incontrare Cristo nei sacramenti. Sussidio teologico per una pastorale sacramentaria* (Milan, Cinisello Balsamo: Paoline, 1988).

————, *Spirit of the Liturgy*, trans. John Saward (San Francisco: Ignatius, 2000).

————, "Zum Begriff des Sakramentes," *Eichstatter Hochschulreden* 15 (Munich, 1979).

————, "Zur Theologie der Ehe," in *Theologie der Ehe*, ed. G. Krems and R. Mumm (Regensburg: Pustet; Göttingen: Vandenhoeck & Ruprecht, 1972), 81-115.

Reali, N., *La ragione e la forma. Il Sacramento nella Teologia di H. U. von Balthasar* (Rome: PUL-Mursia, 1999).

Remy, P., "Le mariage, signe de l'union du Christ et de l'Eglise," *Revue des Sciences Philosophiques et Théologiques* 66 (1982): 397-415.

Rengstorf, K., *Il vangelo secondo Luca* (Brescia: Paideia, 1980).

Ricoeur, P., *The Conflict of Interpretations: Essays in Hermeneutics* (London, New York: Continuum, 2007).

————, *Finitude et culpabilité* (Paris: Aubier, 1960).

————, *From Text to Action: Essays in Hermeneutics II*, trans. Kathleen Blamey (London, New York: Continuum, 2008).

Rochetta, C., "È la relazione uomo-donna che diventa sacramento. Per una sponsalità sacramentale della coppia," in *Cristo Sposo della Chiesa Sposa. Sorgente e modello della spiritualità coniugale e familiare*, ed. R. Bonetti (Rome: Città Nuova 1997), 55-87.

————, *I sacramenti della fede*, vol. 1: *Sacramentaria biblica fondamentale*; vol. 2: *Sacramentaria fondamentale*, 7th edition (Bologna: EDB, 1998).

————, "Il sacramento del matrimonio," in *Incontrare Cristo nei sacramenti*, ed. H. Luthe (Milan: Cinisello Balsamo/Paoline, 1988).

————, *Il sacramento della coppia* (Bologna: EDB, 1996).

————, *Sacramentaria fondamentale. Dal "mysterion" al "sacramentum"* (Bologna: EDB, 1990).

————, "Théologie narrative," in *Dictionnaire de théologie fondamentale*, ed. R. Latourelle and R. Fisichella (Montréal: Bellarmin; Paris: Éd. du Cerf, 1992).

Rondet, H., *Introduction à l'étude de la théologie du mariage* (Paris: Lethielleux, 1960).

Roo, W. A. Van, *The Christian Sacrament* (Rome: PUG, 1992).

Ruffini, E., "Il matrimonio alla luce della teologia cattolica," in *Amore e matrimonio nel pensiero filosofico e teologico moderno*, ed. V. Melchiorre (Milan: Vita e Pensiero, 1976), 100-170.

————, "Il matrimonio-sacramento nei documenti del Vaticano II e del magistero postconciliare," in Aa.Vv., *Il matrimonio cristiano* (Turin, Leumann: LDC, 1978), 40-93.

————, "Il matrimonio-sacramento nella tradizione cattolica. Rilettura teologica," in *Nuova enciclopedia del matrimonio,* ed. T. Goffi (Brescia: Queriniana, 1988), 177-224.

————, "Orientamenti e contenuti della teologia sacramentaria nella riflessione teologica contemporanea," in E. Ruffini and E. Lodi, *"Mysterion" e "sacramentum." La sacramentalità negli scritti dei Padri e nei testi liturgici primitivi* (Bologna: EDB, 1987).

————, "Sacramentalità ed economia sacramentale negli scritti dei Padri della Chiesa," in E. Ruffini and E. Lodi, *"Mysterion" e "sacramentum." La sacramentalità negli scritti dei Padri e nei testi liturgici primitivi* (Bologna: EDB, 1987), 59-204.

————, "Sacramenti," in *Nuovo Dizionario di Teologia,* ed. G. Barbaglio and S. Dianich (Cinisello Balsamo: Paoline, 1985), 1375-97.

Rupert of Deutz, *De divinis officiis,* 1.2.11 (*PL* 170).

Saraiva Martins, J., *I sacramenti della Nuova Alleanza* (Rome: Pontificia Università Urbaniana, 1987).

Sartore, D., "La famiglia, Chiesa domestica," *Lateranum* 45 (1979): 282-30.

Scheeben, M.-J., *The Mysteries of Christianity,* trans. Cyril Vollert (St. Louis, London: B. Herder, 1946), 543-44.

Scheffczyk, L., "Gesù Cristo Sacramento originario della redenzione," in *Incontrare Cristo nei sacramenti. Sussidio teologico per una pastorale sacramentaria,* ed. H. Luthe (Cinisello Balsamo: Paoline, 1988).

————, "La Chiesa, sacramento universale di Gesù Cristo," in *Incontrare Cristo nei sacramenti. Sussidio teologico per una pastorale sacramentaria,* ed. H. Luthe (Cinisello Balsamo: Paoline, 1988).

Schillebeeckx, E., *Christ, the Sacrament of the Encounter with God,* trans. Paul Barrett and N. D. Smith (London, New York: Sheed and Ward, 1965).

————, *Marriage: Human Reality and Saving Mystery* (London: Sheed and Ward, 1965).

————, *Il matrimonio è un sacramento* (Milan: Ancora, 1963).

————, "Les sacrements, organe de la rencontre de Dieu," in *Questions théologiques aujourd'hui* (Paris: Desclée de Brouwer, 1965).

Schlier, H., *Lettera agli Efesini* (Brescia: Paideia, 1965).

Schmaus, M., "Die Ehe," in *Der Glaube der Kirche,* vol. V/4 (Erzabtei St. Ottilien: EOS, 1982), 205-84.

Schnackenburg, R., *Der Brief an die Epheser* (Zurich: Benzinger; Neukirchen-Vluyn: Neukirchener Verlag).

————, "Il matrimonio secondo il Nuovo Testamento," in *La vita cristiana. Esegesi in progresso e in mutamento* (Milan: Jaca Book, 1977), 317-38.

Schökel, L. A., *I nomi dell'amore. Simboli matrimoniali nella Bibbia* (Casale Monferrato: Piemme, 1997).

Schulte, R., "I singoli sacramenti come articolazione del sacramento radicale," in *Mysterium Salutis,* vol. 8 (Brescia: Queriniana, 1975), 51-189.

Schürmann, H., *Comment Jésus a-t-il vécu sa mort?* (Paris: Éd. du Cerf, 1977).

————, *Der Einsetzungsbericht Lk 22, 19-20* (Münster: Aschendorff, 1955).

Scola, A., *Crisi della libertà e vita familiare* (Grosseto: Centro Studi S. Lorenzo–I Portici Editore, 1995).

————, "L'imago Dei e la sessualità umana," *Anthropotes* 1 (1992): 61-73.

————, "La logica dell'incarnazione come logica sacramentale. Avvenimento ecclesiale e libertà umana," in Aa.Vv., *Wer ist die Kirche? Symposion zum 10. Todesjahr von Hans Urs von Balthasar* (Einsiedeln: Johannes Verlag, 1999), 99-135.

―――, "Matrimonio e famiglia luoghi visibili di umanità redenta," *La Rivista* 29, no. 1 (1994).

―――, *The Nuptial Mystery,* trans. Michelle K. Borras (Grand Rapids: Eerdmans, 2005).

―――, "Lo Spirito Santo rivela la verità tutta intera della famiglia cristiana," in *Il matrimonio in Cristo è matrimonio nello Spirito,* ed. R. Bonetti (Rome: Città Nuova, 1998).

―――, "Con Cristo al cuore dell'uomo," *Synesis* 6, no. 1-2 (1989): 47-61.

―――, "La visione antropologica del rapporto uomo-donna. Il significato dell'unità dei due," in Aa.Vv., *Dignità e vocazione della donna* (Vatican City: Libreria Editrice Vaticana, 1989), 91-103.

Semeraro, M., *Il Risorto tra noi. Origine, natura e funzione dei sacramenti* (Bologna: ESD, 1992).

Semmelroth, O., "Die Kirche als Sakrament des Heiles," in *Mysterium Salutis. Grundriß heilsgeschichtlicher Dogmatik,* 4/1, ed. J. Feiner and M. Lohrer (Einsiedeln: Benzinger, 1972), 309-56.

―――, *Die Kirche als Ursakrament* (Frankfurt a. M.: Knecht, 1955, 1963).

―――, *Vom Sinn der Sakramente* (Frankfurt, 1960).

Sepe, C., *La dimensione trinitaria del carattere sacramentale* (Rome: Lateran University Press, 1969).

Sequeira, J. B., *Tout mariage entre baptisés est-il nécessairement sacramentel?* (Paris: Éd. du Cerf, 1985).

Sicari, A., *Breve catechesi sul matrimonio,* 6th edition (Milan: Jaca Book, 1994).

Siewerth, G., *Das Schicksal der Metaphysik von Thomas von Aquin bis Heidegger* (Einsiedeln: Johannes Verlag, 1959).

―――, *Der Thomismus als Identitätssystem,* 2nd edition (Frankfurt am Main: Schulte-Bulmke, 1961).

Silanes, N., *A la Trinidad por los sacramentos* (Salamanca: Ed. Secretariado Trinitario, 1967).

Smulders, P., "L'Église sacrement du salut," in *L'Église de Vatican II,* ed. G. Barauna, vol. 2, *Unam Sanctam,* 51b (Paris: Éd. du Cerf, 1967), 313-38.

Speyr, A. von, *Confession,* trans. Douglas W. Stott (San Francisco: Ignatius, 1985).

―――, *The Cross: Word and Sacrament,* trans. Graham Harrison (San Francisco: Ignatius, 1987).

―――, *Handmaid of the Lord,* trans. E. A. Nelson (San Francisco: Ignatius, 1985).

―――, *John,* vol. 1: *The Word Become Flesh: Meditations on John 1-5* (San Francisco: Ignatius, 1994),

―――, *John,* vol. 4: *The Birth of the Church: Meditations on John 18-21,* trans. David Kipp (San Francisco: Ignatius, 1991).

―――, *The Letter to the Ephesians,* trans. Adrian Walker (San Francisco: Ignatius, 1996).

―――, *Theologie der Geschlechter* (Einsiedeln: Johannes, 1969).

―――, *Das Wort und die Mystik,* vol. 2: *Objektive Mystik* (Einsiedeln: Johannes, 1970).

Stramare, T., "Formulazione di una teologia attuale della santa Famiglia," in Aa.Vv., *La*

Santa Famiglia nei primi XVI secoli della Chiesa. Atti del I Congresso sulla Sacra Famiglia (Barcelona, 1993).

Taymans D'eypernon, F., "Le mariage," in *La Sainte Trinité et les sacrements* (Brussels: Universelle; Paris: Desclée, 1949), 93-107.

Testa, B., *I sacramenti della Chiesa* (Milan: Jaca Book, 1995).

Tettamanzi, D., *I due saranno una carne sola. Saggi teologici su matrimonio e famiglia* (Turin, Leumann: LDC, 1986).

———, "L'Eucaristia al centro della famiglia," *La Famiglia* 97 (1983): 23-42.

———, *La famiglia, via della Chiesa,* 2nd edition (Milan: Massimo, 1991).

———, "La famiglia cristiana 'veluti ecclesia domestica' nell'esortazione apostolica *Familiaris Consortio,*" *La Scuola Cattolica* 111 (1983): 107-52.

———, *Matrimonio cristiano oggi* (Milan: Ancora, 1975).

———, "Il matrimonio e la famiglia nei Padri della Chiesa," *La Famiglia,* six articles from 1970 to 1973.

Thomas Aquinas, *Quaestiones disputatae de potentia.*

———, *Summa contra Gentiles,* III, IV, LVIII.

———, *Summa Theologiae.*

———, *Super IV Sent.,* d. 23-50.

Thurian, M., *L'Eucharistie. Mémorial du Seigneur, sacrifice d'action de grâce et d'intercession* (Neuchâtel: Delachaux et Niestlé, 1959).

Tillard, J.-M., "Église et salut. Sur la sacramentalité de l'Église," *La nouvelle revue théologie* 106 (1984): 658-85.

———, "Le nuove prospettive della teologia sacramentaria," in *Sacra Doctrina* (Bologna, ESD, 1967), 37-58.

Tosato, A., *Il matrimonio nel Giudaismo Antico e nel Nuovo Testamento* (Rome: Città Nuova, 1976).

———, "L'istituto familiare dell'antico Israele e della Chiesa primitiva," *Anthropotes* 13, no. 1 (1997): 109-74.

Tourpe, E., "Le thomisme ontologique de Gustav Siewerth, Ferdinand Ulrich et Hans André à l'arrière-plan de la pensée balthasarienne," *Revista Espanola de Teologia* 65, no. 4 (2005): 467-91.

Tragan, P. R., "Battesimo e fede cristologica nel dialogo fra Gesù e Nicodemo (Gv 3, 1-21)," in *Fede e sacramenti negli scritti giovannei,* ed. P. R. Tragan (Rome: Pontificio Ateneo S. Anselmo, 1985), 47-120.

Tremblay, R., "A proposito della presenza sacrificale di Cristo nell'Eucaristia," in *Gesù Cristo Speranza del mondo,* ed. I. Sanna (Rome: PUL-Mursia, 2000).

Triacca, A. M., " 'Celebrare' il matrimonio cristiano. Suo significato teologico-liturgico (Anamnesis-Méthexis-Epiclesis)," *Ephemerides liturgicae* 93 (1979): 407-56.

———, "Il sangue di Cristo. Mistero di alleanza nella vita coniugale," in *Il mistero del sangue di Cristo e l'esperienza cristiana,* ed. A. M. Triacca (Rome: Centro Studi Sanguis Christi, 1987), 385-417.

———, "La presenza e l'azione dello Spirito Santo nella celebrazione dei sacramenti," *Liturgia* 19 (1985): 26-62.

Ubbiali, S., "Il sacramento e l'istituzione divina. Il dibattito teologico sulla verità del sacramento," *Rivista Liturgica* 81 (1994): 118-50.

————, "Il sacramento cristiano," in *Celebrare il mistero di Cristo,* vol. 2: *La celebrazione dei sacramenti* (Rome: Edizioni Liturgiche, 1996), 13-28.

————, "Il sacramento cristiano e l'agire libero dell'uomo. Per una 'drammatica' dell'azione sacramentale," in Aa.Vv., *Gesù Cristo, Unico Salvatore del Mondo, Pane per la Nuova Vita. Convegno Teologico in preparazione del XLVII Congresso Eucaristico Internazionale* (Rome: PUL, April 27-28, 2000).

————, "Il sacramento e la fede," *La Scuola Cattolica* 127 (1999): 313-44.

Ulrich, F., *Homo Abyssus. Das Wagnis der Seinsfrage,* 2nd edition (Einsiedeln: Johannes, 1998).

Vagaggini, C., *Il senso teologico della liturgia* (Rome: Paoline, 1965).

Voderholzer, R., *Die Einheit der Schrift und ihr geistiger Sinn. Der Beitrag Henri de Lubac zur Erforschung von Geschichte und Systematik christlicher Bibelhermeneutik* (Einsiedeln: Johannes Verlag, 1998).

Vollebregt, G. N., *Le mariage* (Sherbrooke: Éditions Paulines, 1970).

Vorgrimler, H., *Sakramententheologie* (Düsseldorf: Patmos, 1987).

Wattiaux, H., "La famille a-t-elle encore un avenir?" *Esprit et Vie* 40 (1992): 265-69, 529-44.

Westermann, C., *Genesis I–II: A Commentary* (Minneapolis: Augsburg, 1984).

Wojtyla, K., *Love and Responsibility,* trans. Grzegorz Ignatik (Boston: Pauline Books and Media, 2013).

Zani, L., *Lo Spirito e la sposa dicono vieni!: Ap 22, 17* (Trent: Argentarium, 1992).

Zizioulas, J. D., *Being as Communion: Studies in Personhood and the Church* (Crestwood, NY: St. Vladimir's Seminary Press, 1997).